EYEWITNESSES AND OTHERS

**Readings in American History
Volume 2: 1865 to the Present**

HOLT, RINEHART AND WINSTON
Harcourt Brace & Company
Austin • New York • Orlando • Atlanta •
San Francisco • Boston • Dallas • Toronto • London

Reviewers

James M. Bell
Teacher
Poway High School
Poway, California

Thomas R. Frazier
Professor of History
Baruch College
City University of New York
New York, New York

Mary Ellen Godfrey,
Adjunct Instructor in History
Palomar College
San Marcos, California

James M. McPherson
Director of Graduate Studies
Department of History
Princeton University
Princeton, New Jersey

Malcolm Moore, Jr.
Teacher
Thomas Jefferson Middle School
Decatur, Illinois

Acknowledgments

For permission to reprint copyrighted material, grateful acknowledgment is made to the following sources:

Associated Press: From "Remarks by Rep. Newt Gingrich After Election as Speaker," January 1995, by the Associated Press. Copyright © 1995 by the Associated Press.

Bidwell Mansion Cooperating Association: From "Rancho Chico Indians" (Retitled: "Annie Bidwell Attends a Mechoopda Dance") by Annie E. K. Bidwell, edited by Dorothy J. Hill. Copyright © 1980 by Bidwell Mansion Cooperating Association; © 1987 by Bidwell Mansion Association.

Capitola Book Company: From *Chinese Gold: The Chinese in the Monterey Bay Region* (Retitled: "Chinese Railroad Workers on the Frontier") by Sandy Lydon; 1985.

The Crisis Publishing Company: "A Call for Democracy After the War" by W. E. B. Du Bois, from *The Crisis,* XVIII (May 1919). "The Task for the Future—A Program for 1919" by the NAACP.

(*Acknowledgments continued on page 451*)

Contents

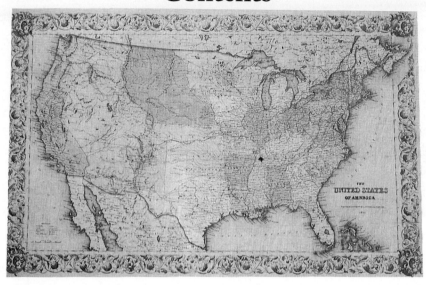

Introduction   1

1 Speeches of Seattle and Ten Bears
  (1854, 1867)   2
  Excerpts from speeches by two Native
  American chiefs

2 A Norwegian Pioneer Woman Describes
  Her New Home in Iowa (1863–1865) .   8
  Excerpts from letters

3 A Teacher Among the Freedmen
  (1864)   15
  Excerpts from Elizabeth Hyde Botume's account

4 Carl Sandburg Describes Lincoln's
  Assassination (1865)   20
  An excerpt from Sandburg's biography of Lincoln

5 Chinese Railroad Workers on the
  Frontier (1865–1890)   26
  Excerpts from a modern historian's account

6 Andrew Carnegie Becomes a
  Businessman (1868)   31
  Excerpts from a magazine article by Carnegie

7 **Annie Bidwell Attends a Mechoopda Dance (1870s)** 39
An excerpt from Bidwell's eyewitness account

8 **The Vaquero (1870s)** 44
An excerpt from a modern historian's account

9 **Wolves and Grasshoppers Plague the Kansas Frontier (1870s)** 49
Excerpts from the reminiscences of pioneer women

10 **Cowpunching on the Texas Trail (1883)** 59
An excerpt from a cowboy's description

Feature: Two Cowboy Songs 64
Music and lyrics

11 **Football Without Helmets (1884)** 68
An excerpt from Amos Alonzo Stagg's account

12 **Thomas Edison Observed (1885)** 72
Excerpts from a biography by Edison's secretary

13 **Clergyman and Critics: A Debate over Imperialism (1885–1899)** 77
Excerpts from Josiah Strong's pro-imperialist argument and the platform of the Anti-Imperialist League

14 **Susan B. Anthony and Senator Joseph Brown Debate a Woman's Suffrage Amendment (1884, 1887)** 83
Excerpts from speeches to the U.S. Senate

15 **A Teacher's Life in the Common Schools (1888)** 91
An excerpt from a Kansas teacher's recollections

16 **An Immigrant Family Goes to School (1880s)** 97
Excerpts from Mary Antin's book *The Promised Land*

17 **Lesson One from McGuffey's *Eclectic Fourth Reader* (1880s)** 100
A lesson from the nineteenth-century textbook

18 Jacob Riis Describes a New York City
   Gang (1880s) 107
   Excerpts from the journalist's book *How
   the Other Half Lives*

19 A Black Georgian Tells of the
   Substitutes for Slavery (1880s) 112
   Excerpts from a laborer's account

20 The Sweatshops of Chicago (1891) . . . 122
   Excerpts from Joseph Kirkland's book *The
   Poor in Great Cities*

21 Booker T. Washington and the "Atlanta
   Compromise" (1895) 125
   Excerpts from Washington's speech at the
   International Exposition in Atlanta

22 A Farm Girl Arrives in the Big City
   (1895) 129
   Excerpts from Hamlin Garland's novel
   Rose of Dutcher's Coolly

23 The Rough Riders Charge San Juan Hill
   (1898) 132
   Excerpts from an account by Richard
   Harding Davis

24 A Farmer in the Grip of the "Octopus"
   (1890s) 137
   An excerpt from the novel *The Octopus* by
   Frank Norris

25 New York in the Golden Nineties
   (1890s) 142
   Excerpts from Henry Collins Brown's
   book about the city

26 Carry Nation Attacks "Dens of Vice"
   (1900) 147
   Excerpts from Nation's autobiography

27 The Squid and the Lobster, from
   Dreiser's *The Financier* (ca. 1900) 153
   An excerpt from Chapter 1

28 Lincoln Steffens Tells How Theodore Roosevelt Began the Square Deal (1901) 158
Excerpts from Steffens' autobiography

29 A View of the Political Machine (ca. 1905) 163
Excerpts from William L. Riordon's book *Plunkitt of Tammany Hall*

30 Jack London Reports on the San Francisco Earthquake (1906) 167
An excerpt from a magazine article

31 Poems of the Chinese Immigrants (ca. 1910) 173
Seven poems about life in the United States

32 General Pershing Arrives in France (1917) 177
Excerpts from a war correspondent's account

33 Two Doughboys in the Great War (1918) 184
Excerpts from soldiers' letters home

34 Senator Henry Cabot Lodge Demands Harsh Peace Terms (1918) 194
Excerpts from a speech by the senator

35 An Ambulance Driver's Story (1919) . . 197
Excerpts from a diary

36 W. E. B. Du Bois Calls for Democracy After the War (1919) 201
A statement about the African American's future in America

37 The NAACP Program of 1919 (1919) 204
A statement of the objectives of the NAACP

38 A Novelist's Portrait of Henry Ford (ca. 1920) 210
An excerpt from John Dos Passos' book *The Big Money*

39 A Minister Calls for Christian Unity
(1920) 216
An excerpt from a lecture by William T. Manning

40 A Portrait of FDR, from *Sunrise at*
***Campobello* (1924)** 221
Final scenes from Dore Schary's play

Feature: An Album of Changes 228
A visual record of home and social life

41 The Great Boom and the Big Crash
(1928–1929) 230
Excerpts from accounts of the Wall Street
events by Frederick Lewis Allen and
Jonathan Norton Leonard

42 Sketches from the Hispanic Southwest
(1920s) 237
Stories about neighborhood people by
Jovita González

43 A Black Texan's School Days (1920s) . . 244
Excerpts from the memoirs of the Rev. C. C. White

44 Life in the Breadlines (1930) 250
Excerpts from a magazine article by
journalist Karl Monroe

45 Roosevelt Defends the New Deal
(1937) 254
An excerpt from Franklin Roosevelt's
Second Inaugural Address

46 Two Poems from Langston Hughes'
***Don't You Want to Be Free?* (1937)** . . . 258
Poems about the African American experience

47 The Impact of the Great Depression
(1930s) 261
Excerpts from Frederick Lewis Allen's
book *Since Yesterday*

48 James Agee Describes the Life of Tenant
Farmers (1930s) 267
An excerpt from the book *Let Us Now
Praise Famous Men*

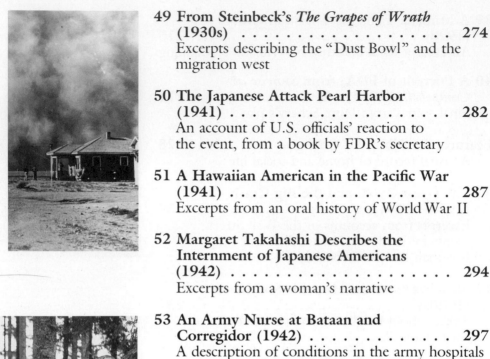

**49 From Steinbeck's *The Grapes of Wrath*
(1930s)** 274
Excerpts describing the "Dust Bowl" and the
migration west

**50 The Japanese Attack Pearl Harbor
(1941)** 282
An account of U.S. officials' reaction to
the event, from a book by FDR's secretary

**51 A Hawaiian American in the Pacific War
(1941)** 287
Excerpts from an oral history of World War II

**52 Margaret Takahashi Describes the
Internment of Japanese Americans
(1942)** 294
Excerpts from a woman's narrative

**53 An Army Nurse at Bataan and
Corregidor (1942)** 297
A description of conditions in the army hospitals

**54 John Hersey Records the Japanese
Experience of Hiroshima (1945)** 304
A description of a survivor's experience,
excerpted from Hersey's book *Hiroshima*

**55 Defense Worker Rachel Wray
Reminisces About Her Wartime
Experiences (1940s)** 310
Excerpts from a factory worker's account

**56 A Black Tank Commander's Story
(1940s)** 313
An excerpt from an oral history

57 America and the Holocaust (1940s) . . . 319
Excerpts from David S. Wyman's book
*The Abandonment of the Jew: America and
the Holocaust*

**58 The Truman Doctrine and the Four
Points (1947, 1949)** 324
Excerpts from two speeches to Congress
by President Harry Truman

59 President Eisenhower Intervenes at
   Little Rock (1957) 330
   Excerpts from a radio speech

60 Victor Navasky Describes the Costs of
   "McCarthyism" (1950s) 334
   Excerpts from the journalist's book *Naming
   Names*

61 Betty Friedan Discusses the Feminine
   Mystique (1950s) 338
   Excerpts from Friedan's *The Feminine Mystique*

62 Two Views of America in the 1950s . . . 342
   Excerpts from a *U.S. News & World Report*
   article and John Kenneth Galbraith's *The
   Affluent Society*

63 A Declaration of Indian Purpose (1961)   350
   An excerpt from the declaration

64 Ambassador Adlai Stevenson Confronts
   the Soviets over Cuba (1962) 354
   Excerpts from Stevenson's UN speech

65 James Meredith Cracks Ole Miss (1962)   358
   An excerpt from Meredith's *Saturday
   Evening Post* article

66 The Reverend Martin Luther King, Jr.,
   Preaches Nonviolence from the
   Birmingham Jail (1963) 367
   Excerpts from King's letter to Alabama
   clergy

67 President Johnson Defines the Great
   Society (1964) 375
   Excerpts from a speech

68 Stokely Carmichael Explains "Black
   Power" (1966) 381
   Excerpts from an essay

69 Senator Fulbright and President Johnson
   Debate the Vietnam War (1966, 1968) . 386
   Excerpts from Fulbright's book *The Arrogance
   of Power* and a speech by President Johnson

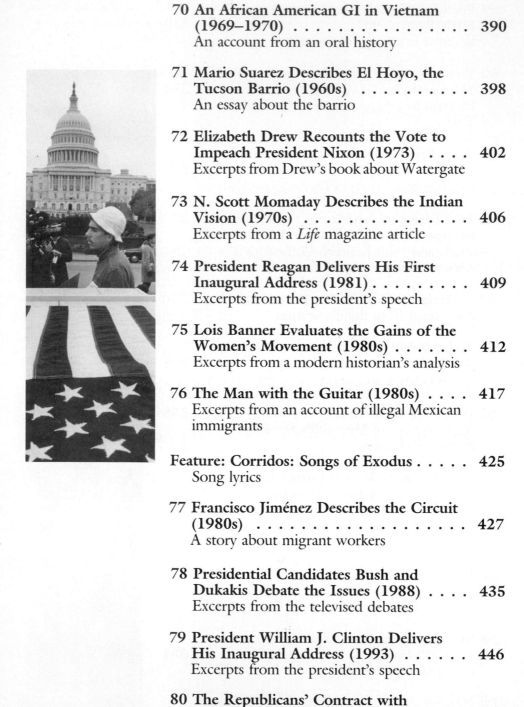

**70 An African American GI in Vietnam
(1969–1970)** 390
An account from an oral history

**71 Mario Suarez Describes El Hoyo, the
Tucson Barrio (1960s)** 398
An essay about the barrio

**72 Elizabeth Drew Recounts the Vote to
Impeach President Nixon (1973)** 402
Excerpts from Drew's book about Watergate

**73 N. Scott Momaday Describes the Indian
Vision (1970s)** 406
Excerpts from a *Life* magazine article

**74 President Reagan Delivers His First
Inaugural Address (1981)** 409
Excerpts from the president's speech

**75 Lois Banner Evaluates the Gains of the
Women's Movement (1980s)** 412
Excerpts from a modern historian's analysis

76 The Man with the Guitar (1980s) 417
Excerpts from an account of illegal Mexican
immigrants

Feature: Corridos: Songs of Exodus 425
Song lyrics

**77 Francisco Jiménez Describes the Circuit
(1980s)** 427
A story about migrant workers

**78 Presidential Candidates Bush and
Dukakis Debate the Issues (1988)** 435
Excerpts from the televised debates

**79 President William J. Clinton Delivers
His Inaugural Address (1993)** 446
Excerpts from the president's speech

**80 The Republicans' Contract with
America (1994)** 449
Excerpts from Gingrich's speech

Introduction

*E*yewitnesses and Others: Readings in American History presents United States history as a collection of written evidence—primary sources—about the past. The readings in this book place you in direct contact with the people who lived and experienced history—the eyewitnesses. As you read the historical evidence they created, you enter the minds of these men and women to view the past through their eyes. Then you step aside from their points of view to make your own historical judgments about the events they describe.

This is the historian's job, and it is absolutely necessary. No two eyewitnesses ever see exactly the same thing, and eyewitness descriptions are often colored and distorted by their authors' personal involvements in the events of their times.

However, an old saying holds that if you would really understand someone you should "walk a mile in his moccasins." *Eyewitnesses and Others* invites you to step into the "moccasins" of Native American chiefs, Chinese railroad workers, pioneers for women's rights, farmers and ranchers, World War I and II soldiers, migrant workers, civil rights leaders, and others. Then you step into the very different shoes of the historian to try to make objective sense of what you have read.

To assist you in your reading, especially difficult words or passages are defined in brackets or in marginal notes.

1

From *I have Spoken: American History Through the Voices of the Indians,* compiled by Virginia Irving Armstrong.

Speeches of Seattle and Ten Bears (1854, 1867)

As the American frontier pushed ever westward, settlers came into frequent and repeated conflict with the Indian societies they encountered. Again and again, treaties were signed with the tribes ceding lands to the Americans in return for guarantees that certain other lands would remain in Indian hands forever. In the 1700s and 1800s these promises were not kept. Frontiersmen would continue to venture into Indian territory, forcing the United States government to return to the tribes to seek new treaties. Ultimately the Indian tribes that had formerly controlled thousands of square miles of the western United States were relocated to small, cramped "Indian reservations."

During this long process of treaty negotiation and renegotiation, Native Americans recorded their protests in political speeches of great power and eloquence. Two of these speeches are excerpted below. Seattle (Seathl) was chief of the Dwamish tribe in what is now Washington state. Ten Bears was one of the principal chiefs of the Yamparika Comanche of the southern Great Plains. Compare and contrast the two speeches as you read.

Seattle

Yonder sky that has wept tears of compassion upon my people for centuries untold, and which to us appears changeless and eternal, may change. Today is fair. Tomorrow it may be overcast with clouds. My words are like the stars that never change. Whatever Seattle says the great chief at Washington can rely upon with as much certainty as he can

upon the return of the sun or the seasons. The White
Chief says that Big Chief at Washington sends us
greetings of friendship and goodwill. That is kind
of him for we know he has little need of our friendship
in return. His people are many. They are like the
grass that covers vast prairies. My people are few.
They resemble the scattering trees of a storm-swept
plain . . . I will not dwell on, nor mourn over, our
untimely decay, nor reproach our paleface brothers
with hastening it, as we too may have been somewhat
to blame. . . .

Your God is not our God. Your God loves
your people and hates mine. He folds his strong
and protecting arms lovingly about the paleface and
leads him by the hand as a father leads his infant
son—but He has forsaken His red children—if they
really are his. Our God, the Great Spirit, seems
also to have forsaken us. Your God makes your people
strong every day. Soon they will fill the land. Our
people are ebbing away like a rapidly receding tide
that will never return. The white man's God cannot
love our people or He would protect them. They
seem to be orphans who can look nowhere for help.
How then can we be brothers? . . . We are two
distinct races with separate origins and separate desti-
nies. There is little in common between us.

To us the ashes of our ancestors are sacred
and their resting place is hallowed ground. You wander far from the graves of your ancestors and seemingly without regret. Your religion was written upon
tables of stone by the iron finger of your God so
that you could not forget. The Red Man could never
comprehend nor remember it. Our religion is the
traditions of our ancestors—the dreams of our old
men, given them in solemn hours of night by the
Great Spirit; and the visions of our sachems [chiefs];
and it is written in the hearts of our people.

Your dead cease to love you and the land of
their nativity [birth] as soon as they pass the portals
of the tomb and wander way beyond the stars. They

**Our people are
ebbing away like
a rapidly
receding
tide . . .**

are soon forgotten and never return. Our dead never forget the beautiful world that gave them being.

Day and night cannot dwell together. The Red Man has ever fled the approach of the White Man, as the morning mist flees before the morning sun. However, your proposition seems fair and I think that my people will accept it and will retire to the reservation you offer them. Then we will dwell apart in peace. . . . It matters little where we pass the remnant of our days. They will not be many. A few more moons; a few more winters—and not one of the descendants of the mighty hosts that once moved over this broad land or lived in happy homes, protected by the Great Spirit, will remain to mourn over the graves of a people once more powerful and hopeful than yours. But why should I mourn at the untimely fate of my people? Tribe follows tribe, and nation follows nation, like the waves of the sea. It is the order of nature, and regret is useless. Your time of decay may be distant, but it will surely come, for even the White Man whose God walked and talked with him as friend with friend cannot be exempt [free] from the common destiny. We may be brothers after all. We will see. . . .

Every part of this soil is sacred . . .

Every part of this soil is sacred in the estimation of my people. Every hillside, every valley, every plain and grove, has been hallowed by some sad or happy event in days long vanished. The very dust upon which you now stand responds more lovingly to their footsteps than to yours, because it is rich with the blood of our ancestors and our bare feet are conscious of the sympathetic touch. Even the little children who lived here and rejoiced here for a brief season will love these somber solitudes and at eventide they greet shadowy returning spirits. And when the last Red Man shall have perished, and the memory of my tribe shall have become a myth among the White Men, these shores will swarm with the invisible dead of my tribe, and when your children's children think themselves alone in the

A Comanche warrior displays typical clothing and weapons for this formal portrait.

field, the store, the shop, upon the highway, or in the silence of the pathless woods, they will not be alone. At night when the streets of your cities and villages are silent and you think them deserted, they will throng with the returning hosts that once filled and still love this beautiful land. The White Man will never be alone.

Let him be just and deal kindly with my people, for the dead are not powerless. Dead, did I say? There is no death, only a change of worlds.

Ten Bears
My heart is filled with joy when I see you here, as the brook fills with water when the snow melts in the spring; and I feel glad as the ponies do when

the fresh grass starts in the beginning of the year. I heard of your coming when I was many sleeps away, and I made but few camps before I met you. . . .

My people have never first drawn a bow or fired a gun against the whites. There has been trouble on the line between us, and my young men have danced with war dance. But it was not begun by us. It was you who sent out the first soldier and we who sent out the second. Two years ago I came upon this road, following the buffalo, that my wives and children might have their cheeks plump and their bodies warm. But the soldiers fired on us, and since that time there has been a noise like that of a thunderstorm, and we have not known which way to go. So it was upon the Canadian [River]. Nor have we been made to cry once alone. The blue-dressed soldiers and the Utes came from out of the night when it was dark and still, and for campfires they lit our lodges. Instead of hunting game they killed my braves, and the warriors of the tribe cut short their hair for the dead. So it was in Texas. They made sorrow come in our camps, and we went out like buffalo bulls when their cows are attacked. When we found them we killed them, and their

The Comanches are not weak and blind . . .

scalps hang in our lodges. The Comanches are not weak and blind, like the pups of a dog when seven sleeps old. They are strong and farsighted, like grown horses. We took their road and we went on it. The white women cried and our women laughed.

But there are things which you have said to me which I do not like. They are not sweet like sugar, but bitter like gourds. You said that you wanted to put us upon a reservation, to build us houses and make us medicine lodges [places of religious practice]. I do not want them. I was born upon the prairie, where the wind blew free and there was nothing to break the light of the sun. I was born where there were no enclosures and where everything drew a free breath. I want to die there and not within walls. I know every stream and every wood between the Rio Grande and the Arkansas. I have hunted and lived over that country. I lived like my fathers before me, and, like them, I lived happily.

When I was at Washington the Great White Father told me that all the Comanche Land was ours, and that no one should hinder us in living upon it. So, why do you ask us to leave the rivers, and the sun, and the wind, and live in houses? Do not ask us to give up the buffalo for the sheep. . . .

If the Texans had kept out of my country, there might have been peace. But that which you now say we must live on is too small. The Texans have taken away the places where the grass grew the thickest and the timber was the best. Had we kept that, we might have done the things you ask. But it is too late. The white man has the country which we loved, and we only wish to wander on the prairie until we die.

REVIEWING THE READING

1. In Seattle's view, how do the dead ancestors of whites and Indians differ?

2. In addition to moving to the reservation, what does Ten Bears say that the United States government is asking the Comanches to do?

3. **Using Your Historical Imagination.** What do the two speeches have in common and how do they differ? What does this indicate about the situation of the Comanches in 1867?

From *Frontier Mother: The Letters of Gro Svendsen,* edited by Pauline Farseth and Theodore C. Blegen.

2

A Norwegian Pioneer Woman Describes Her New Home in Iowa (1863–1865)

During the same decade that the bloodiest war in United States history was being fought, families immigrating to America continued to push the farming frontier further west. As they pushed westward, the immigrants had to adjust to the many differences between life as they had known it at home and their new lives as farmers on the edge of the Great Plains. In the following selection, excerpts from two letters written by pioneer Gro Svendsen to her family back in Norway, we get a glimpse of the immigrant experience on the frontier. As you read the selection, note the differences found by Svendsen between life in Norway and life on the Iowa frontier.

1863

Dear Parents, Sisters, and Brothers (always in my thoughts):

I have often thought that I ought to tell you about life here in the New World. Everything is so totally different from what it was in our beloved Norway. You never will really know what it's like, although you no doubt try to imagine what it might be. Your pictures would be all wrong, just as mine were.

I only wish that I could be with you to tell you all about it. Even if I were to write you countless pages, I still could not tell you everything.

I remember I used to wonder when I heard that it would be impossible to keep the milk here as we did at home. Now I have learned that it is indeed impossible because of the heat here in the summertime. One can't make cheese out of the milk because of flies, bugs, and other insects. I don't know the names of all these insects, but this I do know: If one were to make cheese here in the summertime, the cheese itself would be alive with bugs. Toward late autumn it should be possible to keep the milk. The people who have more milk than they need simply feed it to the hogs.

It's difficult, too, to preserve the butter. One must pour brine over it or salt it; otherwise it gets full of maggots. Therefore it is best, if one is not too far from town, to sell the butter at once. This summer we have been getting from eight to ten cents a pound. Not a great profit. For this reason people around here do not have many cows—just enough to supply the milk needed for the household. It's not wise to have more than enough milk, because the flies are everywhere. Even the bacon must be preserved in brine, and so there are different ways of doing everything.

. . . the flies are everywhere.

I have so much to tell you. We have no twilight here in the summertime. Even in June, on the longest day of the year, the sun doesn't rise before 4:23 and sets at 7:40. The nights are as dark as they are at home in autumn. We never have rain without thunder and lightning. The thunderstorms are so violent that one might think it was the end of the world. The whole sky is aflame with lightning, and the thunder rolls and crashes as though it were right above our heads. Quite often the lightning strikes down both cattle and people, damages property, and splinters sturdy oak trees into many pieces. Even though one did not fear the thunder in Norway, one can easily become frightened here.

Then there is the prairie fire or, as they call it here, "Faieren." This is terrifying, and the fire rages in both the spring and the fall. Whatever it leaves behind in the fall, it consumes in the spring, so there is nothing left of the long grass on the prairies, sloughs, and marshes. It is a strange and terrible sight to see all the fields a sea of fire. Quite often the scorching flames sweep everything along in their path—people, cattle, hay, fences. In dry weather with a strong wind the fire will race faster than the speediest horse. No one dares to travel without carrying matches, so that if there is a fire he can fight it by building another and in this way save his life and prevent burns, which sometimes prove fatal.

Snakes are found here in the summertime and are also a worry to us. I am horribly afraid of them, particularly the rattlesnake. The rattlesnake is the same as the *klapperslange*. I have seen many of them and thousands of ordinary snakes.

On the prairies, where trees were scarce, pioneer families built homes of sod.

I could tell you even more, but possibly many who read this letter may think I am exaggerating. I assure you that all that I have told you I have experienced myself. If they do not believe me, they should come over and find out for themselves. Then they would tell you the same things I tell you.

By the way, no one leaving Norway should sell all his possessions as most people do. Everything that is useful in Norway is also useful here. The women can make use of all their clothes, with the exception of their headdress, bodice, jackets, and kerchiefs. All these they could sell, but all the other clothes they could make over and wear here. Everything Norwegian is of better quality than what can be bought here. So I am very grateful to you, my parents, every time I touch anything I have received from you. Bedding, too, should be brought along, as it's colder here in the winter than in Norway. Even those who criticize Norway and praise America must admit this. I could tell you much more but haven't time.

Estherville, Emmett Co., Iowa
December 3, 1865

Precious Parents, Sisters, and Brothers:

. . . We have had a good year, a rich harvest both from the grain that we sowed as well as from the wild fruit and grain. We have plowed and fenced in three acres of new land. On this plot we raised ninety bushels of corn, twenty-four bushels of potatoes, and a plant called sugar cane or sorghum. This sugar cane is pressed and cooked into syrup or molasses. From our patch of sugar cane we got nine gallons of syrup (a gallon is equal to four *potter*). The man whose pressing and cooking machine we used also got nine gallons so we actually got eighteen gallons all told. We also got some fruit from our garden. It would take too long to list all of it, but I must tell you something about a fruit called "watermelon." We have an enormous quantity of them; I can't compare them to anything I ever saw in Norway. They are as big as a child's head, some are larger. They are round, and the inside is red or yellow. The melons are sweet and juicy. They are eaten just as they are taken from the field, provided they are ripe. I have cooked molasses from them, and I have also brewed juice several times. (Hops [a kind of plant used in making certain alcoholic beverages] grow wild here. They are very plentiful, and we use them throughout the year.) We sometimes sell melons to wayfarers passing by. We usually get ten cents apiece for them. However, most of the melons we shared with our friends and neighbors, many of whom had walked several miles in order to get a chance to taste our watermelons and muskmelons. The latter fruit is not quite so good as the first.

Our harvest was not abundant . . .

Our harvest was not abundant, but since it was enough to supply our needs for the year and since it was raised on land that we call our own, I want to tell you about it.

This summer we plowed up three acres of land that we plan to sow with wheat next year. Had we known that Ole would come back, we would have plowed up more land this summer. Not knowing when he would return, we let it go with just three acres. By the time he did come home, it was too late to plow any more, so we're letting it go till next summer. So you see we haven't so many acres "under the plow" as they say, but it's not so easy to get ahead if one attempts too much.

This winter we are feeding twenty-one head of cattle, two pigs (a sow and a boar), two horses (a mare and a colt), and three sheep belonging to brother Ole. We also have two bulls belonging to brother Sevat Svendsen. We are paid cash for feeding these cattle. All told we have sixteen farm animals of our own, not counting the young cattle.

We have only four cows. The heifer will bear her first calf this winter, and then we shall have

five cows if all goes well. We have only one sheep.
(The lamb died this spring when it was gelded.) I
have sheared the sheep twice this year. The wool,
which was of excellent quality, weighed all of seven
pounds.

We butchered two pigs this week, one fully
grown, the other eight or nine months old. We
had fattened them since last September so they were
quite large.

**We butchered
two pigs this
week . . .**

I also want to tell you that this fall we have
sold butter for thirty-five dollars—not so much, but
I am satisfied for the time being.

Last fall we built a stable for twelve head of
cattle. We built it of timber, and right now we are
building another like it, but this one is a little larger.
They are built a short distance from each other so
that we can have a shed between for the bulls (about
like the Sansat stable). I can't compare them to the
stables in Norway, but around here they are supposed
to be among the best. There are many varieties of
stable to be seen here. Some are built of branches
and hay; others of sod or turf. I have even seen a
barn where the walls were built of layers of manure
piled up one above the other.

Our house is very small and humble, but it's a
shelter from the cold winter. I shall say no more
about it. However, next spring, if we are all here
and all is well, we hope to build a large and comfortable house. We shall build even though it costs a
great deal of money to build houses in this country.

The spring of 1864 we bought twelve and a
half acres of woodland for one hundred dollars, or
eight dollars an acre. We borrowed the money from
old Svend at seven percent interest with five years
to pay. The trees are exceptionally fine, so if we
should want to sell the land again, it would not be
difficult to get twice the amount that we paid for
it. There is not a great deal of woodland here, and
therefore that type of land is much in demand and
the prices are steadily rising.

Our woodland is six miles from home, a long way to haul the wood, but the road is good. The main road is just outside our door, and it runs past the very edge of the woods. The woodland is two miles from the sawmill in the village of Estherville.

We have had very little pastoral [religious] service so far, but we soon hope to get more. A certain Paster Torgersen has taken it upon himself to visit this congregation two or three times a year. I think we have been very fortunate this fall to have had two services. Two years ago we had thirteen Norwegian families in this congregation, and now we have thirty families and more are constantly moving in. Maybe in time we may be so many that we can have our own pastor.

I have told you in part just how we live. It's so incomplete, but as I did want to tell you everything, even the merest trifle, I have included many things that I should have omitted. I hope you will not disapprove.

Now I have used up all the paper, and I still have so much more to tell you. You no doubt will have to pay extra postage for this letter.

REVIEWING THE READING

1. What differences between Iowa and Norway are mentioned in the 1863 letter?

2. What did settlers on the Great Plains do to protect themselves against prairie fires?

3. **Using Your Historical Imagination.** What differences can you detect between the 1863 and 1865 letters of Gro Svendsen in terms of content and personal attitude? What do you think might account for these differences?

A Teacher Among the Freedmen (1864)

3

From *First Days amongst the Contrabands* by Elizabeth Hyde Botume.

Even before the Civil War was over, Elizabeth Hyde Botume was appointed by the New England Freedmen's Aid Society to teach the recently freed slaves at Beaufort, South Carolina. This city was already in Union hands, and former slaves from a wide area in the South took residence there during the war. Many of the freedmen were in desperate circumstances, as the following excerpts from Botume's book make clear. Notice, as you read the selection, the common attitude of the freedmen to Botume's school and the chance to learn to read and write.

"The poor ye have always with you." This was impressed upon me all the time. It was necessary to inspect my district, now crowded with newcomers, to find out the condition and needs of these people.

I went first to the negro quarters at the "Battery Plantation," a mile and a half away. A large number of Georgia refugees who had followed Sherman's army were quartered here. Around the old plantation house was a small army of black children, who swarmed like bees around a hive. There were six rooms in the house, occupied by thirty-one persons, big and little. In one room was a man whom I had seen before. He was very light, with straight red hair and a sandy complexion, and I mistook him for an Irishman. . . . Seven persons occupied this one room. A rough box bedstead, with a layer of moss and a few old rags in it, a hominy pot, two or three earthen plates, and a broken-backed chair, comprised all the furniture of the room. I had previously given one of the women a needle and some thread, and she now sat on the edge of the rough bedstead trying to sew the dress she ought, in decency, to have had on.

In the old kitchen, not far from the house, more refugees had been placed. Two women were very ill, lying on the floor with only moss and corn-husks under them. It was a most pitiful sight. One of these women begged for a blanket, but the other asked for better food.

"I cannot eat only dry hominy, ma'am," she said. "I lived in massa's house, and used to have white bread and coffee, and I want something sweet in my mouth."

She had belonged to kind and careful owners in Georgia, and suffered severely from all these changes. . . .

Both of these women died. Feeling they could not live, to my surprise and consternation [dismay], they willed me their children. In one family there were five children, and in the other but one boy. The old feeling, born of slavery, that the white race had a right of possession over the blacks, still clung to them. They not only gave me their children, but tried to exact from me a promise to keep them and take good care of them. When I hesitated, they implored [begged] me most piteously not to desert them. . . .

On the next plantation was a curious collection of the original people and new-comers. . . .

In one cabin I found a man in a most wretched condition. Years before he had fallen from a building and broken his back. . . . He was only able to use his hands, and he looked like a human ball rolling over the floor.

I had his cabin cleaned and whitewashed, and fresh, clean clothes put on the poor fellow. He tried in vain to find words to express his gratitude. In all my interviews with him I never heard a word

of complaint, although his sufferings must have been extreme.

"Bless the Lord, missis!" he said, "'tain't no use to fret about it, for it can't be helpt; an' I ain't all the time so racket about wid pain as I used to bin. Sometimes at night I'se so painful I can't shet my eye, an' den I look out de doah, up at the stars, an' t'ink dem de eyes of de Lord looking straight down at me one. An' I 'member what de white folks tell me, 'De Lord is my Shepherd, I shall not want;' for in course I is His little sheep, an' I is so glad! It 'pears like the pain don't hurt me no more. I done forget it altogedder." . . .

In my district there were over five hundred contrabands [slaves who escaped to or were brought into Union lines], men, women, and children. All expressed a desire to have their children learn something, if they themselves knew nothing. But all, from the oldest to the youngest, were eager to "come fur larn too."

I found but one person, a young soldier, who disdained [refused] to attempt anything, saying, almost with insolence, that he had a right to learn

Adults as well as children learned to read and write in the freedmen's schools established in the South toward the end of the Civil War.

"... liberty is
so good."

when young, like other boys; this was denied him
then, and he was not allowed to touch a book, and
now it was too late. This man had indomitable will,
with boldness, unceasing activity, and great physical
strength. He was a power with his race. I wished
to gain his influence in school, as well as his own
good, but could never do it.

One contraband said to me, "Liberty is as good
for us as for the birds of the air. Slavery is not so
bad, but liberty is so good."

He spoke with great affection for his master,
who he said had gone to live in Delaware. . . .

Seeing so much destitution [poverty] around
us made our own lives, meagre as they were, seem
luxurious by comparison. But we were not posing
as "saints without bodies," and it was sometimes a
desperate struggle to keep ourselves comfortable.
At first there was nothing by which to note time;
no clocks nor bells nor steam-whistles. There were
two watches belonging to our "mess." When one
was at the schoolhouse there was nothing to guide
the cook at home.

The dial of the contrabands was: "When the
first fowl crow"—"At crack o' day"—"W'en de sun
stan' straight ober head"—"At frog peep"—"When
fust star shine"—"At flood tide," or "ebb tide," or
"young flood"—"On las' moon," or "new moon." Now
they add to this list "quarterly meeting."

But these data did not help our cook to work,
nor us to regular meals. . . .

In some places the first people who were freed
were treated with injudicious [unwise] consideration.
They were told they were by right the owners of
the land upon which they had worked so long, etc.

Whatever sentiment there was in this, we had
to remember we were dealing with people just born
into a new life, who had to learn the meanings of
their new conditions. . . .

For instance, I was advised not to ask the old
house servants to work for me; for they were in

fact the masters and mistresses of the place,—of the situation they were for a time, if they only knew it, but of nothing else. Said my adviser, "I have no more right to ask Cornelia, the old laundress, to wash for me, than she has to ask me to do her washing."

I replied that laundry work had not been my business: I came to teach the freed people to help themselves.

Whatever they could do better than I, in so far they were my superiors. In consideration of their "previous condition," I gave them my time and instruction, whilst I should pay regular wages for their labor. But I should expect good work, and no make-believe.

REVIEWING THE READING

1. In general, what was the attitude of the freed slaves toward Botume's school?

2. What, according to Botume, was the most basic problem of the former slaves around Beaufort, South Carolina?

3. **Using Your Historical Imagination.** Why did the dying women try to give their children to Botume? What was Botume's explanation for why they did this? Using her account of the general situation of the former slaves, can you suggest a second explanation?

From *Abraham Lincoln: The Prairie Years and the War Years* by Carl Sandburg.

4

Carl Sandburg Describes Lincoln's Assassination (1865)

On April 9, 1865, General Lee surrendered to General Grant and the war was all but over. Bells rang out and bands played all across the North. Five days later, on April 14, President Lincoln and his wife Mary Todd Lincoln were attending a play at Ford's Theatre when the event described below took place. This account of Lincoln's assassination is an excerpt from poet Carl Sandburg's biography of Abraham Lincoln. Historians today still argue about the exact circumstances that led to Lincoln's death. Read carefully to see if Sandburg believed that some of Lincoln's own bodyguards were part of the conspiracy.

The carriage left the White House with its four occupants, coachman Francis Burns holding the reins, and alongside him the footman and valet Charles Forbes. At Ford's Theatre, Burns pulled up his horses. Forbes swung down to the sidewalk and opened the carriage door. The President and his wife stepped out, followed by Major Rathbone and Miss Harris. The guard Parker was at hand. The party walked into the theater at about nine o'clock. An usher led them to their box. The audience in their 1,000 seats saw or heard that the President had arrived. They applauded; many rose from their seats; some cheered. The President paused and nodded his acknowledgment of their welcome to him.

On the stage proceeds a play written 14 years before by the English dramatist Tom Taylor; on rehearsal he decided it was not for the British public and later had sent it to the New York producer Lester Wallack, who had told Laura Keene it would fit her. She had put it on, but after a fairly good run it has about reached its limit.

The play proceeds, not unpleasant, often stupid, sprinkled with silly puns, forced humor. The story centers around the Yankee lighting his cigar with an old will, burning the document to ashes and thereby throwing a fortune of $400,000 away from himself into the hands of an English cousin. The audience agrees it is not bad. The applause and laughter say the audience is having a good time.

From the upholstered rocking armchair in which Lincoln sits he can see only the persons in the box with him, the players on the stage and any persons off stage on the left. The box has two doors. The door forward is locked. The President's party has the roominess and convenience of double space, extra armchairs, side chairs, a small sofa. In the privacy achieved he is in sight only of his chosen companions, the actors he has come to see render a play, and the few people who may be off stage to the left.

This privacy however is not as complete as it seems. A few feet behind the President is the box door, the only entry to the box unless by a climb from the stage. In this door is a small hole, bored that afternoon to serve as a peephole—from the outside. Through this peephole it is the intention of the Outsider who made it with a gimlet [small tool] to stand and watch the President, then at a chosen moment to enter the box. This door opens from the box on a narrow hallway that leads to another door opening on the balcony of the theater.

Through these two doors the Outsider must pass in order to enter the President's box. Close to the door connecting with the balcony two inches of plaster have been cut from the brick wall of the narrow hallway. The intention of the Outsider is

> . . . the audience is having a good time.

that a bar placed in this cut-away wall niche and then braced against the panel of the door will hold that door against intruders, will serve to stop anyone from interference with the Outsider while making his observations of the President through the gimleted hole in the box door.

At either of these doors, the one to the box or the one from the balcony to the hallway, it is the assigned duty and expected responsibility of John F. Parker to stand or sit constantly, with unfailing vigil. A Ward Lamon or an Eckert on this duty would probably have noticed the gimleted hole, the newly made wall niche, and been doubly watchful.

"The guard . . . acting as my substitute," wrote the faithful Crook later, "took his position at the rear of the box, close to an entrance leading into the box . . . His orders were to stand there, fully armed, and to permit no unauthorized person to pass into the box. His orders were to stand there and protect the President at all hazards. From the spot where he was thus stationed, this guard could not see the stage or the actors; but he could hear the words the actors spoke, and he became so interested in them that, incredible as it may seem, he quietly deserted his post of duty, and walking down the dimly-lighted side aisle, deliberately took a seat."

The custom was for a chair to be placed in the narrow hallway for the guard to sit in. The doorkeeper Buckingham told Crook that such a chair was provided this evening for the accommodation of the guard. "Whether Parker occupied it at all, I do not know," wrote Crook. "Mr. Buckingham is of the impression that he did. If he did, he left it almost immediately, for he confessed to me the next day that he went to a seat, so that he could see the play." The door to the President's box is shut. It is not kept open so that the box occupants can see the guard on duty.

Either between acts or at some time when the play was not lively enough to suit him or because of an urge for a pony of whisky under his belt, John F. Parker leaves his seat in the balcony and goes down to the street and joins companions in a little whiff of liquor—this on the basis of a statement of the coachman Burns, who declared he stayed outside on the street with his carriage and horses, except for one interlude when "the special police officer [meaning John F. Parker] and the footman of the President [Forbes] came up to him and asked him to take a drink with them; which he did." Thus circumstances favor the lurking and vigilant Outsider.

The play goes on. The evening and the drama are much like many other evenings when the acting is pleasant enough, the play mediocre, the audience having no thrills of great performance but enjoying itself.

Out in a main-floor seat is one Julia Adelaide Shephard, writing a letter to her father about this Good Friday evening at the theater. "Cousin Julia has just told me," she reports, "that the President is in yonder upper right hand private box so handsomely decked with silken flags festooned over a picture of George Washington. The young and

This illustration from a biography of Abraham Lincoln shows John Wilkes Booth preparing to assassinate the president.

lovely daughter of Senator Harris is the only one of his party we see as the flags hide the rest. But we know Father Abraham is there like a Father watching what interests his children. The American cousin has just been making love to a young lady who says she'll never marry but for love but when her mother and herself find out that he has lost his property they retreat in disgust at the left hand of the stage while the American cousin goes out at the right. We are waiting for the next scene."

And the next scene? The next scene is to crash and blare and flare as one of the wildest, one of the most inconceivable, fateful and chaotic that ever stunned and shocked a world that heard the story.

The moment of high fate is not seen by the theater audience. Only one man sees that moment. He is the Outsider, the one who waited and lurked and made his preparations. He comes through the outer door into the little hallway, fastens the strong though slender bar into the two-inch niche in the brick wall, and braces it against the door panel. He moves softly to the box door and through the little hole studies the box occupants and his Human Target seated in an upholstered rocking armchair. Softly he opens the door and steps toward his prey, in his right hand a one-shot brass derringer pistol, a little eight-ounce vest-pocket weapon winged for death, in his left hand a steel dagger. He is cool and precise and times his every move. He raises the derringer, lengthens his right arm, runs his eye along the barrel in a line with the head of his victim less than five feet away—and pulls the trigger.

A lead ball somewhat less than a half-inch in diameter crashes into the left side of the head of the Human Target, into the back of the head, in a line with and three inches from the left ear. "The course of the ball was obliquely forward toward the right eye, crossing the brain in an oblique manner and lodging a few inches behind that eye. In the track of the wound were found fragments of bone, which had been driven forward by the ball, which was embedded in the anterior lobe of the left hemisphere of the brain."

For Abraham Lincoln it is lights out, good night, farewell—and a long farewell to the good earth and its trees, its enjoyable companions, and the Union of States and the world Family of Man he has loved. He is not dead yet. He is to linger in dying. But the living man can never again speak, see, hear or awaken into conscious being.

REVIEWING THE READING

1. What role was played by John F. Parker in the death of Abraham Lincoln?

2. Does Sandburg suggest that Lincoln's death came about as a result of a conspiracy among his bodyguards or other persons close to the president?

3. **Using Your Historical Imagination.** Write a final paragraph (written the next day) completing Julia Adelaide Shephard's letter to her father. How would she describe being present at the death of the man she called "Father Abraham"?

5

From *Chinese Gold: The Chinese in the Monterey Bay Region* by Sandy Lydon.

Chinese Railroad Workers on the Frontier (1865–1890)

During the building of the first transcontinental railroad in the years following the Civil War, thousands of Chinese immigrants did hard and dangerous duty on the construction crews of the Central Pacific Railroad. After the railroad was completed in 1869, these Chinese American workers returned to California to toil on a number of other railroad construction projects, including the Santa Cruz, South Pacific Coast, and Pajaro Valley railroads. Only relatively recently have historians fully acknowledged the role played by the Chinese in settling the West. In the following excerpts from historian Sandy Lydon's book Chinese Gold, *the contribution of Chinese Americans is viewed in perspective. As you read the selection, note the kinds of work performed by the Chinese American railway workers and the wages they received for this work.*

It took one hundred years for the heroic feats of the Chinese who worked on the Transcontinental Railroad to be included in the historical accounts written about the building of the Central Pacific Railroad through and over the Sierra Nevada; the image of Chinese railroad workers hanging over cliffs in baskets as they drilled the blasting holes has finally become part of the history of the American West. When the Central Pacific and Union Pacific Railroads joined in Utah in 1869, the Central Pacific released an estimated five thousand Chinese railroad workers who provided the labor for a decade of railroad building throughout California. In 1870 there were no railroad tracks in the Monterey Bay Region, but by 1880 Chinese railroad builders dug cuts, laid ballast, drilled tunnels, built trestles, laid track, and risked death to build almost one hundred miles of track, bringing Santa Cruz and Monterey counties into the industrial age. . . .

The Monterey and Salinas Valley Railroad

The Monterey and Salinas Valley Railroad was the first of several proposed . . . railroads constructed in central California. . . .

As surveyors moved across the Salinas Valley in April 1874, scrapers, wheelbarrows, and a steam donkey arrived in Monterey by steamer. . . . The first Chinese railroad workers for the project arrived by steamer right behind the steam donkey and wheelbarrows. By May 150 Chinese were cutting the grade between Monterey and the Salinas River. Throughout the next seven months, the M&SVRR tried to supplement its construction crews with white laborers, but few white workers came forward for the arduous [difficult] work, so the Chinese provided the bulk of the labor on the road's construction. . . .

If nineteenth-century Monterey County owed much to the coming of the railroads, Santa Cruz County owed everything, for railroads constructed during the 1870s tied together the isolated communities along the north coast of Monterey Bay and launched an era of unparalleled development. . . .

Between 1875 and 1880 the Chinese built three separate railroads, laid forty-two miles of track, and drilled 2.6 miles of tunnels to stitch Santa Cruz County together and attach it permanently to the world beyond the Santa Cruz Mountains. The Chinese contributed not only their muscle and sweat, but their lives. At least fifty Chinese were killed in accidents while building those railroads. For every mile of railroad, one Chinese died. . . .

Chinese laborers laid track and blasted tunnels through the Sierra Nevada.

Chinese railroad workers on the Santa Cruz Railroad worked six ten-hour days a week and were paid one dollar a day. Two dollars per week was deducted from their pay for food, while expenses such as clothing and recreation chipped away at the remaining four dollars so that they averaged three dollars per week profit. . . .

The [South Pacific Coast Railroad] SPCRR route began on the east side of San Francisco Bay (which was not already locked up by the Southern Pacific), came south along the bay to San Jose, then to Los Gatos and over the mountains to Felton. . . . In August 1878 the SPCRR employed seven hundred men, six hundred of whom were Chinese. Chinese did all the grading, tunneling, track-laying, and ballasting, while whites built trestles and supervised the construction. By 1879, when the tunnels were being drilled and track was being laid in the canyons, approximately one thousand Chinese railroad workers laid track in the Santa Cruz Mountains. . . .

The Chinese crews of twenty to thirty men were supervised by a Chinese contractor who took his orders from a white supervisor and acted as paymaster for the Chinese workers. . . . By the end of the project the white contractors praised the Chinese as hard-working, honest, and "possessed of retentive memories." . . . whites found that the Chinese were not docile, however, for when the Chinese railroad workers felt they were being mistreated or abused, they responded quickly and, on occasion, violently. . . .

The Pajaro Valley Consolidated Railroad was the last railroad project in the Monterey Bay Region in which Chinese railroad workers bore the primary responsibility for construction. The restrictions passed on Chinese immigration in the 1880s had done their work, and the aging, diminishing Chinese population in California was replaced by the younger Japanese immigrants. Crucial to the development of the Monterey Bay Region in the nineteenth century, the railroads had a beneficial impact on agriculture, manufacturing, and tourism. Whether shipping lumber out in flat cars or bringing tourists in parlor cars, the trains came through cuts and tunnels and over grades built by the Chinese. The economic successes of the nineteenth century were built on the sweat and blood of Chinese railroad workers.

REVIEWING THE READING

1. What sorts of work were the Chinese asked to do, and what were they paid for this work?

2. Where did the Chinese construction crews from the Central Pacific Railroad go after the transcontinental line was completed in 1869?

3. **Using Your Historical Imagination.** On the West Coast, public resentment against the Chinese immigrants was growing at the same time they were making their greatest contributions to the development of the West. In 1882 the Chinese Exclusion Act drastically restricted Chinese immigration to the United States. What possible explanations can you think of for this general resentment of the Chinese immigrants?

Andrew Carnegie Becomes a Businessman (1868)

6

From "How I Served My Apprenticeship As a Business Man" by Andrew Carnegie, *Youth's Companion,* Volume LXX, No. 17

Andrew Carnegie came to the United States as a penniless immigrant from Scotland. However, by the end of the nineteenth century he had become a well-known industrialist and one of the wealthiest men in the world. Carnegie launched his business career in 1868 and eventually amassed a fortune in the steel industry. His company produced most of the steel products in the United States by 1900. The selection that follows is taken from an article Carnegie wrote for a magazine called Youth's Companion *in 1896, entitled "How I Served My Apprenticeship As a Businessman." As you read the excerpts, consider what values Carnegie's autobiography reflects.*

I am sure that I should never have selected a business career if I had been permitted to choose.

The eldest son of parents who were themselves poor, I had, fortunately, to begin to perform some useful work in the world while still very young, in order to earn an honest livelihood . . . What I could get to do, not what I desired, was the question.

When I was born my father was a well-to-do master-weaver in Dunfermline, Scotland. He owned no less than four damask looms and employed apprentices. This was before the days of steam factories for the manufacture of linen. A few large merchants took orders and employed "master-weavers," such as my father, to weave the cloth, the merchants supplying the materials.

As the factory system developed, handloom weaving naturally declined, and my father was one

Scottish immigrant Andrew Carnegie rose from poverty to become one of the wealthiest industrialists in the United States.

of the sufferers by the change. The first serious lesson of my life came to me one day when he had taken in the last of his work to the merchant and returned to our little home greatly distressed because there was no more work for him to do. I was then just about ten years of age, but the lesson burned into my heart, and I resolved then that "the wolf of poverty" would be driven from our door some day, if I could do it.

The question of selling the old looms and starting for the United States came up in the family council . . . . It was finally resolved to take the plunge and join relatives already in Pittsburgh. I well remember that neither father nor mother thought the change would be otherwise than a great sacrifice for them, but that "it would be better for our two boys. . . ."

Arriving in Allegheny City, four of us,—father, mother, my younger brother and myself,—father entered a cotton factory. I soon followed and served as a "bobbin boy," and this is how I began my preparation for subsequent apprenticeship as a business man. I received one dollar and twenty cents a week, and was then just about twelve years old.

I cannot tell you how proud I was when I received my first week's own earnings. One dollar and twenty cents made by myself and given to me because I had been of some use in the world! No longer entirely dependent upon my parents, but at last admitted to the family partnership as a contributing member and able to help them! I think this makes a man out of a boy sooner than almost anything else. . . . It is everything to feel that you are useful. . . .

For a lad of twelve to rise and breakfast every morning, except the blessed Sunday morning, and go into the streets and find his way to the factory, and begin work while it was still dark outside, and not be released until after darkness came again in the evening, forty minutes' interval only being al-

lowed at noon, was a terrible task. . . . But I was
young . . . and something within always told
me that . . . I should some day get into a better
position. . . .

A change soon came, for a kind old Scotsman,
who knew some of our relatives, made bobbins and
took me into his factory before I was thirteen. But
here for a time it was even worse than in the cotton
factory, because I was set to fire a boiler in the
cellar, and actually to run the small steam-engine
which drove the machinery.

The firing of the boiler was all right, for fortunately we did not use coal, but the refuse wooden
chips, and I always liked to work in wood. But the
responsibility of keeping the water right and of running the engine, and the danger of my making a
mistake and blowing the whole factory to pieces,
caused too great a strain, and I often awoke and
found myself sitting up in bed through the night
trying the steam-gages. But I never told them at
home that I was having a "hard tussle." No! no!
everything must be bright to them.

This was a point of honor, for every member
of the family was working hard except, of course,
my little brother, who was then a child, and we
were telling each other only all the bright things.
Beside this no man would whine and give up—he
would die first. . . .

My kind employer, John Hay, peace to his ashes!
soon relieved me of the undue strain, for he needed
some one to make out bills and keep his accounts,
and finding that I could write a plain schoolboy
hand, and could [work with numbers], I became
his only clerk. . . .

I come now to the third step in my apprenticeship, for I had already taken two, as you see, the
"cotton factory" and then the "bobbin factory" . . .
I obtained a situation as messenger-boy in the telegraph office of Pittsburgh when I was fourteen. Here
I entered a new world. . . . Amid books, newspapers,

pencils, pen and ink and writing pads, and a clean office, bright windows and the literary atmosphere, I was the happiest boy alive.

My only dread was that I should some day be dismissed because I did not know the city; for it is necessary that a messenger-boy should know all the firms and addresses of men who are in the habit of receiving telegrams. But I was a stranger in Pittsburgh. However, I made up my mind that I would learn to repeat successively each business house in the principal streets, and was soon able to shut my eyes and begin at one side of Wood Street, and call every firm to the bottom. Before long I was able to do this with the business streets generally. . . .

Of course, every ambitious messenger-boy wants to become an operator, and before the operators arrived in the early mornings the boys slipped up to the instruments and practised. This I did and was soon able to talk to the boys in the other offices along the line, who were also practising.

One morning I heard Philadelphia calling Pittsburgh and giving the signal, "Death Message." Great attention was then paid to "Death Messages," and I thought I ought to try to take this one. I answered and did so, and went off and delivered it before the operator came. After that the operators sometimes used to ask me to work for them.

Having a sensitive ear for sound I soon learned to take messages by ear, which was then very uncommon—I think only two persons in the United States could then do it. Now every operator takes by ear, so easy it is to follow and do what any other boy can—if you only have to. This brought me into notice, and finally I became an operator and received the—to me—enormous [salary] of twenty-five dollars per month, three hundred dollars a year!

This was a fortune; the very sum that I had fixed when I was a factory-worker as the fortune I wished to possess, because the family could live on three hundred dollar a year and be almost, or quite independent. Here it was at last! But I was soon to [receive] extra compensation for extra work. The six newspapers of Pittsburgh received telegraphic news in common. Six copies of each despatch were made by a gentleman who received six dollars per week for the work, and he offered me a gold dollar every week if I would do it, of which I was very glad indeed, because I always like to work with news and scribble for newspapers. . . .

I think this last step of doing something beyond one's task is fully entitled to be considered "business." The other revenue, you see, was just salary obtained for regular work; but here was a "little business operation" upon my own account, and I was very proud indeed of my gold dollar every week.

The Pennsylvania Railroad shortly after this was completed to Pittsburgh, and that genius, Thomas A. Scott, was its superintendent. He often came to the telegraph office to talk to his chief . . . and I became known to him in this way.

When that great railway system put up a wire of its own, he asked me to be his "clerk and operator." So I left the telegraph office . . . and became connected with the railways.

> . . . I left the telegraph office . . . and became connected with the railways.

The new appointment was accompanied by a, to me, tremendous increase of salary. It jumped from twenty-five to thirty-five dollars per month. Mr. Scott was then receiving one hundred and twenty-five dollars per month, and I used to wonder what on earth he could do with so much money.

I remained for thirteen years in the service of the Pennsylvania Railroad Company, and was at last superintendent of the Pittsburgh division of the road, successor to Mr. Scott, who had in the meantime risen to the office of vice-president of the company.

One day Mr. Scott, who was the kindest of men, and had taken a great fancy to me, asked if I had or could find five hundred dollars to invest.

Here the business instinct came into play. I felt that as the door was opened for a business investment with my chief, it would be wilful flying in the face of providence if I did not jump at it; so I answered promptly:

"Yes, sir, I think I can."

"Very well," he said, "get it; a man has just died who owns ten shares in the Adams Express Company, which I want you to buy. It will cost you sixty dollars per share, and I can help you with a little balance if you cannot raise it all."

Here was a queer position. The available assets of the whole family were not five hundred dollars. . . .

Indeed, had Mr. Scott known our position he would have advanced it himself, but the last thing in the world the proud Scot will do is to reveal his poverty and rely upon others.

The family had managed by this time to purchase a small house, and paid for it in order to save rent. My recollection is that is was worth eight hundred dollars.

The matter was laid before the council of three that night, and the oracle [wise one, used here in reference to his mother] spoke. "Must be done. Mortgage our house. I will take the steamer in the morning for Ohio and see uncle, and ask him to arrange it. I am sure he can." This was done. Of course her visit was successful—where did she ever fail?

. . . ten shares of Adams Express Company stock was mine . . .

The money was procured; paid over; ten shares of Adams Express Company stock was mine, but no one knew our little home had been mortgaged "to give our boy a start."

Adams Express Stock then paid monthly dividends of one percent, and the first check for ten dollars arrived. I can see it now, and I well remember the signature of "J. C. Babcock, cashier . . ."

Here was something new to all of us, for none of us had ever received anything but from a toil. A return from capital was something strange and new.

How money could make money . . . led to much speculation upon the part of the young fellows

[Carnegie's friends], and I was for the first time hailed
as a "capitalist. . . ."

A very important incident in my life occurred
when one day in a train a nice, farmer-looking gentleman approached me, saying that the conductor had
told him I was connected with the Pennsylvania
Railroad, and he should like to show me something.
He pulled from a small green bag the model of
the first sleeping-car. This was Mr. Woodruff, the
inventor. . . . Its value struck me like a flash. I asked
him to come to Altoona the following week, and
he did so.

Mr. Scott, with his usual quickness, grasped
the idea. A contract was made with Mr. Woodruff
to put two trial cars on the Pennsylvania Railroad.
Before leaving Altoona Mr. Woodruff came and
offered me an interest in the venture which I promptly
accepted. But how I was to make payments rather
troubled me, for the cars were to be paid for in
monthly installments after delivery, and my first
monthly payment was to be two hundred and seventeen dollars and a half.

I had not the money, and I did not see any
way of getting it. But I finally decided to visit the
local banker and ask him for a loan, pledging myself
to repay at the rate of fifteen dollars per month.
He promptly granted it. Never shall I forget his
putting his arm over my shoulder, saying, "Oh, yes,
Andy, you are all right." I then and there signed
my first note. Proud day this; and surely, now, no
one will dispute that I was becoming a "business
man." I had signed my first note and, more important
of all,—for any fellow can sign a note,—I had found
a banker willing to take it as good.

My subsequent payments were made by the
[money received] from the sleeping-cars, and I really
made my first considerable sum from this investment
in the Woodruff Sleeping Car Company, which was
afterward absorbed by Mr. Pullman—a remarkable
man who is now known all over the world.

Shortly after this I was appointed superintendent of the Pittsburgh Division, and returned to my dear old home, smoky Pittsburgh. Wooden bridges were then used exclusively upon the railways, and the Pennsylvania Railroad was experimenting with a bridge built of cast-iron. I saw that wooden bridges would not do for the future, and organized a company in Pittsburgh to build iron bridges.

Here again I had recourse to the bank, because my share of the capital was twelve hundred and fifty dollars and I had not the money; but the bank lent it to me, and we began the Keystone Bridge Works, which proved a great success. . . .

This was my beginning in manufacturing; and from that start all our other works have grown, the profits of the one works building the other. My "apprenticeship" as a business man soon ended, for I resigned my position as an officer of the Pennsylvania Railroad Company to give exclusive attention to business.

I was no longer merely an official working for others . . . but a full-fledged business man working upon my own account.

REVIEWING THE READING

1. Carnegie uses his career to suggest certain values to the youth of the United States. What are these values?

2. What succession of jobs did Carnegie hold before he went into business for himself?

3. **Using Your Historical Imagination.** According to Andrew Carnegie, what did it mean to be a "real businessman"? Do you think it means the same thing today?

Annie Bidwell Attends a Mechoopda Dance (1870s)

From *Rancho Chico Indians* by Annie E. K. Bidwell.

Annie Ellicott Kennedy was born in Meadville, Pennsylvania, in 1839. In 1868 she married California pioneer John Bidwell and went to live on his large ranch, Rancho Arroyo Chico, in Butte County. This began her long association with the band of Mechoopda Indians who lived at the Indian Rancheria on Rancho Chico.

Annie Bidwell was fascinated by Mechoopda customs and concerned with the welfare of the Indians. For almost half a century she was the Indians' patron and protector and arranged for their instruction in both the English language and the Christian religion. The following excerpt is from an account written by Bidwell to document Mechoopda customs in the first decade of her relationship with the Indians. As you read consider what may have been the significance of the dance Bidwell was asked to attend.

After the Indians of my mission learned to speak English, I was invited by the women to attend an Indian dance, which I promised to do, and reported my promise to my husband. His reply was that he did not think it a suitable place for me to go. He had never attended one himself, because he had so understood. My answer was that I must go because I was invited, and because I must know what the Indians were doing in order to be helpful to them. That I would get my pastor and some of my guests to accompany me, which I did, and on arrival at the "Sweat House," was given a seat of honor near the door. This "Sweat House" would hold, I should think, two hundred and fifty people at least. It was made like the dwelling houses only being very much larger. Wooden columns supported the dome, leaving a corridor between the columns and the wall. The doorway was made by cutting a chute through the ground to the ground floor so as not to cut into the dome, and weaken it. A wooden door closed this entrance. In the center of the room was a bright fire of coals which answered for the heat and light. This was kept burning by an Indian who sat by it, throwing little twigs on from time to time to keep it a glowing heat and clear flame without smoke. His only clothing was a pair of trousers. His body was checked up with charcoal. He had drawn a piece of hair between his eyes so that he could look at it so as to give a cross-eyed, wild appearance to his face. He moved his head around as he chanted and kept the fire going. Perfect stillness reigned in the building otherwise. On one side of the building sat the Indian men, in the corridor, with their backs toward the fire, their skins shining like bronze in the lurid light. On their heads were various kinds of feather ornaments. Some looked like magnificient helmets made of the woodpecker's scarlet feathers, giving the appearance of scarlet plush, only more brilliant than could plush possibly be in that fire light. At the back of the helmet were masses of hawk feathers. Wild as it was, it was really an inspiring sight in its weird beauty. On the opposite side sat the women in groups dressed in white costumes, the skirts trimmed around the bottom with lozenges of red calico. In the ears of some were earrings of woodpecker feathers with the little tuft of the quail for pendants. The earring was really a little wooden stick which was thrust through the opening in the ear, leaving the feather ornaments alone exposed to the front view. The man at the fire ceased his chanting, and on the top of the "sweat house" began a sort of intoning. I whispered to the woman next to me, "What does that mean?" pointing toward the man on the outside. She answered in a whisper, with a worshipful accent, "He is talking to God." And gave me to understand that I must not speak in the dance house. After a while this prayer ceased, when suddenly there seemed to be violently thrown past me through the doorway, huge balls of feathers following one after the other, which, to my surprise, were standing on their feet around the fire. This proved to be Indian men clad in very full skirts [capes] of feathers, reaching to the knees and supported over the shoulders by bands of feathers, extending from the front of the skirt to the back of the skirt. Hawk feathers were stuck in their hair. Helmets were rare but they were in evidence. In a twinkle some dozen Indians were dancing around this fire, while the keeper-up of the fire and some half-dozen Indians furnished music for the dancers with their particular chant, (the half-dozen Indians all adding to it by the time they kept with their bare feet on the ground), and a peculiar little musical instrument, (made, I was told, with a few pieces of elder brush), which made a monotonous sound as

The Mechoopda and other California Indians wove beautiful and functional baskets from native grasses.

of one note of a guitar. This was kept up with an intense vigor, dancing and music, until the bronze forms of these Indians shone with moisture, which was fairly streaming down their persons. Suddenly, with almost the same rapidity with which they entered, and with a great shout, they sprang out into the open air, one by one. Had the village been where it was when I came to Rancho Chico, they would have all taken a plunge bath; but as it was, they had to cool off in the open air. I should have said that the baskets of acorn soup were scattered around the border of the room for the refreshment of the dancers. At one time during the evening the music changed to most soft tones, when all in the "sweat house" assumed subdued attitudes while the music continued. When this strange solemnity fell upon these people, I forgot my instructions not to speak, and whispered, "What is it? What does this mean?" My Indian friend who had silenced me before, and who was the daughter of the man who was the chief, when my husband came here, (and a wonderfully strong and interesting man he was) answered me in solemn whisper, "The dead people are dancing now." At the close of this part of the ceremony the Indian men who had been sitting with their backs to the fire, sprang to their feet, and, with those who had gone out, but had returned, mingled with the dancers. Not all danced at once. The contest seemed to be who could dance the longest, and there was great shouting and applause from both men and women at the various feats of agility displayed in these dancers (applauding a part of the service and not considered "talking"). As the different dancers became exhausted they left the dance house to cool off, and usually it was an elderly man who stood it the longest. They seemed to me sometimes to spring almost to the roof of the dome; their agility was marvelous. The next scene was the men and women dancing the "bear dance." The men and women stood opposite each other. One man had a

The contest seemed to be who could dance the longest . . .

piece of bear skin in his hand and acted as if dodging here and there to escape. The women all had in their hands little brushes of tule [probably reeds] which they shook toward the men. The men and women did not touch each other, and I am assured, never do in the Indian dances. This dance was a prayer for game; that is a prayer for God to give them bear of which they used the skins for bedding. We remained until about half past eleven, the service still continuing.

The argument which I presented against the Indian dance was, that when they had a creek to spring into after the dance, it was a benefit to them, purifying their bodies; but that now that they had to sit in the cold wind, it gave them colds and pneumonia. Also that they danced to excess and overtired their bodies so that the next day they were not in condition for good work; that the dance was harmless otherwise for they had told me that God wanted them to dance because they always felt better after the dance, and He wanted them to dance to keep well. I explained to them the Turkish baths and told them the benefit of purifying the body.

They gave up the dance ultimately of their own accord as they have given up all their customs peculiarly their own save a few.

REVIEWING THE READING

1. What precautions did Bidwell take before attending the dance?

2. After it was over, what arguments did Bidwell offer against continuing the custom of the dance?

3. **Using Your Historical Imagination.** How important do you think the dance was to the Mechoopda?

8	# The Vaquero (1870s)

From *The Vaquero* by
Arnold R. Rojas.

Stories about western cowboys provide some of our most colorful moments in American history. But much of what comes to mind when we think of cowboys actually originated in northern Mexico. Mexican American cowboys, or vaqueros, invented most of the objects we associate with life on the range, including the rope lariat, chaps, the broad-brimmed hat, the cotton bandanna, and the western saddle. Moreover, the word cowboy *is a translation from the Spanish word "vaquero." In the following excerpt from the writings of twentieth-century historian Arnold Rojas, we are given a glimpse of what life on the range was like for these first cowboys. As you read the selection, note the special care taken by the vaquero in the treatment of his horse.*

In speaking of the origins of the vaquero we must not forget to mention in passing the first horses to come from Spain. They came with the first Armada [fleet of warships], and were such faithful, heroic horses and played so important, though innocent, a part in the conquest, that a list of them should be included in all books on the American horse. There were sixteen mares and stallions, mostly grays and sorrels, in the original conquest of the New World.

Bernal Diaz gives their colors and the names of the most outstanding. Two were of the famed Valenzuela breed of Spain. There were *El Harriero*, the Driver; *Motilla*, Little Tuft; *El Romo*, the Roman Nosed One; *La Rabona*, the Rat-tailed One (she was the "good gray mare" of Velasquez de Leon). *La*

Rabona was probably an appaloosa because the rat, or stub tail, is a characteristic of that type of horse, and prevails on the appaloosa from Tierra del Fuego through South America, Mexico and western United States to Canada. Diaz called her a gray; but there are many shades of gray and some of the appaloosas are a mottled color which closely approaches, or is, gray. The "blunt old soldier" says of *La Rabona*, "when the battle was going against the Spaniards and the men were weakening, Velasquez de Leon would appear on his good gray mare, and the men would take courage."

The Indians' belief that man and horse were one (the centaur myth) was true in the sense that there existed a perfect affinity [kinship] between horse and rider. This affinity has never been better exemplified [illustrated] than in the Conquest, where man and horse made one terrible creature.

The fabulous amount of gold which the Spaniards took from the New World had at least one benefit to posterity [future generations]. It brought to America the finest horseflesh to be found in Europe. These horses were shipped to New Spain and in time sired the great-hearted mustang, the vaquero's horse. True, before the vaquero went out of existence he rode horses of many breeds and mixtures, but the mustang was the perfect horse for working cattle—sure-footed, utterly loyal, tireless, patient and brave. He was the welder of two continents, a worthy descendant of the Andalusian barb [northern African breed of horse].

The vaquero while working cattle rode hard and was hard on horses, but he never abused them to make a spectacle. The way the vaquero went about taming a horse was not always gentle, but he was not deliberately cruel. He had applied his military riding to the herding of cattle and the roping of grizzly bears, Tule elk, and wild hogs. He never overestimated the intelligence of his mustang, and had studied the degree to which a horse could be

The American cowboy learned many of his roping and stock-handling techniques from the vaquero.

taught. He had learned that patience and repetition were the only means to success in teaching the horse. He never asked the animal to do more than could be expected of it.

The blood of caballeros, bullfighters, Jews, Moors, Basques, and Indian heroes ran in the vaquero's veins. He was a strange mixture of races. He admired his Iberian [Spanish] father, but sided and sympathized with his . . . Indian mother. If food was short he fed his horse before he fed his wife. Though often a strange contradiction, he was, without doubt, the most interesting man in the New World.

He was a descendant of the old conquerors, and retained the language of Spain. In living the free life of the nomad [wanderer] he imitated the Spaniard in the trappings of his horse, and the Indian in his abode [place to live]. He spent his wealth on silver-mounted bits and spurs and often left his home destitute [empty] of necessities. He slept on the ground, but rode a silver-mounted saddle. He may not have combed his hair, but his horse's mane was trimmed, with one tuft for a colt and two for a bridle horse. . . .

The vaquero would lie on the ground with his saddle for a pillow even though the rain was falling, and sleep without a word of complaint, yet he would grumble when his saddle-blankets got wet. Wet saddle-blankets make a horse's back sore.

The vaquero's way of life gave him virtues which do not exist in this modern day, and at this distant time no man can judge a man of that era. His life was hard. He would stand shivering in the early morning cold, holding a cup of coffee in his shaking hand, then sit a horse all day in the driving sleet, chilled to the bone. He would ride from dawn to dusk in a cloud of alkali dust, his tongue parched and swollen, with rippling water in a mirage shimmering in the distance, with visions of all the water he had ever drunk or seen wasted haunting his memory, for memory plays queer, cruel tricks. The want of water was the vaquero's greatest hardship in the burning heat of a San Joaquin Valley summer. He often rode in a daze with visions of springs of cool water bubbling out of the pine-scented Sierra, of canals of water from which he had never bothered to drink. And when he came to drink it would more than likely be out of a reeking waterhole that contained the putrid [rotten] remains of some animal.

But there was another side. A matchless sky overhead. An expanse of wild flowers that spread over the great valley like a purple carpet, so vast that a day's ride would take one only to the middle of it. The bold, brooding Sierra standing in grim outline that stretched away to the northern horizon. A wild chase down a mountainside in the fall when the air is like wine and life is good. The feel of a good horse between one's knees as he sweeps and wheels around a herd of restless cattle. The evening campfire when men broil *costillas*, ribs, on chamiso root coals, and gathered around to tell tales of long ago, of Murrieta, Vasquez, and Garcia [colorful figures in Mexican American history].

REVIEWING THE READING

1. Describe the origin of the American horse.

2. What was the greatest hardship faced by the vaquero? Why would the vaquero complain when his saddle-blankets got wet?

3. **Using Your Historical Imagination.** Why do you think the vaquero put the needs of his horse before his own needs?

Wolves and Grasshoppers Plague the Kansas Frontier (1870s)

9

From *Pioneer Women: Voices from the Kansas Frontier* by Joanna L. Stratton.

Settlers in Kansas faced many hardships as they bravely sought to make new lives for themselves on the frontier. Homesteaders living far away from their neighbors especially feared the prairie fires, which would sweep with horrifying quickness across the open plains. In addition, the hot winds and droughts common to Kansas made life a constant battle between the farmer and nature. But these were not the only ways that nature would plague the Kansas settlers. Animals and even insects could add to the toll. The following selection, excerpted from the accounts of pioneer women in Kansas, tells of nature's more devastating attacks. As you read the selection, note why the Kansas farmers were largely unprepared for the "Grasshopper Year."

Allena A. Clark had her own ways of coping with a lonely day or a sudden emergency. Her daughter Esther remembered:

". . . the unbroken prairies stretched for miles outside, and the wistful-faced sheep were always near at hand. Often mother used to go out and lie down among them, for company, when she was alone for the day.

"When the spring freshets [rising waters] came, the sheep were on the wrong side of the river, and it was my mother who manned one of the three wagons that went back and forth across the rising waters until the last sheep was safely on the home side. She has told me of the terror that possessed her during those hours, with the water coming up steadily to the wagon bed. To this day, there is a superstitious dread of water in the heart of every one of our family.

"Mother has always been the gamest [bravest] one of us. I can remember her hanging on to the reins of a runaway mule team, her black hair tumbling out of its pins and over her shoulders, her face set and white, while one small girl clung with chattering teeth to the sides of the rocking wagon and a baby sister bounced about on the floor in paralyzed wonder. I remember, too, the things the men said about 'Leny's nerve.' But I think, as much courage as it took to hang on to the reins that day, it took more to live twenty-four hours at a time, month in and out, on the lonely and lovely prairie, without giving up to the loneliness."

That loneliness, usually borne with dignity and silence, could at times express itself in unexpected ways. Mary Furguson Darrah recalled a time when "Mr. Hilton, a pioneer, told his wife that he was going to Little River for wood. She asked to go with him . . . She hadn't seen a tree for two years, and when they arrived at Little River she put her arms around a tree and hugged it until she was hysterical."

Nightfall, blanketing the prairie in a dense, boundless [endless] blackness, brought an even keener sense of solitude to the pioneer home. The profound silence was broken only by the occasional chirr of a cricket or the gentle swish of the tall prairie grass—or by the call of the wild. For it was during the black nights that the howl of the coyote and the wolf spread terror throughout every frontier homestead. Often roaming the plains in packs, these rapacious [greedy] animals would attack without provocation or mercy.

"In the summer of 1872 and '73," recalled S. N. Hoisington, "the gray wolves and coyotes were very numerous. It was not safe to go out across the prairies without a weapon of some kind. My mother was a nurse and doctor combined. In early girlhood she used to help her brother mix his medicines, and after she came to Kansas people came for miles for her to doctor their families.

"A man by the name of Johnson had filed on a claim just west of us, and had built a sod house. He and his wife lived there two years, when he went to Salina to secure work. He was gone two or three months, and wrote home once or twice, but his wife grew very homesick for her folks in the east, and would come over to our house to visit mother.

"Mother tried to cheer her up, but she continued to worry until she got bed fast [bedridden] with the fever. At night she was frightened because the wolves would scratch on the door, on the sod and on the windows, so my mother and I started to sit up nights with her. I would bring my revolver and ammunition and axe, and some good-sized clubs.

"The odor from the sick woman seemed to attract the wolves, and they grew bolder and bolder. I would step out, fire off the revolver and they would settle back for a while when they would start a new attack. I shot one through the window and I found him lying dead in the morning.

"Finally the woman died and mother laid her out [prepared her for burial]. Father took some wide boards that we had in our loft and made a coffin for her. Mother made a pillow and trimmed it with black cloth, and we also painted the coffin black.

"After that the wolves were more determined than ever to get in. One got his head in between the door casing and as he was trying to wriggle through, mother struck him in the head with an axe and killed him. I shot one coming through the window. After that they quieted down for about half an hour, when they came back again. I stepped out and fired at two of them but I only wounded one. Their howling was awful. We fought these

. . . the wolves were more determined than ever to get in.

Settlers on the Great Plains use homemade nets in a futile attempt to save their crops from swarming grasshoppers.

wolves five nights in succession, during which time we killed and wounded four gray wolves and two coyotes.

"When Mr. Johnson arrived home and found his wife dead and his house badly torn down by wolves he fainted away. . . . After the funeral he sold out and moved away." . . .

During the first twenty years of its settlement, the Kansas frontier was relatively free from any sizable grasshopper infestation. Although grasshoppers had aggravated the farmer in relatively small numbers from time to time, they had not been a particularly serious problem. As a result, the pioneers were largely unprepared for the massive onslaught [attack] of the insects which would literally eat their way across the state in 1874. In fact, the infestation was so overwhelming and devastating that the year was later identified as the "Grasshopper Year."

In the beginning, 1874 seemed to have the makings of a very good year. "In the spring of 1874," wrote Mrs. Everett Rorabaugh, "the farmers began their farming with high hopes, some breaking the sod for sod corn, others plowing what had been broken the year before, sowing spring wheat, corn and cane, and with plenty of rain everyone was encouraged at the present. The neighbors would meet at some little one-room house and put in the day visiting and eating buffalo meat boiled, and corn-bread and dried 'apple sass' that some relative back east had sent, and the men talking about the bumper crop they were going to have that year."

Although the summer had been typically hot and dry, the crops were growing well. By August, the wheat and the oats were mostly in the shock [collected in small stacks], and the lush green pasture grasses gave promise of fat and healthy herds of cattle. For the farmers evaluating their prospects, a plentiful harvest seemed assured. But their anticipation turned to despair as millions upon millions of grasshoppers blanketed the sky. "They looked like a great, white glistening cloud," recalled one bewildered pioneer, "for their wings caught the sunshine on them and made them look like a cloud of white vapor." Swooping down on the fertile fields, the insects began a feast of destruction.

"August 1, 1874," explained Mary Lyon, "is a day that will always be remembered by the then inhabitants of Kansas. . . . For several days there had been quite a few hoppers around, but this day there was a haze in the air and the sun was veiled almost like Indian summer. They began, toward night, dropping to earth, and it seemed as if we

. . . the grasshoppers covered every inch of ground . . .

were in a big snowstorm where the air was filled with enormous-size flakes."

Alighting to a depth of four inches or more, the grasshoppers covered every inch of ground, every plant and shrub. Tree limbs snapped under their weight, corn stalks bent to the ground, potato vines were mashed flat. Quickly and cleanly, these voracious [gluttonous] pests devoured everything in their paths. No living plant could escape. Whole fields of wheat, corn and vegetables disappeared; trees and shrubs were completely denuded [stripped bare]. Even turnips, tobacco and tansy [a bitter herb] vanished.

"When they came down," remembered Mary Roberts, "they struck the ground so hard it sounded almost like hail. Father had tried to get a start in fruit trees as soon as he could, and we had a greengage plum tree in our yard that was full of plums that were almost ripe, but it was thought too green to pick yet. We had to postpone dinner while 'all hands' gathered garden stuff and plums to save them. We picked every plum, as they would soon have all been devoured by the hoppers had we not done so.

"There was a watermelon patch in our garden and the melons were quite large and long. They were not ripe, so we could not save them, but by the evening of the second day they were all gone. I think we found one or two pieces of rind about the size of the palm of our hand in the whole patch. Such enormous appetites they had! In a few days they had eaten every green thing. They soon had every twig on every tree or bush eaten off and the trees were as bare as in midwinter."

Stunned by the continued onslaught and desperate to save what little remained, the pioneers grabbed whatever coverings they could find to shield their crops and shrubbery. Out came the bedsheets, blankets, quilts and shawls. Even old winter coats and greasy burlap sacks were ripped apart to spread over

precious vegetables. Yet these coverings proved useless; the grasshoppers ate straight through the cloth
or wormed their way underneath. As the settlers
soon learned, these creatures would stop at nothing.

"They devoured every green thing but the prairie grass," continued Mary Lyon. "They ate the leaves
and young twigs off our young fruit trees, and seemed
to relish the green peaches on the trees, but left
the pit hanging. They went from the corn fields as
though they were in a great hurry, and there was
nothing left but the toughest parts of the bare stocks.
Our potatoes had to be dug and marketed to save
them.

"I thought to save some of my garden by covering it with gunny sacks, but the hoppers regarded
that as a huge joke, and enjoyed the awning thus
provided, or if they could not get under, they ate
their way through. The cabbage and lettuce disappeared the first afternoon; by the next day they
had eaten the onions. They had a neat way of eating
onions. They devoured the tops, and then ate all
of the onion from the inside, leaving the outer shell.

"The garden was soon devoured, and when all
of these delicacies were gone, they ate the leaves
from the fruit trees. They invaded our homes, and
if our baking was not well guarded by being enclosed
in wood or metal, we would find ourselves minus
the substantial part of our meals; and on retiring
to bed, we had to shake them out of the bedding,
and were fortunate if we did not have to make a
second raid before morning."

Within hours, no part of the countryside was
left unscathed [untouched]. Having eliminated all
the crops and foliage, grasshoppers by the thousands
moved on into barns and houses. Besides devouring
the food left in cupboard, barrel and bin, they attacked anything made of wood, destroying kitchen
utensils, furniture, fence boards and even the rough
siding on cabins. Window curtains were left hanging
in shreds, and the family's clothing was heartily

. . . the insects took a special liking to the handles of pitchforks . . .

consumed. Craving anything sweaty, the insects took a special liking to the handles of pitchforks and the harnesses of horses. Lumbering cattle stood by helplessly as the pests crawled all over their bodies, tickling their ears, eyes and nostrils. Young children screamed in terror as the creatures writhed through their hair and down their shirts. Men tied strings around their trouser cuffs to keep them from wriggling up their legs.

Lillie Marcks was a child of twelve when the grasshoppers scourged [destroyed] these prairies. In her memoirs, she relived the anguish of witnessing the unexpected devastation of her family's homestead. "Several days before the plague of grasshoppers, my father and his hired man, Jake, came home from the near-by village with tales of trains that could not start or stop because the tracks were slick with crushed grasshoppers. So thick were the grasshoppers that the sun could scarcely be seen.

"One morning, I had a chill and shook for hours. Mother made a pallet for me on the floor near the front door and covered me. I fell asleep. After a long rest, I awoke burning with fever. Mother had placed a wet cool towel over my face to reduce the fever. The sun was shining over my pallet and I felt so ill. Oh dear! Then Jake's voice rang loud and clear. 'Mrs.! Oh, Mrs.! They're come! They're come! The grasshoppers is here! You can jes' see the trees bein' ett up!' I raised the towel from my face and eyes, looked toward the sun. Grasshoppers by the millions in a solid mass filled the sky. A moving gray-green screen between the sun and earth.

"Riding his pony like the wind, father came home telling us more tales of destruction left in the path of the pests. They hit the house, the trees and picket fence. Father said, 'Go get your shawls, heavy dresses and quilts. We will cover the cabbage and celery beds. Perhaps we can save that much.' Celery was almost an unseen vegetable in that time and place—they wished to save it. They soon were busy spreading garments and coverings of all sorts over the vegetables.

"The hired man began to have ideas. Everyone was excited trying to stop the devastation. Bonfires began to burn thru the garden. 'Now I'll get some of them,' Jake said. Picking up a shovel, he ran thru the gate. Along the fence they were piled a foot deep or more, a moving struggling mass. Jake began to dig a trench outside the fence about two feet deep and the width of the shovel. Father gathered sticks and dead leaves. In a few minutes, the ditches were filled with grasshoppers, but they soon saw the fire covered and smothered by grasshoppers. Think of it, grasshoppers putting out a fire.

"Ella, my five-year-old sister, was shooing and beating them off the covered garden by means of a long branch someone had given her. I was ill and so excited over all of this battle and could only be up a few seconds at a time. Then all at once, Ella's voice rang out in fear. 'I'm on fire!' Forgotten was my fever. I ran to the door and saw a flame going up the back of her dress. In less time that I can tell this, I ran to her and tore off her dress from the shoulders down. Then I turned and looked at the writhing mass of grasshoppers on the garments covering the vegetables and called, 'Ma! Ma! Come here! They are eating up your clothes!'"

At least the clothes the grasshoppers ate in the Marcks household were on the ground and not being worn. Adelheit Viets was not as lucky: "The storm of grasshoppers came on Sunday. I remember that I was wearing a dress of white with a green stripe. The grasshoppers settled on me and ate up every bit of green stripe in that dress before anything could be done about it."

For the beleaguered [troubled] settlers, the devastation continued long after the grasshoppers had moved on. To their dismay, everything reeked with the taste and odor of the insects. The water in the ponds, streams and open wells turned brown with their excrement [bodily waste] and became totally unfit for drinking by either the pioneers or their livestock. Bloated from consuming the locusts, the barnyard chickens, turkeys and hogs themselves tasted so strongly of grasshoppers that they were completely inedible.

REVIEWING THE READING

1. What did Mrs. Hilton do when she arrived at Little River? According to S. N. Hoisington, why did she and her mother stay at the Johnson house?

2. Why were the Kansas farmers largely unprepared for the "Grasshopper Year"? Why was it useless for the farmers to try to save their gardens by covering them with burlap sacks and clothing?

3. **Using Your Historical Imagination.** What do you think the Kansas settlers did for food after everything was destroyed by the grasshoppers?

Cowpunching on the Texas Trail (1883)

10

From *We Pointed Them North: Recollections of a Cowpuncher* by E. C. Abbott and Helena Huntington Smith.

From 1867 to 1886, hundreds of thousands of Texas cattle were driven north to the railhead towns of Kansas, where they were shipped east to market. For a time—and the heyday of the great trail drives lasted less than two decades—great profits were possible. Scrub longhorns from the mesquite thickets of south Texas were next to worthless at home, but— if you could get them there—they sold for $25 to $50 each in Kansas.

Little of this money went into the pockets of the ordinary cowpunchers, who endured great hardships in the long drive north. In the following excerpt from his book of reminiscences, cowpuncher "Teddy Blue" Abbott gives an account of what life was like for the cowpunchers on the Texas Trail. As you read the selection, note what Abbott says was the greatest hardship the men had to face.

In 1883 all the cattle in the world seemed to be coming up from Texas. On the trail we were hardly ever out of sight of a herd, and when we got to that big flat country along the North Platte [River] we could see the dust of the others for twenty miles. One afternoon I was out hunting some of our horses—because we had brought a lot of wild range horses up from Texas with us, and bought more at North Platte, and they were always getting away. And I rode up on a little hill to look for the horses, and from the top of the hill I could see seven herds behind us; I knew there were eight herds ahead of us, and I could see the dust from thirteen more of them on the other side of the river.

On another hill on the north side of the North Platte, near Cold Water, was where I left the herd and lay down in the shade. That was counted a disgrace, but I had been in the saddle two nights and three days.

The first night after we crossed the river with the F U F [initials of a ranch] herd I was on night guard, ten to twelve, and it came up an awful hailstorm. I told my partner, a kid from Boston, to ride to one side and take the saddle off and hold it over his head. And pretty soon I had to quit, too, and hold my saddle over my head, and there were still dents in that saddle when I traded it off in Buffalo, Wyoming, a year later. Nobody knows now what those storms were like, because nobody has to stay out in them any more, but believe me, they were awful. If you had to take that drumming on your head, it would drive you crazy.

I lost my horse that night, because a big hailstone hit my hand, and it hurt so bad I let go the reins as he plunged. The rest of the night I was afoot and helpless. Nobody came out from camp to relieve us, because camp was on the other side of a big coulee—arroyo, they call it down there— and it was swimming water and they couldn't get across. So all that night my partner and I were out there with the herd alone.

The next night another storm came up and . . . it was my relief again. The second night nobody in the outfit got any sleep, but the rest of them only had one night of it, and my partner and I had two. Five herds was camped close together when that storm struck, and next day 10,000 range cattle was all mixed up. We rounded up and cut our cattle out; it was hot as hell, and in that country along the Platte there wasn't a tree nor even any brush for fifty or sixty miles.

About three in the afternoon, on Cold Water Creek, I saw a sod house that some cow outfit had built there for a line camp, and I saw where this

little bit of a house made a patch of shade. So I rode over to it, and got off my horse and I took my rope down and laid on it, so the horse couldn't leave me. And I just died.

Watching over the herd was an important part of the cowboy's job.

When I woke up, it was dark. I could see our campfire away up the flat. I rode out there and asked the boss to figure out what he owed me, because I thought I would get fired for quitting the herd and I wanted to beat him to it.

But all he said was: "Ted, I thought you was going to do that yesterday."

They used to have some terrible storms on the North and South Platte. The year before this, in '82, I was in one that killed fourteen head of cattle and six or seven horses and two men, on the different herds. One man was so scared he threw his six-shooter away, for fear it would draw the lightning. . . .

Lots of cowpunchers were killed by lightning, and that is history. I was knocked off my horse by it twice. The first time I saw a ball of fire coming toward me and felt something strike me on the head. When I came to, I was lying under old Pete and the rain was pouring down on my face. The second time I was trying to get under a railroad bridge when it hit me, and I came to in the ditch. The cattle were always restless when there was a storm at night, even if it was a long way off, and that was when any little thing would start a run. Lots of times I have ridden around the herd, with lightning playing and thunder muttering in the distance, when the air was so full of electricity that I would see it flashing on the horns of the cattle, and there would be balls of it on the horse's ears and even on my mustache, little balls about the size of a pea. I suppose it was static electricity, the same as when you shake a blanket on a winter night in a dark room.

. . . the worst hardship we had on the trail was loss of sleep.

But when you add it all up, I believe the worst hardship we had on the trail was loss of sleep. There was never enough sleep. Our day wouldn't end till about nine o'clock, when we grazed the herd onto the bed ground. And after that every man in the outfit except the boss and horse wrangler and cook would have to stand two hours' night guard. Suppose my guard was twelve to two. I would stake my night horse, unroll my bed, pull off my boots, and crawl in at nine, get about three hours' sleep, and then ride two hours. Then I would come off guard and get to sleep another hour and a half, till the cook yelled, "Roll out," at half past three. So I would get maybe five hours' sleep when the weather was nice and everything smooth and pretty, with cowboys singing under the stars. If it wasn't so nice, you'd be lucky to sleep an hour. But the wagon rolled on in the morning just the same.

That night guard got to be part of our lives. They never had to call me. I would hear the fellow coming off herd—because laying with your ear to the ground you could hear that horse trotting a mile off—and I would jump up and put my hat and boots on and go out to meet him. We were all just the same. I remember when we got up to the mouth of the Musselshell [River] in '84 we turned them loose, and Johnny Burgess, the trail boss, said: "We won't stand no guard tonight, boys," and it sounded good. But every man in that outfit woke when his time to go on guard came, and looked around and wanted to know why they didn't call him.

Sometimes we would rub tobacco juice in our eyes to keep awake. It was rubbing them with fire. I have done that a few times, and I have often sat in my saddle sound asleep for just a few minutes. In '79, when we hit the Platte River with that Olive herd, a strong north wind was blowing waves two feet high in their faces, and they bulled on us, which means they won't do nothing, only stand and look at you. So since they wouldn't take the water we had to hold them, and we had one of those bad electric storms and they run nearly all night. We got them across the river the next day, and that night on guard my partner, Joe Buckner, says: "Teddy, I am going to Greenland where the nights are six months long, and I ain't agoing to get up until ten o'clock next day."

For a cowboy on the trail drive north, the broad-brimmed felt hat had many practical uses.

REVIEWING THE READING

1. According to Abbott, what was the greatest hardship faced by the cowpunchers on the Texas Trail?

2. How did Abbott lose his horse one night? Why did he ask his boss to figure out how much he owed him?

3. **Using Your Historical Imagination.** Why do you think the Texas cowpunchers failed to seek shelter during lightning storms?

Two Cowboy Songs

Many a cowboy was lulled to sleep on the Texas trail listening
to his fellow cowboys singing songs under the night stars.

From *He Was Singin' This Song* by Jim Bob Tinsley.

Little Joe the Wrangler

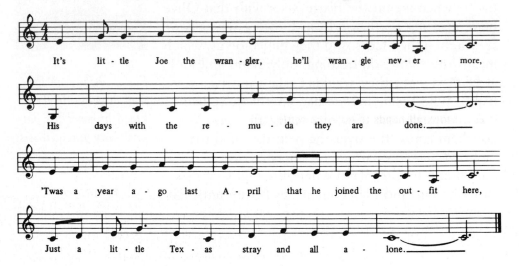

It was long late in the evening he rode up to our herd,
    On a little old brown pony he called Chaw;
With his brogan shoes and overalls, a harder looking kid
    You never in your life had seen before.

His saddle was a southern kack built many years ago,
    An OK spur on one foot idly hung,
His hot roll in a cotton sack was loosely tied behind,
    And a canteen from the saddle horn he'd slung.

He said he had to leave his home, his paw had married twice,
    And his new maw beat him every day or two.
So he saddled up old Chaw one night and lit a shuck this way,
    Thought he'd try and paddle now his own canoe.

He said he'd do the best he could if we'd only give him
    work,
    Though he didn't know straight up about a cow.
So the boss he cut him out a mount and kinda put him on,
    For he sorter like the little stray somehow.

We taught him how to herd the string and learn to know them all,
    To round 'em up by daylight, if he could.
To follow the chuck wagon and always hitch the team
    And help the *cosinero* rustle wood.

We'd driven to Red River and the weather had been fine;
    We were camped down on the south side in a bend.
When a norther commenced blowing and we doubled up our guards,
    For it took all hands to hold the cattle then.

Little Joe the wrangler was called out with the rest,
    And scarcely had the kid got to the herd,
When the cattle they stampeded, like a hailstorm
    round they flew,
    And all of us were riding for the lead.

'Tween the streaks of lightning we could see
    a horse far out ahead,
    It was little Joe the wrangler in the lead.
He was riding old Blue Rocket with his slicker
    above his head
    Trying to check the leaders in their speed.

At last we got them milling and kinda quieted down,
    And the extra guard back to the camp did go
But one of them was missing, and we all knew at a
    glance
    'Twas our little Texas stray—poor wrangler Joe.

Next morning just at sunup we found where Rocket fell,
    Down in a washout twenty feet below.
Beneath his horse, mashed to a pulp, his spurs had rung the knell.
    Was our little Texas stray—poor wrangler Joe.

Sam Bass

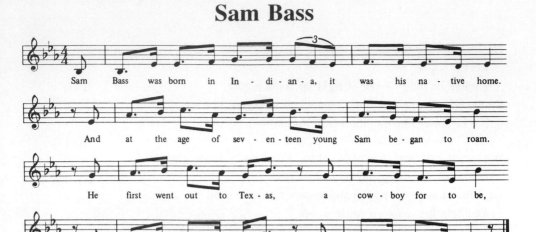

Sam Bass was born in In - di - an - a, it was his na - tive home.

And at the age of sev - en - teen young Sam be - gan to roam.

He first went out to Tex - as, a cow - boy for to be,

A kind - er - heart - ed fel - low you sel - dom ev - er see.

Sam used to deal in race stock, one called the ''Denton mare.''
    He watched her in scrub races and took her to the fair.
He used to coin the money and spend it just as free,
    He always drank good whiskey wherever he might be.

Sam Bass had four companions, all bold and daring lads.
    They were Underwood and Jackson, Joel Collins and Old Dad.
More bold and reckless cowboys the Wild West never knew,
    They whipped the Texas Rangers and chased the boys in blue.

Young Sam he left the Collins ranch in the merry month of May,
    With a herd of Texas cattle for the Back Hills far away.
Sold out in Custer City and then went on a spree
    With a harder set of cowboys you seldom ever see.

On the way back to Texas, they robbed the U. P. train;
    They then split up in couples and started out again.
Joe Collins and his pardner were overtaken soon,
    With all their hard-earned money, they had to meet their doom.

Sam made it back to Texas, all right side up with care;
    Rode in the town of Denton with all his friends to share.
But his stay was short in Texas, three robberies did he do,
    He robbed the Longview passenger, express, and mail cars too.

Sam had another comrade, called "Arkansaw" for short;
   Killed by a Texas Ranger by the name of Thomas Floyd.
Jim Murphy was arrested and then released on bail;
   He jumped his bond at Tyler and took the train for Terrell.

But Major Jones had posted Jim and that was all a stall.
   It was only a plan to capture Sam before the coming fall.
He met his fate at Round Rock, July the twenty-first,
   They pierced poor Sam with rifle balls and emptied out his purse.

Sam Bass he is a corpse now and six feet under clay,
   And Jackson's in the bushes a-trying to get away.
Murphy borrowed Sam's hard money and didn't want to pay;
   The only way he saw to win was give poor Sam away.

And so he sold out Sam and Barnes and left their friends to mourn.
   O what a scorching Jim will get when Gabriel blows his
      horn!
Perhaps he got to heaven, there's none of us can say,
   But if I'm right in my surmise, he's gone the other way.

11

From *Touchdown!* by
Amos Alonzo Stagg and
Wesley Winans Stout.

Football Without Helmets (1884)

Although football has a long history, it did not at its beginning resemble the game we see today. In 1884, when Amos Alonzo Stagg came to Yale as a freshman and went out for the team, football was still an informal and irregular sport, one played mostly for fun. As Stagg says, injuries in practice or in games "were disregarded" and incoming freshmen (all volunteers) were expected to learn the game on their own. But even in 1884, change was coming. Over the objections of some of its faculty, Yale had just purchased its first athletic field, and at Princeton the students had forced their football squad to stop smoking. Things were clearly getting serious! Beginning his career in these "dark ages" of football, Stagg stayed to see the sport come of age. His coaching career lasted over 50 years. As you read this excerpt from Stagg's account of those early years, consider what factors may have contributed to the rise in importance of the game of football.

I arrived at Yale in September, 1884, and turned out for the squad. The college bought its first athletic field that year, the one hundred and eighty-third of its history. Being situated in the heart of New Haven, it had to go far out to the farther bank of the West River to find sufficient cheap vacant land. Paying good money for a playground caused talk and revived faculty criticism of the attention being given to athletics. Prof. E. L. Richards, who promoted the present Yale gym, dug into the records on his own initiative, proved that disciplinary cases had decreased sharply and progressively since 1875, and silenced the conservatives.

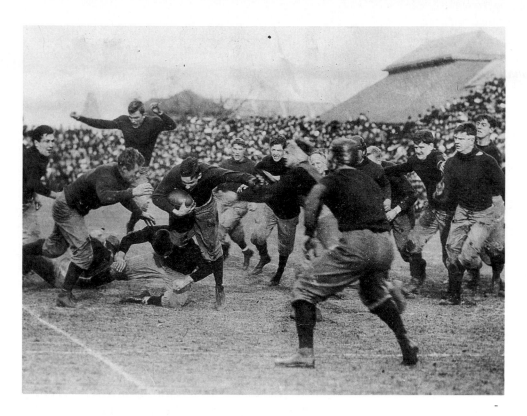

The old gym was a primitive thing where freshmen were marshaled [gathered] in street dress and forced to swing Indian clubs and dumbbells. No bath followed and the drill probably did as much harm as good. One of the joys of growing to sophomore stature was escaping the gym. Informal football and baseball practice customarily was held on the gym lot, where Harkness Dormitory now stands. Conditions at Yale were representative of [similar to] the larger colleges.

There were no coaches, trainers, rubbers [persons who give rubdowns], or even a water boy. Occasional graduated players were drifting back to advise the football team, but the captain still was a captain, not a coach's foreman. He chose the team, ran it, and was not always above playing favorites. Once elected, he was answerable to no one. . . . Once under Camp's [Walter Camp—often called the "father of American football" because of his

In the earliest days of American-style football, helmets were rarely worn. This is the game between Yale and Harvard in 1907.

contributions to the game as coach, Yale athletic director, and author] captaincy the Yale squad came near dissolving in mid-season over a quarrel between the forwards and the backs. Camp and his fellow backs favored the newer running mass style of play. The rush line was unanimous naturally for the old open, kicking, passing, individual running game in which they could be as spectacular as the backs.

Camp was particularly fearful of a muddy field for the Thanksgiving Day game with Princeton, with Eaton and Fred Remington, heavy ends, and insisted on drilling the line in mass formations. The line revolted. That night Camp summoned the squad to his room in Durfee Hall, told them that the responsibility was his, that he either would run the team or get off, resigned and left the room. Ten minutes of heated debate followed. The rush line was as little convinced as ever, but so disturbed at the threatened loss of Camp's leadership that they coaxed him back. Camp led the eleven against Princeton and won, but Yale played the old game.

Camp resigned another time. There were no training rules or training table, but the squad had pledged themselves not to leave the campus for ten days before the Princeton game, and to be in bed by eleven each night. Catching Johnny Moorehead sneaking back from the theater one night late, Camp called every man out of bed and quit on the spot. Moorehead offered his own resignation instead, and Camp reconsidered. As Moorehead played in the Princeton game, he seems to have been restored to grace.

At Princeton as early as 1879 the students had so criticized the football squad for smoking that the players gradually gave up tobacco during the season. In those years at Princeton the team customarily practiced at noon and jogtrotted half a mile to a mile at sundown. A full three-quarters-of-an-hour period of continuous playing against the scrubs was Yale's daily practice, and injuries were disregarded. There was no freshman rule, but no particular attempt was made to interest the incoming class. Two or three dependable substitutes were all that a team thought of needing. The freshman who made the varsity was either a natural player or had played in prep school. The bulk of the newcomers never had seen the game. If they turned out, they were expected to teach themselves.

REVIEWING THE READING

1. What things did a university football program *not* have in 1884 that it had at the time of Stagg's writing (1927)?

2. What was the reason for the conflict among the Yale team members?

3. **Using Your Historical Imagination.** What factors do you think might explain the rise of the sport of university football to its current prominence?

12

From *Edison's Open Door: The Life Story of Thomas A. Edison* by Alfred O. Tate.

Thomas Edison Observed (1885)

Alfred O. Tate served as Thomas Edison's secretary for years, and in 1938 he published this description of the personal character of the great inventor. As the inventor of the phonograph, the incandescent lamp, and a hundred other practical and profitable machines and mechanical processes, Edison left a deep mark on industry and society. He was also a very human man, as Tate's account demonstrates. Consider, as you read these excerpts, how Edison used mathematics in his research.

O ne of Edison's friends in eulogizing him [praising him in a speech] after his death said that he was the last great empirical experimenter. The dictionary defines empirical as "depending on experience alone with due regard to science or theory," and an empirical experimenter as "one who relies on practical experience." Edison certainly at times employed methods that might be regarded as unorthodox [unusual], but it would be wrong to assume that he was not abreast of science. He not only subscribed to but read all the scientific journals. He had a thoroughly modern scientific library which constantly was augmented [added to] and which did not remain unread.

No one but himself could know to what extent he drew upon science and theory. He must have employed theory, because no forward step can be taken in experimentation unless the mind is projected ahead of it. Science may be described as "systemized knowledge." It has many branches, but in those which Edison pursued he unquestionably was familiar with all "systemized knowledge" associated with them, and demonstrated at times his ability to project it.

In the year 1875 he discovered the waves that now enter every household "through the air" to provide entertainment. They were called the "Edison Effect" or "Etheric Force," and a number of patents were issued to him covering devices designed to utilize them.

Edison was not a mathematician. He had a method of his own of solving mathematical problems. His lack of knowledge of this science never seemed to be a handicap. His mind seemed to alight on the answer in one swift flight which perhaps he himself could not explain. It has been said that [Isaac] Newton never could demonstrate a problem in Euclid [geometry based on the work of the Greek mathematician Euclid]. The answers were to him so obvious that he could not restrain his mental processes long enough to follow the steps of a demonstration. That is the way Edison's mind seemed to work. His esteem for mathematicians could not be described as extravagant. He had been subjected to the ridicule of these scientists in his earlier days when he was conducting his "empirical" experiments on the incandescent lamp. They lived to regret it.

One day I walked into a room where Edison was working at a bench. Arthur Kennelley, his mathematician, was just leaving the room and he was laughing. I went over to Edison and asked him what was the joke.

"Tate," he exclaimed impatiently, "these mathematicians make me tired. When you ask them to work out a sum they take a piece of paper, cover it with rows of A's and B's and X's and Y's, decorate them with a lot of little numbers, scatter a mess of flyspecks over them (his disrespectful synonym for decimals was much more Rabelaisian [crude] than this) and then give you an answer that's all wrong!"

. . . . I recall one of Edison's empirical experiments. He wanted to find a solvent [solution that dissolves] of hard rubber. Science had not discovered it. Theory was helpless. So he resorted to empiricism.

> His mind seemed to alight on the answer in one swift flight . . .

Thomas Edison, the famous inventor, established his reputation while still a young man.

He had a storeroom of scientific chemicals that was complete. He immersed in vials containing one of each of these chemicals a small section of hard rubber. I do not recall how many there were, but it was an impressive collection. Later on I asked him how the experiment had turned out. "I got it," he said, and mentioned the name of the solvent which, not being a chemist, I have forgotten, except that it was an acetate.

But I have Edison's word for it that he was not a scientist. He subscribed to a newspaper clipping bureau and when the basket containing letters to be submitted to him was put before him each morning these clippings were placed on top, as he always wanted to read them first. It was not vanity. It was curiosity.

On one of these occasions when I was sitting beside him, he passed a clipping over to me in which he was referred to as a scientist. Then he said, "That's wrong! I'm not a scientist. I'm an inventor. [Michael] Faraday was a scientist. [Faraday was a leading researcher of the time in electricity.] He didn't work for money. Said he hadn't time. But I do. I measure everything I do by the size of a silver dollar [silver dollars were current coin then]. If it don't come up to that standard then I know it's no good."

His meaning was clear. If his work would sell, if the public would buy and pay their silver dollars for it, then he would know that it was useful. And that was his vocation—the production of new and useful inventions. He was a utilitarian [practical] inventor, and money was the only barometer [gauge] that could be employed to indicate success. But I do not concur [agree] in his disclaimer. He also was a Scientist most highly esteemed and admired by his contemporaries throughout the world.

Edison had beautiful hands, more sensitive than those of a woman. Often I have watched them hovering over an instrument to make delicate adjustments, with the rest of his body as rigid as a statue. At

these times they seemed to assume an individuality
of their own. Always I associated them with the
strings of a harp. They seemed to belong there.
But there was one thing those hands were unable
to accomplish. They could not count money.

One evening we were dining together at Del-
monico's to go later to the apartment of Ed Rice
of the famous theatrical firm of Rice and Dixey. At
that time Henry Dixey was appearing in *Adonis,* which
ran for a period that broke all previous records and
made Dixey the most popular stage artist in New
York. Rice played some of his delightful piano com-
positions for us and Dixey entertained us with some
of his wonderful card tricks. After dinner, when the
bill was presented, Edison took a roll of notes [paper
money] out of his pocket, flattened it on the table,
and began to pick at it. He disarranged it. Then
he patted it around the edges, smoothed it out, and
began to pick at it again. Then in disgust he pushed
the pile across the table to me and said: "Here,
Tate! . . . Stick it in your pocket and pay our
bills tonight."

The reason for this was that he never, or very
seldom, carried money, and while he made large
sums, little of it passed through his hands in the
form of currency. At his laboratory in Orange, if
he had occasion to go to New York, I had carefully
to see that he was provided with money. Otherwise
he would have started without any. He derived no
pleasure from the expenditure of money for personal
gratification [his own needs]. He was indifferent concerning food with the exception of pie. When inten-
sively preoccupied with work in his laboratory his
meals were sent there from his home, but invariably
he would let them stand until cold and frequently
I have seen him eat the pie which always formed a
part of his fare [meal] and leave everything else
untouched. This irregularity was the habit of a lifetime and undoubtedly was the cause of the stomach
acidity which assailed him at not infrequent intervals.

But in the expenditure of money for experimentation he never stopped to count the cost. It made no difference to him what the cost might be when he had an objective in view. This factor never entered his mind. He evaluated money not as something to be conserved or accumulated but as a vehicle essential to the progress of his work. If beyond this a surplus was accumulated, he was gratified, not because it represented wealth, but because it constituted tangible [real] evidence of the utility of his inventions.

In those early days when the Edison Electric Light Company shares were quoted at an enormous premium, and when he had relatively little money, he never sold a share. He was bitterly opposed to speculation [buying and selling stocks based on what the market might do in the future]. There was no title of reproach and contempt that he could confer on anyone more withering than that of speculator. I can hear him now annihilating [destroying] someone of whose pursuits in this hazardous field he disapproved with the blasting denunciation, "Oh! he's a speculator!" And yet he staked, lost and won millions in his own field of adventure. It is the objective that reveals and establishes character in the great gamble of industrial development. Edison played a square game.

REVIEWING THE READING

1. According to Tate, what was Edison's attitude toward money?

2. What was Edison's attitude toward food?

3. **Using Your Historical Imagination.** Why did Edison say that he was an inventor, not a scientist, and what was his attitude toward mathematics?

Clergyman and Critics: A Debate over Imperialism (1885–1899)

13

From *Our Country: Its Possible Future and Its Present Crisis* by Josiah Strong; and *Platform of the American Anti-Imperialist League.*

Imperialism, the expansion of national power abroad and the acquisition of foreign territories, aroused strong opinions among Americans for and against. Generally, however, the imperialists were more convincing to most Americans in the decades of the 1880s and 1890s. Imperialism seemed the reasonable—even the Christian—thing to do. European nations were engaged in a scramble for territories in Africa and elsewhere around the world. Many persons in the United States sincerely believed it was in our national interest to do the same. Major foreign territories were acquired from Spain after the quick American victory in the war of 1899, and the United States soon set out to administer its own foreign empire.

In the following excerpts, the Reverend Josiah Strong and the American Anti-Imperialist League (a political group opposed to imperialist adventures abroad) offer arguments for and against American imperialism. Study their arguments closely before turning to the questions at the end of the selection.

Josiah Strong

Every race which has deeply impressed itself on the human family has been the representative of some great idea—one or more—which has given direction to the nation's life and form to its civilization. Among the Egyptians this seminal [the most important] idea was life, among the Persians it was light, among the Hebrews it was purity, among the

Greeks it was beauty, among the Romans it was law. The Anglo-Saxon is the representative of two great ideas, which are closely related. One of them is that of civil liberty. Nearly all of the civil liberty in the world is enjoyed by Anglo-Saxons: the English, the British colonists, and the people of the United States. . . . The noblest races have always been lovers of liberty. That love ran strong in early German blood, and has profoundly influenced the institutions of all the branches of the great German family; but it was left for the Anglo-Saxon branch fully to recognize the right of the individual to himself, and formally to declare it the foundation stone of government.

The other great idea of which the Anglo-Saxon is the exponent [supporter] is that of a pure *spiritual* Christianity. It was no accident that the great reformation of the sixteenth century originated among a Teutonic [northern European], rather than a Latin people. It was the fire of liberty burning in the Saxon heart that flamed up against the absolutism of the Pope. . . .

It is not necessary to argue to those for whom I write that the two great needs of mankind, that all men may be lifted up into the light of the highest Christian civilization, are, first, a pure, spiritual Christianity, and, second, civil liberty. Without controversy, these are the forces which, in the past, have contributed most to the elevation of the human race, and they must continue to be, in the future, the most efficient ministers to its progress. It follows, then, that the Anglo-Saxon, as the great representative of these two ideas, the depository of these two greatest blessings, sustains peculiar relations to the world's future, is divinely commissioned to be, in a peculiar sense, his brother's keeper. . . .

There can be no reasonable doubt that North America is to be the great home of the Anglo-Saxon, the principal seat of his power, the center of his life and influence. Not only does it constitute seven-elevenths of his possessions, but his empire is unsevered, while the remaining four-elevenths are fragmentary and scattered over the earth. Australia will have a great population; but its disadvantages, as compared with North America, are too manifest [obvious] to need mention. Our continent has room and resources and climate, it lies in the pathway of the nations, it belongs to the zone of power, and already, among Anglo-Saxons, do we lead in population and wealth. . . .

Our continent has room and resources and climate . . .

Mr. [Charles] Darwin is not only disposed to see, in the superior vigor of our people, an illustration of his favorite theory of natural selection [survival of the fittest], but even intimates [suggests] that the world's history thus far has been simply preparatory for our future, and tributary [contributes] to it. He says: "There is apparently much truth in the belief that the wonderful progress of the United States, as well as the character of the people, are the results of natural selection; for the more energetic, restless, and courageous men from all parts of Europe have emigrated during the last ten or twelve generations to that great country, and have succeeded best. . . ."

The time is coming when the pressure of population on the means of subsistence will be felt here as it is now felt in Europe and Asia. Then will the world enter upon a new stage of its history—*the final competition of races, for which the Anglo-Saxon is being schooled.* Long before the thousands millions are here, the mighty *centrifugal* tendency [movement outward from the center], inherent [inborn] in this stock and strengthened in the United States, will assert itself. Then this race of unequaled energy, with all the majesty of numbers and the might of wealth behind it—the representative, let us hope, of the largest liberty, the purest Christianity, the highest civilization—having developed peculiarly aggressive traits calculated to impress its institutions upon mankind, will spread itself over the earth. If I read not amiss, this powerful race will move down upon

Mexico, down upon Central and South America, out upon the islands of the sea, over upon Africa and beyond. And can any one doubt that the result of this competition of races will be the "survival of the fittest"? . . .

In my own mind, there is no doubt that the Anglo-Saxon is to exercise the commanding influence in the world's future; but the exact nature of that influence is, as yet, undetermined. How far his civilization will be materialistic and atheistic, and how long it will take thoroughly to Christianize and sweeten it, how rapidly he will hasten the coming of the kingdom wherein dwelleth righteousness, or how many ages he may retard it, is still uncertain; but *it is now being swiftly determined.* . . .

Notwithstanding the great perils which threaten it, I cannot think our civilization will perish; but I believe it is fully in the hands of the Christians of the United States, during the next fifteen or twenty years, to hasten [hurry] or retard [slow] the coming of Christ's kingdom in the world by hundreds, and perhaps thousands, of years. We of this generation and nation occupy the Gibraltar of the ages which command the world's future.

American Anti-Imperialist League

We hold that the policy known as imperialism is hostile to liberty and tends toward militarism, an evil from which it has been our glory to be free. We regret that it has become necessary in the land of Washington and Lincoln to reaffirm that all men,

In this editorial cartoon from 1899, Uncle Sam cheers the imperialistic exploits of the conquering U.S. Navy.

of whatever race or color, are entitled to life, liberty and the pursuit of happiness. We maintain that governments derive [get] their just powers from the consent of the governed. We insist that the sub-jugation [conquering] of any people is "criminal aggression." . . .

We earnestly condemn the policy of the present National Administration in the Philippines. It seeks to extinguish the spirit of 1776 in those islands. We deplore [regret] the sacrifice of our soldiers and sailors, whose bravery deserves admiration even in an unjust war. We denounce the slaughter of the Filipinos as a needless horror. We protest against the extension of American sovereignty by Spanish methods [force].

The United States have always protested against the doctrine of international law which permits the subjugation of the weak by the strong. A self-govern-ing state cannot accept sovereignty over an unwilling people. The United States cannot act upon the an-cient heresy [unpopular view] that might makes right.

. . . Much as we abhor [hate] the war of "crimi-nal aggression" in the Philippines, greatly as we regret that the blood of the Filipinos is on American hands, we more deeply resent the betrayal of American institutions at home. . . .

Whether the ruthless slaughter of the Filipinos shall end next month or next year is but an incident in a contest that must go on until the Declaration of Independence and the Constitution of the United States are rescued from the hands of their betrayers. Those who dispute about standards of value while the foundation of the Republic is undermined will be listened to as little as those who would wrangle about the small economies of the household while the house is on fire. The training of a great people for a century, the aspiration [striving] for liberty of a vast immigration are forces that will hurl aside those who in the delirium of conquest seek to destroy the character of our institutions.

We deny that the obligation of all citizens to support their Government in times of grave national peril applies to the present situation. If an Administration may with impunity [without any cost] ignore the issues upon which it was chosen, deliberately create a condition of war anywhere on the face of the globe, debauch [corrupt] the civil service for spoils to promote the adventure, organize a truth-suppressing censorship and demand of all citizens . . . their unanimous support while it chooses to continue the fighting, representative government itself is imperiled. . . .

We hold, with Abraham Lincoln, that "no man is good enough to govern another man without that other's consent. When the white man governs himself and also governs another man, that is more than self-government—that is despotism." "Our reliance is in the love of liberty which God has planted in us. Our defense is in the spirit which prizes liberty as the heritage of all men in all lands. Those who deny freedom to others deserve it not for themselves, and under a just God cannot long retain it."

REVIEWING THE READING

1. According to Strong, what are the two great ideas introduced to the world by the "Anglo-Saxon race"?

2. What arguments for imperialism are made by Josiah Strong, and what arguments against it are offered by the American Anti-Imperialist League?

3. **Using Your Historical Imagination.** Evaluate the arguments for and against imperialism, and express your own opinions about the issue.

Susan B. Anthony and Senator Joseph Brown Debate a Woman's Suffrage Amendment (1884, 1887)

14

From *American Forum: Speeches on Historic Issues: 1788–1900*, edited by Ernest J. Wrage and Barnet Baskerville.

Forty years after the Seneca Falls Declaration on woman's rights, women in the United States still could not vote. It would be more than 30 years after the following statements were made until women received the vote in 1920. Susan B. Anthony was one of the most important activists in the fight for woman's suffrage. In the first excerpt, Anthony testifies in favor of a suffrage amendment before a Senate committee in 1884. In the second excerpt, from 1887, Georgia Senator Joseph Brown tells the Senate why he cannot support such an amendment. As you read consider the arguments made by Anthony and Brown to justify their positions on woman's suffrage.

Susan B. Anthony

Mr. Chairman and Gentlemen: Mrs. Spencer said that I would make an argument. I do not propose to do so, because I take it for granted that the members of this committee understand that we have all the argument on our side, and such an argument would be simply a series of platitudes and maxims [common sayings or slogans] of government. The theory of this Government from the beginning has been perfect equality to all the people. That is shown by every one of the fundamental principles, which I need not stop to repeat. Such being theory, the application would be, of course, that all persons not having forfeited their right to representation in the Government should be possessed of it at the age of twenty-one. But instead of adopting a practice in conformity with the theory of our Government, we began first by saying that all men of property were the people of the nation upon whom the Constitution conferred [gave] equality of rights. The next step was that all white men were the people to whom should be practically applied the fundamental theories. There we halt to-day and stand at a deadlock, so far as the application of our theory may go. We women have been standing before the American republic for thirty years, asking the men to take yet one step further and extend the practical application of the theory of equality of rights to all the people to the other half of the people—the women. That is all that I stand here to-day to attempt to demand. . . .

I voted in the State of New York in 1872 under the construction of those amendments, which we felt to be the true one, that all persons born in the United States, or any State thereof, and under the jurisdiction of the United States, were citizens, and entitled to equality of rights, and that no State could deprive them of their equality of rights. I found three young men, inspectors of elections, who were simple enough to read the Constitution and understand it in accordance with what was the letter and what should have been its spirit. Then, as you will remember, I was prosecuted by the officers of the Federal court [for voting], and the cause was carried through the different courts in the State of New York, in the northern district, and at last I was brought to trial at Canandaigua.

When Mr. Justice Hunt was brought from the supreme bench to sit upon that trial, he wrested my case from the hands of the jury altogether, after having listened three days to testimony, and brought in a verdict himself of guilty, denying to my counsel

even the poor privilege of having the jury polled.
Through all that trial when I, as a citizen of the
United States, as a citizen of the State of New York
and city of Rochester, as a person who had done
something at least that might have entitled her to
a voice in speaking for herself and for her class
[women], in all that trial I not only was denied my
right to testify as to whether I voted or not, but
there was not one single woman's voice to be heard
nor to be considered, except as witnesses, save when
it came to the judge asking, "Has the prisoner anything to say why sentence shall not be pronounced?"
Neither as judge, nor as attorney, nor as jury was I
allowed any person who could be legitimately called
by peer to speak for me.

> . . . there was
> not one single
> woman's voice to
> be heard . . .

Then, as you will remember, Mr. Justice Hunt
not only pronounced the verdict of guilty, but a
sentence of $100 fine and costs of prosecution. I
said to him, "May it please your honor, I do not
propose to pay it"; and I never have paid it, and I
never shall. . . .

Let me remind you that in the case of all other
classes of citizens under the shadow of our flag you
have been true to the theory that taxation and representation are inseparable. Indians not taxed are not
counted in the basis of representation, and are not
allowed to vote; but the minute that your Indians
are counted in the basis of representation and are
allowed to vote they are taxed. . . .

When the fourteenth and fifteenth amendments
were attached to the Constitution they carried to
the black man of Connecticut the boon of the ballot
as well as the burden of taxation, whereas they carried
to the black woman of Connecticut the burden
of taxation, but no ballot by which to protect her
property. . . .

Then you ask why we do not get suffrage by
the popular-vote method, State by State? I answer,
because there is no reason why I, for instance, should
desire the women of one State of this nation to

vote any more than the women of another State. I have no more interest as regards the women of New York than I have as regards the women of Indiana, Iowa, or any of the States represented by the women who have come up here. The reason why I do not wish to get this right by what you call the popular-vote method, the State vote, is because I believe there is a United States citizenship. I believe that this is a nation, and to be a citizen of this nation should be a guaranty to every citizen of the right to express my opinion. You deny to me my liberty, my freedom, if you say that I shall have no voice whatever in making, shaping, or controlling the conditions of society in which I live. . . .

The franchise [vote] to you men is not secure. You hold it to-day, to be sure, by the common consent of white men, but if at any time, on your principle of government, the majority of any of the States should choose to amend the State constitution so as to disfranchise this or that portion of the white men by making this or that condition, by all the decisions of the Supreme Court and by the legislation thus far there is nothing to hinder them.

Susan B. Anthony and Joseph E. Brown were in bitter opposition over the issue of rights for women.

Therefore the women demand a sixteenth amendment to bring to women the right to vote, or if you please to confer upon women their right to vote, to protect them in it, and to secure men in their right, because you are not secure. . . .

The amendment which has been presented before you reads:

Article XVI.

Section I. The right of suffrage in the United States shall be based on citizenship, and the right of citizens of the United States to vote shall not be denied or abridged by the United States, or by any State, on account of sex, or for any reason not equally applicable to all citizens of the United States.

Section 2. Congress shall have power to enforce this article by appropriate legislation.

. . . We were all born into the idea that the proper sphere of women is subjection [inferiority], and it takes education and thought and culture to lift us out of it. Therefore when men go to the ballot-box they all vote "no," unless they have actual argument on it. . . . It is a question that the unthinking masses never have thought upon. They do not care about it one way or the other, only they have an instinctive feeling that because women never did vote therefore it is wrong that they ever should vote.

Joseph Emerson Brown

Mr. President: The joint resolution introduced by my friend, the Senator from New Hampshire [Mr. Blair], proposing an amendment to the Constitution of the United States, conferring the right to vote upon the women of the United States, is one of paramount [utmost] importance. . . .

I believe that the Creator intended that the sphere of the males and females of our race should be different, and that their duties and obligations, while they differ materially, are equally important

The different classes of outdoor labor which require physical strength . . . are by nature assigned to man . . .

and equally honorable, and that each sex is equally well qualified by natural endowments [qualities] for the discharge of the important duties which pertain to each, and that each sex is equally competent to discharge those duties.

Man, by reason of physical strength, and his other endowments and faculties, is qualified for the discharge of those duties that require strength and ability to combat with the sterner realities and difficulties of life. The different classes of outdoor labor which require physical strength and endurance are by nature assigned to man, the head of the family, as part of his task. He discharges such labors as require greater physical endurance and strength than the female sex are usually found to possess.

It is not only his duty to provide for and protect the family, but as a member of the community it is also his duty to discharge the laborious and responsible obligations which the family owe to the State, and which obligations must be discharged by the head of the family, until the male members of the family have grown up to manhood and are able to aid in the discharge of those obligations, when it becomes their duty each in his turn to take charge of and rear a family, for which he is responsible.

Among other duties which the head of the family owes to the State, is military duty in time of war, which he, when able-bodied, is able to discharge, and which the female members of the family are unable to discharge. . . .

On the other hand, the Creator has assigned to woman very laborious and responsible duties, by no means less important than those imposed upon the male sex, though entirely different in their character. In the family, she is a queen. She alone is fitted for the discharge of the sacred trust of wife and the endearing relation of mother. . . .

Mr. President, it is no part of my purpose in any manner whatever to speak disrespectfully of the large number of intelligent ladies, sometimes called strong-minded, who are constantly going before the public, agitating this question of female suffrage. While some of them may, as is frequently charged, be courting notoriety, I have no doubt they are generally engaged in a work which, in their opinion, would better their condition and would do no injury to society.

In all this, however, I believe they are mistaken.

I think the mental and physical structure of the sexes, of itself, sufficiently demonstrates the fact that the sterner, more laborious, and more difficult duties of society are to be performed by the male sex; while the more delicate duties of life, which require less physical strength, and the proper training of youth, with the proper discharge of domestic duties, belong to the female sex. Nature has so ar- ranged it that the male sex can not attend properly to the duties assigned by the law of nature to the female sex, and that the female sex can not discharge the more rigorous duties required of the male sex.

> . . . the more delicate duties of life . . . belong to the female sex.

This movement is an attempt to reverse the very laws of our being, and to drag woman into an arena for which she is not suited, and to devolve upon [pass on to] her onerous [burdensome] duties which the Creator never intended that she should perform.

While the husband discharges the laborious and fatiguing duties of important official positions, and conducts political campaigns, and discharges the du- ties connected with the ballot-box, or while he bears arms in time of war, or discharges executive or judicial duties, or the duties of juryman, requiring close con- finement and many times great mental fatigue; or while the husband in a different sphere of life dis- charges the laborious duties of the plantation, the workshop, or the machine shop, it devolves upon the wife to attend to the duties connected with home life, to care for infant children, and to train carefully and properly those who in the youthful period are further advanced towards maturity.

The woman with the infant at the breast is in no condition to plow on the farm, labor hard in the workshop, discharge the duties of a juryman, conduct causes as an advocate in court, preside in important cases as a judge, command armies as a general, or bear arms as a private. These duties, and others of like character, belong to the male sex; while the more important duties of home, to which I have already referred, devolve upon the female sex. We can neither reverse the physical nor the moral laws of our nature, and as this movement is an attempt to reverse these laws, and to devolve upon the female sex important and laborious duties for which they are not by nature physically competent, I am not prepared to support this bill.

My opinion is that a very large majority of the American people, yes, a large majority of the female sex, oppose it, and that they act wisely in doing so. I therefore protest against its passage.

REVIEWING THE READING

1. For what crime was Anthony prosecuted and convicted in New York state in 1872?

2. What does Anthony mean when she says that woman's suffrage will be another step in the "practical application of the theory of equality of rights to all the people"?

3. **Using Your Historical Imagination.** What arguments do Anthony and Brown make for their positions on woman's suffrage? Do you think their arguments would be considered valid today? Why or why not?

A Teacher's Life in the Common Schools (1888)

15

From *Pioneer Women: Voices from the Kansas Frontier* by Joanna L. Stratton.

In the decades following the Civil War, Horace Mann's "common schools" spread westward with the advance of the frontier. Local Common School Districts would be organized by the pioneers, taxes would be assessed to support them, and the local districts (this one was known as Prairie Range CSD) would come under the control of an elected county school superintendent. That control was minimal, however, because frontier counties were large, with scores of rural schools, and travel was limited by bad roads. The county superintendent might make an appearance once a year, but the rural teacher was otherwise left quite on her own to run her school as she saw fit.

The following selection, from a book on the pioneer women of Kansas, is an excerpt from the account of India Harris Simmons, a teacher on the Kansas frontier. As you read the selection, consider the physical conditions under which the first Prairie Range School got underway.

India Harris Simmons came to Kansas from Ohio to join her homesteading parents and was soon appointed as the first schoolteacher of the Prairie Range district of northwest Kearny County. The story of her first year shows that though a true school system was evolving, the circumstances in the local prairie schoolhouse were slow to improve.

"School opened in October of 1888 with nineteen pupils [Simmons writes]. Not wishing to postpone the opening of school until a suitable building could be secured, the patrons decided to use a dugout

The floors and walls were just plain dirt . . .

which had served as a dwelling for a pre-empter [land holder], who had 'proved up' [improved the land] and gone.

"The outlook, or speaking more exactly, the inlook, was not reassuring. The floor and walls were just plain dirt, not even adobe plaster, and the one window and the cellar type of doorway gave scant illumination. Plain benches without backs ran around three sides of the room. There were no blackboards or other school equipment. Decorating it, or improving it in any substantial way would take at least a little money which could not be spared by the district until more land was 'proved up' and made taxable.

"So, clean 'gunny bags,' a kind of coarse burlap bag, were ripped apart and fastened against the walls to keep the dirt away from the clothing. Use had somewhat packed and hardened the floor, which they cleared of loose dirt, and then laid down old rugs and pieces of carpet, on which the children's feet could rest. They cleaned the tiny four-paned window, at each side of which they hung a bright piece of cheap drapery, being careful not to obscure [block] any of the precious light.

"A small wooden box, with a clean paper on top, held the water jug and the common drinking cup. A taller box, with a shelf inside and a pretty stand cover on it, served as the teacher's desk, and her chair was one of the home-made kind with a broad board nailed on slantingly for a back, quite common in the dugout homes. A little Topsy stove, on which the bachelor claim holder had baked his morning flap-jacks, was the final piece of furniture.

"When a little group had been called in, and nineteen happy expectant faces greeted her from the row of benches, the young teacher had a sense of misgiving as to her ability to change that crude little dirt-walled room into a hall of learning. Of course, she knew about Mark Hopkins and the log and the student making a University [Hopkins was an educator about whom his former student President

James A. Garfield is supposed to have said, "The
ideal college is Mark Hopkins on one end of a log
and a student on the other."], but Alas! That took
a Mark Hopkins, and he wasn't present, but breathing
a prayer that plain surroundings, like plain living,
might be conducive to [lead to] high thinking, she
began the opening exercises which dedicated the
lowly dwelling to its new high use.

"The nondescript supply of books which each
pupil had brought from whatever state was 'back
home' to him was placed on the bench by his side.
Slates, which had to take the place of both blackboard and tablets, were of all sizes and descriptions,
from Jimmy's tiny one with the red felt covered
frame and pencil tied to it with a string, to Mary's
big double one with the wide home-made frames
fastened together with strong hinges and cut deep
with initials and hearts. She had found it packed
away among grandfather's books which he had used
away back in Ohio. There were histories from Illinois,
spellers and writing books from Iowa, readers from
St. Louis city schools, and even some old blue-backed
spellers, with their five-syllabled puzzlers.

"From this motley [varied] array the teacher
made the assignments and arranged the classifica-
tions, depending entirely upon her own judgment.
The pupils had been without school privileges long
enough to be glad to have an opportunity to study,
and their rapid progress showed they came, for the
most part, from intelligent families. True, there was
not a suspension globe for explaining mathematical
geography, but an apple and a ball did very well.
There was no case of the latest wall maps on rollers,
but the large ones in the books answered the purpose
when care was taken to hold them correctly.

"As for a library, well, the contribution from
the homes, kept on the shelf of the teacher's box
desk, made a good substitute. There were a whole
year's numbers of Youth's Companion, whose stories,
informational articles, pictures and puzzles furnished

recreation for all ages. Volumes of the Chatterbox, Harper's Young People and a few books of the right sort, including some of Louisa May Alcott's, made a sufficient variety of literature for our needs. The books were read aloud and the different characters were assumed by the pupils, who often 'played them out' as they called it, at recess time. We call it 'dramatization' now, and make it part of our daily program. But whatever the name, it surely helped to implant a deep and abiding love for good literature. . . .

"Towards spring, an unfinished frame building was secured at a bargain from a nearby townsite, and it was moved into the district, where it was permanently located and fitted up as much as possible for school purposes. No one could be secured at the time to plaster it, but the school took possession as soon as it was on its foundation, and they were so thankful for a floor, plenty of light, comfortable seats and desks, and a 'really truly' blackboard, that they didn't mind if the walls were as yet only lathed [prepared for plastering].

"There was very little passing on the roads at that time, and there was no need to have the windows even partly frescoed with soap or scouring powders, to keep pupils from looking out too much. It really was very lonely when lessons or games did not engage the attention of the pupils, and sometimes they, and the teacher as well, paused in their engrossing pursuit of knowledge to look through the open door at a speck of black on a distant swell of ground, hoping that it might chance to be a human being riding or driving their way, being disappointed later to see that it was no more than a clump of soap weeds which some mirage or some play of light or shadow had magnified and lifted into view.

"They had just one visitor that spring, the County Superintendent, Mr. Cyrus Russel, who descended upon them in his little open buggy, driving a white-maned sorrel horse—a familiar sight to the country school of this county for several years. A

few days previous, to give variety to the playtime activities, they had visited a nearby gypsum bed, bringing back a goodly supply of the clay-like deposit. With no thought of manual art or visualized instruction, they had modeled the beautiful white material into flat maps and relief maps of the continents and into vases and plaques, decorated with flowers, and one ambitious girl had even attempted a bust of George Washington. They did not realize at the time that this work was the beginning of Manual Art in our rural schools, and it seemed to them a most important and disconcerting [upsetting] time for the school inspector to appear on the scene. However, he must have had the vision to see some educational value in their display, for he made a favorable report of the school and recommended the teacher to an excellent teaching position in the county seat for the next year.

"The next incident made an exciting break in their daily program. One afternoon the sky took on a peculiar coppery hue and to the southeast small clouds of dust kept rising above the swells, and ridges that marked the horizon line, expanding and thinning until lost in the surrounding air, similar clouds constantly rising to take their places. At the recess period

In this typical rural classroom, students of different ages and grades study together in a single room.

they stood watching this curious display of color and formation, when suddenly they saw a well-defined funnel-shaped cloud separate itself from the dusty mass and move rapidly in their direction. They were almost panic stricken when they saw it so near that it obscured [blocked] from their view an old sod house that stood two miles to the southeast.

"There was a cyclone cellar under the school house, but no door had yet been made leading to it. They all ran into the house, where the teacher seized the kindling hatchet with the idea of chopping a hole in the floor or prying up some boards, when one of the white-faced children cried out from the doorway. 'It's done turned, teacher. It's going straight north.' And sure enough, in that freakish way that tornadoes have, it had shifted its course.

"The people in the district never grew tired of teasing the teacher about scaring away a tornado with a hatchet and said discipline ought to come easy to her after that."

REVIEWING THE READING

1. Why does Simmons say her first school did not look reassuring?

2. How did Simmons acquire books for a library in her new school?

3. **Using Your Historical Imagination.** One of the most basic questions that the historian must be aware of as he or she analyzes historical sources is "How typical is this account?" Simmons' Prairie Range School was highly typical of American frontier schools from Wisconsin to Texas. Using the Prairie Range example, describe the basic features of the pioneer school.

An Immigrant Family Goes to School (1880s)

16

From *The Promised Land* by Mary Antin.

During the decades from 1870 to 1910, hundreds of thousands of European immigrants came to the United States to make new lives for themselves. They came from many different countries and for many different reasons, but to many of them free public education was the means by which their children were to become fully Americanized. In her classic account The Promised Land, *Mary Antin eloquently describes the immigrant experience through the history of her own family. In the following excerpts from her account, Antin tells what being in America meant to her father and what happened the day he first took his children to a public school. As you read consider what a free education meant to a Jewish immigrant from Russia in the 1880s.*

The public school has done its best for us foreigners, and for the country, when it made us into good Americans. I am glad it is mine to tell how the miracle was wrought [accomplished] in one case. You should be glad to hear it, you born Americans; for it is the story of the growth of your country. . . . And you will be glad to hear it, my comrades in adoption; for it is a rehearsal of your own experience. . . .

In America . . . everything was free, as we had heard in Russia. Light was free; the streets were as bright as a synagogue on a holy day. Music was free. . . .

Education was free. That subject my father had written about repeatedly, as comprising his chief hope for us children, the essence of American opportunity, the treasure that no thief could touch, not even misfortune or poverty. . . . No application made, no questions asked, no examinations, rulings, exclusions; no machinations [plotting], no fees. The doors stood open for every one of us. . . .

Father himself conducted us to school. He would not have delegated that mission to the President of the United States. He had awaited the day with impatience equal to mine, and the visions he saw as he hurried us over the sun-flecked pavements transcended all my dreams . . . he had left home in search of bread for his hungry family, but he went blessing the necessity that drove him to America. The boasted freedom of the New World meant to him far more than the right to reside, travel, and work wherever he pleased; it meant the freedom to speak his thoughts, to throw off the shackles [chains] of superstition, to test his own fate, unhindered by political or religious tyranny. He was only a young man when he landed—thirty-two; and most of his life he had been held in leading-strings [he had been restrained]. . . .

So it was with a heart full of longing and hope that my father led us to school on that first day. He took long strides in his eagerness, the rest of us running and hopping to keep up.

Students of many different ethnic backgrounds stand to salute the flag in a New York City classroom in 1889.

At last the four of us stood around the teacher's desk; and my father, in his impossible English, gave us over in her charge, with some broken words of his hopes for us that his swelling heart could no longer contain. I venture to say that Miss Nixon was struck by something uncommon in the group we made, something outside of Semitic [Jewish] features and the abashed [self-conscious] manner of the alien. . . . This foreigner, who brought his children to school as if it were an act of consecration [a holy ceremony], who regarded the teacher of the primer class with reverence, who spoke of visions, like a man inspired, in a common schoolroom, was not like other aliens, who brought their children in dull obedience to the law; was not like the native fathers, who brought their unmanageable boys, glad to be relieved of their care. I think Miss Nixon guessed what my father's best English could not convey. I think she divined that by the simple act of delivering our school certificates to her he took possession of America.

REVIEWING THE READING

1. What was the most basic reason that Mary Antin's father had taken his family to the United States?

2. According to Antin, what most impressed an immigrant from Russia about life in the United States?

3. **Using Your Historical Imagination.** Explain what Antin meant by the last two sentences in the reading: "I think Miss Nixon guessed what my father's best English could not convey. I think she divined that by the simple act of delivering our school certificates to her he took possession of America."

17

From *The Eclectic Fourth Reader: Containing Elegant Extracts in Prose and Poetry, From the Best American and English Writers. With Copious Rules for Reading, and Directions for Avoiding Common Errors* by William McGuffey.

Lesson One from McGuffey's *Eclectic Fourth Reader* (1880s)

During the last two-thirds of the nineteenth century and even into the early twentieth century, the school textbooks of William McGuffey were in widespread use in United States public and private schools. Written for grades one through six, McGuffey's "Eclectic Readers" were—like the earlier Columbian Orator*—intended to be read aloud. Also like many of the readings in the* Orator, *most of the readings in McGuffy had Christian lessons to accompany the instructions in vocabulary and the rules of proper speech. Consider what moral lesson is being taught in the following excerpt from the* Eclectic Fourth Reader.

Lesson I

RULE.—Be careful to pronounce every syllable distinctly, and not to join the words together. Nothing is more important to good reading than attention to this rule, and yet most young readers violate it.

EXERCISES UNDER THE RULE. To be read over several times by all the pupils.

In the following exercises difficult sounds have been introduced, which are commonly spoken indistinctly or entirely omitted. Let every pupil, before commencing [beginning] the reading lesson, read them over several times slowly and distinctly. The difficult sounds are put in Italics.

He was *incapable of* it. (Here take care not to join *ble* and *of.*)

He was *amiable, respectable, formidable, unbearable, intolerable, unmanageable, terrible.* (Here the sound *ble* must be fully sounded.)

He was *branded* as a traitor.

Thou *prob'st* my wound.

He was *stretched on* the floor.

But *Ruth clave* unto her.

The above rule is so important, that the first twelve lessons will all be under it.

Remarkable Preservation
Prof. Wilson

1. You have often asked me to describe to you on paper an event in my life, which thirty years later, I cannot look back to without horror. No words can give an adequate image of the miseries I suffered during that fearful night; but I shall try to give you something like a faint shadow of them, that from it your soul may conceive what I must have suffered.

2. I was, you know, on my voyage back to my native country after an absence of five years spent in unintermitting toil in a foreign land, to which I had been driven by a singular fatality. Our voyage had been most cheerful and prosperous, and on Christmas day we were within fifty leagues [200 miles] of port. Passengers and crew were all in the highest spirits, and the ship was alive with mirth and jollity.

3. The ship was sailing at the rate of seven knots [about 8 miles per hour] an hour. A strong snowstorm blew, but steadily and without danger, and the ship kept boldly on her course, close reefed, and mistress of the storm. While leaning over the gunwale, admiring the water rushing by like a foaming cataract, by some unaccountable accident, I lost my balance, and in an instant fell overboard into the sea.

4. I remember a convulsive shuddering all over my body, and a hurried leaping of my heart as I felt myself about to lose hold of the vessel, and

. . . I lost my balance, and in an instant fell overboard into the sea.

afterwards a sensation of the most icy chillness, from immersion in the waves, but nothing resembling a fall or precipitation. When below the water, I think that a momentary belief rushed across my mind that the ship had suddenly sunk, and that I was but one of a perishing crew. I imagined that I felt a hand with long fingers clutching at my legs and made violent efforts to escape, dragging after me as I thought, the body of some drowning wretch.

5. On rising to the surface, I recollected in a moment what had befallen me, and uttered a cry of horror, which is in my ears to this day. It often makes me shudder, as if it were the mad shriek of another person in perilous agony! Often have I dreamed over again that dire moment, and the cry I utter in my sleep is said to be something more horrible than a human voice. No ship was to be seen. She was gone forever.

6. The little happy world to which a moment before, I had belonged, had been swept by, and I felt that God had flung me at once from the heart of joy, delight, and happiness, into the uttermost abyss of mortal misery and despair. Yes! I felt that the Almighty God had done this—that there was an act, a fearful act of Providence. Miserable worm that I was, I thought that the act was cruel, and a sort of wild, indefinite, objectless rage and wrath assailed me, and took for awhile the place of that first shrieking terror. I gnashed my teeth, and cursed myself—and, with bitter tears and yells, blasphemed [cursed] the name of God.

7. It is true, my friend, that I did so. God forgave that wickedness. The Being, whom I then cursed, was, in his tender mercy, not unmindful of me,— of me, a poor, blind miserable, mistaken worm. The waves dashed over me and struck me on the face, and howled at me. The winds yelled, and the snow beat like drifting sand into my eyes, and the ship, the *ship* was *gone*, and there was I left to struggle, and buffet, and gasp, and sink, and perish, alone,

The waves dashed over me . . .

unseen, and unpitied by man, and, as I thought too, by the everlasting God.

8. I tried to penetrate the surrounding darkness with my glaring eyes, that felt as if leaping from their sockets. I saw, as if by miraculous power, to a great distance through the night—but no *ship*—nothing but white-crested waves, and the dismal noise of thunder.

9. I shouted, shrieked, and yelled, that I might be heard by the crew, until my voice was gone—and that too, when I knew that there were none to hear me. At last I became utterly speechless, and when I tried to call aloud, there was nothing but a silent gasp and convulsion, while the waves came upon me like stunning blows, reiterated [repeated], and drove me along, like a log of wood, or a dead animal.

> . . . I knew there were none to hear me.

10. All this time I was not conscious of any act of swimming, but I soon found that I had instinctively been exerting all my power and skill, and both were requisite [needed] to keep me alive in the tumultuous wake of the ship. Something struck me harder than a wave. What it was I knew not, but I grasped it with a passionate violence, for the hope of salvation came suddenly over me, and with a sudden transition from despair, I felt that I was rescued.

11. I had the same thought as if I had been suddenly heaved on shore by a wave. The crew had thrown overboard everything they thought could afford me the slightest chance of escape from death, and a hencoop had drifted towards me. At once all the stories I had even read of mariners [sailors] miraculously saved at sea rushed across my recollection. I had an object to cling to, which I knew would enable me to prolong my existence.

12. I was no longer helpless on the cold weltering world of waters, and the thought that my friends were thinking of me, and doing all they could for me, gave to me a wonderful courage. I may yet

McGuffey's famous readers were in wide use in American classrooms by the 1880s.

pass the night in the ship, I thought, and I looked round eagerly to hear the rush of her prow, or to see through the snowdrift the gleaming of her sails.

13. This was but a momentary gladness. The ship I knew could not be far off, but for any good she could do me, she might as well have been in the heart of the Atlantic Ocean. Before she could have altered her course, I must have drifted a long way to leeward [downwind], and in the dim snowy night how was such a speck to be seen? I saw a flash of lightning, and then there was thunder. It was the ship firing a gun to let me know, if still alive, that she was somewhere lying to.

14. But where? I was separated from her by a dire necessity, by many thousand fierce waves that would not let my shrieks be heard. Each succeeding

gun was heard fainter and fainter, till at last I cursed the sound that, scarcely heard above the hollow rumbling of the tempestuous sea, told me that the ship was farther and farther off, until she and her heartless crew had left me to my fate.

15. Why did they not send out all their boats to row round and round all that night through, for the sake of one whom they pretended to love so well? I blamed, blessed, and cursed them by fits, until every emotion of my soul was exhausted, and I clung in sullen despair to the wretched piece of wood that still kept me from eternity.

16. Everything was now seen in its absolute dreadful reality. I was a castaway—no hope of rescue. It was broad daylight, and the storm had ceased, but clouds lay round the horizon, and no land was to be seen. What dreadful clouds! Some black as pitch, and charged with thunder, others like cliffs of fire, and here and there all streamered over with blood. It was indeed a sullen, wrathful, and despairing sky.

17. The sun itself was a dull brazen orb [sphere], cold, dead, and beamless. I saw three ships afar off, but all their heads were turned away from me. For whole hours they would adhere motionless to the sea, while I drifted away from them, and then a rushing wind would spring up, and carry them, one by one, into the darkness of the stormy distance. Many birds came close to me, as if to flap me with their large spreading wings, screamed round and round me, and then flew away in their strength, and beauty, and happiness.

18. I now felt myself indeed dying. A calm came over me. I prayed devoutly for forgiveness of my sins, and for all my friends on earth. A ringing was in my ears, and I remember only the hollow fluctuations of the sea with which I seemed to be blended, and a sinking down and down an unfathomable depth, which I thought was Death, and into the kingdom of the eternal Future.

19. I awoke from insensibility and oblivion with a hideous, racking pain in my head and loins, and in a place of utter darkness. I heard a voice say, "Praise the Lord." My agony was dreadful, and I cried aloud. Wan [pale], glimmering, melancholy lights kept moving to and fro. I heard dismal whisperings, and now and then a pale silent ghost glided by. A hideous din [noise] was over head, and around me the fierce dashing of the waves. Was I in the land of spirits?

20. But, why strive to recount the mortal pain of my recovery, the soul-humbling gratitude that took possession of my being? I was lying in the cabin of a ship and kindly tended by a humane and skillful man. I had been picked up, apparently dead, and cold. The hand of God was there. Adieu, my dear friend. It is now the hour of rest, and I hasten to fall down on my knees before the merciful Being who took pity upon me, and who, at the intercession of our Redeemer, may, I hope, pardon all my sins.

REVIEWING THE READING

1. As students were asked in the reader: "What were the Professor's feelings when he first fell into the water?"

2. Also from McGuffey are these questions: "What did he imagine was clutching at his heels? How did he act upon rising to the surface?"

3. **Using Your Historical Imagination.** State in your own words the moral lesson that is being taught in this reading? Do you think this lesson is still relevant today?

Jacob Riis Describes a New York Gang (1880s)

18

From *How the Other Half Lives* by Jacob A. Riis.

Jacob Riis was a journalist and social reformer who came to the United States in 1870 when he was 21. Riis wrote a number of descriptions of New York tenement life, and in 1890 published this account of the youthful gangs of the great city. Heavy immigration, poverty, crowding, and the rapid growth of cities like New York were factors contributing to a high rate of crime. Then as now, many of the younger members of the criminal class organized themselves into informal gangs that staked out territories across the city, battled the police, and terrorized the general public. Consider, as you read the following excerpts from his book, whether Riis thought these gangs were transplanted from Europe with the waves of immigration or were native to America.

The gang is an institution in New York. The police deny its existence while nursing the bruises received in nightly battles with it that tax their utmost resources. The newspapers chronicle its doings daily, with a sensational minuteness of detail that does its share toward keeping up its evil traditions and inflaming the ambition of its members to be as bad as the worst. The gang is the ripe fruit of tenement-house growth. It was born there, endowed with a heritage of instinctive hostility to restraint by a generation that sacrificed home to freedom, or left its country for its country's good. . . . New York's tough represents the essence of reaction against the old and the new oppression, nursed in the rank soil of its slums. Its gangs are made up of the American-born sons of English, Irish, and German parents. They reflect exactly the conditions of the tenements from which they sprang. Murder is as congenial [common] to Cherry Street or to Battle Row, as quiet and order to Murray Hill. The "assimilation" [Americanizing] of Europe's oppressed hordes, upon which our Fourth of July orators are fond of dwelling, is perfect. The product is our own.

Such is the genesis [root] of New York's gangs. Their history is not so easily written. It would embrace the largest share of our city's criminal history for two generations back, every page of it dyed red with blood.

. . . Bravado [defiance] and robbery are the real purposes of the gangs; the former prompts the attack upon the policeman, the latter that upon the citizen. Within a single week last spring, the newspapers recorded six murderous assaults on unoffending people, committed by young highwaymen in the public streets. How many more were suppressed by the police, who always do their utmost to hush up such outrages "in the interests of justice," I shall not say. There has been no lack of such occurrences since, as the records of the criminal courts show. In fact, the past summer has seen, after a period of comparative quiescence [inactivity] of the gangs, a reawakening to renewed turbulence of the East Side tribes, and over and over again the reserve forces of a precinct have been called out to club them into submission. It is a peculiarity of the gangs that they usually break out in spots, as it were. When the West Side is in a state of eruption, the East Side gangs "lie low," and when the toughs along the North River are nursing broken heads at home, or their revenge in Sing Sing [a prison], fresh trouble breaks out in the tenements east of Third Avenue. This result is brought about by the very efforts made by the police to put down the gangs. In spite of local feuds, there is between them a species of ruffianly Freemasonry [criminal brotherhood] that readily admits to full fellowship a hunted rival in the face of the common enemy. The gangs belt the city like a huge chain from the Battery to Harlem—the collective name of the "chain gang" has been given to their scattered groups in the belief that a much closer connection exists between them than commonly supposed—and the ruffian for whom the East Side has become too hot, has only to step across town and change his name, a matter usually much easier for him than to change his shirt, to find a sanctuary in which to plot fresh outrages. The more notorious he is, the warmer the welcome, and if he has "done" [killed] his man he is by common consent accorded the leadership in his new field.

From all this it might be inferred that the New York tough is a very fierce individual, of indomitable courage and naturally as blood-thirsty as a tiger. On the contrary he is an arrant [obvious] coward. His instincts of ferocity are those of the wolf rather than the tiger. It is only when he hunts with the pack that he is dangerous. Then his inordinate vanity makes him forget all fear or caution in the desire to distinguish himself before his fellows, a result of his swallowing all the flash literature and penny-

This photo by Jacob Riis shows the slum district of Mulberry Bend (also called "Bandit's Roost")—one of the toughest and most neglected parts of New York City in the 1890s.

dreadfuls [cheap adventure literature] he can beg, borrow, or steal—and there is never any lack of them—and of the strongly dramatic element in his nature that is nursed by such a diet into rank and morbid growth. He is a queer bundle of contradictions at all times. Drunk and foul-mouthed, ready to cut the throat of a defenceless stranger at the toss of a cent, fresh from beating his decent mother black and blue to get money for rum, he will resent as an intolerable insult the imputation [suggestion] that he is "no gentleman." Fighting his battles with the coward's weapons, the brass-knuckles and the deadly sand-bag, or with brick-bats from the house-tops, he is still in all seriousness a lover of fair play, and as likely as not, when his gang has downed a policeman in a battle that has cost a dozen broken heads, to be found next saving a drowning child

Ready wit he has at all times . . .

or woman at the peril of his own life. . . . Ready wit he has at all times, and there is less meanness in his makeup than in that of the bully of the London slums; but an intense love of show and applause, that carries him to any length of bravado, which his twin-brother across the sea entirely lacks. I have a very vivid recollection of seeing one of his tribe, a robber and murderer before he was nineteen, go to the gallows unmoved, all fear of the rope overcome, as it seemed, by the secret, exultant pride of being the centre of a first-class show, shortly to be followed by that acme [highest point] of tenement-life bliss, a big funeral. . . .

Inspector Byrnes is authority for the statement that throughout the city the young tough has more "ability" and "nerve" than the thief whose example he successfully emulates [copies]. He begins earlier, too. Speaking of the increase of the native element among criminal prisoners exhibited in the census returns of the last thirty years, the Rev. Fred H. Wines says, "their youth is a very striking fact." Had he confined his observations to the police courts of New York, he might have emphasized the remark and found an explanation of the discovery that "the ratio of prisoners in cities is two and one-quarter times as great as in the country at large," a computation that takes no account of the reformatories for juvenile delinquents, or the exhibit would have been still more striking. Of the 82,200 persons arrested by the police in 1889, 10,505 were under twenty years old. The last report of the society for the Prevention of Cruelty to Children enumerates, as "a few typical cases," eighteen "professional cracksmen," between nine and fifteen years old, who had been caught with burglars' tools, or in the act of robbery. Four of them hardly yet in long trousers, had "held up" a wayfarer in the public street and robbed him of $73. One, aged sixteen, "was the leader of a noted gang of young robbers in Forty-ninth Street. He committed murder, for which he is now serving a term of nineteen years in State's Prison." Four of the eighteen were girls and quite as bad as the worst. In a few years they would have been living with the toughs of their choice without the ceremony of a marriage, egging them on by their pride in their lawless achievements, and fighting side by side with them in their encounters with the "cops."

REVIEWING THE READING

1. According to Riis, what was the origin of the New York gangs?

2. What was the attitude of the municipal police toward the gangs? Why do you think they took this approach?

3. **Using Your Historical Imagination.** What were the characteristics of a New York gang "tough" of the 1880s? How do you think urban gangs may be similar or different today?

19

From *The Life Stories of Undistinguished Americans as Told by Themselves,* edited by Hamilton Holt.

A Black Georgian Tells of the Substitutes for Slavery (1880s)

Reconstruction of the former states of the Confederacy ended in the 1870s. Republican state governments backed by the military were replaced by governments dominated by southern Democrats. Under this reasserted southern control, the conditions of life for southern blacks worsened. Landowners and local and state governments often cooperated to keep black agricultural workers under conditions of bondage that resembled those of slavery. Sometimes blacks (and whites, for that matter) worked a landowner's land for a share of the crop; sometimes they signed a contract and worked for wages. Both these arrangements were used by unscrupulous white landowners to place their black employees in a system of debt slavery from which they could not easily escape. If they tried, the full power of law enforcement would be brought to bear.

In the following excerpts from a collection of life stories, an anonymous black man from Georgia tells how the system drew him into a state of bondage in many ways worse than slavery. This man never had a chance to attend school and so could not read or write. As you read the account, consider why it was entirely to the advantage of the white landowner that his workers remain illiterate.

I am a Negro and was born sometime during the war in Elbert County, Ga., and I reckon by this time I must be a little over forty years old. My mother was not married when I was born, and I

never knew who my father was or anything about
him. Shortly after the war my mother died, and I
was left to the care of my uncle. All this happened
before I was eight years old, and so I can't remember
very much about it. When I was about ten years
old my uncle hired me out to Captain ———. I had
already learned how to plow, and was a good hand
at picking cotton. I was told that the Captain wanted
me for his houseboy, and later on he was going to
train me to be his coachman. To be a coachman
in those days was considered a post of honor, and
young as I was, I was glad of the chance.

But I had not been at the Captain's a month
before I was put to work on the farm, and with
some twenty or thirty other Negroes—men, women
and children. From the beginning the boys had the
same tasks as the men and women. There was no
difference. We all worked hard during the week,
and would frolic on Saturday nights and often on
Sundays. And everybody was happy. The men got
$3 a week and the women $2. I don't know what
the children got. Every week my uncle collected
my money for me, gave me a place to sleep, and
allowed me ten or fifteen cents a week for "spending
change," as he called it.

I must have been seventeen or eighteen years
old before I got tired of that arrangement, and felt
that I was man enough to be working for myself
and handling my own wages. The other boys about
my age and size were "drawing" their own pay, and
they used to laugh at me and call me "Baby," because
my old uncle was always on hand to "draw" my
pay. Worked up by these things, I made a break ·
for liberty. Unknown to my uncle or the Captain I
went off to a neighboring plantation and hired myself
out to another man. The new landlord agreed to
give me forty cents a day and furnish me one meal.
I thought that was doing fine. Bright and early one
Monday morning I started for work, still not letting
the others know anything about it. But they found

it out before sundown. The Captain came over to the new place and brought some kind of officer of the law. The officer pulled out a long piece of paper from his pocket and read it to my employer. When this was done I heard my new boss say:

"I beg your pardon, Captain. I didn't know this Negro was bound out to you, or I wouldn't have hired him."

"He certainly is bound out to me," said the Captain. "He belongs to me until he is twenty-one, and I'm going to make him know his place."

So I was carried back to the Captain's. That night he made me strip off my clothing down to the waist, ordered his foreman to give me thirty lashes with a buggy whip across my bare back, and stood by until it was done. After that experience the Captain made me stay on his place night and day—but my uncle still continued to "draw" my money.

I was a man nearly grown before I knew how to count from one to one hundred . . .

I was a man nearly grown before I knew how to count from one to one hundred. I was a man nearly grown before I ever saw a colored teacher. I never went to school a day in my life. Today I can't write my own name, though I can read a little. I was a man nearly grown before I ever rode on a railroad train, and then I went on an excursion from Elberton to Athens. What was true of me was true of hundreds of other Negroes around me—'way off there in the country, fifteen or twenty miles from the nearest town.

When I reached twenty-one the Captain told me I was a free man, but he urged me to stay with him. He said he would treat me right, and pay me as much as anybody else would. The Captain's son and I were about the same age, and the Captain said that, as he had owned my mother and uncle during slavery, and as his son didn't want me to leave them (since I had been with them so long), he wanted me to stay with the old family. And I stayed. I signed a contract—that is, I made my

mark—for one year. The Captain was to give me
$3.50 a week, and furnish me a little house on the
plantation—a one-room log cabin similar to those
used by his other laborers.

During that year I married Mandy. For several
years Mandy had been the house-servant for the
Captain, his wife, his son and his three daughters,
and they all seemed to think a good deal of her.
As an evidence of their regard they gave us a suit
of furniture, which cost about $25, and we set up
housekeeping in one of the Captain's two-room shan-
ties. I thought I was the biggest man in Georgia.
Mandy still kept her place in the "Big House" after
our marriage. We did so well for the first year that
I renewed my contract for the second year, and
for the third, fourth and fifth year I did the same
thing. Before the end of the fifth year the Captain
had died, and his son, who had married some two
or three years before, took charge of the plantation.
Also, for two or three years, this son had been serving
at Atlanta in some big office to which he had been
elected. I think it was in the Legislature or something
of that sort—anyhow, all the people called him Senator. At the end of the fifth year the Senator suggested
that I sign up a contract for ten years; then, he
said, we wouldn't have to fix up papers every year.
I asked my wife about it; she consented; and so I
made a ten-year contract.

Not long afterward the Senator had a long,
low shanty built on his place. A great big chimney,
with a wide, open fireplace, was built at one end
of it and on each side of the house, running length-
wise, there was a row of frames or stalls just large
enough to hold a single mattress. The places for
these mattresses were fixed one above the other;
so that there was a double row of these stalls or
pens on each side. They looked for all the world
like stalls for horses. Since then I have seen cabooses
similarly arranged as sleeping quarters for railroad
laborers.

Nobody seemed to know what the Senator was fixing for. All doubts were put aside one bright day in April when about forty able-bodied Negroes, bound in iron chains, and some of them handcuffed, were brought out to the Senator's farm in three big wagons. They were quartered in the long, low shanty, and it was afterward called the stockade. This was the beginning of Senator's convict camp. These men were prisoners who had been leased by the Senator from the State of Georgia at about $200 each per year, the State agreeing to pay for guards and physicians, for necessary inspection, for inquests, all rewards for escaped convicts, the cost of litigation and all other incidental expenses.

When I saw these men in shackles, and the guards with their guns, I was scared nearly to death. I felt like running away, but I didn't know where to go. And if there had been any place to go to, I would have had to leave my wife and child behind. We free laborers held a meeting. We all wanted to quit. We sent a man to tell the Senator about it. Word came back that we were all under contract for ten years and that the Senator would hold us to the letter of the contract, or put us in chains and lock us up—the same as the other prisoners. It was made plain to us by some white people we talked to that in the contracts we had signed we had all agreed to be locked up in a stockade at night or at any other time that our employer saw fit; further, we learned that we could not lawfully break our contract for any reason and go and hire ourselves to somebody else without the consent of our employer; and, more than that, if we got mad and ran away, we could be run down by bloodhounds, arrested without process of law, and be returned to our employer, who, according to the contract, might beat us brutally or administer any kind of punishment that he thought proper. In other words, we had sold ourselves into slavery—and what could we do about it? The white folks had all the courts, all the

A black sharecropper discovers how much he is in debt at the "company store."

guns, all the hounds, all the railroads, all the telegraph wires, all the newspapers, all the money, and nearly all the land—and we had only our ignorance, our poverty and our empty hands. We decided that the best thing to do was to shut our mouths, say nothing, and go back to work. And most of us worked side by side with those convicts during the remainder of the ten years.

But this first batch of convicts was only the beginning. Within six months another stockade was built, and twenty or thirty other convicts were brought to the plantation, among them six or eight women! The Senator had bought an additional thousand acres of land, and to his already large cotton plantation he added two great big sawmills and went into the lumber business. Within two years the Senator had in all 200 Negroes working on his plantation—about half of them free laborers, so called, and about half of them convicts. The only difference between the free laborers and the others was that the free laborers could come and go as they pleased,

. . . when we thought that our bondage was at an end we found that it had really just begun.

at night—that is, they were not locked up at night, and were not, as a general thing, whipped for slight offenses.

The troubles of the free laborers began at the close of the ten-year period. To a man they all refused to sign new contracts—even for one year, not to say anything of ten years. And just when we thought that our bondage was at an end we found that it had really just begun. Two or three years before, or about a year and a half after the Senator had started his camp, he had established a large store, which was called the commissary. All of us free laborers were compelled to buy our supplies—food, clothing, etc.—from that store. We never used any money in our dealings with the commissary, only tickets or orders, and we had a general settlement once each year, in October. In this store we were charged all sorts of high prices for goods, because every year we would come out in debt to our employer. If not that, we seldom had more than $5 to $10 coming to us—and that for a whole year's work. Well, at the close of the tenth year, when we kicked and meant to leave the Senator, he said to some of us with a smile (and I never will forget that smile—I can see it now):

"Boys, I'm sorry you're going to leave me. I hope you will do well in your new places—so well that you will be able to pay the little balances which most of you owe me."

Word was sent out for all of us to meet him at the commissary at 2 o'clock. There he told us that, after we had signed what he called a written acknowledgement of our debts, we might go and look for new places. The storekeeper took us one by one and read to us statements of our accounts. According to the books there was no man of us who owed the Senator less than $100; some of us were put down for as much as $200. I owed $165, according to the bookkeeper. These debts were not accumulated during one year, but ran back for three

and four years, so we were told—in spite of the
fact that we understood that we had had a full settlement at the end of each year. But no one of us
would have dared to dispute a white man's word—
oh, no; not in those days. Besides, we fellows didn't
care anything about the amounts—we were after
getting away; and we had been told that we might
too, if we signed the acknowledgment. We would
have signed anything, just to get away. So we stepped
up, we did, and made our marks. That same night
we were rounded up by a constable and ten or twelve
white men, who aided him, and we were locked
up, every one of us, in one of the Senator's stockades.
The next morning it was explained to us by the
two guards appointed to watch us that, in the papers
we had signed the day before, we had not only
made acknowledgement of our indebtedness, but
that we had also agreed to work for the Senator
until the debts were paid by hard labor. And from
that day forward we were treated just like convicts.
Really we had made ourselves lifetime slaves, or
peons, as the laws called us. But call it slavery,
peonage, or what not, the truth is we lived in a
hell on earth what time we spent in the Senator's
peon camp. . . .

    The stockades in which we slept, were, I believe,
the filthiest places in the world. They were cesspools
of nastiness. During the thirteen years that I was
there I am willing to swear that a mattress was never
moved after it had been brought there, except to
turn it over once or twice a month. No sheets were
used, only dark-colored blankets. Most of the men
slept every night in the clothing that they had worked
in all day. Some of the worst characters were made
to sleep in chairs. The doors were locked and barred,
each night, and tallow-candles were the only lights
allowed. Really the stockades were but little more
than cow sheds, horse stables, or hog pens. Strange
to say, not a great number of these people died
while I was there, though a great many came away

> . . . **we were
> treated just like
> convicts.**

maimed and bruised and, in some cases, disabled for life. As far as I can remember only about ten died during the last ten years that I was there, two of these being killed outright by the guards for trivial offenses. . . .

The working day on a peon farm begins with sunrise and ends when the sun goes down; or, in other words, the average peon works from ten to twelve hours each day, with one hour (from 12 o'clock to 1 o'clock) for dinner. Hot or cold, sun or rain, this is the rule. As to their meals, the laborers are divided up into squads or companies, just the same as soldiers in a great military camp would be. Two or three men in each stockade are appointed as cooks. From thirty to forty men report to each cook. In the warm months (or eight or nine months out of the year) the cooking is done on the outside, just behind the stockades; in the cold months the cooking is done inside the stockades. Each peon is provided with a great big tin cup, a flat tin pan, and two big tin spoons. No knives and forks are ever seen, except those used by the cooks. At meal time the peons pass in single file before the cooks, and hold out their pans and cups to receive their allowances. Cow peas, (red or white, which when boiled turn black), fat bacon and old-fashioned Georgia cornbread, baked in pones from one to two and three inches thick, made up the chief articles of food. Black coffee, black molasses and brown sugar are also used abundantly. Once in a great while, on Sundays, biscuits would be made, but they would always be made from the kind of flour called "shorts." As a rule, breakfast consisted of coffee, fried bacon, cornbread, and sometimes molasses—and one "helping" of each was all that was allowed. Peas, boiled with huge hunks of fat bacon, and a hoe-cake [a cornmeal cake], as big as a man's hand, usually answered for dinner. Sometimes this dinner bill of fare gave place to bacon and greens (collard or turnip) and pot liquor [cooking liquid left in the pot].

REVIEWING THE READING

1. What were the terms of the narrator's first one-year work contract with the "Captain" at age twenty-one?

2. What was the arrangement between the state of Georgia and the senator regarding the convict labor?

3. **Using Your Historical Imagination.** Explain how the narrator's ten-year work contract became a situation of "peonage," in which he worked as a convict to pay his debt—how did this new arrangement come about? Also, what role did the illiteracy of the senator's black field hands play in this process?

20

From *The Poor in Great Cities* by Joseph Kirkland.

The Sweatshops of Chicago (1891)

Prior to the passage of laws regulating wages and working conditions, many of the poor living in the big cities of the nineteenth century worked in sweatshops. Sweatshops were makeshift factories where large numbers of people worked long hours for little pay on a piecework basis. These factories were usually crowded, dimly lighted, poorly ventilated, unsafe, and unsanitary places. Although a number of industries used the sweatshop system, the worst working conditions were found in the garment industry. As you read the following excerpts from a book about the poor in big cities in the late 1800s, look for reasons that help to explain why people were willing to work under these terrible conditions.

The *sweat-shop* is a place where, separate from the tailor-shop or clothing-warehouse, a "sweater" (middleman) assembles journeyman tailors and needle-women, to work under his supervision. He takes a cheap room outside the dear [expensive] and crowded business centre, and within the neighborhood where the work-people live. Thus is rent saved to the employer, and time and travel to the employed. The men can and do work more hours than was possible under the centralized system, and their wives and children can help, especially when, as is often done, the garments are taken home to "finish." (Even the very young can pull out basting-threads.) This "finishing" is what remains undone after the machine has done its work, and consists in "felling" [sewing the raw edges of] the waists and leg-ends of trousers (paid at one and one-half cents a pair), and, in short, all the "felling" necessary on any garment of any kind. For this service, at the prices paid, they cannot earn more than from twenty-five to forty cents a day, and the work is largely done by Italian, Polish, and Bohemian women and girls.

The entire number of persons employed in these vocations [jobs] may be stated at 5,000 men (of whom 800 are Jews), and from 20,000 to 23,000 women and children. The wages are reckoned by piece-work and (outside the "finishing") run about as follows:

Girls, hand-sewers, earn nothing for the first month, then as unskilled workers they get $1 to $1.50 a week, $3 a week, and (as skilled workers) $6 a week. The first-named class constitutes fifty per cent of all, the second thirty per cent, and the last twenty per cent. In the general work, men are only employed to do button-holing and pressing, and their earnings are as follows: "Pressers," $8 to $12 a week; "under-pressers," $4 to $7. Cloak operators earn $8 to $12 a week. Four-fifths of the sewing-machines are furnished by the "sweaters" (middlemen); also needles, thread, and wax.

The "sweat-shop" day is ten hours; but many take work home to get in overtime; and occasionally the shops themselves are kept open for extra work, from which the hardest and ablest workers sometimes make from $14 to $16 a week. On the other hand, the regular work-season for cloakmaking is but seven

This illustration from Scribner's Magazine *in 1898 shows a sweatshop in full operation in a private home.*

months, and for other branches nine months, in the year. The average weekly living expenses of a man and wife, with two children, as estimated by a self-educated workman named Bisno, are as follows: Rent (three or four small rooms), $2; food, fuel, and light $4; clothing, $2, and beer and spirits, $1. . . .

A city ordinance enacts that rooms provided for workmen shall contain space equal to five hundred feet of air for each person employed; but in the average "sweat-shop" only about a tenth of that quantity is to be found. In one such place there were fifteen men and women in one room, which contained also a pile of mattresses on which some of the men sleep at night. The closets were disgraceful. In an adjoining room were piles of clothing, made and unmade, on the same table with the food of the family. Two dirty little children were playing about the floor. . . .

The "sweating system" has been in operation about twelve years, during which time some firms have failed, while others have increased their production tenfold. Meantime certain "sweaters" have grown rich; two having built from their gains tenement-houses for rent to the poor workers. The wholesale clothing business of Chicago is about $20,000,000 a year.

REVIEWING THE READING

1. Who was the "sweater"?

2. What was "finishing" and how much could be made doing it?

3. **Using Your Historical Imagination.** What were the advantages of the sweatshop system to the "sweater"? How do you explain the fact that workers were willing to come to work in the sweatshops?

Booker T. Washington and the "Atlanta Compromise" (1895)

21

From *The Negro and the Atlanta Exposition* by Booker T. Washington.

Few speeches by private citizens have had the historical impact of Booker T. Washington's so-called "Atlanta compromise" speech of 1895. Washington, a former slave, was the founder and director of the Tuskegee Institute in Alabama and perhaps the best-known African American leader in the United States. Washington had been invited to speak at the opening ceremony of the Cotton States and International Exposition in Atlanta, and his 20-minute talk on the theme "Cast down your bucket where you are" was very favorably received by his mixed audience of southern blacks and whites—seated in separate sections—and northern whites. As you read these excerpts from Washington's speech, pay careful attention to what he means by his story of the "bucket."

One-third of the population of the South is of Negro race. No enterprise seeking the material, civil, or moral welfare of this section can disregard this element of our population and reach the highest success. I but convey to you, Mr. President and Directors, the sentiment of the masses of my race, when I say that in no way have the value and manhood of the American Negro been more fittingly and generously recognized, than by the managers of this magnificent Exposition at every stage of its progress. . . .

Booker T. Washington, the founder of Tuskegee Institute, was the best-known spokesman for African Americans in the decade of the 1890s.

A ship lost at sea for many days suddenly sighted a friendly vessel. From the mast of the unfortunate vessel was seen the signal: "Water, water, we die of thirst." The answer from the friendly vessel at once came back, "Cast down your bucket where you are." A second time the signal, "Water, water, send us water," ran up from the distressed vessel and was answered, "Cast down your bucket where you are," and a third and fourth signal for water was answered, "Cast down your bucket where you are." The captain of the distressed vessel, at last heeding the injunction [order], cast down his bucket and it came up full of fresh, sparkling water from the mouth of the Amazon River. To those of my race who depend on bettering their condition in a foreign land, or who underestimate the importance of cultivating friendly relations with the Southern white man who is their next door neighbor, I would say cast down your bucket where you are, cast it down in making friends, in every manly way, of the people of all races by whom we are surrounded. Cast it down in agriculture, in mechanics, in commerce, in domestic service, and in the professions. And in this connection it is well to bear in mind that, whatever other sins the South may be called upon to bear, when it comes to business pure and simple it is in the South that the negro is given a man's chance in the commercial world; and in nothing is this Exposition more eloquent than in emphasising this chance. Our greatest danger is that, in the great gap from slavery to freedom, we may overlook the fact that the masses of us are to live by the productions of our hands, and fail to keep in mind that we shall prosper in proportion as we learn to dignify and glorify common labor and put brains and skill into the common occupations of life; shall prosper in proportion as we learn to draw the line between the superficial and the substantial, the ornamental gewgaws of life and the useful. No race can prosper till it learns that there is as much dignity in tilling a field as in writing a poem. It is at the bottom of life we must begin and not the top. Nor should we permit our grievances to overshadow our opportunities.

To those of the white race who look to the incoming of those of foreign birth and strange tongue and habits for the prosperity of the South, were I permitted, I would repeat what I say to my own race, "Cast down your bucket where you are." Cast it down among the 8,000,000 negroes whose habits you know, whose loyalty and love you have tested in days when to have proved treacherous meant the ruin of your firesides. Cast it down among these people who have, without strikes and labor wars, tilled your fields, cleared your forests, builded your railroads and cities, and brought forth treasures from the bowels of the earth and helped make possible this magnificent representation of the progress of the South. Casting down your bucket among my people, helping and encouraging them as you are doing on these grounds, and to education of head, hand, and heart, you will find that they will buy your surplus land, make blossom the waste places in your fields, and run your factories. While doing this you can be sure in the future, as you have been in the past, that you and your families will be surrounded by the most patient, faithful, law-abiding, and unresentful people that the world has seen. . . . .

Nearly sixteen millions of hands [of blacks] will aid you pulling the load upwards, or they will pull against you the load downwards. We shall constitute one-third and much more of the ignorance and crime of the South, or one-third its intelligence and progress; we shall contribute one-third to the business and industrial prosperity of the South, or we shall prove a veritable body of death, stagnating, depressing, retarding every effort to advance the body politic. . . .

The wisest among my race understand that the agitation of questions of social equality is the extremest folly, and that progress in the enjoyment of all the privileges that will come to us must be the result of severe and constant struggle, rather than of artificial forcing. No race that has anything to contribute to the markets of the world is long in any degree ostracized [excluded]. It is important and right that all privileges of the law be ours, but it is vastly more important that we be prepared for the exercise of these privileges. The opportunity to earn a dollar in a factory just now is worth infinitely more than the opportunity to spend a dollar in an opera house.

REVIEWING THE READING

1. According to Washington, what did the story of the bucket mean for southern blacks?

2. What did the story mean for southern whites?

3. **Using Your Historical Imagination.** What was Washington telling southern blacks to do? What part of his message might arouse the greatest opposition among present-day African Americans concerned with civil rights?

A Farm Girl Arrives in the Big City (1895)

22

From *Rose of Dutcher's Coolly* by Hamlin Garland.

Hamlin Garland was a novelist who himself experienced the enormous transition between life on the farm and life in the great city. He left his farm family in 1884 to pursue a literary career in Chicago and Boston. The subject of his novels and short stories was often this aspect of his own experience—the ambitious young person from the country confronted by the new world of the city, with its diversity, mystery, excitement, and promise. In the excerpts below from Rose of Dutcher's Coolly, *one of Garland's heroines encounters Chicago for the first time. As you read the selection, consider the things that impressed her most about Chicago in 1895.*

The next day Rose went to town alone. The wind had veered to the south, the dust blew, and the whole terrifying panorama [view] of life in the street seemed some way blurred together, and forms of men and animals were like figures in tapestry. The grind and clang and clatter and hiss and howl of the traffic was all about her. . . .

So it was—the wonderful and the terrifying appealed to her mind first. In all the city she saw the huge and the fierce. She perceived only contrasts. She saw the ragged newsboy and the towering policeman. She saw the rag-pickers, the street vermin, with a shudder of pity and horror, and she saw also the gorgeous show windows of the great stores. She saw the beautiful new gowns and hats, and she saw also the curious dress of swart [dark] Italian girls scavenging with baskets on their arms. Their faces were old and grimy, their voices sounded like

Electric streetcars and a variety of horse-drawn vehicles crowd the streets of Chicago around 1890.

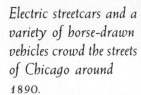

the chattered colloquies [conversations] of monkeys in the circus.

It all seemed a battlefield. There was no hint of repose or home in it all. People were just staying here like herself, trying to get work, trying to make a living, trying to make a name. They had left their homes as she had, and though she conceived of them as having a foothold she could not imagine them having reached security. The home-life of the city had not revealed itself to her.

She made her way about the first few blocks below Water street, looking for Dr. Herrick's address. It was ten o'clock, and the streets were in a frenzy of exchange. The sidewalks were brooks, the streets rivers of life which curled into doors and swirled around mountainous buildings.

It was almost pathetic to see how helpless she seemed in the midst of these alien sounds. It took away from her the calm, almost scornful, self-reliance which characterized her in familiar surroundings. Her senses were as acute as a hare's and sluiced [washed] in upon her a bewildering flood of sights and sounds. She did not appear childish, but she seemed slow and stupid, which of course she was not. She thought and thought till she grew sick with thought. She struggled to digest all that came to her, but it was like trampling sand; she apparently gained nothing by her toil.

The streets led away into thunderous tunnels, beyond which some other strange hell of sound and stir imaginatively lay. The brutal voices of drivers of cabs and drays [wagons] assaulted her. The clang of gongs drew her attention, now here, now there, and her anxiety to understand each sound and to appear calm added to her confusion.

She heard crashes and yells that were of murder and sudden death. It was the crash of a falling bundle of sheet iron, but she knew not that. She looked around thinking to see some savage battle scene.

She saw women with painted faces and bleached hair whom she took to be those mysterious and appalling women who sell themselves to men. They were in fact simple-minded shop girls or vulgar little housewives with sad lack of taste.

Every street she crossed, she studied, looking both up and down it, in the effort to see some end of its mystery. They all vanished in lurid [yellowish and hazy], desolate distance, save toward the lake. Out there she knew, the water lay serene and blue.

This walk was to her like entrance into war. It thrilled and engaged her at every turn. She was in the center of human life. To win here was to win all she cared to have.

REVIEWING THE READING

1. What were Rose's first impressions of the city?

2. What indications does the novelist give of Rose's essential character, and how she may react to the city?

3. **Using Your Historical Imagination.** In your opinion, are the reactions of Rose to Chicago still typical of young people moving to the big city? Explain.

23

From *The Cuban and Porto (sic) Rican Campaigns* by Richard Harding Davis.

The Rough Riders Charge San Juan Hill (1898)

By May of 1898, Spain's Atlantic fleet was trapped in the harbor of Santiago, Cuba, by an American naval force. Within a few weeks, some 18,000 United States troops were landed on the nearby coast and the American generals made plans to capture the city of Santiago. The United States attack focused on the two major defensive positions of El Caney Hill and San Juan Hill. Once these were seized, the city could no longer be effectively defended by the Spanish.

American forces attacked on the first of July. Assigned to take San Juan Hill were the divisions of J. L. Kent and Theodore Roosevelt, who commanded his famous (but until now untried) "Rough Riders." Newspaper reporter Richard Harding Davis published an eyewitness account of what happened next. As you read the following excerpts from his book, consider who—in Davis' opinion—deserved most of the credit for the victory.

General Kent's division, which was to have been held in reserve, according to the plan, had been rushed up in the rear of the First and Tenth, and the Tenth had deployed [scattered] in skirmish order to the right. The trail was now completely blocked by Kent's division. Lawton's division, which was to have reinforced on the right, had not appeared, but incessant firing from the direction of El Caney showed that he and Chaffee were fighting mightily. The situation was desperate. Our troops could not retreat, as the trail for two miles behind them was wedged with men. They could not remain where they were for they were being shot to pieces. There was only one thing they could do—go forward and take the San Juan hills by assault. It was as desperate as the situation itself. To charge earthworks [mounds of earth forming barricades] held by men with modern rifles, and using modern artillery, until after the earthworks have been shaken by artillery, and to attack them in advance and not in the flanks, are both impossible military propositions. But this campaign had not been conducted according to military rules, and a series of military blunders had brought

Teddy Roosevelt (just to the left of the flag) and his Rough Riders pose for the camera after taking San Juan Hill.

**. . . there was
no escape . . .**

seven thousand American soldiers into a chute of
death, from which there was no escape except by
taking the enemy who held it by the throat, and
driving him out and beating him down. So the generals of the divisions and brigades stepped back and
relinquished [gave up] their command to the regimental officers and the enlisted men.

"We can do nothing more," they virtually said.
"There is the enemy."

Colonel Roosevelt, on horseback, broke from
the woods behind the line of the Ninth, and finding
its men lying in his way, shouted: "If you don't wish
to go forward, let my men pass, please." The junior
officers of the Ninth, with their Negroes, instantly
sprang into line with the Rough Riders, and charged
at the blue block-house on the right.

I speak of Roosevelt first because, with General
Hawkins, who led Kent's division, notably the Sixth
and Sixteenth Regulars, he was, without doubt, the
most conspicuous figure in the charge. General Hawkins, with hair as white as snow, and yet far in
advance of men thirty years his junior, was so noble
a sight that you felt inclined to pray for his safety;
on the other hand, Roosevelt, mounted high on
horseback, and charging the rifle-pits at a gallop
and quite alone, made you feel that you would like
to cheer. He wore on his sombrero a blue polka-
dot handkerchief, *à la* Havelock [a British general],
which, as he advanced, floated out straight behind
his head, like a guidon [small flag]. Afterward, the
men of his regiment who followed this flag, adopted
a polka-dot handkerchief as the badge of the Rough
Riders. These two officers were notably conspicuous
in the charge, but no one can claim that any two
men, or any one man, was more brave or more daring,
or showed greater courage in that slow, stubborn
advance than did any of the others. . . .

I think the thing which impressed one the most,
when our men started from cover, was that they
were so few. It seemed as if someone had made an

awful and terrible mistake. One's instinct was to call them to come back. You felt that someone had blundered and that these few men were blindly following out some madman's mad order. It was not heroic then, it seemed merely terribly pathetic. The pity of it, the folly of such a sacrifice was what held you.

They had no glittering bayonets, they were not massed in regular array. There were a few men in advance, bunched together, and creeping up a steep, sunny hill, the top of which roared and flashed with flame. The men held their guns pressed across their breasts and stepped heavily as they climbed. Behind these first few, spreading out like a fan, were single lines of men, slipping and scrambling in the smooth grass, moving forward with difficulty, as though they were wading waist high through water, moving slowly, carefully, with strenuous effort. It was much more wonderful than any swinging charge could have been. They walked to greet death at every step, many of them, as they advanced, sinking suddenly or pitching forward and disappearing in the high grass, but the others waded on, stubbornly, forming a thin blue line that kept creeping higher and higher up the hill. It was as inevitable as the rising tide. It was a miracle of self-sacrifice, a triumph of bull-dog courage, which one watched breathless with wonder. The fire of the Spanish riflemen, who still stuck bravely to their posts, doubled and trebled in fierceness, the crests of the hills crackled and burst in amazed roars, and rippled with waves of tiny flame. But the blue line crept steadily up and on, and then, near the top, the broken fragments gathered together with a sudden burst of speed, the Spaniards appeared for a moment outlined against the sky and poised for instant flight, fired a last volley and fled before the swift-moving wave that leaped and sprang up after them.

The men of the Ninth and the Rough Riders rushed to the blockhouse together, the men of the

They walked to greet death at every step . . .

Sixth, of the Third, of the Tenth Cavalry, of the Sixth and Sixteenth Infantry, fell on their faces along the crest of the yellow silk flags of the cavalry and the Stars and Stripes of their country into the soft earth of the trenches, and then sank down and looked back at the road they had climbed and swung their hats in the air. And from far overhead, from these few figures perched on the Spanish rifle-pits, with their flags planted among the empty cartridges of the enemy, and overlooking the walls of Santiago, came, faintly, the sound of a tired, broken cheer.

REVIEWING THE READING

1. Why was the charge up San Juan Hill a military necessity?

2. What two basic propositions of modern warfare did the charge violate?

3. **Using Your Historical Imagination.** The Rough Riders were an elite cavalry unit, recruited by their leader from the ranks of cowboys, polo players, professional jockeys, and other excellent riders. What was unusual about their charge up San Juan Hill?

A Farmer in the Grip of the "Octopus" (1890s)

From *The Octopus* by Frank Norris.

24

In 1901 Frank Norris published The Octopus, *a novel about the bitter conflict between the railroad and farmers in California. The "octopus" of the novel was the railroad itself. Its steel tentacles caught farmers in its grasp and squeezed the profit from farming, primarily by controlling the rates at which farmers could ship crops to market. Norris presents only the point of view of the exploited farmers, but historians confirm that the railroads actually practiced many of the ethical abuses the novelist condemns. As you read the following excerpt from Norris' book, consider what principle lay behind the action of the railroad in the case of Mr. Dyke.*

"I'll be wanting some cars of you people before the summer is out," observed Dyke to the clerk as he folded up and put away the order that the other had handed him. He remembered perfectly well that he had arranged the matter of transporting his crop some months before, but his role of proprietor amused him and he liked to busy himself again and again with the details of his undertaking.

"I suppose," he added, "You'll be able to give 'em to me. There'll be a big wheat crop to move this year and I don't want to be caught in any car famine."

"Oh, you'll get your cars," murmured the other.

"I'll be the means of bringing business your way," Dyke went on; "I've done so well with my hops that there are a lot of others going into the business next season. Suppose," he continued, struck with an idea, "suppose we went into some sort of pool, a sort of shippers' organization, could you give us special rates, cheaper rates—say a cent and a half?"

The other looked up.

"A cent and a half! Say *four* cents and a half and maybe I'll talk business with you."

"Four cents and a half," returned Dyke, "I don't see it. Why, the regular rate is only two cents."

"No, it isn't," answered the clerk, looking him gravely in the eye, "it's five cents."

"Well, there's where you are wrong, m'son," Dyke retorted, genially. "You look it up. You'll find the freight on hops from Bonneville to 'Frisco is two cents a pound for carload lots. You told me that yourself last fall."

"That was last fall," observed the clerk. There was a silence. Dyke shot a glance of suspicion at the other. Then, reassured, he remarked:

"You look it up. You'll see I'm right."

S. Behrman came forward and shook hands politely with the ex-engineer.

"Anything I can do for you, Mr. Dyke?"

Dyke explained. When he had done speaking, the clerk turned to S. Behrman and observed respectfully:

"Our regular rate on hops is five cents."

"Yes," answered S. Behrman, pausing to reflect; "yes, Mr. Dyke, that's right—five cents."

The clerk brought forward a folder of yellow paper and handed it to Dyke. It was inscribed at the top "Tariff Schedule No. 8," and underneath these words, in brackets, was a smaller inscription, *"Supersedes* [takes the place of] *No. 7 of Aug. 1."*

"See for yourself," said S. Behrman. . . .

In the list that was printed below, Dyke saw that the rate for hops between Bonneville or Guadalajara and San Francisco was five cents.

For a moment Dyke was confused. Then swiftly the matter became clear in his mind. The Railroad had raised the freight on hops from two cents to five.

All his calculations as to a profit on his little investment he had based on a freight rate of two cents a pound. He was under contract to deliver his crop. He could not draw back. The new rate ate up every cent of his grains. He stood there ruined.

"Why, what do you mean?" he burst out. "You promised me a rate of two cents and I went ahead with my business with that understanding. What do you mean?"

S. Behrman and the clerk watched him from the other side of the counter.

"The rate is five cents," declared the clerk doggedly.

"Well, that ruins me," shouted Dyke. "Do you understand? I won't make fifty cents. *Make!* Why, I will *owe,*—I'll be—be— That ruins me, do you understand?"

The other raised a shoulder.

"We don't force you to ship. You can do as you like. The rate is five cents."

". . . I'm under contract to deliver. What am I going to do? Why, you told me—you promised me a two-cent rate."

"I don't remember it," said the clerk. "I don't know anything about that. But I know this; I know that hops have gone up. I know the German crop

In this 1885 political cartoon, the Grange, a farmers' organization, tries to alert citizens to their exploitation by the railroad.

was a failure and that the crop in New York wasn't worth the hauling. Hops have gone up to nearly a dollar. You don't suppose we don't know that, do you, Mr. Dyke?"

"What's the price of hops got to do with you?"

"It's got *this* to do with us," returned the other with a sudden aggressiveness, "that the freight rate has gone up to meet the price. We're not doing business for our health. My orders are to raise your rate to five cents, and I think you are getting off easy."

Dyke stared in blank astonishment. For the moment, the audacity [shamelessness] of the affair was what most appealed to him. He forgot its personal application.

"Good Lord," he murmured, "good Lord! What will you people do next? Look here. What's your basis of applying freight rates anyhow?" he suddenly vociferated [said] with furious sarcasm. "What's your rule? What are you guided by?"

But at the words, S. Behrman, who had kept silent during the heat of the discussion, leaned abruptly forward. For the only time in his knowledge, Dyke saw his face inflamed with anger and with the enmity [bitterness] and contempt of all this farming element with whom he was contending.

"Yes, what's your rule? What's your basis?" demanded Dyke, turning swiftly to him.

S. Behrman emphasized each word of his reply with a tap of one forefinger on the counter before him:

"All—the—traffic—will—bear."

The ex-engineer stepped back a pace, his fingers on the ledge of the counter, to steady himself. He felt himself grow pale, his heart became a mere leaden weight in his chest, inert, refusing to beat.

In a second the whole affair, in all its bearings, went speeding before the eye of his imagination like the rapid unrolling of a panorama [series of pictures]. Every cent of his earnings was sunk in this hop business of his. More than that, he had borrowed money to carry it on, certain of success— borrowed of S. Behrman, offering his crop and his little home as security. Once he failed to meet his obligations, S. Behrman would foreclose. Not only would the Railroad devour every morsel of his profits, but also it would take from him his home; at a blow he would be left penniless and without a home. What would then become of his mother—and what would become of the little tad? She, whom he had been planning to educate like a veritable [true] lady. For all that year he had talked of his ambition for his little daughter to every one he met. All Bonneville knew of it. What a mark for gibes he had made of himself. The workingman turned farmer! What a target for jeers—he who had fancied he could elude [escape] the Railroad! He remembered he had once said the great Trust had overlooked his little enterprise, disdaining to plunder such small fry. He should have known better than that. How had he ever imagined the Road would permit him to make any money?

REVIEWING THE READING

1. What did Dyke plan to ship, and to where? What had been the freight cost quoted to him last fall?

2. What determined the increase in the rate from 2¢ to 5¢ a pound, according to the clerk, and what underlying principle did this illustrate?

3. **Using Your Historical Imagination.** Can you think of any way Dyke could have avoided higher freight rates? Why do you think the railroads at this time were able to manipulate freight rates generally as they wished?

25

From *In the Golden Nineties* by Henry Collins Brown.

New York in the Golden Nineties (1890s)

With the coming of electric lights and power in the 1890s, city life changed drastically. Nevertheless, as this account from Henry Brown's book In the Golden Nineties demonstrates, things were still very different from what we are accustomed to today. As you read the following excerpts from Brown's book, note the various forms of transport used in New York City during the 1890s.

It was the advent of the Bicycle that created the present enormous vogue for [popularity of] athletics amongst women. Of course, there had previously been some ladylike tennis and croquet playing, skating and archery on the distaff [feminine] side, but it was only by a small minority, in a spirit of high adventure, or as an excuse to wear some jaunty, if tight fitting, sporting costumes. The real beginning of swimming the Channel for mommer, popper, and the babies on our block, and the Star Spangled Banner; of tennis quarrels, and similar amenities [pleasantries] of feminine sport, is found in the great bicycle craze of the Nineties, which put the world awheel. "Daisy Bell" and her bicycle built for two, was the lyric expression of this furore [uproar]. Bicycles were at first constructed for skirted females. Then some intrepid [courageous] women revived the bloomer, which had caused so much laughter and indignation way back in the Fifties, and rode men's bikes in them. Society took up the fad, and organized the Michaux Club on Broadway near 53rd Street, then still an equine [horse] neighborhood. Pictures of society belles in fetching bicycle costumes, including

the popular Tyrolean [Austrian-style] hat, appeared
in the Sunday papers, and of course, what Society favored, who could resist? It took only a few
months for the fad to make a conquest of the entire
population. . . .

Another mode of transit, supplementing the pioneer work of the bicycle in carrying people afield,
was the trolley. This newly-invented vehicle had
by this time about wholly superseded [taken the
place of] the old, slow-moving horse car. The greater
speed of this new transportation system made it a
popular vehicle, especially in those remote sections
of Greater New York where lamps were still lighted
only in the dark of the moon.

The power that furnished the transit also furnished the light. The small incandescent lamp was
perfected by this time and the cheerful brightness
of the trolley car at night soon suggested its use
for a novel purpose—neighborhood outings. For a
trifling expense a car could be illuminated from one
end to the other in a perfect blaze of multi-colored
lights, producing at once a carnival spirit that was
quite irresistible. Many of the companies bedecked
[decorated] these cars at their own expense and found
the added patronage adequately justified the cost.
In these outlying districts, especially in Brooklyn
and the small towns around the city, these trolley
parties became quite the fad and all through the
summer this delightful pastime was vastly popular
and entertained whole communities.

In the city itself this same attraction made itself
felt, and encouraged a new class of passengers known
as "pleasure riders," who paid their nickels merely
for the sake of the ride and the cooling breezes
incidental thereto. This had hitherto been the mo-
nopoly of the poorer East Side classes. Particularly
on Broadway did it flourish, the cars then running
without change from Harlem to the Battery. The
noisy family parties of the Third Avenue line found
an antithesis [opposite] in the more sedate, and also

During the bicycle boom of the 1890s, thousands of New York residents took to the streets on two-wheelers.

more varied types, of the Broadway line. Down Columbus Avenue, curving into the "White Light" district, then into the semi-gloom below Madison Square, and the deserted wholesale and financial quarters the car sped. After a pleasant hour or less it finally disgorged [let off] its cooled and gratified passengers into the still delightful precincts of Battery Park, with its view of the bay and the twinkling lights of the moving craft on its dark and romantic waters. . . .

It was not until the early nineties that the hansom [two-wheeled horse-drawn two-passenger cab in which the driver's seat is above and behind the cab] appeared on our streets in any numbers. Its four-wheeled predecessor in the cab ranks was generally termed a "coupe." The New Yorker of that day was not a cab-riding biped [creature with two feet].

Except on those rare occasions when for some particular reason he desired to create an impression, the
street cars served his purpose quite adequately and
cheaply. . . .

The coming of the hansom gave a considerable
impetus [push] to cab riding here. There was an
old maxim among cab patrons—"Never ride in a
cab with two men on the box." This harmless observation carried a world of meaning to the initiated;
numerous robberies occurred when the warning was
disregarded. The lure of driving has always held
an irresistible appeal to ex-convicts, ticket of leave
men, robbers, etc. Perhaps it is the temporary contact
with genteel life that fascinates them. At all events
not only in the Nineties but even in our own day
[the 1920s] this same attraction persists, and the
taxi cab bandit is only the legitimate successor of
the two men on the box of which we speak.

The hansom had only room for two passengers,
and its open front made it very pleasant for sightsee-
ing. It was also much handier to navigate than the
old four-wheeler. Ladies, in particular, liked the hansom to see and be seen, and it soon became the
most popular form of *de luxe* transit. In fact, the
first taxicabs on our streets were built on the hansom
pattern.

New York's first "rubber-neck" wagon was the
old Fifth Avenue stage which rumbled over the granite stones of that renowned thoroughfare drawn by
a pair of dejected steeds that often excited the com-
miseration [pity] of the S.P.C.A. [Society for the
Prevention of Cruelty to Animals] and were the occasion of their official interference. The original stages
had not outside accommodation for passengers. In
fact, business on the line was not very brisk as it
ran parallel with the Madison Avenue cars and public
preference for the smooth rails instead of jolting
stones was pronounced. But the strangers and the
sightseers all wanted to see the outside of the millionaires' mansions along the 'bus line. The company

issued little booklets containing a directory of these fabled domiciles [homes] which were faithfully consulted by the passengers interested. The tendency to this form of "rubber necking" became so pronounced that the company installed seats on the roofs of its vehicles and, to the great relief of the general public, also improved their horse power. Business picked up wonderfully, and thus began the present admirable system in vogue.

REVIEWING THE READING

1. To what does the author give credit for sparking an interest in serious athletics among women?

2. What was the meaning of the New York saying: "Never ride in a cab with two men on the box"?

3. **Using Your Historical Imagination.** Imagine yourself standing on a busy street corner in present-day downtown New York. Based on what you have learned in the reading, what would be the likely differences in what you would see, hear, and smell now and in the 1890s?

Carry Nation Attacks "Dens of Vice" (1900)

26

From The Use and Need of the Life of Carry A. Nation by Carry A. Nation.

As one of the leaders of the movement to prohibit saloons, Carry Nation attracted national attention. Nation believed she was divinely inspired to attack the evils of drink, and in the early 1900s published her autobiography, from which the following excerpts are taken. As you read consider how most people reacted to the actions of Carry Nation.

On the 6th of June, before retiring, as I often did, I threw myself face downward at the foot of my bed and told the Lord to use me any way to suppress the dreadful curse of liquor. The next morning, before I awoke, I heard these words very distinctly: "Go to Kiowa [Kansas], and" (as in a vision and here my hands were lifted and cast down suddenly.) "I'll stand by you."

I got a box that would fit under my buggy seat, and every time I thought no one would see me, I went out in the yard and picked up some brick-bats [pieces of brick], for rocks are scarce around Medicine Lodge, and I wrapped them up in newspapers to pack in the box under my buggy seat. I also had four bottles I had bought from Southworth, the druggist, with "Schlitz-Malt" in them, which I used to smash with.

I hitched my horse to the buggy, put the box of "smashers" in, and at half past three o'clock in the afternoon, the sixth of June, 1900, I started to Kiowa.

I got there at 8:30 P.M. and stayed all night with a friend. Early next morning I had my horse put to the buggy and drove to the first place, kept by Mr. Dobson. I put the smashers on my right arm and went in. He and another man were standing behind the bar. These rocks and bottles being wrapped in paper looked like packages bought from a store. Be wise as devils and harmless as doves. I did not wish my enemies to know what I had.

I said: "Mr. Dobson, I told you last spring, when I held my county convention here (I was W. C. T. U. [Women's Christian Temperance Union] president of Barber County), to close this place, and you didn't do it. Now I have come with another remonstrance [protest]. Get out of the way. I don't want to strike you, but I am going to break up this den of vice."

I began to throw at the mirror and the bottles below the mirror. Mr. Dobson and his companion jumped into a corner, seemed very much terrified. From that I went to another saloon, until I had destroyed three, breaking some of the windows in the front of the building. In the last place, kept by Lewis, there was quite a young man behind the bar. I said to him: "Young man, come from behind that bar, your mother did not raise you for such a place." I threw a brick at the mirror, which was a very heavy one, and it did not break, but the brick fell and broke everything in its way. I began to look around for something that would break it. I was standing by a billiard table on which there was one ball. I said: "Thank God," and picked it up, threw it, and it made a hole in the mirror. While I was throwing these rocks at the dives in Kiowa, there was a picture before my eyes of Mr. McKinley, the President, sitting in an old arm chair and as I threw, the chair would fall to pieces.

The other dive keepers closed up, stood in front of their places and would not let me come in. By this time the streets were crowded with people; most of them seemed to look puzzled. There was one boy about fifteen years old who seemed perfectly

wild with joy, and he jumped, skipped and yelled
with delight. I have since thought of that as being
a significant sign. For to smash saloons will save
the boy.

When I reached Medicine Lodge the town was
in quite an excitement, the news having been tele-
graphed ahead. I drove through the streets and told
the people I would be at the postoffice corner to
tell why I had done this. A great crowd had gathered
and I began to tell them of my work in the jail
here, and the young men's lives that had been ruined,
and the broken hearted mothers, the taxation that
had been brought on the county, and other wrongs
of the dives of Kiowa. . . .

On the 27th of December, 1900, I went to
Wichita, almost seven months after the raid in Kiowa.
Mr. Nation went to see his brother, Mr. Seth Nation,
in eastern Kansas and I was free to leave home.

I took a valise [small suitcase] with me, and
in that valise I put a rod of iron perhaps a foot
long, and as large around as my thumb. I also took
a cane with me. I found out by smashing in Kiowa
that I would use a rock but once, so I took the
cane with me. I got down to Wichita about seven
o'clock in the evening, that day, and went to the
hotel near the Santa Fe depot and left my valise. I
went up town to select the place I would begin at
first. I went into about fourteen places, where men
were drinking at bars, the same as they do in licensed
places. The police standing with the others.

I finally came to the "Carey Hotel," next to
which was called the Carey Annex or Bar. The first
thing that struck me was the life-size picture of a
naked woman, opposite the mirror.

I went back to the hotel and bound the rod
and cane together, then wrapped paper around the
top of it. I slept but little that night, spending most
of the night in prayer. I wore a large cape. I took
the cane and walked down the back stairs the next
morning, and out in the alley I picked up as many

*Carry Nation was a fi-
ery crusader against
saloons.*

rocks as I could carry under my cape. I walked into the Carey Bar-room, and threw the rocks at the picture; then turned and smashed the mirror that covered almost the entire side of the large room. Some men drinking at the bar ran at break-neck speed; the bar-tender was wiping a glass and he seemed transfixed to the spot and never moved. I took the cane and broke up the sideboard, which had on it all kinds of intoxicating drinks. Then I ran out across the street to destroy another one. I was arrested at 8:30 A.M., my rocks and cane taken from me, and I was taken to the police headquarters, where I was treated very nicely by the Chief of Police, Mr. Cubbin, who seemed to be amused at what I had done. This man was not very popular with the administration, and was soon put out.

At 6:30 P.M., I was tried and taken to Wichita jail; found guilty of malicious mischief. . . .

The way I happened to think of a hatchet as a souvenir, some one brought me one and told me I ought to carry them. I then selected a pattern and got a party in Providence, R. I., to make them. These have been a great financial aid to me; helped me pay my fines and expenses. People have often bought them from me, at my prison cell window. I sell them everywhere I go. . . .

From Holt I went to Topeka. I stopped with the United Brethren minister there, and spoke in his church. The saloons were all over Topeka. I went down town after dark, to see the condition of things. It was soon learned that I was on the streets, and a crowd gathered. I went to some dives and joints. I could not get in. One had his mistress stationed at the door with a broomstick. She gave me four blows before I could get away, poor creature. I met her niece after that, who told how the saloon-keeper cast her off and that she died a miserable death.

While I was there the State Temperance Union had a meeting in the First Presbyterian church. Capt.

Cook, from Chetopa, got up in the meeting and said: "Here is ten dollars towards giving a medal to the bravest woman in Kansas, Carry Nation." One hundred and twenty dollars was raised.

I said: "I would prefer that the money be used to pay my lawyers, rather than be put into a medal as I did not wear gold in any way."

We held a good many meetings. I spoke in several churches and held meetings in Dr. Eva Harding's office, where we prepared to take measures to break up saloons in Topeka, where sworn officials were perjuring themselves [breaking formal promises] from the governor down to constable.

I passed on down to the "Senate" saloon and went in. This was about daylight. The bartender ran towards me with a yell, wrenched my hatchet out of my hand and shot off his pistol toward the ceiling; he then ran out of the back door, and I got another hatchet from a lady with us. I ran behind the bar, smashed the mirror and all the bottles under it; picked up the cash register, threw it down; then broke the faucets of the refrigerator, opened the door and cut the rubber tubes that conducted the beer. Of course it began to fly all over the house. I threw over the slot machine, breaking it up and I got from it a sharp piece of iron with which I opened the bungs of the beer kegs, and opened the faucets of the barrels, and then the beer flew in every direction and I was completely saturated [soaked]. A policeman came in and very good-naturedly arrested me. For this I was fined $100 and put in jail. . . .

I spoke in Austin, Texas, at the state university. When I arrived in the city I was met by "Uncle Tom" Murrah. "Uncle Tom" is a true type of the old fashion gentleman. Had it not been for the chivalry of this dear old friend I expect I would have had some trouble with the police of Austin.

I went into a saloon and was led out in very forcible manner by the proprietor, who was one of the city council. I stood in front of this man's man-

I threw over the slot machine . . .

trap and cried out against this outrageous business. The man kept a phonograph going to drown my voice. The police would have interfered but "Uncle Tom" told me to say what I pleased, and he would stand by me. I went up to the state university with students who tried to get a hall for me to speak to them but they could not. I spoke from the steps. In the midst of the speech and the cheers from the boys I heard a voice at my side. I looked and there stood the Principal, Prexley Prather. He was white with excitement, saying: "Madam, we do not allow such." I said: "I am speaking for the good of these boys." "We do not allow speaking on the campus." I said: "I have spoken to the students at Ann Arbor, at Harvard, at Yale, and I will speak to the boys of Texas." The boys gave a yell. The mail man was driving up at this time. The horse took fright, the letters and papers flew in every direction. The man jumped from the sulky; the horse ran up against a tree and was stopped. I offered to pay for the broken shafts but the mail carrier would take nothing. There was no serious damage and all had a good laugh, except perhaps, the dignified principal.

REVIEWING THE READING

1. What was Carry Nation's customary prayer before retiring?

2. In what way did Nation make money to support her cause?

3. **Using Your Historical Imagination.** What were the various reactions to Nation's attacks on saloons? How do you explain these reactions?

The Squid and the Lobster, from Dreiser's *The Financier* (ca. 1900)

27

From *The Financier* by Theodore Dreiser.

Novelist Theodore Dreiser wrote about American big business in its most colorful and ruthless era. The Financier, Dreiser's first widely successful novel, was published in 1912. It told the story of Frank Cowperwood, whose life embodied the brutal struggle for wealth and power in the no-holds-barred world of business and banking. In the following excerpt from Chapter 1, we meet Cowperwood at age ten just forming his vision of how the world was organized. Consider what lesson he thought that he had learned from the affair of the squid and the lobster.

Frank Cowperwood, even at ten, was a natural-born leader. At the day school he attended, and later at the Central High School, he was looked upon as one whose common sense could unquestionably be trusted in all cases. He was a sturdy youth, courageous and defiant. From the very start of his life, he wanted to know about economics and politics. He cared nothing for books. He was a clean, stalky, shapely boy, with a bright, clean-cut, incisive [forceful] face; large, clear, gray eyes; a wide forehead; short, bristly, dark-brown hair. He had an incisive, quick-motioned, self-sufficient manner, and was forever asking questions with a keen desire for an intelligent reply. He never had an ache or pain, ate his food with gusto, and ruled his brothers with a rod of iron. "Come on, Joe!" "Hurry, Ed!" These commands were issued in no rough but always a sure way, and Joe and Ed came. They looked up to Frank from the first as a master, and what he had to say was listened to eagerly.

He was forever pondering, pondering—one fact astonishing him quite as much as another—for he could not figure out how this thing he had come into—this life—was organized. How did all these people get into the world? What were they doing here? Who started things, anyhow? His mother told him the story of Adam and Eve, but he didn't believe it. There was a fish-market not so very far from his home, and there, on his way to see his father at the bank, or conducting his brothers on after-school expeditions, he liked to look at a certain tank in front of one store where were kept odd specimens of sea-life brought in by the Delaware Bay fishermen. He saw once there a sea-horse—just a queer little sea-animal that looked somewhat like a horse—and another time he saw an electric eel which Benjamin Franklin's discovery had explained. One day he saw a squid and a lobster put in the tank, and in connection with them was witness to a tragedy which stayed with him all his life and cleared things up considerably intellectually. The lobster, it appeared from the talk of the idle bystanders, was offered no food, as the squid was considered his rightful prey. He lay at the bottom of the clear glass tank on the yellow sand, apparently seeing nothing—you could not tell in which way his beady, black buttons of eyes were looking—but apparently they were never off the body of the squid. The latter, pale and waxy in texture, looking very much like pork fat or jade, moved about in torpedo fashion; but his movements were apparently never out of the eyes of his enemy, for by degrees small portions of his body began to disappear, snapped off by the relentless claws of his pursuer. The lobster would leap like a catapult to where the squid was apparently idly dreaming, and the squid, very alert, would dart away, shooting out at the same time a cloud of ink, behind which it would disappear. It was not

Novelist Theodore Dreiser was famous for his realistic descriptions of the world of American big business.

always completely successful, however. Small portions of its body or its tail were frequently left in the claws of the monster below. Fascinated by the drama, young Cowperwood came daily to watch.

One morning he stood in front of the tank, his nose almost pressed to the glass. Only a portion of the squid remained, and his ink-bag was emptier than ever. In the corner of the tank sat the lobster, poised apparently for action.

The boy stayed as long as he could, the bitter struggle fascinating him. Now, maybe, or in an hour or a day, the squid might die, slain by the lobster, and the lobster would eat him. He looked again at the greenish-copperish engine of destruction in the corner and wondered when this would be. To-night, maybe. He would come back to-night.

He returned that night, and lo! the expected had happened. There was a little crowd around the tank. The lobster was in the corner. Before him was the squid cut in two and partially devoured.

"He got him at last," observed one bystander. "I was standing right here an hour ago, and up he leaped and grabbed him. The squid was too tired.

He wasn't quick enough. He did back up, but that
lobster he calculated on his doing that. He's been
figuring on his movements for a long time now.
He got him to-day."

Frank only stared. Too bad he had missed this.
The least touch of sorrow for the squid came to
him as he stared at it slain. Then he gazed at the
victor.

"That's the way it has to be, I guess," he com-
mented to himself. "That squid wasn't quick enough."
He figured it out.

"The squid couldn't kill the lobster—he had
no weapon. The lobster could kill the squid—he
was heavily armed. There was nothing for the squid
to feed on; the lobster had the squid as prey. What
was the result to be? What else could it be? He
didn't have a chance," he concluded finally, as he
trotted on homeward.

The incident made a great impression on him.
It answered in a rough way that riddle which had
been annoying him so much in the past: "How is
life organized?" Things lived on each other—that
was it. Lobsters lived on squids and other things.
What lived on lobsters? Men, of course! Sure, that
was it! And what lived on men? he asked himself.
Was it other men? Wild animals lived on men. And
there were Indians and cannibals. And some men
were killed by storms and accidents. He wasn't so
sure about men; but men did kill each other. How
about wars and street fights and mobs? He had seen
a mob once. It attacked the *Public Ledger* building
as he was coming home from school. His father
had explained why. It was about the slaves. That
was it! Sure, men lived on men. Look at the slaves.
They were men. That's what all this excitement was
about these days. Men killing other men—negroes.

He went on home quite pleased with himself
at his solution.

"Mother!" he exclaimed, as he entered the house,
"he finally got him!"

"Got who? What got what?" she inquired in amazement. "Go wash your hands."

"Why, that lobster got that squid I was telling you and pa about the other day."

"Well, that's too bad. What makes you take any interest in such things? Run, wash your hands."

"Well, you don't often see anything like that. I never did."

He went out in the back yard, where there was a hydrant and a post with a little table on it, and on that a shining tin-pan and a bucket of water. Here he washed his face and hands.

"Say, papa," he said to his father, later, "you know that squid?"

"Yes."

"Well, he's dead. The lobster got him."

His father continued reading. "Well, that's too bad," he said, indifferently.

But for days and weeks Frank thought of this and of the life he was tossed into, for he was already pondering on what he should be in this world, and how he should get along. From seeing his father count money, he was sure that he would like banking; and Third Street, where his father's office was, seemed to him the cleanest, most fascinating street in the world.

REVIEWING THE READING

1. How does the author describe his hero, Cowperwood?

2. What was the lesson learned from the squid and the lobster?

3. **Using Your Historical Imagination.** How do you think this vision of how the world is organized may influence Cowperwood's subsequent career in business?

28

From *The Autobiography of Lincoln Steffens* by Lincoln Steffens.

Lincoln Steffens Tells How Theodore Roosevelt Began the Square Deal (1901)

Lincoln Steffens was one of the most famous of the "muckraking" journalists of the reform era at the turn of the century. In this selection, excerpted from his autobiography, Steffens describes the first days in power of the reform president, Theodore Roosevelt. Roosevelt had returned as a national hero from the Spanish-American War, and in 1898, the same year he led the charge up San Juan Hill, he was elected governor of New York. The conservative Republicans of the New York state political machine were frightened of Roosevelt and more than happy to help him move into the vice presidency under McKinley—a position, they thought, of little power. But then McKinley was killed by an assassin's bullet, and suddenly, on September 14, 1901, Roosevelt was president.

Steffens was a friend of Roosevelt and well records the president's first days in office. As you read the following selection, consider Steffens' assessment of Theodore Roosevelt as a political reformer.

The gift of the gods to Theodore Roosevelt was joy, joy in life. He took joy in everything he did, in hunting, camping, and ranching, in politics, in reforming the police or the civil service, in organizing and commanding the Rough Riders. . . .

But the greatest joy in T. R.'s life was at his succession to the Presidency. I went to Washington to see him; many reformers were there to see the first reformer president take charge. We were like

the bankers T. R. described to me later, much later,
when his administration suddenly announced a bond
issue.

"It was just as if we had shot some big animal
and the carcass lay there exposed for a feast. The
bankers all over the country rose like buzzards, took
their bearings, and then flew in a flock straight here
to—the carrion [dead body]."

So we reformers went up in the air when President McKinley was shot, took our bearings, and
flew straight to our first president, T. R. And he
understood, he shared, our joy. He was not yet living
in the White House. He used the offices, which
were then in the main building, upstairs on the second
floor; he worked there by day, but he had to go
home at night to his own residence till the McKinleys
were moved out and the White House was made
ready for Mrs. Roosevelt. His offices were crowded
with people, mostly reformers, all day long, and
the president did his work among them with little
privacy and much rejoicing. He strode triumphant
around among us, talking and shaking hands, dictat-
ing and signing letters, and laughing. Washington,
the whole country, was in mourning, and no doubt
the president felt that he should hold himself down;
he didn't; he tried to, but his joy showed in every
word and movement. I think that he thought he
was suppressing his feelings and yearned for release,
which he seized when he could. One evening after
dusk, when it was time for him to go home, he
grabbed William Allen White with one hand, me
with the other, and saying, "Let's get out of this,"
he propelled us out of the White House into the
streets, where, for an hour or more he allowed his
gladness to explode. With his feet, his fists, his face
and with free words he laughed at his luck. He
laughed at the rage of Boss Platt and at the tragic
disappointment of Mark Hanna; these two had not
only lost their President McKinley but had been
given as a substitute the man they had thought to

He strode triumphant around among us, talking and shaking hands . . .

President Theodore Roosevelt was a man of vigor, energy, and determination—qualities of character readily visible in this early twentieth-century photograph.

bury in the vice-presidency. T. R. yelped at their downfall. And he laughed with glee at the power and place that had come to him. The assassination of McKinley had affected him, true, but in a romantic way. He described what he would do if an assassin attacked him. He looked about him in the shadows of the trees we were passing under—he looked for the dastardly coward that might pounce upon him, and, it seemed to me, he hoped the would-be murderer would appear then and there—say at the next dark corner—as he described, as he enacted, what he, the president, would do to him, with his fists, with his feet, with those big, clean teeth. It would have frightened the assassin to see and hear what it was T. R. would have done to him; it may have filled Bill White with terror; what I sensed was the passionate thrill the president was actually finding in the assassination of his assassin.

I had come to Washington to find out whether the fighting reformer president, who used to see things as I saw them, saw them now as I saw them now, and what he meant to do with them. I spent my afternoons in the press gallery of the Senate and the House, watching the senators and representatives I knew about in the States at work representing—what? . . . The Senate was the chamber of the bosses. Two senators from each State, one represented the political machine that betrayed the people of his State, the other one represented the leading business men of his State whom the boss worked for there. The U. S. Senate represented corruption, business, as I saw it in those days; it was a chamber of traitors, and we used to talk about the treason of the Senate. . . .

"The representatives and the senators," I said, "those that I know, those who come from States that I have investigated are picked men, chosen for their tried service to the system in their States. They stand for all you are against; they are against all you are for. They have the departments filled with men they have had sent here to be rewarded for anti-social service, and as vacancies occur, they will want you to appoint rascals of similar records."

He nodded. He knew that. T. R. saw the machine; he did not see the system. He saw the party organizations of the politicians; he saw some of the "bad" trusts back of the bad politics, but he did not see the good trusts back of the bad trusts that were back of the bad machines. He did not see that the corruption he resisted was a process to make the government represent business rather than politics and the people.

"I am on to the crooked machines," he said, "and the machinists, too. Yes, even in the Congress."

"What are you going to do about them and their demands for jobs for their heelers?"

"Deal with them," he snapped. "If they'll vote for my measures I'll appoint their nominees to Federal jobs. And I'm going to tell them so. They think I won't, you know. I'm going to call in a couple of machine senators and a few key congressmen and tell them I'll trade". . . .

That was his policy with the bosses, the political and the business agents in and out of the Senate and the House. He played the game with them; he did business with them; and he told them he would, from the very start. He did not fight, he helped build up, the political machine—and he made it partly his. I think that that was one of his purposes: to build up the party organization with enough of his appointees and to lead it with such an expectation of reward and punishment that it would nominate and help elect him to the presidency. T. R. was a politician much more than he was a reformer; in the phraseology of the radicals, he was a careerist, an opportunist with no deep insight into issues, but he was interesting, picturesque.

I accused him of this superficiality once during his first term, when he was keeping his promise to carry out McKinley's policies. That was his excuse for doing "nothing much." He was "being good" so as to be available for a second term.

"You don't stand for anything fundamental," I said and he laughed. He was sitting behind his desk; I was standing before it. He loved to quarrel amiably [in a friendly way] with his friends, and it was hard to hit him. So now, to get in under his guard and land on his equanimity [calmness], I said with all the scorn I could put into it, "All you represent is the square deal."

"That's it," he shouted, and rising to his feet, he banged the desk with his hands. "That's my slogan: the square deal. I'll throw that out in my next statement. The square deal." And he did.

REVIEWING THE READING

1. How does Steffens describe Roosevelt's reaction to McKinley's death?

2. What was Roosevelt's interpretation of the move among Republican politicians to run him as vice president under McKinley?

3. **Using Your Historical Imagination.** What does Steffens say was Roosevelt's attitude toward the Republican political machine that dominated the United States Senate? Why does Steffens say "T.R. was a politician more than he was a reformer"?

A View of the Political Machine (ca. 1905)

29

From *Plunkitt of Tammany Hall* by William L. Riordon.

Soon after European immigrants came to the United States and settled into the large cities of the Northeast they encountered the political "machine." The machine was run by "bosses," who were often recent immigrants themselves. In return for the votes of the new immigrants, the bosses provided a variety of political favors— jobs, direct financial help in times of trouble, and a variety of other things. The social services offered by city government were poor to nonexistent, so immigrants were heavily dependent on help from the political machine. Many political reformers dismissed the big city machines as corrupt, and in a real sense they were, but the immigrants often had a different point of view. Similarly, so did the bosses.

In the reading that follows, George Washington Plunkitt, one of the bosses of the notorious Tammany Hall machine of New York City, justifies the machine and tells how it worked. This remarkable interview was recorded by reporter William L. Riordon and published in his book Plunkitt of Tammany Hall. *As you read the excerpts from Riordon's interview, note the kinds of services provided by the Tammany political machine.*

There's only one way to hold a district: you must study human nature and act accordin'. . . .

To learn real human nature you have to go among the people, see them and be seen. I know every man, woman, and child in the Fifteenth District, except them that's been born this summer— and I know some of them, too. I know what they

like and what they don't like, what they are strong
at and what they are weak in, and I reach them by
approachin' at the right side.

For instance, here's how I gather in the young
men. I hear a young feller that's proud of his voice,
thinks that he can sing fine. I ask him to come
around to Washington Hall and join our Glee Club.
He comes and sings, and he's a follower of Plunkitt
for life. Another young feller gains a reputation as
a baseball player in a vacant lot. I bring him into
our baseball club. That fixes him. You'll find him
workin' for my ticket at the polls next election day.
Then there's the feller that likes rowin' on the river,
the young feller that makes a name as a waltzer on
his block, the young feller that's handy with his
dukes—I rope them all in by givin' them opportunities to show themselves off. I don't trouble them
with political arguments. I just study human nature
and act accordin'. . . .

As to the older voters, I reach them, too. No,
I don't send them campaign literature. That's rot.
People can get all the political stuff they want to
read—and a good deal more, too—in the papers.
Who reads speeches, nowadays, anyhow? It's bad
enough to listen to them. You ain't goin' to gain
any votes by stuffin' the letter boxes with campaign
documents. . . .

What tells in holdin' your grip on your district
is to go right down among the poor families and
help them in different ways they need help. I've
got a regular system for this. If there's a fire in Ninth,
Tenth, or Eleventh Avenue, for example, any hour
of the day or night, I'm usually there with some of
my election district captains as soon as the fire engines. If a family is burned out I don't ask whether
they are Republicans or Democrats, and I don't refer
them to the Charity Organization Society, which
would investigate their case in a month or two and
decide they were worthy of help about the time
they are dead from starvation. I just get quarters

for them, buy clothes for them if their clothes were burned up, and fix them up till they get things runnin' again. It's philanthropy, but it's politics, too—mighty good politics. Who can tell how many votes one of these fires brings me? The poor are the most grateful people in the world, and, let me tell you, they have more friends in their neighborhoods than the rich have in theirs. . . .

Former senator George Washington Plunkitt (on the shoeshine stand) dominated the New York City political machine around the turn of the century.

Another thing, I can always get a job for a deservin' man. I make it a point to keep on the track of jobs, and it seldom happens that I don't have a few up my sleeve ready for use. I know every big employer in the district and in the whole city, for that matter, and they ain't in the habit of sayin' no to me when I ask them for a job. . . .

There's no crime so mean as ingratitude in politics. . . .

The politicians who make a lastin' success in politics are the men who are always loyal to their friends, even up to the gate of State prison, if neces-sary; men who keep their promises and never lie. . . .

The question has been asked: Is a politician ever justified in goin' back on his district leader? I answer: "No; as long as the leader hustles around and gets all the jobs possible for his constituents." When the voters elect a man leader, they make a sort of contract with him. They say, although it ain't written out: "We've put you here to look out for our interests. You want to see that this district gets all the jobs that's comin' to it. Be faithful to us, and we'll be faithful to you."

REVIEWING THE READING

1. How did Plunkitt go about enlisting young persons to become political work-ers for the Tammany machine?

2. What sorts of social services were pro-vided by the political machine?

3. **Using Your Historical Imagination.** Why do you think the Tammany Hall machine was so successful in getting the votes of new immigrants? And what does Plunkitt mean when he says "the poor are the most grateful people in the world"?

Jack London Reports on the San Francisco Earthquake (1906)

30

From *Collier's Weekly*,
May 5, 1906.

On April 17, 1906, San Francisco, California, was devastated by one of the most destructive earthquakes to strike the North American continent—a quake several times more powerful than the earthquake that struck the area in October 1989. Novelist Jack London, a resident of the city, wrote about the quake and the great fire that followed. As you read the following excerpt from London's report, consider which disaster accounted for most of the damage.

San Francisco is gone! Nothing remains of it but memories and a fringe of dwelling houses on the outskirts. Its industrial section is wiped out. Its social and residential section is wiped out. The factories and warehouses, the great stores and newspaper buildings, the hotels and the palaces of the nabobs [wealthy], are all gone. Remains only the fringe of dwelling houses on the outskirts of what was once San Francisco.

Within an hour after the earthquake shock the smoke of San Francisco's burning was a lurid tower visible a hundred miles away. And for three days and nights this lurid tower swayed in the sky, reddening the sun, darkening the sky, and filling the land with smoke.

On Wednesday morning at a quarter past five came the earthquake. A minute later the flames were leaping upward. In a dozen different quarters south of Market Street, in the working-class ghetto, and in the factories, fires started. There was no opposing the flames. There was no organization, no communication. All the cunning adjustments of a twentieth-century city had been smashed by the earthquake. The streets were humped into ridges and depressions and piled with debris of fallen walls. The steel rails were twisted into perpendicular and horizontal angles. The telephone and telegraph systems were disrupted. And the great water mains burst. All the shrewd contrivances and safeguards of man had been thrown out of gear by thirty seconds' twitching of the earth crust.

By Wednesday afternoon, inside of twelve hours, half the heart of the city was gone. At that time I watched the vast conflagration [fire] from out on the bay. It was dead calm. Not a flicker of wind stirred. Yet from every side wind was pouring in upon the city. East, west, north, and south, strong winds were blowing upon the doomed city. The heated air rising made an enormous suck. Thus did the fire of itself build its own colossal chimney through the atmosphere. Day and night this dead calm continued, and yet, near to the flames, the wind was often half a gale, so mighty was the suck.

The edict which prevented the chaos was the following proclamation by Mayor E. E. Schmitz:

"The Federal Troops, the members of the Regular Police Force, and all Special Police Officers have been authorized to KILL any and all persons found engaged in looting or in the commission of any other crime.

"I have directed all Gas and Electric Lighting Companies not to turn on gas or electricity until I order them to do so; you may therefore expect the city to remain in darkness for an indefinite time.

"I request all citizens to remain at home from darkness until daylight every night until order is restored.

"I warn all citizens of the danger of fire from damaged or destroyed chimneys, broken or leaking gas pipes or fixtures, or any like cause."

Wednesday night saw the destruction of the very heart of the city. Dynamite was lavishly used, and many of San Francisco's proudest structures were crumbled by man himself into ruins, but there was no withstanding the onrush of the flames. Time and again successful stands were made by the fire fighters, and every time the flames flanked around on either side, or came up from the rear, and turned to defeat the hard-won victory. . . .

At nine o'clock Wednesday evening I walked down through miles and miles of magnificent buildings and towering skyscrapers. Here was no fire. All was in perfect order. The police patrolled the streets. Every building had its watchman at the door.

Survivors of the San Francisco earthquake of 1906 eat dinner near the ruins of their home on Franklin Street.

And yet it was doomed, all of it. There was no water. The dynamite was giving out. And at right-angles two different conflagrations were sweeping down upon it.

At one o'clock in the morning I walked down through the same section. Everything still stood intact. There was no fire. And yet there was a change. A rain of ashes was falling. The watchmen at the doors were gone. The police had been withdrawn. There were no firemen, no fire engines, no men fighting with dynamite. The district had been absolutely abandoned. I stood at the corner of Kearney and Market, in the very innermost heart of San Francisco. Kearney Street was deserted. Half-a-dozen blocks away it was burning on both sides. The street was a wall of flame. And against this wall of flame, silhouetted sharply, were two United States cavalry-men sitting their horses, calmly watching. That was all. Not another person was in sight. In the intact heart of the city two troopers sat their horses and watched.

Surrender was complete. There was no water. The sewers had long since been pumped dry. There was no dynamite. Another fire had broken out further uptown, and now from three sides conflagrations were sweeping down. The fourth side had been burned earlier in the day. In that direction stood the tottering walls of the Examiner Building, the burned-out Call Building, the smouldering ruins of the Grand Hotel, and the gutted, devastated, dynamited Palace Hotel.

The following will illustrate the sweep of the flames and the inability of men to calculate their spread. At eight o'clock Wednesday evening I passed through Union Square. It was packed with refugees. Thousands of them had gone to bed on the grass. Government tents had been set up, supper was being cooked, and the refugees were lining up for free meals.

At half-past one in the morning three sides of

. . . A rain of ashes was falling.

Union Square were in flames. The fourth side, where stood the great St Francis Hotel, was still holding out. An hour later, ignited from top and sides, the St Francis was flaming heavenward. Union Square, heaped high with mountains of trunks, was deserted. Troops, refugees, and all had retreated.

It was at Union Square that I saw a man offering a thousand dollars for a team of horses. He was in charge of a truck piled high with trunks from some hotel. It had been hauled here into what was considered safety, and the horses had been taken out. The flames were on three sides of the square, and there were no horses.

Also, at this time, standing beside the truck, I urged a man to seek safety in flight. He was all but hemmed in by several conflagrations. He was an old man and he was on crutches. Said he: "Today is my birthday. Last night I was worth thirty thousand dollars. I bought five bottles of wine, some delicate fish, and other things for my birthday dinner. I have had no dinner, and all I own are these crutches."

I convinced him of his danger and started him limping on his way. An hour later, from a distance, I saw the truckload of trunks burning merrily in the middle of the street.

On Thursday morning, at a quarter past five, just twenty-four hours after the earthquake, I sat on the steps of a small residence of Nob Hill. With me sat Japanese, Italians, Chinese, and Negroes—a bit of the cosmopolitan flotsam of the wreck of the city. All about were the palaces of the nabob pioneers of Forty-nine. To the east and south, at right-angles, were advancing two mighty walls of flame.

I went inside with the owner of the house on the steps of which I sat. He was cool and cheerful and hospitable. "Yesterday morning," he said, "I was worth six hundred thousand dollars. This morning this house is all I have left. It will go in fifteen minutes." He pointed to a large cabinet. "That is my wife's collection of china. This rug upon which we stand is a present. It cost fifteen hundred dollars. Try that piano. Listen to its tone. There are few like it. There are no horses. The flames will be here in fifteen minutes."

Outside, the old Mark Hopkins residence, a palace, was just catching fire. The troops were falling back and driving refugees before them. From every side came the roaring of flames, the crashing of walls, and the detonations of dynamite.

I passed out of the house. Day was trying to dawn through the smoke pall. A sickly light was creeping over the face of things. Once only the sun broke through the smoke pall, blood-red, and showing quarter its usual size. The smoke pall itself, viewed from beneath, was a rose colour that pulsed and fluttered with lavender shades. Then it turned to mauve and yellow and dun. There was no sun. And so dawned the second day on stricken San Francisco.

REVIEWING THE READING

1. Which of the two related disasters, the earthquake and the fire, actually destroyed most of San Francisco?

2. Why did the fire burn so fiercely at a time when the wind was calm?

3. **Using Your Historical Imagination.** Why could nothing be done to stop the spread of the fire? Given an earthquake as powerful as that of 1906, how many of these same problems would be present in a large city today?

Poems of the Chinese Immigrants (ca. 1910)

31

From *Songs of Gold Mountain: Cantonese Rhymes From San Francisco Chinatown*, edited by Marlon K. Hom.

In 1849 news of the discovery of gold in California reached China, and thousands of immigrants came to America in later decades as mining, farming, and railroad construction boomed. Most Chinese workers came from the province of Canton in southeast China, and most immigrated to the United States under the "credit system." A man would repay the loan for his passage by working under contract for a certain period, after which he was free to do what he wished.

Many of the Chinese immigrants settled in San Francisco, living in a part of the city the Anglo Americans called "Chinatown" and the Chinese Americans called the "Canton of the West." From the earliest stages of their immigrant experience, the Cantonese recorded their reactions to America in poems. As you read the following poems, all written by different individuals, note the conflicting opinions about the desirability of changing traditional Chinese ways to American ways.

Since I left South China,
I have changed my clothes to the Western style.
I seek praise for being neat and fashionable
Though I have yet to speak with an American tongue.
Smart in appearance—
Who dares to call me an ignorant fool?
A loose gown with wide sleeves brings only scurrilous
    [abusive] remarks
And it gets you nowhere, even if you are modern
    in education.

Spring returns to the continent.
Soothing is the misty scenery.
Flowers by the hundreds in red, by the thousands
    in purple, all noble and rich;
Everywhere, towers and terraces, all decorated with
    brilliant lanterns.
It's a delight to the heart.
I sightsee in the Golden City,
Eyes darting around, spirit dashing about, what
    genuine joy—
Entertaining myself, I have forgotten about going
    home.

School lets out for the summer.
No need to go home right away.
Bustling are the parks and museums;
So, hurry and rent a bicycle
Just to ride around.
Start pedaling, roll down the streets!
It's soothing and pleasing to the soul, a truly dashing
    experience.
But my companions tease me about what a big show-
    off I am.

A son is not totally dependable,
The toil of raising him is all but futile.
Blood kin becoming strangers in the streets is not
    at all a strange sight;
That's the practice, especially in Europe and America.
Each one flies his own way.
Liberty is not concerned with filial piety [devotion
    from children].
You should save enough for later while you're still
    able;
Spare yourself from suffering cold and hunger when
    you are old.

The emancipated women are the most shameful;
Their mouths are filled with foreign speech.
They loiter around with men day and night,
   everywhere,
Showing no respect for the husbands they married.
They are out of control.
How can a decent man challenge such a woman?
He resorts to remonstrating [protesting] with kind
   and wise words;
Pity no shrews can appreciate such kind intent.

So many Chinese immigrants came to live in a certain section of San Francisco that it came to be called Chinatown.

The oppression of women has been around for a
   long, long time.
So many women live in sorrow.

Progress and civilization are gradually removing the
restrictions.
So, let's stretch out and free our minds; no more
suffocation!
Wisdom unfolds,
Acquiring knowledge of East and West through
education.
Equality has been won, and must be maintained.
How can we tolerate the confines of those dated
moral conventions?

Following the practice of the Western countries,
I am free to make my marriage choice.
I cheer that the obsolete rituals are abolished.
No longer can matchmakers manipulate our lives.
It's a brand new world.
I am married in a civilized way.
I have found a good husband on my own, as I have
wished.
Our hearts and views are at one, our brows beam
with joy.

REVIEWING THE READING

1. Why does one poet say that clothes are
   more important than language in getting
   ahead in the United States?

2. What seems to be the common element
   of the poems that praise the social changes
   brought about by living in America?

3. **Using Your Historical Imagination.** Judg-
   ing from these poems, what seem to be
   the areas of greatest conflict between the
   old ways of traditional Chinese society
   and the new ways of Chinese American
   society?

General Pershing Arrives in France (1917)

32

From "And They Thought We Wouldn't Fight" by Floyd Gibbons.

President Woodrow Wilson selected Major General John J. Pershing to command the American Expeditionary Force sent to France in World War I. In June 1917, General Pershing and the first Americans reached war-weary France and received the remarkable welcome described in the account that follows. The reporter of these events was Chicago Tribune *war correspondent Floyd Gibbons. As you read the excerpts from Gibbons' account, note the general reaction of the French to the arrival of Pershing and the first American troops.*

We landed that day at Boulogne, June 13th, 1917. Military bands massed on the quay [wharf], blared out the American National Anthem as the ship was warped [hauled with ropes] alongside the dock. Other ships in the busy harbour began blowing whistles and ringing bells, loaded troop and hospital ships lying near by burst forth into cheering. The news spread like contagion along the harbour front.

As the gangplank was lowered, French military dignitaries in dress uniforms resplendent [dazzling] with gold braid, buttons and medals, advanced to that part of the deck amidships where the General stood. They saluted respectfully and pronounced elaborate addresses in their native tongue. They were followed by numerous French Government officials in civilian dress attire. The city, the department and the nation were represented in the populous delegations who presented their compliments, and conveyed to the American commander the unstinted

[unlimited] and heartfelt welcome of the entire people of France.

Under the train sheds on the dock, long stiff-
standing ranks of French poilus [soldiers] wearing
helmets and their light blue overcoats pinned back
at the knees, presented arms as the General walked
down the lines inspecting them. At one end of the
line, rank upon rank of French marines, and sailors
with their flat hats with red tassels, stood at attention
awaiting inspection.

The docks and train sheds were decorated with
French and American flags and yards and yards of
the mutually-owned red, white and blue. Thousands
of spectators began to gather in the streets near
the station, and their continuous cheers sufficed to
rapidly augment [add to] their own numbers.

Accompanied by a veteran French colonel, one
of whose uniform sleeves was empty, General Pershing, as a guest of the city of Boulogne, took a
motor ride through the streets of this busy port
city. He was quickly returned to the station, where
he and his staff boarded a special train for Paris. I
went with them. . . .

The sooty girders of the Gare du Nord shook
with cheers when the special train pulled in. The
aisles of the great terminal were carpeted with red
plush. A battalion of bearded poilus of the Two
Hundred and Thirty-seventh Colonial Regiment was
lined up on the platform like a wall of silent grey,
bristling with bayonets and shiny trench helmets.

General Pershing stepped from his private car.
Flashlights boomed and batteries of camera men ma-
noeuvred into positions for the lens barrage. The
band of the Garde Republicaine blared forth the
strains of the "Star Spangled Banner," bringing all
the military to a halt and a long standing salute. It
was followed by the "Marseillaise."

At the conclusion of the train-side greetings
and introductions, Marshall Joffre and General
Pershing walked down the platform together. The

tops of the cars of every train in the station were crowded with workmen. As the tall, slender American commander stepped into view, the privileged observers on the car-tops began to cheer.

A minute later, there was a terrific roar from beyond the walls of the station. The crowd outside had heard the cheering within. They took it up with thousands of throats. They made their welcome a ringing one. Paris took Pershing by storm. . . .

General Pershing and M. Painlevé, Minister of War, took seats in a large automobile. They were preceded by a motor containing United States Ambassador Sharp and former Premier Viviani. The procession started to the accompaniment of martial

General J. J. Pershing (right) lands at Boulogne, France, on June 13, 1917.

. . . **women
and children
tossed down
showers of
flowers . . .**

music by massed military bands in the courtyard
of the station. . . .

The crowds overflowed the sidewalks. They
extended from the building walls out beyond the
curbs and into the streets, leaving but a narrow lane
through which the motors pressed their way slowly
and with the exercise of much care. From the crowded
balconies and windows overlooking the route,
women and children tossed down showers of flowers
and bits of coloured paper.

The crowds were so dense that other street
traffic became marooned in the dense sea of joyously
excited and gesticulating [gesturing] French people.
Vehicles thus marooned became islands of vantage.
They were soon covered with men and women and
children, who climbed on top of them and clung
to the sides to get a better look at the khaki-clad
occupants of the autos.

Old grey-haired fathers of French fighting men
bared their heads and with tears streaming down
their cheeks shouted greetings to the tall, thin, grey-
moustached American commander who was leading
new armies to the support of their sons. Women
heaped armfuls of roses into the General's car and
into the cars of other American officers that followed
him. Paris street gamins [children] climbed the lamp-
posts and waved their caps and wooden shoes and
shouted shrilly.

American flags and red, white and blue bunting
waved wherever the eye rested. English-speaking
Frenchmen proudly explained to the uninformed that
"Pershing" was pronounced "Peur-chigne" and not
"Pair-shang."

Paris was not backward in displaying its knowledge of English. Gay Parisiennes were eager to make
use of all the English at their command, that they
might welcome the new arrivals in their native
tongue.

Some of these women shouted "Hello," "Heep,
heep, hourrah," Good morning," "How are you,

keed?" and "Cock-tails for two." Some of the expressions were not so inappropriate as they sounded.

Occasionally there came from the crowds a good old genuine American whoop-em-up yell. This happened when the procession passed groups of American ambulance workers and other sons of Uncle Sam, wearing the uniforms of the French, Canadian and English Corps.

They joined with Australians and South African soldiers on leave to cheer on the new-coming Americans with such spontaneous expressions as "Come on, you Yanks," "Now let's get 'em," and "Eat 'em up, Uncle Sam."

The frequent stopping of the procession by the crowds made it happen quite frequently that the automobiles were completely surrounded by enthusiasts, who reached up and tried to shake hands with the occupants. Pretty girls kissed their hands and blew the invisible confection [sweetness] toward the men in khaki. . . .

Through such scenes as these, the procession reached the great Place de la Concorde. In this wide, paved, open space an enormous crowd had assembled. As the autos appeared the cheering, the flower throwing, and tumultuous kiss-blowing began. It increased in intensity as the motors stopped in front of the Hotel Crillon into which General Pershing disappeared, followed by his staff.

Immediately the cheering changed to tremendous clamorous [noisy] demand for the General's appearance on the balcony in front of his apartments.

"*Au balcon, au balcon,*" were the cries that filled the Place. The crowd would not be denied.

General Pershing stepped forth on the balcony. . . . A soft breeze from the Champs Elysees touched the cluster of flags on the General's right and from all the Allied emblems fastened there it selected one flag.

The breeze tenderly caught the folds of this flag and wafted them across the balcony on which the General bowed. He saw and recognised that flag. He extended his hand, caught the flag in his fingers and pressed it to his lips. All France and all America represented in that vast throng [crowd] that day cheered to the mighty echo when Pershing kissed the tri-colour of France.

It was a tremendous, unforgettable incident. It was exceeded by no other incident during those days of receptions and ceremonies, except one. That was an incident which occurred not in the presence of thousands, but in a lonely old burial ground on the outskirts of Paris. This happened several days after the demonstration in the Place de la Concorde.

On that day of bright sunshine, General Pershing and a small party of officers, French and American, walked through the gravel paths of Picpus Cemetery in the suburbs of Paris, where the bodies of hundreds of those who made the history of France are buried.

Several French women in deep mourning curtsied as General Pershing passed. His party stopped in front of two marble slabs that lay side by side at the foot of a granite monument. From the General's party a Frenchman stepped forward and, removing his high silk hat, he addressed the small group in quiet, simple tones and well-chosen English words. He was the Marquis de Chambrun. He said:

"On this spot one can say that the historic ties between our nations are not the result of the able schemes of skilful diplomacy. No, the principles of liberty, justice and independence are the glorious links between our nations.

"These principles have enlisted the hearts of our democracies. They have made the strength of their union and have brought about the triumph of their efforts.

"To-day, when, after nearly a century and a half, America and France are engaged in a conflict for the same cause upon which their early friendship was based, we are filled with hope and confidence.

"We know that our great nations are together with our Allies invincible [unbeatable], and we rejoice to think that the United States and France are reunited in the fight for liberty, and will reconsecrate, in a new victory, their everlasting friendship of which your presence to-day at this grave is an exquisite and touching token."

General Pershing advanced to the tomb and placed upon the marble slab an enormous wreath of pink and white roses. Then he stepped back. He removed his cap and held it in both hands in front of him. The bright sunlight shone down on his silvery grey hair. Looking down at the grave, he spoke in a quiet, impressive tone four simple, all-meaning words:

"Lafayette, we are here."

REVIEWING THE READING

1. Where did Pershing land, and where did he go from there?

2. How would you describe the French reaction to Pershing and the Americans?

3. **Using Your Historical Imagination.** What was the significance of General Pershing's visit to the grave and his spoken phrase "Lafayette, we are here"? (You may need to consult your American History textbook to answer this question.)

33

From *Our Soldiers Speak:
1775–1918*, by William
Matthews and Dixon
Wecter.

Two Doughboys in the Great War (1918)

World War I (1914-1918) had been raging in Europe for nearly three years before the United States entered the war in 1917. The bravery of those Americans who fought the ground war during those last two years of the war, however, would long be remembered. And none were more brave than the hard-fighting infantrymen, who would become known as the "doughboys" because of the cakes and bread that were part of their rations.

The doughboys lived in and fought from deep, hand-dug muddy trenches, waiting for the call to go "over the top" into hand-to-hand combat with the Germans. Marine Sergeant Karl P. Spencer, wrote home about the battle of Belleau Wood in France in June 1918. Infantryman Norman Roberts, recalled the war at Saint-Mihiel in France in September of the same year. As you read the following excerpts from their letters, which were gathered in a collection of soldiers' accounts, consider the sacrifices made by the doughboys during the war. Also think about why their personal bravery was an important part of the Allied victory.

Karl P. Spencer

My Dear Mother: I am taking this opportunity to write. The Lord only knows when I will be able to get the letter off. Yesterday and today I received beaucoup [much] first-class mail and a package of eats from Paris, plum pudding and chocolate bars. Believe me, Mother, one appreciates such luxuries after existing for six days on Argentine bully

beef, French bread, salmon and water. Twice the
Red Cross and Y.M.C.A. (God bless them!) have
sent us jam and cakes and chocolates and cigarettes.
I smoke cigarettes (when I have them) like a trooper,
and especially when I am lying in my hole in the
ground and the shells are breaking all around, they
quiet one's nerves, I believe.

In my last letter I spoke of our moving to the
rear; instead, that very day word came for us to go
into the front line that night. Were we disgusted?
Gee, but you should have heard us rave and swear!
We have been in the trenches since March 14th,
and in this sector nearly four weeks; no leaves; no
liberty; no rest; they must think the Marines are
supermen or maybe mechanical devices for fighting.
But then we have it straight from General Pershing
that what's left of the Marine Corps will parade in
Paris July 4th. Glory be, if this is only true. According
to the fighting we've done we rate something out
of the ordinary, and, of course, you know the Marines
are credited with saving Paris. You have read exagger-
ated accounts of our exploits, perhaps you would
be pleased to hear the truth. It is a long, long story
so don't weaken.

Get you a map, locate Chateau-Thierry, back
up ten kilometres toward Paris by way of Meaux
(Meaux was being evacuated when we arrived), and
there you find the location of our battle-ground.
The Germans were advancing ten kilometres a day
when in swept the Marines, relieving the retreating
boys and with the Eighty-second and Eighty-third
Companies in skirmish formation, attacking, the
Huns [slang for Germans] were stopped and in three
hours were pushed back four kilometres. Our losses
were slight, for the Germans were not prepared to
meet a stone wall resistance such as they bumped
up against and certainly they had no idea of an
offensive movement being launched.

The German infantry had been moving at so
rapid a pace that their artillery could not keep up

with them. As a result it was easy sailing for us. You should have seen those Huns running; they dropped everything and started toward Berlin. Twenty German planes were counted overhead that evening; they wanted to find out what the devil had interfered with their well-laid plans; what they saw was a wheat-field full of Marines and for miles behind the lines hundreds of trucks going forward at full speed, loaded with men, provisions and munitions [weapons]. The Kaiser certainly had a set-back.

To continue with the battle, our objective was a railway station, but between us and our objective was a machine-gun Hill 142, and here the Germans made a last stand. The hill is sort of a plateau rising out of Belleau Woods, but between it and the woods are patches of wheat and beyond the hill the ground slopes gently down to the railway station. The hilltop is covered with immense rock and behind these the Germans placed their machine guns and made their stand, and held out for three weeks. The Eighty-second and Eighty-third made one attack against this position. We formed in the wheat-field in wave formation, and with our captain and major leading we rushed up that hill in the face of twenty machine guns. The woods were also full of German snipers.

The attack failed; we lost all our officers and half our company. We were just starting when out from behind a rock comes an unarmed German with arms up in the air shouting, "Kamerad!" A dozen Marines rushed forward with fixed bayonets and stuck that man full of holes—orders were to take no prisoners. Many a brave Marine fell that day. That was our last attack. Since then six separate attacks were made on that hill and not until the other night did the Marines take it. Between the time of our attack and the successful one, the German artillery was moved up and we suffered much from shell fire.

The attack the 25th was wonderfully successful. We, the Eighty-second Company, were in support [held in reserve to send in if needed], but were not called upon. At 3 P.M. the American artillery opened up on the hill. The Germans suspected something and immediately began gassing our rear and shelling the support—us. After two hours of fearful bombarding, at 5:05 P.M. two companies of Marines marched up that hill in wave formation and never halted until they had taken the position. Their losses were heavy, for the whizz-bangs, 77's, and other German guns were playing a tune all over that hill and about one hundred Maxims were spitting fire into the ranks of our brave men, but at heart those Germans are cowards, and when they saw the jig was up they surrendered. Six hundred prisoners, old men, and boys of eighteen and nineteen years, and fifty machine guns were taken. One Marine private took sixty prisoners, and by himself marched them away.

The inevitable followed. A counter-attack. Four hundred Huns attempted to retake the hill; a great many were taken prisoners, and several hundred gassed by our battery. To-day we hold the hill and the prospect of an early relief is bright. Not a great deal is to be feared from these defeated divisions, for the Marines have their "Nanny."

Finish to-morrow, Mother, for it's getting too dark to write.

June 28, 1918. I saw a wonderfully thrilling sight several days ago—an air battle. For several hours a Hun plane had been flying low, up and down our lines, observing our activities and probably signaling his artillery our range. He was loafing over our position, when out from the clouds above darts a frog [slang for French] plane straight for the Hun, when within range the frog opened up with his machine gun and the next minute the German plane was nothing but a ball of fire. The aviator tried his best to get back to the German lines, but the wind was blowing our way, so Heinie [slang for German] darn near burned himself to death; but he turned and

. . . a great many were taken prisoners . . .

volplaned [glided with the engine turned off] toward our line, and when within a few feet of the ground he sprang out of his machine, killing himself. Three Boche planes were down that day in this one sector. Some of our men went out this morning to salvage the dead Germans. They returned with watches, razors, iron crosses, pictures, knives, German money, *gats* [pistols], and all sorts of souvenirs. I don't like salvaging, for the odor of a dead German is stifling. Nix on that stuff. The only souvenir I care to bring back to U.S.A. is yours truly.

This has been a banner day for us. Our ration detail returned this A.M. with Y.M.C.A. donations— chocolate, cookies, raisins, sugar and syrup, and cigarettes. This P.M. more mail arrived, K.C. [Kansas City, his home] papers and two pair of white lisle sox from Jones Store, Paris. I put one pair on immediately, although my feet were dirty and darn near black, due to the absence of water and abundance of sand. Two weeks ago I had a bath. That was a memorable day. The major decided that his boys needed washing, so he marched the whole battalion about twelve kilometres to the rear to a small village on the Marne River. The town had been evacuated, so we made ourselves at home. New potatoes, green peas, onions, and honey. I had honey that day, but I certainly paid for it. Several of us put on respirators, wrapped up well and invaded the beehives. I finished with eleven bee stings and a great quantity of excellent honey. After that escapade I filled my tummy and then went for a plunge in the river Marne. We were a happy crew that evening.

Water up here is scarce. We send after drinking-water at night. One dares not wander very far from his hole during the day, except on duty, of course, for those deadly whizz-bangs are very muchly in evidence. A whizz-bang (so-called because of the sound it makes when hitting near by—you hear the whizz and immediately a bang) is a trench-mortar affair, calibre 88 cm., shot from a small gun about

. . . Two weeks ago I had a bath.

one and one half to two feet long, and smooth-bore. The shell has very little trajectory (in fact, the Germans use them for sniping), is filled with shrapnel, and its concussion is terrific. Damn it, I certainly hate these things! You can hear other shells coming and quite often can dodge them, but these whizz-bangs come fast and low.

The only writing I shall ever do when I return home will be a theme or so for some English Prof. There will be so much war bunk after this affair is over that people will become sick of the word "war." I used to be ambitious. I desired a war cross and honor, but my ideas have changed. I have seen too many men with those ambitions go down riddled with bullets. (One of our lieutenants was shot twenty times while trying to rush a machine-gun position.) So I've come to the conclusion that I am of more value and credit to my country, to you and myself, as a live soldier, obedient and ready for duty, than as a dead hero. No grand-standing—just good honest team work and common sense. Don't be disillusioned—if I live long enough I may rate a sir.

I hope Bill enjoys his work this summer. What wouldn't I give to spend several months in Denver! When I get back behind the lines and have a few moments' time I shall write him. I am truly glad that he cannot get into the service. We have several kids his age with us; they are always ailing. Their feet hurt or something is always wrong, so they generally end up by being musics or galley slaves. The hiking about the country with a heavy pack and the irregular life of the trenches is just naturally too much for one so young. There is not a man in the outfit who does not lose weight doing hitch [time of service] in the trenches. About two months ago while we were at Verdun our captain and one lieutenant both went to the hospital physical wrecks.

Mother, I find I can spend a pleasant hour or so writing about different things, so I shall not close, but write a few words each day until we are relieved.

United States soldiers operate a machine gun during the Saint-Mihiel advance of 1918.

When I finish this document I wish you would send it to Grandpa—he will probably enjoy reading about our scrap.

Sunday afternoon, June 30, 1918. Oh, what a relief! Last night we were relieved on the front line. . . . We were many miles behind the lines. We struck camp in a large woods. At 3 A.M. we had a hot meal; turned in later and slept until 11 A.M. when we ate again. Since then I have been swimming and feel like a different man. Received your June 10th letter a short while ago. More Y.M.C.A. supplies blew in, so with a full stomach and a feeling of security from those "Dutch" shells I am fairly happy. From a reliable source we are told that our battalion will parade in Paris July 4th and will be decorated for the fighting we have done this month. Will write you later whether or not this comes to pass.

With love, Karl.

Norman Roberts

Sept. 11, '18. Started for the front at 6 P.M. Raining and wind blowing. Very cold. All boys wet to the skin. Roads very muddy and all shot to pieces from the Germans big guns. Very bad walking. Falling in holes to one's waist, these holes being full of water. Germans shelling this road as we advance.

No one allowed to talk. All noise unnecessary prohibited. When near the woods the Germans dropped a H. E. [high explosive] shell near us and threw mud all over us. Believe me I was some frightened, after entering the woods the shelling was something terrible. Iron falling like hail. Our Major was there directing the placing of the men in the trenches. Dark as pitch except when a shell would explode. Some of the boys praying and some swearing. No place to swear. So dark each man had to take the other by the straps on his haversack to keep from getting lost. With that the detail that I was with became lost but finally found the trench which we had been allotted. Some mud. Over the knees. About 12 o'clock all were in the trenches waiting for the zero hour that we were to make our attack upon Fritz [slang for Germans]. At 1:30 A.M. 12th the barrage of our guns broke loose upon the first line trenches and oh what a noise there was, a great number of 16 inch Navel guns which was with our 75s. Then the Germans came back with their guns. Oh me what noise and not be allowed to talk. All of us were wet and cold and SCARED. The boy sitting next to me shot himself in the foot to keep from going over the top.

Sept. 12. At five o'clock A.M. the words came down the trench to get ready for attack. Over the Top we are going after Fritz. I was the fourth man of my platoon to go over. A baptism of fire was my reception in my first battle and first all-American offensive, St.-Mihiel drive. This sector had been the scenes of many battles during the war by the French and English troops—to capture this would mean the straightening of the line of the Allies. But both had failed to take same. Day had not broke and you could hardly tell where to go. Bullets, million of them, flying like rain drops. Rockets and flares in all directions. Shrapnel bursting the air and sending down its deadly iron. High explosives bursting in the ground and sending forth bricks, mud and iron to the destruction of man. Oh what a morning. Machine gun bullets flying past you as the wind. Whistling as a bird going its travel. Dead and wounded all around you. Comrades falling directly in front and you not allowed to assist them. The command ONWARD. Every minute looking for the next to be gone to the great beyond. A mad dash for 50 feet and then look for cover. A stop for a minute and then the barrage would lift to a farther point and then another mad rush. Always leaving some of your comrades cold in the face of death. Men crying for the Allmighty God to have mercy upon them. Asking the men to shoot them and place them out of their misery. Oh what a pleading before your very eyes for death. Men making all kinds of promises to God if He would only protect them at this time. Airplanes sweeping down upon you and firing their guns almost in your face. Barbed wire in all directions. I became tangled in this and thought surely before I could free myself that I would be killed. We having supremacy of the air during this battle. Day breaks and oh how pleased to welcome same. Now capturing prisoners in wholesale lots. One of our boys captured 29 by himself. Our Major Brewer wounded twice before he retired from the battle and Capt. Lainson taking command of the battalion. I assisted in capture and had prisoners carrying our wounded to the first aid station upon their shoulders. I assisted in dressing the wounded as the first aid men was scarce. One man in particular asked me to shoot him and end his misery. Some were wounded in the legs, arms, throat, stomach, lungs. Some having their legs blown entirely away, some with the head blown off. Arms missing, some blinded, some became crazy. Oh what a sight to behold that had been inflicted upon innocent men. In this battle our company lost 12 killed, 80 wounded, 2 lieutenants killed and one wounded, one having been wounded in every battle that he had taken part in. The Americans flanking Mount Falcon on right. English lost 30,000 men in 1916

I assisted in dressing the wounded . . .

and failed to capture it. French also tryed and failed. This was some fight. Took up position on hillside. A German rest camp here. Cold and windy. The field of dead a terrible sight. Both American and German. A day never to be forgotten.

Oct. 6. Rested all day, now dug in the Verdun woods, this place has seen the very hottest fighting of the Worlds war. Ground nothing but shell holes, trees look like sticks. Preaching services by Chaplain Robb assisted by Chaplain Hatch. We taking communion. The cloth was found in a German dugout and a table of sheet iron on a stump of an old tree. While being served with communion and during the preaching service there were 5 conversions and one of the prettiest sights that I have ever seen. The noise of bursting shells and the noise of our heavy artillery, air battles going on, we could hardly hear Chaplain Robb when he would try to speak to us.

Oct. 14. 5:30 A.M. awaiting orders to move to front. First Battalion having gone over the top. Heavy shelling and losses. Very heavy resistance. Our guns putting over a terrible barrage. Orders were to take hill 288 regardless of cost. Captured hill.

REVIEWING THE READING

1. In what way did the doughboys show great personal bravery?

2. In both battles the infantrymen were aided by other military forces. What were they, and how important was their role in aiding the infantry?

3. **Using Your Historical Imagination.** Imagine yourself as an American doughboy during World War I. What do you think your greatest challenge would be? Your greatest fear? Why?

From *History of U.S. Political Parties*, Volume III, edited by Arthur M. Schlesinger.

34

Senator Henry Cabot Lodge Demands Harsh Peace Terms (1918)

On November 11, 1918, representatives of the German army met with Allied military leaders to sign the armistice that ended more than four years of fighting, signaling the end of The Great War, or World War I. Even before this, however, there had been much debate over the terms of peace.

President Wilson and others supported the idea of a "peace without victory," an end to the war in which Germany would not be unduly punished or held solely responsible for the damages of the conflict. In this way the deep resentments that could lead to another war would be avoided. In practical terms this meant that Germany should not be saddled with huge reparation payments—"fines"—as punishment for the war. Others, such as U.S. Senator Henry Cabot Lodge, chairperson of the Foreign Affairs Committee and one of the more influential Republican leaders, disagreed with Wilson's proposals. They wanted a peace based on Germany's unconditional surrender. In a speech made on August 23, 1918, Senator Lodge explained why he believed as he did. As you read the following excerpts from Lodge's speech, try to determine his reasons for supporting a policy of unconditional surrender.

These [concessions and compensations] are the principal conditions which alone will give us a victory worth having, and when we talk about a complete peace and a just and righteous peace, let

Senator Henry Cabot Lodge favored harsh punishments for Germany after the end of World War I. Consequently, he was an unyielding foe of President Wilson's peace plan.

it be known to all the world that this is what we mean. It is idle to talk about our annihilating [destroying] the German people. Nobody, of course, has any such idea. It could not be done even if we wished to do it. We are not engaged in this way to try to arrange a government for Germany. The German people must do that themselves, and they will get precisely the government which they desire and deserve—just as they now have the government they prefer, whose purposes and ambitions and barbarism they share and sustain. Our part and our business is to put Germany in a position where she can do no more harm in the future to the rest of the world. Unless we achieve this we shall have fought in vain. Congress and the President had no right to declare war unless they meant to do precisely this thing. Nothing less should justify our action. We are pouring out the best blood of the country, the blood of our chosen youth, upon the altar of patriotism. We are making every sort of pecuniary [monetary] sacrifice. We are bearing an immense burden of taxation. We are mortgaging with our loans the future of coming generations. We have set aside for the time being the Constitution under which individual liberty has been preserved and the country has grown and prospered. . . . It is our intention to return, as our laws show, to the old restrictions, protections, and rights of the ordered freedom of the Constitution. We are taking these vast risks, we are bearing these huge burdens, we are making these unspeakable sacrifices of life with a brave and cheerful spirit; but we have no right to do all these things unless we win the prize and reach the goal which alone can warrant and justify them. . . . The only peace for us is one that rests on hard physical facts, the peace of unconditional surrender. No peace that satisfied Germany in any degree can ever satisfy us. It can not be a negotiated peace. It must be a dictated peace, and we and our allies must dictate it. The victory bringing such a peace must be won inside, not outside, the German frontier. It must be won finally and thoroughly in German territory, and can be so won nowhere else.

REVIEWING THE READING

1. What was Lodge's primary reason for supporting a policy of unconditional surrender for Germany?

2. According to Lodge, what was the only reason the United States entered the war?

3. **Using Your Historical Imagination.** Assume that you are a member of the United States Senate in 1918. Remembering that Lodge's speech calling for unconditional surrender was made *before* the war had ended, what argument might you make in opposition to his demands?

An Ambulance Driver's Story (1919)

35

From *The Compensations of War: The Diary of an Ambulance Driver during the Great War* by Guy Emerson Bowerman, Jr., edited by Mark C. Carnes.

Among the many unsung heroes of World War I were the ambulance drivers who risked their own lives in the midst of battle to save others. Most of the ambulance drivers were volunteers. American writer Ernest Hemingway, who served as an ambulance driver after failing the army's physical examination, later used his experiences in the war as background for some of his best-selling novels.

Another ambulance driver, Guy Emerson Bowerman, Jr., kept his own personal account of the life of an ambulance driver during The Great War. As you read the following excerpts from Bowerman's account of the final days of the war, think about how he and the soldiers around him must have felt when they heard that the war was over.

*T*hurs. Oct. 31. The attack started early this morning with two French divisions on the flanks and one American at the center. The Americans went too fast and got ahead of their barrage which was put up by the French artillery so that there are many wounded and their ambulances don't seem to be able to handle them. At Zult this morning a young Frenchman walked a quarter of a kilometer holding his entrails [intestines] in with his hands. After being bandaged he asked for a cigarette and when we put him into a car he was smiling as if nothing had happened. I don't suppose he will live but he surely had unlimited nerve. A little later I drove a captain up to an advanced poste, a little thatched cottage at the end of a lane. While I was waiting outside I heard a terrible scream from within. I rushed inside but was too late to see the cause of the scream—an amputation without ether of a young Boche's [German's] leg. Never in my life have I seen anything which could compare to the pain and anguish in the face and every muscle of the body of that German. . . .

Mon. Nov. 4. The attack has been very successful and is at last terminated. The Americans added additional glory to their record in France and one may count numbers of khaki bodies lying half concealed by the [beet] tops of Belgian farms. . . . The Germans surely did retreat in a hurry tho in good order. . . .

Tues. Nov. 5. Section moves from Noker[e] to Vive St. Eloi. On our way over we were greatly surprised to be bombed by a German airplane which was flying so high that we never imagined he would try to hit us. We were not only surprised to have him throw his bombs at us but we were utterly astounded when he succeeded in wounding an American officer. . . .

Frid. Nov. 8. Every one is positive that two German generals came across the lines today with a white flag to demand an armistice. Foch [the French commander-in-chief who became commander of the unified command in April 1918] has given them

In this photo, World War I casualties lie on stretchers awaiting removal by an ambulance unit.

72 hours to accept or refuse his terms and meanwhile
preparations for another big attack are being made
in this sector. . . .

Sun. Nov. 10. 10 P.M. LA PAIX EST SIGNEE
[the peace is signed]. All the sky is lighted up with
Verey Lights and gun flashes. All the Frenchmen
are shouting and shooting and we're so plain . . .
happy we don't know where we are. All the Section
is out.

LA GUERRE EST FINIE!
[Undated entry beginning at top of page 55 of re-
copied diary; (equivalent entry in original diary dated
Nov. 17):] Really the entry for Nov. 10 should end
on page 54. The make up of the bottom of that
page portrays exactly our, or should I say my? feelings
but those few lines were written while the daze
had not left me. Then all was supreme gladness,
un-adulterated, supreme, ecstatic joy. Joy, pure joy,
but thoughtless joy. The entry under Nov. 10 does
not explain why our joy was insane nor why, a little
later when the spasm had spent itself, we drew within
ourselves and went quietly back to our bunks where
some of us laid till almost morning, silent, but wide
awake. I remember how Rouget the French sergeant
threw up his arms and fell limply into his cot exclaim-
ing "Bon Dieu [Good God], it is the end of a bad
dream." And so it was but like the awakening from
a bad dream we were troubled to assure ourselves
that the dream had ended, that now we were awake
safe from the hideous thing which pursued us in
our slumbers. . . . We had heard so many rumors
that we [thought] this but the fabled cry of "wolf."
We had hoped so long and passionately for this
hour to come and had been so long disappointed
that our minds could not grasp the meaning of it
when it was here. As I have said before, after our
first few months in the war we had so far identified
with war that we were as men who have had a
lapse of memory. The old life was gone forever

and each succeeding day and each succeeding horror drove the peaceful part farther behind us till at last it was gone completely from our ken [memory]. Here we were, men made for war, men born to war, men whose life is filled from beginning to end with war and we felt secretly in our hearts that there could be no other life. Then to those of us who had been enough in war to lose our peace identity completely were suddenly, precipitately and unwarned flung into another life, a life of peace. We could have been no more awed, no more bewildered than would the men of Mars could they suddenly find themselves on this planet. Then gradually we came to realize what it all meant though we walked warily like men fearing ambush, fearful of having this new-found joy snatched fom our grasp. Even, when after a week the guns were still [quiet], though we outwardly were jovial and carefree, certain of seeing home again, yet within ourselves we questioned, doubted nor were we ever sure deep down within us till we got our final pay, took off our uniforms and again sat at our family table.

REVIEWING THE READING

1. How did Bowerman and the soldiers around him react to the news that the peace armistice had been signed?

2. Why do you think the soldiers were afraid to believe that the war was really over?

3. **Using Your Historical Imagination.** Although Bowerman was glad to see an end to the war, he also had concerns about a life of peace. What do you think he was afraid of? What adjustments would he and the soldiers now have to make in their lives?

W. E. B. Du Bois Calls for Democracy After the War (1919)

36

"A Call for Democracy After the War" by W. E. B. Du Bois, *The Crisis*, XVIII, May 1919.

Black men as well as white were drafted into the military during World War I. As they had in every previous war, the African Americans served their country valiantly. At war, however, just as at home, blacks were segregated from the white soldiers.

A few years before the war, a black leader, W. E. B. Du Bois, had joined with several white liberals to form the National Association for the Advancement of Colored People (NAACP) to fight for equal rights for blacks. Although some progress had been made during the years before and during the war, more would have to be done before blacks could take their rightful place in America. Du Bois used his position as editor of the NAACP publication The Crisis *to call for some of the many needed changes. As you read his "Call for Democracy After the War," think about the basic human rights Du Bois wanted for African Americans in America.*

We are returning from war! *The Crisis* and tens of thousands of black men were drafted into a great struggle. For bleeding France and what she means and has meant and will mean to us and humanity and against the threat of German race arrogance, we fought gladly and to the last drop of blood; for America and her highest ideals, we fought in far-off hope; for the dominant southern oligarchy [elite governing group] entrenched in Washington, we fought in bitter resignation. For the America that represents and gloats in lynching, disfranchisement,

W. E. B. Du Bois led the campaign for fairer treatment of black Americans after the end of World War I.

caste, brutality and devilish insult—for this, in the hateful upturning and mixing of things, we were forced by vindictive fate to fight also.

But today we return! We return from the slavery of uniform which the world's madness demanded us to don [wear], to the freedom of civil garb. We stand again to look America squarely in the face and call a spade a spade. We sing: This country of ours, despite all its better souls have done and dreamed, is yet a shameful land.

It *lynches.*

And lynching is barbarism of a degree of contemptible nastiness unparalleled in human history. Yet for fifty years we have lynched two Negroes a week, and we have kept this up right through the war.

It *disfranchises* its own citizens.

Disfranchisement is the deliberate theft and robbery of the only protection of poor against rich and black against white. The land that disfranchises its citizens and calls itself a democracy lies and knows it lies.

It encourages *ignorance.*

It has never really tried to educate the Negro. A dominant minority does not want Negroes educated. It wants servants, dogs, whores, and monkeys. And when this land allows a reactionary group by its stolen political power to force as many black folk into these categories as it possibly can, it cries in contemptible hypocrisy: "they threaten us with degeneracy; they cannot be educated."

It *steals* from us.

It organizes industry to cheat us. It cheats us out of our land; it cheats us out of our labor. It confiscates our savings. It reduces our wages. It raises our rent. It steals our profit. It taxes us without representation. It keeps us consistently and universally poor, and then feeds us on charity and derides [ridicules] our poverty.

It *insults* us.

It has organized a nation-wide and latterly [recently] a world-wide propaganda of deliberate and continuous insult and defamation of black blood wherever found. It decrees that it shall not be possible in travel nor residence, work nor play, education nor instruction for a black man to exit without tacit [silent] or open acknowledgment of his inferiority to the dirtiest white dog. And it looks upon any attempt to question or even discuss this dogma as arrogance, unwarranted assumption and treason.

This is the country to which we Soldiers of Democracy return. This the fatherland for which we fought! But it is *our* fatherland. It was right for us to fight. The faults of *our* country are *our* faults. Under similar circumstances, we would fight again. But by the God of Heaven, we are cowards and jackasses if now that that war is over, we do not marshal every ounce of our brain and brawn to fight a sterner, longer, more unbending battle against the forces of hell in our own land.

We return. We return from fighting. We return fighting.

Make way for Democracy! We saved it in France, and by the Great Jehovah, we will save it in the United States of America, or know the reason why.

REVIEWING THE READING

1. What basic human rights did Du Bois seek for blacks in the United States?

2. How did Du Bois feel about blacks fighting in World War I?

3. **Using Your Historical Imagination.** Du Bois said, "We return. We return from fighting. We return fighting." What do you think he meant by this? What future do you think he envisioned for African Americans in the United States?

37

The NAACP Program of 1919 (1919)

In the late 1800s, African Americans in the United States suffered numerous setbacks. In the South laws legalizing racial segregation were passed. Other laws kept blacks from voting. In the North blacks faced economic and social barriers. Throughout the country, lynchings of blacks made headlines.

In 1910 a group of blacks and whites joined together to form the National Association for the Advancement of Colored People (NAACP) in an effort to secure equal protection under the Constitution for blacks. At the end of its first decade of existence in 1919, the organization published a document that clearly stated its goals and objectives. As you read the document, try to determine the main objective of the NAACP at the time the document was written.

First and foremost among the objectives for 1919 must be the strengthening of the Association's organization and resources. Its general program must be adapted to specific ends. Its chief aims have many times been stated:

1. A vote for every Negro man and woman on the same terms as for white men and women.

2. An equal chance to acquire the kind of an education that will enable the Negro everywhere wisely to use this vote.

3. A fair trial in courts for all crimes of which he is accused, by judges in whose election he has participated without discrimination because of race.

4. A right to sit upon the jury which passes judgment upon him.

5. Defense against lynching and burning at the hands of mobs.

6. Equal service on railroad and other public carriers. This to mean sleeping car service, dining car service, Pullman service, at the same cost and upon the same terms as other passengers.

7. Equal right to use of public parks, libraries and other community services for which he is taxed.

8. An equal chance for a livelihood in public and private employment.

9. The abolition of color-hyphenation and the substitution of "straight Americanism."

If it were not a painful fact that more than four-fifths of the colored people of the country are denied the above named elementary rights, it would seem an absurdity that an organization is necessary to demand for American citizens the exercise of such rights. One would think, if he were from Mars, or if he knew America only by reading the speeches of her leading statesmen, that all that would be needful would be to apply to the courts of the land and to the legislatures. Has not slavery been abolished? Are not all men equal before the law? Were not the Fourteenth and Fifteenth Amendments passed by the Congress of the United States and adopted by the states? Is not the Negro a man and a citizen?

. . . **Are not all men equal before the law?**

When the fundamental rights of citizens are so wantonly denied and that denial justified and defended as it is by the lawmakers and dominant forces of so large a number of our states, it can be realized that the fight for the Negro's citizenship rights means a fundamental battle for real things, for life and liberty.

This fight is the Negro's fight. "Who would be free, himself must strike the blow." But, it is no less the white man's fight. The common citizenship rights of no group of people, to say nothing of nearly 12,000,000 of them, can be denied with impunity [without any cost] to the State and the social order which denies them. This fact should be plain to the dullest mind among us, with the upheavals of Europe before our very eyes. Whoso loves America and cherishes its institutions, owes it to himself and his country to join hands with the members of the National Association for the Advancement of Colored People to "Americanize" America and make the kind of democracy we Americans believe in to be the kind of democracy we shall have in *fact*, as well as in theory.

The Association seeks to overthrow race prejudice but its objective may better be described as a fight against *caste*. Those who seek to separate the Negro from the rest of Americans are intent upon establishing a caste system in America and making of all black men an *inferior caste*. As America could not exist "half slave and half free" so it cannot exist with an upper caste of whites and a lower caste of Negroes. Let no one be deceived by those who would contend that they strive only to maintain "the purity of the white race" and that they wish to separate the races but to do no injustice to the black man. The appeal is to history which affords no example of any group or element of the population of any nation which was separated from the rest and at the same time treated with justice and consideration. Ask the Jew who was compelled [forced] to live in the proscribed Ghetto whether being held separate he was afforded the common rights of citizenship and "equal protection of the laws?" To raise the question is to find the answer "leaping to the eyes," as the French say.

Nor should any one be led astray by the tiresome talk about "social equality." Social equality is a private question which may well be left to individual decision. But, the prejudices of individuals cannot be accepted as the controlling policy of a state. The National Association for the Advancement of Colored People is concerned primarily with *public equality*. America is a nation—not a private club. The privileges no less than the duties of citizenship be-

long of right to no *separate class* of the people but to *all* the people, and to them as *individuals*. The constitution and the laws are for the protection of the minority and of the unpopular, no less than for the favorites of fortune, or they are of no meaning as American instruments of the government.

Such a fight as has been outlined is worthy of the support of all Americans. The forces which seek to deny, and do deny, to the Negro his citizenship birthright, are powerful and intrenched. They hold the public offices. They administer the law. They say who may, and who may not vote, in large measure. They control and edit, in many sections, the influential organs [publications] of public opinion. They dominate. To dislodge them by legal and constitutional means as the N.A.A.C.P. proposes to endeavor to dislodge them, requires a strong organization and ample funds. These two things attained, victory is but a question of time, since justice will not forever be denied.

The lines along which the Association can best work are fairly clear. Its fight is of the brain and

The National Association for the Advancement of Colored People (NAACP), whose early offices are shown here, became a very effective political organization fighting for civil rights of African Americans.

the soul and to the brain and soul of America. *It seeks to reach the conscience of America.* America is a large and busy nation. It has many things to think of besides the Negro's welfare. In Congress and state legislatures and before the bar of public opinion, the Association must energetically and adequately defend the Negro's right to fair and equal treatment. To command the interest and hold the attention of the American people for *justice to the Negro* requires money to print and circulate literature which states the facts of the situation. And the appeal must be on the basis of the facts. It is easy to talk in general terms and abstractly. The presentation of concrete data necessitates ample funds.

Lynching must be stopped. Many Americans do not believe that such horrible things happen as do happen when Negroes are lynched and burned at the stake. Lynching can be stopped when we can reach the hearts and consciences of the American people. Again, money is needed.

Legal work must be done. Defenseless Negroes are every day denied the "equal protection of the laws" because there is not money enough in the Association's treasury to defend them, either as individuals or as a race.

Legislation must be watched. Good laws must be promoted wherever that be possible and bad laws opposed and defeated, wherever possible. Once more, money is essential.

The public must be kept informed. This means a regular press service under the supervision of a trained newspaper man who knows the difference between news and gossip, on the one hand, and mere opinion on the other. That colored people are contributing their fair share to the well-being of America must be made known. The war has made familiar the heroic deeds of the colored soldier. The colored civilian has been, and is now, contributing equally to America's welfare. If men have proven to be heroes in warfare, they must have had virtues in peace time. That law-abiding colored people are denied the commonest citizenship rights, must be brought home to all Americans who love fair play. Once again, money is needed.

The facts must be gathered and assembled. This requires effort. Facts are not gotten out of one's imagination. Their gathering and interpretation is skilled work. Research workers of a practical experience are needed. Field investigations, in which domain the Association has already made some notable contributions, are essential to good work. More money.

The country must be thoroughly organized. The Association's nearly 200 branches are a good beginning. A field staff is essential to the upbuilding of this important branch development. A very large percentage of the branch members are colored people. As a race they have less means, and less experience in public organization, than white people. But, they are developing rapidly habits of efficiency in organization. Money, again is needed.

But, not money alone is needed. Men and women are vital to success. Public opinion is the main force upon which the Association relies for a *victory of justice.*

REVIEWING THE READING

1. What do you think was the main objective of the NAACP at the time the document was written?

2. According to the document, why should all Americans, black and white, be concerned with democracy for blacks?

3. **Using Your Historical Imagination.** Why do you think the NAACP placed greater emphasis on *public equality* than on *social equality?* Do you think that one could be achieved without the other? Explain your answer.

38

From *The Big Money* by
John Dos Passos.

A Novelist's Portrait of Henry Ford (ca. 1920)

Americans coming of age in the early 1920s faced a world their parents had not even dreamed of. Industrialization and technology were expanding at a dizzying rate. Radios, airplanes, and automobiles were common sights. The Jazz Age was in full swing. People swarmed to the movies and to sporting events. For most people times were good.

Henry Ford, one of America's greatest industrial pioneers, helped bring about those good times. Ford helped change the automobile from a toy for the rich to a practical form of transportation for the common person. The following selection is an excerpt from a novel written by American author John Dos Passos. In it the author uses an almost poetic style of writing—often ignoring the spacing and punctuation usually found in narratives—to characterize many of the events and people of the early twentieth century. As you read the author's characterization of Henry Ford, try to determine how Ford's production methods revolutionized the automobile industry.

"*M*r. Ford the automobileer," *the featurewriter wrote in 1900,*

"*Mr. Ford the automobileer began by giving his steed three or four sharp jerks with the lever at the righthand side of the seat; that is, he pulled the lever up and down sharply in order, as he said, to mix air with gasoline and drive the charge into the exploding cylinder. . . . Mr. Ford slipped a small electric switch handle and there followed a puff, puff, puff. . . . The puffing of the machine assumed a higher key. She was flying along about eight miles an hour. The ruts in the road were deep, but the machine certainly went with a*

dreamlike smoothness. There was none of the bumping common
even to a streetcar. . . . By this time the boulevard had
been reached, and the automobileer, letting a lever fall a little,
let her out. Whiz! She picked up speed with infinite rapidity.
As she ran on there was a clattering behind, the new noise
of the automobile."

For twenty years or more,

ever since he'd left his father's farm when he
was sixteen to get a job in a Detroit machineshop,
Henry Ford had been nuts about machinery. First
it was watches, then he designed a steamtractor,
then he built a horseless carriage with an engine
adapted from the Otto gasengine he'd read about
in *The World of Science,* then a mechanical buggy with
a one cylinder fourcycle motor, that would run forward but not back;

at last, in ninetyeight, he felt he was far enough
along to risk throwing up his job with Detroit Edison
Company, where he'd worked his way up from night
fireman to chief engineer, to put all his time into
working on a new gasoline engine,

(in the late eighties he'd met Edison at a meeting
of electriclight employees in Atlantic City. He'd gone
up to Edison after Edison had delivered an address
and asked him if thought gasoline was practical as
a motor fuel. Edison had said yes. If Edison said it,
it was true. Edison was the great admiration of Henry
Ford's life);

and in driving his mechanical buggy, sitting
there at the lever jauntily dressed in a tight-buttoned
jacket and high collar and a derby hat, back and
forth over the level illpaved streets of Detroit,

scaring the big brewery horses and the skinny
trotting horses and the sleekrumped pacers with the
motor's loud explosions,

looking for men scatterbrained enough to invest
money in a factory for building automobiles.

He was the eldest son of an Irish immigrant
who during the Civil War had married the daughter
of a prosperous Pennsylvania Dutch farmer and

This photograph from 1919 shows Henry Ford seated in his office.

settled down to farming near Dearborn in Wayne County, Michigan;

like plenty of other Americans, young Henry grew up hating the endless sogging through the mud about the chores, the hauling and pitching manure, the kerosene lamps to clean, the irk and sweat and solitude of the farm.

He was a slender, active youngster, a good skater, clever with his hands; what he liked was to tend the machinery and let the others do the heavy work. His mother had told him not to drink, smoke, gamble, or go into debt, and he never did.

When he was in his early twenties his father tried to get him back from Detroit, where he was working as mechanic and repairman for the Drydock

Engine Company that built engines for steamboats,
by giving him forty acres of land.

Young Henry built himself an uptodate square
white dwellinghouse with a false mansard roof [roof
with two slopes on each of four sides] and married
and settled down on the farm,

but he let the hired men do the farming;

he bought himself a buzzsaw and rented a sta-
tionary engine and cut the timber off the woodlots.

He was a thrifty young man who never drank
or smoked or gambled or coveted his neighbor's
wife, but he couldn't stand living on the farm.

He moved to Detroit, and in the brick barn
behind his house tinkered for years in his spare time
with a mechanical buggy that would be light enough
to run over the clayey wagonroads of Wayne County,
Michigan.

By 1900 he had a practicable car to promote.

He was forty years old before the Ford Motor
Company was started and production began to move.

Speed was the first thing the early automobile
manufacturers went after. Races advertised the makes
of cars.

Henry Ford himself hung up several records
at the track at Grosse Pointe and on the ice on
Lake St. Clair. In his 999 he did the mile in thirtynine
and fourfifths seconds.

But it had always been his custom to hire others
to do the heavy work. The speed he was busy with
was speed in production, the records in efficient
output. He hired Barney Oldfield, a stunt bicyclerider
from Salt Lake City, to do the racing for him.

Henry Ford had ideas about other things than
the designing of motors, carburetors, magnetos, jigs
and fixtures, punches and dies; he had ideas about
sales:

that the big money was in economical quantity
production, quick turnover, cheap interchangeable
easilyreplaced standardized parts:

it wasn't until 1909, after years of arguing with

his partners, that Ford put out the first Model T.

Henry Ford was right.

That season he sold more than ten thousand tin lizzies, ten years later he was selling almost a million a year.

In these years the Taylor plan was stirring up plantmanagers and manufacturers all over the country. Efficiency was the word. The same ingenuity that went into improving the performance of a machine could go into improving the performance of the workmen producing the machine.

. . . In 1913 they established the assembly line at Ford's.

In 1913 they established the assemblyline at Ford's. That season the profits were something like twentyfive million dollars, but they had trouble in keeping the men on the job, machinists didn't seem to like it at Ford's.

Henry Ford had ideas about other things than production.

He was the largest automobile manufacturer in the world; he paid high wages; maybe if the steady workers thought they were getting a cut (a very small cut) in the profits, it would give trained men an inducement [a reason] to stick to their jobs,

wellpaid workers might save enough money to buy a tin lizzie; the first day Ford's announcement that cleancut properlymarried American workers who wanted jobs had a chance to make five bucks a day (of course it turned out that there were strings to it; always there were strings to it)

such an enormous crowd waited outside the Highland Park plant

all through the zero January night

that there was a riot when the gates were opened; cops broke heads, jobhunters threw bricks; property, Henry Ford's own property, was destroyed. The company dicks [armed guards] had to turn on the firehose to beat back the crowd.

The American Plan; automotive prosperity seeping down from above; it turned out there were strings to it.

But that five dollars a day
paid to good, clean American workmen
who didn't drink or smoke cigarettes or read
or think,
and who didn't commit adultery
and whose wives didn't take in boarders,
made America once more the Yukon [reference
to the Alaska gold rush] of the sweated workers of
the world;
made all the tin lizzies and the automotive age,
and incidentally,
made Henry Ford the automobileer, the admirer
of Edison, the birdlover,
the great American of his time.

REVIEWING THE READING

1. In what way did Ford revolutionize the automobile industry? How did his new methods make it possible for the common person to buy a car for the first time?

2. Why did Ford give his workers a small cut in the profits of the company?

3. **Using Your Historical Imagination.** Henry Ford and many other industrialists of his time were opposed to labor unions and laws governing the rights of workers. What policies do you think workers at the Ford plant might have changed if they had had a choice?

39

From *The Call To Unity: The Bedell Lectures for 1919 Delivered at Kenyon College May 24th and 25th, 1920,* by William T. Manning.

A Minister Calls for Christian Unity (1920)

In the sixteenth century, a phenomenal religious up-heaval—the Reformation—took place in Europe and resulted in the founding of Protestantism and the break-ing away of millions of Christians from the Roman Catholic church. Over the centuries, groups of religious reformers formed many different denominations of Christian churches, each with its own doctrines and traditions.

By the twentieth century, there was a growing concern among many Christian leaders about the lack of cooperation among the churches. Many believed that this lack of cooperation was interfering with the ability of any of the churches to be truly effective in bringing the message of Christianity to the world. In the following excerpt from his book of collected lectures, William T. Manning, Rector of Trinity Church in New York, calls for Christian unity. As you read the selection, written in 1920, try to determine the reasons that Manning and others believed Christian unity was so important.

The whole world to-day is moved by the thought of fellowship. It is not surprising therefore that we feel more than ever the incongruity [disharmony] of our lack of fellowship in the Christian Church. The desire for fellowship among Christians has in fact reached a new point of progress. It has ceased to be merely a pious aspiration [religious hope], and has become a world wide movement. Never since the divisions in the Church of Christ took place has the need of reunion been felt as it is now.

And this necessity is being forced home upon us from many sides. Hard facts are driving us to see the evils, and the perils of our present situation.

The outbreak of the world war burned into our souls the weaknesses of a divided Christianity. We saw that, as a power to preserve peace among men, the Church did not seriously count. Its voice was not heard speaking unitedly and clearly for those principles of justice and righteousness upon which alone peace can rest. Its influence in the hour of the world's crisis was negligible. And the whole course of events since has served to make this inadequacy clearer to us. Whatever explanation, or defense, or palliation [excuse] there may be for them, it is plain that our divisions are a disaster to the cause of Christ. Before the present unprecedented need of the world, the Christian Church stands with her life enfeebled, her witness weakened, her message in large measure discredited by her own differences and dissensions [disagreements].

Christian Unity is no mere ecclesiastical [religious] problem. It is the greatest, and the most far reaching of all present day questions. It lies back of, and holds the key to, all our other problems, national and international, social, political and economic. As men face the tremendous responsibilities and tasks of this new time, they are feeling the need of support and guidance. They know that if there is to be a new order it must be filled with a new spirit. They are looking for moral and spiritual strength and help. But they are not looking, with confidence, to the Church for this. A disunited Church cannot call forth the faith of men, nor give the message of Christ to the world. Its own inconsistency, and self-contradiction are too evident. How can the world learn the Gospel of fellowship from an organization which is at variance with itself? What power is there in an appeal for a united world issued by a divided Church? What force is there in a plea for brotherhood by those who fail to give evidence

A disunited Church cannot call forth the faith of men . . .

Episcopal minister William T. Manning was one of the first American Protestants to argue for greater cooperation between Christian denominations in the United States.

of brotherliness? Such an appeal suggests at once the retort: "Physician, heal thyself."

The Christian Church is commissioned to show the world the true meaning of human brotherhood. It is for this that the Church is set here among men. It is to preach and to be, the truest realization of fellowship ever seen on this earth; a fellowship which transcends all bounds of nation, or race, or color; a fellowship blessed, made holy and complete, in oneness with Jesus Christ. This fellowship was to be the proof of the Church's Divine mission and of the power of Him in Whose Name she speaks. While the Church fails to furnish this proof, can we wonder if the world listens to her message with doubt and uncertainty?

The Church should be the inspiration and guiding force of the present movements for social advance. Changes far greater than any of us realize are taking place. We have entered into a new era. Vast problems are pressing for solution. The truer order of cooperation, fellowship, brotherhood is to be established. In all this the Church should be not a spectator, nor a mere sympathetic influence, but the great guiding power. The one true hope for the world is that these movements shall be actuated [motivated] by the spirit, and the principles, of Christ. There should now be a world-wide call from the Church for a redeemed social order, in which the spirit and law of Christ shall rule, for the bringing of Christian principles into the whole fabric of modern civilization; for the Christianization of every department of life. Who but the Church can issue such a call? What other power but that of religion is able to bring the spirit of brotherhood into human relationships and "to make justice and love the controlling motive in all social conditions"? But her own divided state makes it impossible for the Church to give such a call with effect. "Doth a fountain send forth at the same place sweet water and bitter?" Can a Church which is divided by the spirit of sect liberate men's hearts from the spirit of class and of caste? Can a Church which maintains barriers of religious antagonism and division be the herald of cooperation, and of the common life? Can a Church in which men are separated into competitive and rival groups preach effectively the social message of the Gospel? In his interesting essay on "Christianity and the Working Classes," Mr. Arthur Henderson very pointedly asks "Is Christianity, as we have it represented to-day, split up as it is into almost innumerable denominational churches, capable of dealing adequately with the growing forces of reaction?" and he adds: "However much Christians may console themselves that a Church divided into numerous sects is justified and, as many think, a source of strength, the multitude is slow to believe in a Christianity so divided."

Of the practical waste, the squandering of energy, time and resources, occasioned by our divisions it is scarcely necessary to speak. We see the evidences of this on every hand. It is obvious that the energies, which as Christians, we devote to controversy and conflict with each other should be concentrated on the one great purpose for which the Church exists. But the overlapping, the duplication of effort, the competition and rivalry among Christians are worse than mere waste of power, serious as this is. They are a spectacle which lessens the faith of men, which brings religion into disrepute [disfavor], and which does daily hurt to the cause of Christ. Men generally are not hostile to religion, but the message of Christ seems to them confused and uncertain. Amid the controversies of the churches they cannot hear the great central message of the Church. The fact which they see clearly is that, however the divisions may be accounted for, they conflict with the Church's own teaching, and contradict her own fundamental principles. They know that whatever else the Church of Christ stands for it must, if it truly represents Him, stand for harmony, not for discord, for peace, not for dissension, for fellowship, brotherhood and love. A divided Church is giving us a non-believing world.

REVIEWING THE READING

1. What reasons did Manning give to support his call for Christian unity?

2. According to Manning, what is the primary purpose of the Christian church? How does he believe churches have failed in this mission?

3. **Using Your Historical Imagination.** Why do you think the minister believed that the period of time in which he spoke— in 1920—was a good time to call for unity of the Christian churches after so many centuries of disunity?

A Portrait of FDR, from *Sunrise at Campobello* (1924)

40

From *Sunrise at Campobello* by Dore Schary.

In June 1924 Franklin Delano Roosevelt, who would later become the thirty-second president of the United States, clicked heavy braces into place on his legs, positioned crutches under his arms, and slowly began a long ten steps forward. Then, leaning against the lectern for support, Roosevelt electrified the delegates of the Democratic convention with a rousing speech nominating Alfred E. Smith for president.

More than 30 years later, playwright Dory Schary captivated theater audiences with his play Sunrise at Campobello. *The play dramatically captured Roosevelt's struggle from the onset of the polio that crippled him in 1921 to his courageous return to the political arena at the 1924 Democratic convention. As you read the final two scenes from the play, consider the courage Roosevelt displayed as he faced those ten difficult steps.*

Scene Two

*W*e *are in a small room of Madison Square Garden. We are aware of the roaring sound of the Convention hall, which is swarming with delegates. The sound is constant and present in the room, but not loud enough to distract us. It is June 26, 1924, about 11:30 P.M.*

In the room is FDR, seated in a more conventional wheel chair than the ones he has used in his home. He is bronzed and beaming with vitality. JAMES, *the eldest son, stands near the back wall, on which his father's crutches lean.* ELEANOR [Eleanor Roosevelt, FDR's wife] *is seated to the left of FDR, knitting.* HOWE [Louis M. Howe, aide and close advisor to FDR] *is standing by.* MISSY

[Missy LeHand, FDR's private secretary] *is seated to the right of FDR. A uniformed* POLICEMAN *is on duty, guarding the door. A screen is in one corner of the room, large enough to cover FDR and his wheel chair. FDR's braces are on the desk. A roar goes up outside.* HOWE *looks at his watch.*

HOWE: That, very likely is the finish of Miss Kennedy's address to the brethren.

ELEANOR: Now what?

HOWE: Now Bill Sweet, to second the nomination of McAdoo—then the roll call—and if Connecticut remembers its cue, it yields to New York—and—
(*He points to FDR*)

FDR: Then they get one half-hour of little ol' me.
(DALY, *a young man, dashes in. He is frantic*)

DALY: Mr. Roosevelt, I've checked everything again and again—and everything should be all right.

FDR: I'm certain it will be, Daly.

DALY: You're feeling okay?

FDR: (*Nodding*) Fine.

DALY: Is there anything I can do for you, sir?

FDR: No, thank you.

HOWE: (*Noticing* DALY's *tension*) Say, Daly—

DALY: Yes—

HOWE: I'd like to make sure that everything is on schedule. Take a look—size up the crowd—get some impressions and then report back. Will you do that?

DALY: Of course.

HOWE: Thanks. Thanks very much.
(HOWE *motions to* MISSY *to open the door. She does, as* DALY *approaches it. We see the* POLICEMAN *and hear the crowd, louder now.* DALY *goes out, and the door closes*)

FDR: Thanks, Louie.

HOWE: I wasn't thinking about you. He was driving me crazy. (*He crosses to* FDR) You'd better get ready, Franklin.

FDR: Jimmy—

JIMMY: I've got them, Father.

> (JIMMY *takes the braces from the desk and goes behind the screen with* FDR. HOWE *takes a step toward the screen and calls over*)

HOWE: Franklin, I want to take another crack at you about the finish of the speech. FDR: (*Back of the screen*) Louie, not again.

HOWE: Yes, again. Listen, Franklin, this phrase of Proskauer's is a rich one, and I think you're murdering it by not using it at the finish.

FDR: (*Back of the screen*) It's close enough to the finish.

HOWE: I think it ought to be the last thing you say. "I give you—the Happy Warrior of the Political Battlefield—Al Smith." Period. Crash.

FDR: (*Back of the screen*) I don't think so. Period. Crash.

HOWE: You're wrong. It's a sock phrase and will stick. It ought to be the punch line.

ELEANOR: Franklin, may I say a word?

FDR: (*Back of the screen*) Certainly. If you're going to agree with me.

ELEANOR: Then I've nothing to say.

FDR: (*Back of the screen, annoyed*) That's hardly a sign of wifely devotion.

HOWE: Your being here and doing this is the most important thing. I only feel you're losing the value of the last minute or two of a good speech.

FDR: (*Back of the screen*) Louie—I'm not sold on changing it. I'm sorry.

HOWE: Further deponent [one who gives sworn testimony] sayeth not.

> (*At that moment* FDR *appears with* JIMMY *from behind the screen*)

JIMMY: Did I get it too tight, Father?

FDR: I don't think so, Jimmy. No, that's fine.

> (*At this moment* SARA ROOSEVELT *enters. The noise is suddenly louder.*)

SARA: Franklin, they hardly let me through to you—

FDR: Mama, ever the lady. You came in just at the right time—just as I stepped into my pants.

. . . That howling mob consists of ladies and gentlemen conducting the business of democracy.

SARA: Oh, Franklin—

FDR: Welcome to the smoke-filled back room of politics.

SARA: That howling mob outside is frightening.

FDR: That howling mob consists of ladies and gentlemen conducting the business of democracy.

SARA: How anything of consequence can be accomplished out of such a babble is a miracle.

FDR: Mama—I'm all for noisy congregations. God help us if our conventions ever turn into high school pageants.

SARA: Franklin, this is hardly the time to give me lessons in politics. I wanted only a moment to say God bless you.

FDR: (*Simply*) He has given me many blessings. (SARA *kisses him*)

SARA: And, Franklin, speak out loudly and clearly. (SARA *exits*)

HOWE: Franklin, if I know Mama, in a couple of months she'll be working on a political primer. (*He looks at his watch*) I know this is awful—but I'm getting nervous.

ELEANOR: And I have dropped three stitches.

FDR: He's only been on a few minutes. It just seems long.
(*The noise swells as the door bursts open. The* POLICEMAN *is gripping* DALY)

DALY: Mr. Howe—Mr. Howe—for God's sake, Miss LeHand, will you tell this man I belong here!

MISSY: (*To* POLICEMAN) He does. He does. (*The* POLICEMAN *unhands* DALY, *who moves into the room, excited*)

DALY: Sorry I got panicky. Mr. Howe, you ought to get ready. The crowd is enormous and busting with excitement. Senator Walsh says it's time to get Mr. Roosevelt to the platform.

HOWE: Missy—will you check the press handouts. Take Daly here with you for anything you need.

MISSY: Right. (*Crosses to* FDR, *shakes his hand*) Boss, I know you'll be tremendous.

FDR: Thanks, Missy. For everything.
(MISSY *starts for the door*)
DALY: Good luck, Mr. Roosevelt—and to you, Mrs. Roosevelt—and to you, Elliott.
JIMMY: James—Jimmy.
DALY: Yes—thank you.
HOWE: Okay, Daly. Good luck to you.
(DALY *waves and goes out with* MISSY)
FDR: Jimmy, are you all set?
JIMMY: Yes, Father. In my mind I have gone over it a hundred times. (*He smiles*) You make the speech, and I'll worry about everything else.
FDR: (*With a laugh*) That's my son—man of iron.
(*Now* FDR *leans over his legs*) Better check the braces.
(*He clicks them into place—turns them with his hands and then releases them, leaving his knees limp again.* JIMMY *brings the crutches over*) They should be fine. Jimmy, if I slip, pick me up in a hurry.
(ELEANOR *comes to him and they caress each other*)

This 1924 photo shows Franklin Delano Roosevelt at the time he returned to politics after his recovery from polio.

**. . . I'm ready.
Jimmy—battle
stations!**

FDR: (*He takes the crutches from Jimmy*) I'm ready.
  Jimmy—battle stations!
  (JIMMY *starts to push the chair as* DALY *bursts in excitedly*)
DALY: Mr. Roosevelt—

The Curtain Falls

Scene Three

*The scene reveals the platform in Madison Square Garden.
We are looking toward the rear platform. Facing us are huge
drapes of bunting and pictures of Wilson and Jefferson. Stage
front is the speaker's lectern, about twenty feet from the rear,
where are grouped* FDR *in his wheel chair,* JIMMY, *holding
the crutches next to him, the other children,* ELEANOR ROOSE-
VELT, SARA ROOSEVELT, MISSY, LOUIS HOWE, *and the*
POLICEMAN.

  At the lectern is a SPEAKER. *Next to him is* SENATOR
WALSH *of Montana, the Chairman. The crowd noise swells,
loud and turbulent. It comes from all sides. There is no micro-
phone, and the speakers must yell to be heard. It is bedlam
as the* SPEAKER *tries to be heard.*

WALSH: (*Banging gavel and screaming*) Ladies and
  Gentlemen! Please—give the speaker your
  attention—
  (*There is some measure, small but noticeable, of attention*)
SPEAKER: (*Also yelling*) There is a good deal of mail
  accumulating for the delegates in the Convention
  post office—and we urge you, please, to pick up
  your mail. It's getting very crowded. Please pick
  up your mail! Thank you!
  (*There is cheering and screaming again.* WALSH *takes
    the gavel*)
WALSH: (*After hammering the audience into some quiet*) We
  will continue with the calling of the roll.
  Connecticut!
VOICE: (*From the pit*) Connecticut, the Nutmeg State,
  yields to the great Empire State of New York!
  (*An enormous cheer and more yelling*)

WALSH: (*Banging for quiet*) Ladies and Gentlemen! (*He hammers away with his gavel and finally gets some attention*) The Chair recognizes the Honorable Franklin D. Roosevelt of the State of New York!

(*As he says this, there is applause.* JIMMY *hands* FDR *the crutches; he gets to his feet and then, proud, smiling and confident, he starts to walk on his crutches to the lectern, as the applause mounts in intensity. Slowly, but strongly and surely,* FDR *walks those ten great steps. The cheering starts— whistles, screams, and rebel yells—and the band plays "Sidewalks of New York."* FDR *reaches the lectern and hands the crutches to* JIMMY, *who takes them and steps down. The screaming crowd continues to sound off.* FDR *stands there, holding the lectern with his left hand. Now he waves his right hand at the crowd in that familiar gesture. He smiles broadly, basking in the warmth of this genuine and wholehearted tribute to his appearance, his courage and his future. The cheering continues as:*)

The Curtain Falls

REVIEWING THE READING

1. In what way did Roosevelt show tremendous courage by agreeing to give the nominating address at the convention?

2. How did the delegates of the convention show their respect for Roosevelt?

3. **Using Your Historical Imagination.** In 1928 Roosevelt was elected governor of New York, and just five years later he would be elected to the first of four terms as president. (He died in office before completing his fourth term.) What effect do you think Roosevelt's choice to walk, rather than use his wheelchair, at the 1924 convention had on his future career in politics?

An Album of Changes

1

2

3

"Good Bye, Dad, I'm Off To Fight For Old Glory. You Buy U.S. GOVT BONDS"

THIRD LIBERTY LOAN

4

SUNDAY MAGAZINE
of the SUNDAY RECORD-HERALD

5

8

9

1. Child's bicycle, 1882; 2. early 1900s wringer washer; 3. World War I poster; 4. 1912 magazine cover; 5. 1872 revenue bond scrip; 6. Henry Ford's 1929 Model A, successor to the Model T; 7. the teddy bear, named after Theodore Roosevelt; 8. 1920s college dance; 9. 1930 model telephone.

7

6

From *Only Yesterday* by
Frederick Lewis Allen;
and *Three Years Down* by
Jonathan Norton
Leonard.

41

The Great Boom and the Big Crash (1928–1929)

The years immediately following World War I in the United States would be remembered as the "Roaring Twenties." Things were booming. Most people were earning more money than ever before, and they had many new gadgets and products on which to spend their money. People soon began to look for new ways to participate in the great prosperity. Many invested in stocks as a way to get rich quick.

By mid-1929, investments in the stock market were at an all-time high. Business and industry earnings and profits skyrocketed. People became millionaires—at least on paper—overnight. There seemed to be no end to the excitement. But it could not last forever. The beginning of the end came on Thursday, October 24, 1929, when the stock market crashed. As you read the following excerpts from Frederick Lewis Allen's description of the Great Boom and Jonathan Leonard's account of the Big Crash that followed, try to determine the cause of the crash.

Frederick Lewis Allen

Gradually the huge pyramid of capital rose. While supersalesmen of automobiles and radios and a hundred other gadgets were loading the ultimate consumer with new and shining wares, supersalesmen of securities were selling him shares of investment trusts which held stock in holding companies which owned the stock of banks which had affiliates which in turn controlled holding companies—and so on *ad infinitum* [without end]. Though

the shelves of manufacturing companies and jobbers
and retailers were not overloaded, the shelves of
the ultimate consumer and the shelves of the distribu-
tors of securities were groaning. Trouble was brew-
ing—not the same sort of trouble which had visited
the country in 1921, but trouble none the less. Still,
however, the cloud in the summer sky looked no
bigger than a man's hand.

How many Americans actually held stock on
margin [money or collateral deposited with a broker
to help insure the broker against loss on transactions
undertaken for a buyer or seller of stocks] during
the fabulous summer of 1929 there seems to be no
way of computing, but it is probably safe to put
the figure at more than a million. . . . The additional number of those who held common stock
outright and followed the daily quotations with an
interest nearly as absorbed as that of the margin
trader was, of course, considerably larger. As one
walked up the aisle of the 5:27 local [train], or found
one's seat in the trolley car, two out of three newspapers that one saw were open to the page of stock-
market quotations. Branch offices of the big Wall
Street houses blossomed in every city and in numerous suburban villages. In 1919 there had been five
hundred such offices; by October, 1928, there were
1,192; and throughout most of 1929 they appeared
in increasing numbers. The broker found himself
regarded with a new wonder and esteem. Ordinary
people, less intimate with the mysteries of Wall Street
than he was supposed to be, hung upon his every
word. Let him but drop a hint of a possible split-
up in General Industries Associates and his neighbor
was off hot-foot the next morning to place a buying
order.

The rich man's chauffeur drove with his ears
laid back to catch the news of an impending move
in Bethlehem Steel; he held fifty shares himself on
a twenty-point margin. The window-cleaner at the
broker's office paused to watch the ticker, for he

**Branch offices of
the big Wall
Street houses
blossomed in
every city . . .**

was thinking of converting his laboriously accumulated savings into a few shares of Simmons. Edwin Lefèvre told of a broker's valet who had made nearly a quarter of a million in the market, of a trained nurse who cleaned up thirty thousand following the tips given her by grateful patients; and of a Wyoming cattleman, thirty miles from the nearest railroad, who bought or sold a thousand shares a day,—getting his market returns by radio and telephoning his orders to the nearest large town to be transmitted to New York by telegram. An ex-actress in New York fitted up her Park Avenue apartment as an office and surrounded herself with charts, graphs, and financial reports, playing the market by telephone on an increasing scale and with increasing abandon. Across the dinner table one heard fantastic stories of sudden fortunes; a young banker had put every dollar of his small capital into Niles-Bement-Pond and now was fixed for life; a widow had been able

A desperate man tries to sell his late-model car for $100 after losing all his money in the stock market crash.

to buy a large country house with her winnings in
Kennecott. Thousands speculated—and won, too—
without the slightest knowledge of the nature of
the company upon whose fortunes they were relying,
like the people who bought Seaboard Air Line under
the impression that it was an aviation stock. Grocers,
motormen, plumbers, seamstresses, and speakeasy
waiters were in the market. Even the revolting intellectuals were there: loudly as they might lament
the depressing effects of standardization and mass
production upon American life, they found themselves quite ready to reap the fruits thereof. Literary
editors whose hopes were wrapped about American
Cyanamid B lunched with poets who swore by Cities
Service, and as they left the table, stopped a moment
in the crowd at the broker's branch office to catch
the latest quotations; and the artist who had once
been eloquent only about Gauguin laid aside his
brushes to proclaim the merits of national Bellas
Hess. The Big Bull market had become a national
mania.

In September the market reached its ultimate
glittering peak.

Jonathan Leonard

That Saturday and Sunday Wall Street hummed with
week-day activity. The great buildings were ablaze
with lights all night as sleepy clerks fought desperately to get the accounts in shape for the Monday
opening. Horrified brokers watched the selling orders
accumulate. It wasn't a flood; it was a deluge. Everybody wanted to sell—the man with five shares and
the man with ten thousand. Evidently the week-end
cheer barrage had not hit its mark.

Monday was a rout [retreat] for the banking
pool, which was still supposed to be "on guard." If
it did any net buying at all, which is doubtful, the
market paid little attention. Leading stocks broke
through the support levels as soon as trading started
and kept sinking all day. Periodically the news would

. . . the big
financial
interests had
abandoned the
market to its
fate.

circulate that the banks were about to turn the tide
as they had done on Thursday, but it didn't happen.
A certain cynicism developed in the board rooms
as the day wore on. Obviously the big financial
interests had abandoned the market to its fate, probably intending to pick up the fragments cheap when
the wreck hit the final bottom. "Very well," said
the little man, "I shall do the same."

When the market finally closed, 9,212,800
shares had been sold. The *Times* index of 25 industrials
fell from 367.42 to 318.29. The whole list showed
alarming losses, and margin calls were on their way
to those speculators who had not already sold out.

That night Wall Street was lit up like a Christmas tree. Restaurants, barber shops, and speakeasies
were open and doing a roaring business. Messenger
boys and runners raced through the streets whooping
and singing at the tops of their lungs. Slum children
invaded the district to play with balls of ticker tape.
Well-dressed gentlemen fell asleep in lunch counters.
All the downtown hotels, rooming houses, even flop-
houses [cheap hotels] were full of financial employees
who usually slept in the Bronx. It was probably Wall
Street's worst night. Not only had the day been
bad, but everybody down to the youngest office
boy had a pretty good idea of what was going to
happen tomorrow.

The morning papers were black with the story
of the Monday smash. Except for rather feeble hopes
that the great banks would step into the gap they
had no heart for cheerful headlines. In the inside
pages, however, the sunshine chorus continued
as merry as ever. Bankers said that heavy buying
had been sighted on the horizon. Brokers were loud
with "technical" reasons why the decline could not
continue.

It wasn't only the financial bigwigs who spoke
up. Even the outriders of the New Era felt that if
everybody pretended to be happy, their phoney
smiles would blow the trouble away. Jimmy Walker

[mayor of New York], for example, asked the movie houses to show only cheerful pictures. *True Story Magazine*, currently suffering from the delusions of grandeur, ran full page advertisements in many papers urging all wage earners to buy luxuries on credit. That would fix things right up. McGraw-Hill Company, another publishing house with boom-time megalomania [delusions of grandeur], told the public to avert its eyes from the obscene spectacle in Wall Street. What they did not observe would not affect their state of mind and good times could continue as before.

These noble but childish dabbles in mass psychology failed as utterly as might have been expected. Even the more substantial contributions of U.S. Steel and American Can in the shape of $1 extra dividends had the same fate. Ordinarily such action would have sent the respective stocks shooting upward, but in the present mood of the public it created not the slightest ripple of interest. Steel and Can plunged down as steeply as if they had canceled their dividends entirely. The next day, Tuesday, the 29th of October, was the worst of all. In the first half hour 3,259,800 shares were traded, almost a full day's work for the laboring machinery of the Exchange. The selling pressure was wholly without precedent. It was coming from everywhere. The wires to other cities were jammed with frantic orders to sell. So were the cables, radio and telephones to Europe and the rest of the world. Buyers were few, sometimes wholly absent. Often the specialists stood baffled at their posts, sellers pressing around them and not a single buyer at any price.

This was real panic. It was what the banks had prevented on Thursday, had slowed on Monday. Now they were helpless. Reportedly they were trying to force their associated corporations to toss their buying power into the whirlpool, but they were getting no results. Albert Conway, New York State Superintendent of Insurance, took the dubious step of urging the companies under his jurisdiction to buy common stocks. If they did so, their buying was insufficient to halt the rout.

When the closing bell rang, the great bull market was dead and buried. 16,410,000 shares had changed hands. Leading stocks had lost as much as 77% of their peak value. The Dow Jones index was off 40% since September 3. Not only the little speculators, but the lordly, experienced big traders had been wiped out by the violence of the crash and the whole financial structure of the nation had been shaken to its foundations. Many bankers and brokers were doubtful about their own solvency, for their accounting systems had broken down. The truth was buried beneath a mountain of scribbled paper which would require several days of solid work to clear away.

REVIEWING THE READING

1. What caused the Great Boom in the stock market?

2. What did publisher McGraw-Hill suggest as a remedy for falling stock prices, according to Leonard?

3. **Using Your Historical Imagination.** People from all walks of life made investments in the stock market during the 1920s' Great Boom period. What do you think was the biggest mistake made by most people?

Sketches from the Hispanic Southwest (1920s)

42

From *Tone the Bell Easy* by Jovita González.

Life was hard for the rural Mexican Americans who lived on the Texas-Mexico border in the early 1900s. While groups were fighting for the rights of women and blacks, worrying about worldwide war, and enjoying the benefits of growing industrialization, the Spanish-speaking Hispanics led a life far removed from these concerns. They had to work hard simply to make a living in the harsh desert land of the Southwest.

Writer Jovita González grew up in this environment. Later, she wrote about her childhood and the people who made up her close-knit community. As you read the following three stories from González' book, think about why these people meant so much to her, and the things they did to create such lasting bonds.

Shelling Corn by Moonlight

In August, down towards the Rio Grande, the rays of the sun beat vertically upon the sandy stretches of land, from which all tender vegetation has been scorched, and the white, naked land glares back at the sun; the only palpitating [moving] things discoverable between the two poles of heat are heat devils. The rattlesnakes are as deeply holed up and as quiet as in midwinter. In the thickets of brush the roadrunners, rusty lizards, mockingbirds, and all other living things pant. Whirlwinds dance across the stretches of prairie interspersed between the thickets of thorn. At six o'clock it is hotter than at midday. Seven o'clock, and then the sun, a ball of orange-pink, descends below the horizon at one stride. The change is magical. A soft cooling breeze, the pulmotor [breathing apparatus] of the Border lands, springs up from the south.

Down in the *cañada* [brook between mountains], which runs by the ranch, doves coo. Out beyond, cattle are grazing and calves are frisking. In the cottonwood tree growing beside the dirt "tank" near the ranch house the redbird sings. Children shout and play. From the corrals come the voices of vaqueros [cowboys] singing and jesting. Blended with the bleatings of goats and sheep are the whistles and hisses of the *pastor* (shepherd). The locusts complete the chorus of evening noises. Darkness subdues them; then, as the moon rises, an uncounted mob of mongrel curs set up a howling and barking at it that coyotes out beyond mock.

It was on a night like this that the ranch folk gathered at the Big House to shell corn. All came: Tio Julianito, the *pastor*, with his brood of sunburned half-starved children ever eager for food; Alejo the fiddler; Juanito the idiot, called the Innocent, because the Lord was keeping his mind in heaven; Pedro the hunter, who had seen the world and spoke English; the vaqueros; and, on rare occasions, Tio Esteban, the mail carrier. Even the women came, for on such occasions supper was served.

A big canvas was spread outside, in front of the kitchen. In the center of this canvas, ears of corn were piled in pyramids for the shellers, who sat about in a circle and with their bare hands shelled the grains off the cobs.

. . . **we heard stories of witches, buried treasures, and ghosts.**

It was then, under the moonlit sky, that we heard stories of witches, buried treasures, and ghosts. I remember one in particular that sent chills up and down my spine.

"The night was dark, gloomy; the wind moaned over the treetops, and the coyotes howled all around. A knock was heard; the only occupant limped across the room and opened the door. A blast of cold wind put out the candle.

" 'Who is there?' he asked, looking out into a night as dark as the mouth of a wolf.

" 'Just a lost hermit,' answered a wailing voice. 'Will you give a stranger a lodging for the night?'

"A figure wrapped in a black cape entered, and as he entered, a tomblike darkness and coldness filled the room.

" 'Will you take off your hat and cape?' the host asked solicitously of his mysterious guest.

" 'No—but—I shall—take off my head.' And saying this, the strange personage placed his head, a skull, upon the table nearby."

Then the *pastor* told of how he had seen spirits in the shape of balls of fire floating through the air. They were souls doing penance for their past sins. As a relief to our fright, Don [a title of respect] Francisco suggested that Tio Julianito do one of his original dances to the tune of Alejo's fiddle. A place was cleared on the canvas, and that started the evening's merriment.

Pedro the Hunter

Pedro was a wonderful person among all the people of the ranch. Besides being the most renowned hunter, he had seen the world, and conscious of his superiority, he strutted among the vaqueros and other ranch hands like an only rooster in a small barnyard. Besides, he spoke English, which he had learned on one of his trips up North. Yes, Pedro was a traveled man; he had been as far away as Sugar Land and had worked in sugar-cane plantations. Many strange things he had seen in his travels. He had seen how the convicts were worked on the plantations and how they were whipped for the least offense. Yes, he, Pedro, had seen that with his own eyes.

He did not stay in the Sugar Land country long; the dampness was making him have chills. So he hired himself as a section hand. His auditors should have seen that big black monster, *el Tren*

Volador [the Flying Train]. It roared and whistled and belched fire and smoke as it flew over the land. He would have liked being a section hand on the railroad had it not been for the food—cornbread and salt pork.

He had been told that if he ate salt pork, he would soon learn to speak English. Bah! What a lie! He had eaten it three times a day and had only learned to say "yes." But being anxious to see a city, he came to Houston. As he walked through the downtown streets one Saturday evening, he saw some beautiful American ladies singing at a corner. And that made him homesick for the ranch. He stopped to listen, and the beautiful ladies talked to him and patted him on the back. They took him with them that night and let him sleep in a room above the garage.

He could not understand them but they were very kind and taught him to play the drum, and every evening the ladies, after putting on a funny hat, took the guitars and he the drum, and they went to town. They sang beautifully, and he beat the drum in a way that must have caused the envy of the passers-by, and when he passed a plate, many people put money in it. During the winter he learned English. But with the coming of spring he got homesick for the *mesquitales* [mesquite trees], the fragrant smell of the *huisache* [desert flowers], the lowing of the cattle at sundown, and above all, for the mellow, rank smell of the corral. What would he not give for a good cup of black, strong ranch coffee, and a piece of jerky broiled over the fire! And so one night, with his belongings wrapped up in a blanket, he left south by west for the land of his youth. And here he was again, a man who had seen the world but who was happy to be at home.

The Mail Carrier
No people of the North feel cold more than do the Border people when the winter norther sweeps

down. In the teeth of one of these northers we left Las Viboras ranch just before dawn, bound for the nearest railroad station, Hebbronville. The day proved to be as dreary as the dawn, and I amused myself counting the stiff jack rabbits that crossed our path. At a turn of the road the car almost collided with a forlorn-looking two-wheeled vehicle drawn by the sorriest-looking nag I had ever seen. On the high seat, perched like a bright-colored tropical bird, sat a figure wrapped up in a crazy quilt. On seeing us he stopped, motioned us to do the same, and in mumbled tones bade us good morning, asked where we were going, what might be the news at the ranches, and finally, were we all right. He seemed to ask these questions for the sake of asking, not waiting for a reply to any one of them. At last, having paused in his catechism [series of questions]

A water vendor peddles his wares by donkey cart in the lower Rio Grande valley of early twentieth-century Texas.

long enough for some sort of reply to be given, he put out one of his hands gingerly from under his brilliant cape to wave us good-bye.

"That's Tío Esteban, the mail carrier," grandfather said. And that is how I met this employee of Uncle Sam. Six months later, suitcase and all, I rode with him twenty miles as a passenger, for the sum of two dollars and fifty cents. That summer we became intimate friends. He was the weather-beaten, brown-faced, black-eyed Cupid of the Community. Often when some lovesick vaquero did not have a two-cent stamp to pay for the delivery of the love missive [letter], he personally delivered the letter. Not only did he carry letters, but he served as secretary to those who could not write. He possessed a wonderful memory and could recite ballads and love poems by the hour. If the amorous [romantic] outburst was in verse, his fee was double. He was a sly old fellow and knew all the love affairs of the community. I am not so sure of his honorableness as a mail carrier. I am afraid he sometimes opened the love missives. Once as he handed a love letter to Serafina, our cook, he said in a mellifluous [sweet and smooth] voice, "My dear Serafina, as the poet says, we are like two cooing doves." Poor Serafina blushed even to the whites of her eyes. Later she showed me that very phrase in the letter.

Tío Esteban knew not only all the love affairs but also all the scandal of the two counties through which he passed. And because of that, he was the welcome guest of every ranch house. He made grandfather's house his headquarters and could always have a bed with the ranch hands. He needed little encouragement to begin talking. He usually sat on a low stool, cleared his throat, and went through all the other preliminaries of a long-winded speaker. Ah, how we enjoyed his news! What did he care for what the papers said? They told of wars in Europe, of the Kaiser's surrender [the surrender of German armed forces at the end of World War I]. But what was all this compared with what Tío Esteban had to tell us?

Did we know Chon had left his wife because she did not wash her face often enough? And about Felipe's hog eating all the soap his wife had made? Pablo's setting hen, which had all white Leghorn eggs, had hatched all black chickens. A strange event, but not so strange if you remembered that Pablo's sister-in-law had black chickens. And with such news he entertained us until the roosters began to crow.

REVIEWING THE READING

1. What things did the people in the stories do that built lasting bonds between them?

2. How did the people in the stories earn a living?

3. **Using Your Historical Imagination.** Why do you think the people in "The Mail Carrier" had so little concern for what was going on in the rest of the country?

A Black Texan's School Days (1920s)

43

From *No Quittin' Sense* by the Reverend C. C. White and Ada Morehead Holland.

In 1852 Massachusetts became the first state to require students between the ages of 6 and 16 to attend school. By 1918 school attendance was required in every state. In those days, African American children were not allowed to attend the same schools as white children, and in many states, especially in the South, very little effort was made to ensure that African American children attended school at all. The following selection is excerpted from a book written by the Reverend C. C. White, a black man who grew up in Texas. As you read from White's account of his childhood in Texas during the early 1900s, and about his chance to go to school, think about the obstacles he had to overcome to obtain even an elementary education.

That fall a man we'd never seen before come to our house. He was riding a mule. He talked to Mama about how us children ought to go to school. He said, "The government's spending a lot of money trying to fix schools for these children and you ought to let them go. Why, it costs thirty dollars a month just to pay the teacher."

Mama said, "Yes, but the government ain't gonna buy the slates and slate pencils, is they?"

The man said, "Well, are you so poor you can't buy your children a slate and pencil?"

Mama drawed her little bitty self up as tall as she could and stuck her face up at that man and said just as nasty as she knowed how, "The ones that's old enough'll be there when school starts." And she whirled around and marched back in the house. Liza stayed to give the man our names, but I followed Mama.

"And what about them books you're gonna be needing later on? Who's gonna pay for them?" she grumbled. I didn't say nothing. I sure did want to go to school. But now wasn't the time to say it. "Po', is we?" snorted Mama.

Mama had stopped working for the Smith family in Shelbyville. She wasn't doing housework now because we were trying to make a crop on the shares and we all had to work in the field. But once when it come a rainy spell she went back over there and worked a week so's Mr. Smith would let her have slates and pencils and a dinner bucket for us out of his store.

School didn't start till the middle of the winter. They just had four months a year. Had two in the winter and two in the summer. They tried to have school when it wasn't the right time for the children to be working in the fields. I could hardly wait for it to begin.

Mama worked every night now, carding, spinning, knitting, and sewing—to have clothes for us to wear to school. I was always there watching, and one day she said, "Charley, if you're bound to be under foot, you might as well help." So she taught me to card cotton. After while I learned to spin, too. . . .

Mama knitted us some socks. We didn't have no shoes, but when it got real cold we could put on our socks and tie a piece of old tow sack or something around our feet. I liked to watch Mama knit. She could make them little needles just *go*—*clickety, clickety, click.*

Liza and me was up early the first day of school. Mama had made us bring the washtub in the night before, and put warm water in it, and take us a bath. Now we put on our new clothes and Mama fixed us some corn bread and cane syrup and a couple pieces of fried fatback to put in our dinner pail. As we walked to school other children come along, too, and several of us went together. Part of the way we walked along the road, but we went through the woods, too, across fences and along trails. A squirrel jumped out of our way and run up on a limb and shook his tail at us. And one of them great big black woodpeckers, that's as big as a cow and has a red topknot, was pounding on a big old oak tree. Liza said, "There's a Old Lord God over there, trying to chop down that tree."

When we got almost underneath him, he took off saying "Kuk, kuk, kuk, kuk, kuk."

Everybody was laughing and having fun. I sure was glad Liza and me was there.

I knowed where the school was. I'd seen it when we'd been to visit Aunt Big Lucy. She was a big fat woman that was one of Mama's friends, and us children liked to go there because she always had more to eat than we did. You always got something good to eat at Aunt Big Lucy's. And the school was just across the road from her house.

The schoolhouse was a old log building, just one room. It had one door and one window, and in the end was a big fireplace that was made out of sticks and mud, like the fireplaces in the houses we'd lived in. That's the kind of chimneys and fireplaces they used then. They called them "stock and cat" chimneys. They made a framework of sticks and daubed it good with balls of mud they called "cats."

There was a blackboard at school. And in one corner the teacher had a barrel where he kept lots of switches, of all sizes. He used big ones on the big kids and little ones on the little-uns. We didn't have no desks. We set on anything we could get. There was some benches. The boys set on one side of the room and the girls on the other. We put our dinner buckets down in one corner. There was a old wooden water bucket there, with a couple of gourds that we drunk out of.

The teacher wrote the ABC's on the board and made us say them over after him. Then we had to write them on our slates. He made us do that every day, and after we got so we could write them pretty good he started making us learn them by heart, forwards and backwards. I got to where I knowed what every one of them was when he pointed to it, but seemed like I just couldn't say them in the right order. The teacher thought I wasn't trying. He said I couldn't start learning to read till I got through with the ABC's. But he did start me doing a little arithmetic.

Some of the other children had been to school before and they already knew their ABC's so he was teaching them to read, and spell. He'd put a word on the board and they'd have to tell him what it was. Then he'd wipe it off and tell them to spell it. Sometimes they couldn't. I just loved to watch them. I got so I knowed a lot of words, just to look at them, and I could spell some of them, too. . . .

I made up my mind I was gonna learn them ABC's somehow. It was hard. Couldn't nobody at home help me. Mama couldn't read. And Liza didn't know as much as I did. She wasn't much interested in learning. . . .

I practiced reading in the evenings, too. I'd put pine knots in the fireplace, to make it blaze up so I'd have light to see by. We didn't have no light except the fireplace. Mama sewed by light from the

In the common school districts of the rural South, blacks, whites, and Hispanics (when present) usually attended separate schools. Sometimes boys and girls had separate entrances.

fireplace. Sometimes I'd write words in the ashes with a stick, like "cat," or "dog," or "house," and try to teach Mama to read a little. But I never did get very far with that. She tried to act interested, but she'd always be so tired, or some grownup would come in and she'd have to talk to them.

Uncle Ossie bought me a pair of shoes to wear to school. When he bought shoes for his own children he bought Frank and Liza and me some, too. This was my second pair of shoes, first ones since the little red boots. Now I had a new book and new shoes, too. I thought I was rich.

The teacher said he could tell I'd been studying . . .

School started out real good [his second year]. The teacher said he could tell I'd been studying because I read better than the others. Going through the woods on the way home that evening, seemed like I was so full of myself I didn't know what to do. I run, and jumped, and kicked, and felt all bouncy, like a ball. I punched Frank so many times, just playing, that he finally went crying home and told Mama, and she said, "Charley, I'm warning you, if you don't behave yourself I'm gonna wear you out. I don't feel like putting up with no foolishness."

That night, after I went to bed, I got to thinking about school, and remembering some of the stories I'd heard the others reading out of the third reader. Maybe if I worked real hard at learning I could get promoted to the third grade by next year. Boy . . . Mama really would be proud of me then.

Before we left for school the next morning we got in plenty wood and water. Mama hadn't been feeling too good, and she'd had trouble stooping to pick up anything. But we didn't think much about it. Mama had had rheumatiz off and on about as long as we could remember. It didn't stop her. It just made her fuss at us more.

But on the third day of school that year Mama couldn't get out the bed. I know she tried, but she just couldn't make it. Everybody said it was the rheumatiz, and I suppose it was.

She called me and said when I got through eating breakfast to come there she wanted to talk to me. I went and leaned against the wall at the foot of her bed, all pleased with myself because I'd had Frank help me and we'd got in lots of wood and water while Liza cooked breakfast, so Liza wouldn't have nothing much to do but take care of Mama till we got home. I figured we'd already done what she was going to tell me to do. I sure wasn't ready for what come.

She said, "Charley, it looks like you're gonna have to quit school and go to work."

I pushed my hands hard against the wall behind me, and tried not to let her see how my insides was churning up and down.

She said, "Mr. Tom Barlow talked to me the other day about getting you to work for him, but I said no, I wanted you to go to school. Now I can't work, so I guess you'll have to. You can do it. You're a big boy now. You're ten years old."

O-o-o-oh, I hated to quit school. And just now when everything was going so good. But I'd a done *anything* for Mama, of course. So I went to work for old man Barlow.

REVIEWING THE READING

1. What obstacles did Charley have to overcome in order to do well in school? Why did he have to quit school at the age of ten?

2. What made Charley's mother agree to allow him to attend school?

3. **Using Your Historical Imagination.** Although the public school Charley attended was free, his family had to make many sacrifices so that he could attend. What sacrifices did Charley's mother make?

<table>
<tr><td>

44

From "No Men Wanted"
by Karl Monroe, *The
Nation*, August 6, 1930.

</td><td>

Life in the Breadlines (1930)

</td></tr>
</table>

*The Roaring Twenties, and the belief that there was
no end to the spiraling growth in business and industry,
came to an abrupt and devastating end with the
crash of the stock market in October 1929. In just
a few short days millionaires became poor, and people
who had invested their life savings in the market
found themselves penniless. Within a few months,
businesses failed, unemployment soared, and people
from all walks of life were forced into the streets,
homeless, hungry, and with no hope of finding a
way to earn a living. People looked to soup kitchens,
breadlines, and lodging houses for food and shelter.
In the following excerpts from a magazine article
written in 1930, journalist Karl Monroe describes
the agony felt by many during these hard times. As
you read his account of life in the breadlines, try to
imagine the hopelessness Monroe must have felt.*

With assets of perhaps twenty dollars and some
nine years' experience as a reporter in New
England I came to New York to find a job. The
round of newspaper offices and news bureaus netted
me a series of polite but firm statements to the effect
that "there's nothing open just now, but you might
leave your name and address." After two weeks of
this I set myself to what I believed would be the
much easier task of securing a clerical place, or even
something like ushering in a theater, "hopping the
bells" at a hotel, or running an elevator in an office
building.

Innocently enough, I followed the crowd to
the agencies in Sixth Avenue. Visions of being sent
to a position where a percentage would be taken

from the first month's salary for a fee were quickly dissolved in the face of the cold fact that any position must be paid for in full and in advance. I learned from one young man that he had paid $10 for a job at which he had worked only four days, receiving $13.50, or a net profit of $3.50 for his four days of work. He and other victims told me, apparently from experience, that many of the agencies make a regular practice of sending men to jobs for which they are obviously unfitted, so that the same job might be sold several times. Many of the men, I learned, realized this, but were willing to "take a gypping" in order to earn a few dollars.

My funds were getting low, and rather than spend any more of the bit of cash I still had I resolved to ride the subways for the night. Not only did I find this fairly easy, but I found that hundreds of others were doing it. Experts at the game—men who lived a hand-to-mouth existence by panhandling and petty racketeering—told me that the most satisfactory system was to ride the B.M.T. trains which run from Times Square to Coney Island, swinging around a loop and returning. The trip consumes nearly two hours if a local train is taken. A good corner seat gives the rider a change to get a fair nap, and the thing can be repeated endlessly. When morning came I went to the Grand Central Terminal, where I washed for a nickel.

Sleeping in the parks, I found, was much less satisfactory than the comfort offered by the rapid-transit companies. Tired, hungry, and cold, I stretched out on the bench, and despite the lack of downy mattress and comforter eventually fell asleep. The soles of my feet were swollen with blisters, because my shoes had not been removed in at least seventy-two hours and I had tramped the sidewalks for three days. Suddenly I was awakened by a patrolman who had swung his night stick sharply against the soles of my feet, sending an indescribable electric pain through my hunger-racked body.

. . . I resolved to ride the subways for the night.

Cooks serve a meal to some of the more than 200 jobless and homeless men housed in a New York City church during the Great Depression.

For three nights I slept in an institution on Twenty-third Street maintained for the benefit of released prisoners, who were given food and lodging until they found work. Along with others, I was given a hearty breakfast in the morning and a good meal at six at night, but none but jail-birds were aided in finding work. When I entered the place, on recommendation of a social-service agency, I had walked the streets for two days and nights, and my first real pleasure came when I found I could wash with hot water and soap. At the end of the three days the superintendent told me I must leave, explaining that the institution was maintained solely for ex-prisoners.

Finally, I stood in the bread line in Twenty-fifth Street. . . . To my surprise, I found in the line all types of men—the majority being skilled craftsmen unable to find work. One of them told me he had been a civil engineer and had earned $8,000 a year. Since losing his job almost a year ago, he had drifted from bad to worse, occasionally picking up odd jobs, until he had sunk to the bread line. The professional bums usually found at such a place were conspicuously lacking. True, there were several unemployables—men in the sixties, who stood no chance in competition with the thousands of younger healthier men. There were also a number of middle-aged men who had long since given up the idea of finding work. Having started honestly enough in a sincere effort to get placed, they had met disappointment so consistently that their ambition was broken. . . . Such men never think of the future in terms of more than one or two days.

Perhaps more to be pitied than this class is the young family whose ambition has been stifled. . . .

There are many men who still hope despite months of failure. Of a dozen men in the park of nights, at least eight will tell you that they have something in mind for the following day, and they actually convince themselves. A few nights later a casual search will reveal the same men, still with "something in mind for tomorrow." For most of them that tomorrow is many months ahead. Perhaps it will never come. In the meantime, they read, under the arc lights in the park, in second-hand newspapers, predictions that business will be normal again within sixty days.

REVIEWING THE READING

1. Why did Monroe come to New York? What was he told by the newspaper offices and news bureaus he visited?

2. How did Monroe try to solve the problem of having no place to sleep?

3. **Using Your Historical Imagination.** People from all walks of life found themselves unemployed and homeless in the 1930s. Which group of people—young, old, professional, skilled, unskilled, and so on— do you think would find it the most difficult to cope with the circumstances? Explain your answer.

45

From "Second Inaugural
Address of President
Franklin D. Roosevelt."

Roosevelt Defends the New Deal (1937)

When Franklin D. Roosevelt was first elected president in 1932, the country was in the midst of the worst economic depression of its history. Unemployment and homelessness were a way of life for millions of Americans, and business and industry had still not recovered from the disastrous stock market crash of 1929. In his campaign Roosevelt had called for a New Deal, his plan for economic recovery. Four years later he was reelected by an overwhelming majority, although the country was still not out of the depression. In his second inaugural address, on January 20, 1937, Roosevelt talked about the accomplishments of the New Deal during the previous four years and the things that still needed to be done. As you read this excerpt from Roosevelt's second inaugural address, try to determine what lessons he believed could be learned from the problems faced during the depression.

When four years ago we met to inaugurate a President, the Republic, single-minded in anxiety, stood in spirit here. We dedicated ourselves to the fulfillment of a vision—to speed the time when there would be for all the people that security and peace essential to the pursuit of happiness. We of the Republic pledged ourselves to drive from the temple of our ancient faith those who had profaned it; to end by action, tireless and unafraid, the stagnation and despair of that day. We did those first things first.

But our covenant [pact] with ourselves did not stop there. Instinctively we recognized a deeper need—the need to find through government the instrument of our united purpose to solve for the individual the ever-rising problems of a complex

civilization. Repeated attempts at their solution without the aid of government had left us baffled and
bewildered. For, without that aid, we had been unable
to create those moral controls over the services of
science which are necessary to make science a useful
servant instead of a ruthless master of mankind. To
do this we knew that we must find practical controls
over blind economic forces and blindly selfish men.

We of the Republic sensed the truth that democratic government has innate [natural] capacity to
protect its people against disasters once considered
inevitable—to solve problems once considered un-
solvable. We would not admit that we could not
find a way to master economic epidemics just as,
after centuries of fatalistic suffering, we had found
a way to master epidemics of disease. We refused
to leave the problems of our common welfare to
be solved by the winds of chance and the hurricanes
of disaster.

In this we Americans were discovering no
wholly new truth; we were writing a new chapter
in our book of self-government.

This year marks the one hundred and fiftieth
anniversary of the Constitutional Convention which
made us a nation. At that Convention our forefathers
found the way out of the chaos which followed
the Revolutionary War; they created a strong government with powers of united action sufficient then
and now to solve problems utterly beyond individual
or local solution. A century and a half ago they
established the Federal Government in order to promote the general welfare and secure the blessings
of liberty to the American people.

Today we invoke [call forth] those same powers
of government to achieve the same objectives.

Four years of new experience have not belied
[disguised] our historic conflict. They hold out the
clear hope that government within communities,
government within the separate States, and government of the United States can do the things the

President Franklin Roosevelt delivers his inaugural address defending the New Deal, January 20, 1937.

times require, without yielding its democracy. Our tasks in the last four years did not force democracy to take a holiday.

Nearly all of us recognize that as intricacies of human relationships increase, so power to govern them also must increase—power to stop evil; power to do good. The essential democracy of our Nation and the safety of our people depend not upon the absence of power but upon lodging it with those whom the people can change or continue at stated intervals through an honest and free system of elections. The Constitution of 1787 did not make our democracy impotent [powerless].

In fact, in these last four years, we have made the exercise of all power more democratic; for we have begun to bring private autocratic [self-governing] powers into their proper subordination to the public's government. The legend that they were in-vincible—above and beyond the processes of a de-mocracy—has been shattered. They have been challenged and beaten.

Our progress out of the depression is obvious. But that is not all that you and I mean by the new order of things. Our pledge was not merely to do a patch-work job with second-hand materials. By using the new materials of social justice we have undertaken to erect on the old foundations a more enduring structure for the better use of future genera-tions.

In that purpose we have been helped by achieve-ments of mind and spirit. Old truths have been re-learned; untruths have been unlearned. We have always known that heedless self-interest was bad morals; we know now that it is bad economics. Out of the collapse of a prosperity whose builders boasted their practicality has come the conviction that in the long run economic morality pays. We are begin-ning to wipe out the line that divides the practical from the ideal; and in so doing we are fashioning an instrument of unimagined power for the establish-ment of a morally better world.

REVIEWING THE READING

1. According to Roosevelt, what lessons could be learned from the problems faced during the depression?

2. What actions did Roosevelt say were first taken during his administration?

3. **Using Your Historical Imagination.** Presi-dent Roosevelt compares the problems of the 1930s with the problems faced 150 years earlier at the Constitutional Con-vention. What did the two events have in common?

46

Poems from *Don't You Want to be Free?* by Langston Hughes.

Two Poems from Langston Hughes' *Don't You Want to Be Free?* (1937)

During the 1920s many African Americans moved from their homes in the South for what they hoped would be a better life in the northern cities. Many of them ended up in Harlem, in New York City. Most of them succeeded in getting only the most lowly of jobs, and were forced into rundown segregated ghettos where their opportunities were few. When the Great Depression hit the nation in the 1930s, things became even more difficult for African Americans, who were usually the last hired and the first fired.

During this time, a group of black writers, artists, poets, and musicians began making a name for themselves in Harlem. Their work was so impressive that the period became known as the Harlem Renaissance. In 1937 one of the most famous Harlem Renaissance poets, Langston Hughes, wrote a play called Don't You Want to be Free?, *which showcased several of his poems. It opened that same year at the Harlem Suitcase Theater. As you read Hughes' poems, try to determine why they would be such a great hit with the mostly black audiences.*

I am a Negro:
Black as the night is black,
  Black like the depths of my Africa.

I've been a slave:
  Caesar told me to keep his door-steps clean.
  I brushed the boots of Washington.

I've been a worker:
   Under my hand the pyramids arose.
   I made mortar for the Woolworth Building.

I've been a singer:
   All the way from Africa to Georgia
   I carried my sorrow songs.
   I made ragtime.

I've been a victim:
   The Belgians cut off my hands in the Congo.
   They lynch me now in Texas.

I am a Negro:
   Black as the night is black,
   Black like the depths of my Africa.

Langston Hughes was the most famous African American poet of the early twentieth century and a leader of the literary movement called the Harlem Renaissance.

Clean the spitoons,* boy.
   Detroit,
   Chicago,
   Atlantic City,
   Palm Beach.
Clean the spitoons.
The steam in hotel kitchens,
And the smoke in hotel lobbies,
And the slime in hotel spitoons:
Part of my life.
   Hey, boy!
   A nickel,
   A dime,
   A dollar,
Two dollars a day.
Hey, boy!
   A nickel,
   A dime,
   A dollar,
   Two dollars
Buy smokes, shoes,
A ticket to the movies.

*Containers in public places into which people spit, especially those who chewed tobacco.

House rent to pay,
Gin on Saturday,
Church on Sunday.
   My God!
Movies and church
and women and Sunday
all mixed up with dimes and
dollars and clean spitoons
and house rent to pay.
   Hey, boy!
A bright bowl of brass is beautiful to the Lord.
Bright polished brass like the cymbals
Of King David's dancers,
Like the wine cups of Solomon.
   Hey, boy!
A clean spitoon on the altar of the Lord.
A clean bright spitoon all newly polished,—
At least I can offer that.

REVIEWING THE READING

1. Why would Hughes' poems appeal to the mostly black theater audiences?

2. In the poem that begins "I am a Negro:" what message about being black do you think Hughes was trying to get across to his audience?

3. **Using Your Historical Imagination.** What do you think Hughes was trying to accomplish through his poetry?

The Impact of the Great Depression (1930s)

47

From *Since Yesterday* by Frederick Lewis Allen.

The stock market crash of 1929 signaled the beginning of more than a decade of the worst economic depression in American history. The great industrial growth of the 1920s came to an abrupt halt, throwing tens of thousands of people out of work almost overnight. People had no money to spend, and manufacturers, finding fewer and fewer people to buy their goods, slowed to a crawl, putting even more people out of work. It was a vicious cycle. Businesses of all types failed. Thousands of banks around the country had to close their doors, taking with them the life savings of millions of Americans. As you read the following excerpts from writer Frederick Lewis Allen's account of the Great Depression, identify the four signs of the depression that Allen said could be found if a person knew where to look.

Walking through an American city, you might find few signs of the depression visible—or at least conspicuous—to the casual eye. You might notice that a great many shops were untenanted, with dusty plate-glass windows and signs indicating that they were ready to lease; that few factory chimneys were smoking; that the streets were not so crowded with trucks as in earlier years, that there was no uproar of riveters to assail the ear, that beggars and panhandlers were on the sidewalks in unprecedented numbers (in the Park Avenue district of New York a man might be asked for money four or five times in a ten-block walk). Traveling by railroad, you might notice that the trains were shorter, the Pullman cars fewer—and that fewer freight trains were on the line. Traveling overnight, you might find only two or three other passengers in your sleeping car. (By contrast, there were more filling stations by the motor highways than ever before, and of all the retail businesses in "Middletown" [the name given to a town studied by sociologists during these years] only the filling stations showed no large drop in business during the black years; for although few new automobiles were being bought, those which would still stand up were being used more than ever—to the dismay of the railroads.)

Otherwise things might seem to you to be going on much as usual. The major phenomena of the depression were mostly negative and did not assail the eye.

But if you knew where to look, some of them would begin to appear. First, the breadlines in the poorer districts. Second, those bleak settlements ironically known as "Hoovervilles" [sarcastic reference to President Hoover, who was blamed by many for the depression] in the outskirts of the cities and on vacant lots—groups of makeshift shacks constructed out of packing boxes, scrap iron, anything that could be picked up free in a diligent [thorough] combing of the city dumps: shacks in which men and sometimes whole families of evicted people were sleeping on automobile seats carried from auto-graveyards, warming themselves before fires of rubbish in grease drums. Third, the homeless people sleeping in doorways or on park benches, and going the rounds of the restaurants for leftover half-eaten biscuits, piecrusts, anything to keep the fires of life burning. Fourth, the vastly increased number of thumbers [hitchhikers] on the highways, and particularly of freight-car transients on the railroads: a huge army of drifters ever on the move, searching half-aimlessly for a place where there might be a job.
. . . It was estimated that by the beginning of 1933, the country over, there were a million of these transients on the move. . . .

Among the comparatively well-to-do people of the country (those, let us say, whose pre-depression incomes had been over $5,000 a year) the great majority were living on a reduced scale, for salary cuts had been extensive, especially since 1931, and dividends were dwindling. These people were discharging servants, or cutting servants' wages to a minimum, or in some cases "letting" a servant stay

During the 1930s many people were forced to live in shanty towns like this one in New York City's Central Park.

on without other compensation than board and lodging. In many pretty houses, wives who had never
before—in the revealing current phrase—"done their
own work" were cooking and scrubbing. Husbands
were wearing the old suit longer, resigning from
the golf club, deciding, perhaps, that this year the
family couldn't afford to go to the beach for the
summer, paying seventy-five cents for lunch instead
of a dollar at the restaurant or thirty-five instead
of fifty at the lunch counter. When those who had
flown high with the stock market in 1929 looked
at the stock-market page of the newspapers nowadays
their only consoling thought (if they still had any
stock left) was that a judicious [wise] sale or two
would result in such a capital loss that they need
pay no income tax at all this year.

Alongside these men and women of the well-
to-do classes whose fortunes had been merely reduced by the depression were others whose fortunes
had been shattered. The crowd of men waiting for
the 8:14 train at the prosperous suburb included
many who had lost their jobs, and were going to
town as usual not merely to look stubbornly and
almost hopelessly for other work but also to keep
up a bold front of activity. (In this latter effort they
usually succeeded: one would never have guessed,
seeing them chatting with their friends as train-time
approached, how close to desperation some of them
had come.) There were architects and engineers
bound for offices to which no clients had come in
weeks. There were doctors who thought themselves
lucky when a patient paid a bill. Mrs. Jones, who
went daily to her stenographic job, was now the
economic mainstay of her family, for Mr. Jones was
jobless and was doing the cooking and looking after
the children (with singular distaste and inefficiency).
Next door to the Joneses lived Mrs. Smith, the widow
of a successful lawyer: she had always had a comfortable income, she prided herself on her "nice things,"
she was pathetically unfitted to earn a dollar even

if jobs were to be had; her capital had been invested in South American bonds and United Founders stock and other similarly misnamed "securities," and now she was completely dependent upon hand-outs from her relatives, and didn't even have carfare in her imported pocketbook. . . .

Further down in the economic scale, particularly in those industrial communities in which the factories were running at twenty per cent of capacity or had closed down altogether, conditions were infinitely worse. . . . In every American city, quantities of families were being evicted from their inadequate apartments; moving in with other families till ten or twelve people would be sharing three or four rooms; or shivering through the winter in heatless houses because they could afford no coal, eating meat once a week or not at all. If employers sometimes found that former employees who had been discharged did not seem eager for re-employment ("They won't take a job if you offer them one!"), often the reason was panic: a dreadful fear of inadequacy which was one of the depression's commonest psychopathological results. A woman clerk, offered piecework after being jobless for a year, confessed that she almost had not dared to come to the office, she had been in such terror lest she wouldn't know where to hang her coat, wouldn't know how to find the washroom, wouldn't understand the boss's directions for her job. . . .

At the very bottom of the economic scale the conditions may perhaps best be suggested by two brief quotations. The first, from Jonathan Norton Leonard's *Three Years Down*, describes the plight of Pennsylvania miners who had been put out of company villages after a blind and hopeless strike in 1931: "Reporters from the more liberal metropolitan papers found thousands of them huddled on the mountainsides, crowded three or four families together in one-room shacks, living on dandelions and wild weed-roots. Half of them were sick, but

> . . . ten or twelve people would be sharing three or four rooms.

no local doctor would care for the evicted strikers.
All of them were hungry and many of them were
dying of those providential [fortunate] diseases
which enable welfare authorities to claim that no
one has starved." The other quotation is from Louise
V. Armstrong's *We Too Are the People,* and the scene
is Chicago in the late spring of 1932:—

"One vivid, gruesome moment of those dark
days we shall never forget. We saw a crowd of some
fifty men fighting over a barrel of garbage outside
the back of a restaurant. American citizens fighting
for scraps of food like animals!"

REVIEWING THE READING

1. According to Allen, what four signs of
   the depression could be found if a person
   knew where to look?

2. Every class of people was affected by the
   Great Depression. What two examples
   does Allen give of those people at the
   very bottom of the economic scale?

3. **Using Your Historical Imagination.** Why
   do you think gas stations thrived during
   the Great Depression when every other
   business was failing?

James Agee Describes the Life of Tenant Farmers (1930s)

48

From *Let Us Now Praise Famous Men* by James Agee and Walker Evans.

From the earliest days of American history tenant farming, a situation in which landowners rented out a portion of their land for others to farm, had been popular. By 1900 one out of three farms in the United States was operated by tenants, many of whom hoped to earn enough money from their crops to eventually buy the land from their landlords. During the Great Depression of the 1930s, farm tenancy reached its highest peak. Many of the landowners lost their land during the hard times and were forced to become tenants themselves. Others worked land belonging to other people because it was their only means of earning a living. Tenant farming was especially popular in the South, and by the 1930s more than half of all southern farms were operated by tenants. As you read the following excerpt from a book written by James Agee and Walker Evans about tenant farmers, think about why it was unlikely that a tenant farmer would ever be able to own the land he worked.

Woods and Ricketts work for Michael and T. Hudson Margraves, two brothers, in partnership, who live in Cookstown. Gudger worked for the Margraves for three years; he now (1936) works for Chester Boles, who lives two miles south of Cookstown.

On their business arrangements, and working histories, and on their money, I wrote a chapter too long for inclusion in this volume without sacrifice of too much else. I will put in its place here as extreme a précis [summary] as I can manage.

Gudger has no home, no land, no mule; none of the more important farming implements. He must get all these of his landlord. Boles, for his share of the corn and cotton, also advances him rations [food] money during four months of the year, March through June, and his fertilizer.

Gudger pays him back with his labor and with the labor of his family.

At the end of the season he pays him back further: with half his corn; with half his cotton; with half his cottonseed. Out of his own half of these crops he also pays him back the rations money, plus interest, and his share of the fertilizer, plus interest, and such other debts, plus interest, as he may have incurred.

What is left, once doctors' bills and other debts have been deducted, is his year's earnings.

Gudger is a straight half-cropper, or share-cropper.

Woods and Ricketts own no home and no land, but Woods owns one mule and Ricketts owns two, and they own their farming implements. Since they do not have to rent these tools and animals, they work under a slightly different arrangement. They give over to the landlord only a third of their cotton and a fourth of their corn. Out of their own parts of the crop, however, they owe him the price of two thirds of their cotton fertilizer and three fourths

Most tenant farmers of the 1930s used mules or horses to power their plows and cultivators.

of their corn fertilizer, plus interest; and, plus interest, the same debts or rations money.

Woods and Rickets are tenants: they work on third and fourth.

A very few tenants pay cash rent: but these two types of arrangement, with local variants (company stores; food instead of rations money; slightly different divisions of the crops) are basic to cotton tenantry all over the South.

From March through June, while the cotton is being cultivated, they live on the rations money.

From July through to late August, while the cotton is making, they live however they can.

From late August through October or into November, during the picking and ginning season, they live on the money from their share of the cottonseed.

From then on until March, they live on whatever they have earned in the year; or however they can.

During six to seven months of each year, then— that is, during exactly such time as their labor with the cotton is of absolute necessity to the landlord— they can be sure of whatever living is possible in rations advances and in cottonseed money.

During five to six months of the year, of which three are the hardest months of any year, with the worst of weather, the least adequacy of shelter, the worst or least of food, the worst of health, quite normal and inevitable, they can count on nothing except that they may hope least of all for any help from their landlords.

Gudger—a family of six—lives on ten dollars a month rations money during four months of the year. He has lived on eight, and on six. Woods—a family of six—until this year was unable to get better than eight a month during the same period; this year he managed to get it up to ten. Ricketts—a family of nine—lives on ten dollars a month during this spring and early summer period.

This debt is paid back in the fall at eight per cent interest. Eight per cent is charged also on the fertilizer and on all other debts which tenants incur in this vicinity.

At the normal price, a half-sharing tenant gets about six dollars a bale from his share of the cotton-seed. A one-mule, half-sharing tenant makes on the average three bales. This half-cropper, then, Gudger, can count on eighteen dollars, more or less, to live on during the picking and ginning: though he gets nothing until his first bale is ginned.

Working on third and fourth, a tenant gets the money from two thirds of the cottonseed of each bale: nine dollars to the bale. Woods, with a mule, makes three bales, and gets twenty seven dollars. Ricketts, with two mules, makes and gets twice that, to live on during the late summer and fall.

What is earned at the end of a given year is never to be depended on . . .

What is earned at the end of a given year is never to be depended on and, even late in a season, is never predictable. It can be enough to tide through the dead months of the winter, sometimes even better: it can be enough, spread very thin, to take through two months, and a sickness, or six weeks, or a month: it can be little enough to be completely meaningless: it can be nothing: it can be enough less than nothing to insure a tenant only of an equally hopeless lack of money at the end of his next year's work: and whatever one year may bring in the way of good luck, there is never any reason to hope that that luck will be repeated in the next year or the year after that.

The best that Woods has ever cleared was $1300 during a war year. During the teens and twenties he fairly often cleared as much as $300; he fairly often cleared $50 and less; two or three times he ended the year in debt. During the depression years he has more often cleared $50 and less; last year he cleared $150, but serious illness during the winter ate it up rapidly.

The best that Gudger has ever cleared is $125. That was in the plow-under year. He felt exceedingly hopeful and bought a mule: but when his landlord warned him of how he was coming out the next year, he sold it. Most years he has not made more than $25 to $30; and about one year in three he has ended in debt. Year before last he wound up $80 in debt; last year, $12; of Boles, his new landlord, the first thing he had to do was borrow $15 to get through the winter until rations advances should begin.

Years ago the Ricketts were, relatively speaking, almost prosperous. Besides their cotton farming they had ten cows and sold the milk, and they lived near a good stream and had all the fish they wanted. Ricketts went $400 into debt on a fine pair of mules. One of the mules died before it had made its first crop; the other died the year after; against his fear, amounting to full horror, of sinking to the half-crop level where nothing is owned, Rickets went into debt for other, inferior mules; his cows went one by one into debts and desperate exchanges and by sickness; he got congestive chills; his wife got pellagra [disease caused by dietary deficiency]; a number of his children died; he got appendicitis and lay for days on end under the ice cap; his wife's pellagra got into her brain; for ten consecutive years now, though they have lived on so little rations money, and have turned nearly all their cottonseed money toward their debts, they have not cleared or had any hope of clearing a cent at the end of the year.

It is not often, then, at the end of the season, that a tenant clears enough money to tide him through the winter, or even an appreciable part of it. More generally he can count on it that, during most of the four months between settlement time in the fall and the beginning of work and the resumption of rations advances in the early spring, he will have no money and can expect none, nor any help, from his landlord: and of having no money during the six midsummer weeks of laying by, he can be still more sure. Four to six months of each year, in other words, he is much more likely than not to

. . . All he can hope to do is find work.

have nothing whatever, and during these months he must take care for himself: he is no responsibility of the landlord's. All he can hope to do is find work. This is hard, because there are a good many chronically unemployed in the towns, and they are more convenient to most openings for work and can at times be counted if they are needed; also there is no increase, during these two dead farming seasons, of other kinds of work to do. And so, with no more jobs open than at any other time of year, and with plenty of men already convenient to take them, the whole tenant population, hundreds and thousands in any locality, are desperately in need of work.

A landlord saves up certain odd jobs for these times of year: they go, at less than he would have to pay others, to those of his tenants who happen to live nearest or to those he thinks best of; and even at best they don't amount to much.

When there is wooded land on the farm, a landlord ordinarily permits a tenant to cut and sell firewood for what he can get. About the best a tenant gets of this is a dollar a load, but more often (for the market is glutted, so many are trying to sell wood) he can get no better than half that and less, and often enough, at the end of a hard day's peddling, miles from home, he will let it go for a quarter or fifteen cents rather than haul it all the way home again: so it doesn't amount to much. Then, too, by no means everyone has wood to cut and sell: in the whole southern half of the county we were working mainly in, there was so little wood that the negroes, during the hard winter of 1935–36, were burning parts of their fences, outbuildings, furniture and houses, and were dying off in great and not seriously counted numbers, of pneumonia and other afflictions of the lungs.

WPA work [Works Progress Administration: a federal agency offering employment to the jobless during the Great Depression] is available to very few tenants: they are, technically, employed, and thus have no right to it: and if by chance they manage to get it, landlords are more likely than not to intervene. They feel it spoils a tenant to be paid wages, even for a little while. A tenant who so much as tries to get such work is under disapproval.

There is not enough direct relief even for the widows and the old of the county.

Gudger and Ricketts, during this year, were exceedingly lucky. After they, and Woods, had been turned away from government work, they found work in a sawmill. They were given the work on condition that they stay with it until the mill was moved, and subject strictly to their landlords' permission: and their employer wouldn't so much as hint how long the work might last. Their landlords quite grudgingly gave them permission, on condition that they pay for whatever help was needed in their absence during the picking season. Gudger hired a hand, at eight dollars a month and board. Ricketts did not need to: his family was large enough. They got a dollar and a quarter a day five days a week and seventy-five cents on Saturday, seven dollars a week, ten hours' work a day. Woods did not even try for this work: he was too old and too sick.

REVIEWING THE READING

1. What chance do you think the sharecropper and tenant farmers had of ever being in a position to buy the land they worked? Explain your answer.

2. Why were most of the tenant farmers unable to get work on government projects?

3. **Using Your Historical Imagination.** In what way did the feelings of the landlords and the townspeople differ from those of the tenant farmers when the cotton was almost ready for picking?

49

From *The Grapes of Wrath* by John Steinbeck.

From Steinbeck's *The Grapes of Wrath* (1930s)

During the early 1920s, while business and industry in the United States was growing at a rapid pace, farming was one of the "sick industries" that did not prosper. When the overall economy of the country began to suffer during the Great Depression, things got even worse for the farmers. In the midst of all this, the farmers, especially those in the high plains states that reached from Texas and Oklahoma to South and North Dakota, were hit by an unrelenting drought that killed their crops and destroyed their land. By 1934 the drought became so bad that the soil turned to a powdery dust that was swept across the plains in choking black clouds. The region became known as the Dust Bowl.

Thousands of farmers, unable to earn a living, packed up their families and belongings in the family car and headed west to California, where they hoped to find work as migrant farmers. Author John Steinbeck wrote about them in his novel The Grapes of Wrath. *As you read the following excerpts from the book, try to determine how the families made their hard journey west more bearable.*

The Dust Bowl

The surface of the earth crusted, a thin hard crust, and as the sky became pale, so the earth became pale. . . .

And as the sharp sun struck day after day, the leaves of the young corn became less stiff and erect; they bent in a curve at first, and then, as the central ribs of strength grew weak, each leaf tilted downward. Then it was June, and the sun shone more fiercely.

The brown lines on the corn leaves widened and moved in on the central ribs. The weeds frayed and edged back toward their roots. The air was thin and the sky more pale; and every day the earth paled.

In the roads where the teams moved, where the wheels milled the ground and the hooves of the horses beat the ground, the dirt crust broke and the dust formed. Every moving thing lifted the dust into the air; a walking man lifted a thin layer as high as his waist, and a wagon lifted the dust as high as the fence tops, and an automobile boiled a cloud behind it. . . .

The dust from the roads fluffed up and spread out and fell on the weeds beside the fields, and fell into the fields a little way. Now the wind grew strong and hard and it worked at the rain crust in the corn fields. Little by little the sky was darkened by the mixing dust, and the wind felt over the earth, loosened the dust, and carried it away. The wind grew stronger. The rain crust broke and the dust lifted up out of the fields and drove gray plumes into the air like sluggish smoke. The corn threshed the wind and made a dry, rushing sound. The finest dust did not settle back to earth now, but disappeared into the darkening sky.

The dust from the roads fluffed up and spread out and fell on the weeds beside the fields . . .

The wind grew stronger, whisked under stones, carried up straws and old leaves, and even little clods, marking its course as it sailed across the fields. The air and the sky darkened and through them the sun shone redly, and there was a raw sting in the air. During a night the wind raced faster over the land, dug cunningly among the rootlets of the corn, and the corn fought the wind with its weakened leaves until the roots were freed by the prying wind and then each stalk settled wearily sideways toward the earth and pointed the direction of the wind.

The dawn came, but no day. In the gray sky a red sun appeared, a dim red circle that gave a little light, like dusk; and as that day advanced, the dusk slipped back toward darkness, and the wind cried and whimpered over the fallen corn.

Men and women huddled in their houses, and they tied handkerchiefs over their noses when they went out, and wore goggles to protect their eyes.

When the night came again it was black night, for the stars could not pierce the dust to get down, and the window lights could not even spread beyond their own yards. Now the dust was evenly mixed with the air, an emulsion [mixture] of dust and air. Houses were shut tight and cloth wedged around doors and windows, but the dust came in so thinly that it could not be seen in the air, and it settled like pollen on the chairs and tables, on the dishes. The people brushed it from their shoulders. Little lines of dust lay at the door sills.

In the middle of that night the wind passed on and left the land quiet. The dust-filled air muffled sound more completely than fog does. The people, lying in their beds, heard the wind stop. They awakened when the rushing wind was gone. They lay quietly and listened deep into the stillness. Then the roosters crowed, and their voices were muffled, and the people stirred restlessly in their beds and wanted the morning. They knew it would take a long time for the dust to settle out of the air. In the morning the dust hung like fog, and the sun was as red as ripe new blood. All day the dust sifted down from the sky, and the next day it sifted down. An even blanket covered the earth. It settled on the corn, piled up on the tops of the fence posts, piled up on the wires; it settled on roofs, blanketed the weeds and trees.

In the morning the dust hung like fog . . .

The Migration West

The cars of the migrant people crawled out of the side roads onto the great cross-country highway, and they took the migrant way to the West. In the daylight they scuttled like bugs to the westward; and as the dark caught them, they clustered like bugs near to shelter and to water. And because they were lonely and perplexed [confused], because they had all come from a place of sadness and worry and defeat, and because they huddled together; they talked together; they shared their lives, their food, and the things they hoped for in the new country. Thus it might be that one family camped near a spring, and another camped for the spring and for company, and a third because two families had pioneered the place and found it good. And when the sun went down, perhaps twenty families and twenty cars were there.

. . . they shared their lives, their food, and the things they hoped for in the new country.

In the evening a strange thing happened: the twenty families became one family, the children were the children of all. The loss of home became one loss, and the golden time in the West was one dream. And it might be that a sick child threw despair into the hearts of the twenty families, of a hundred people; that a birth there in a tent kept a hundred people quiet and awestruck through the night and filled a hundred people with birth-joy in the morning. A family which the night before had been lost and fearful might search its goods to find a present for a new baby. In the evening, sitting about the fires, the twenty were one. They grew to be units of the camps, units of the evenings and the nights. A guitar unwrapped from a blanket and tuned—and the songs, which were all of the people, were sung in the nights. Men sang the words, and women hummed the tunes.

Every night a world created, complete with furniture—friends made and enemies established; a world complete with braggarts and with cowards, with quiet men, and humble men, with kindly men. Every night relationships that make a world, established; and every morning the world torn down like a circus.

At first the families were timid in the building and tumbling worlds, but gradually the technique of building worlds became their technique. Then leaders emerged, then laws were made, then codes

This migrant farmer of the 1930s is having mechanical problems on the road. All his worldly possessions are on the car or in the trailer.

came into being. And as the worlds moved westward they were more complete and better furnished, for their builders were more experienced in building them.

The families learned what rights must be observed—the right of privacy in the tent; the right to keep the past black hidden in the heart; the right to talk and to listen; the right to refuse help or to accept, to offer help or to decline it; the right of son to court and daughter to be courted; the right of the hungry to be fed; the rights of the pregnant and the sick to transcend all other rights.

And the families learned, although no one told them, what rights are monstrous and must be destroyed: the right to intrude upon privacy, the right to be noisy while the camp slept, the right of seduction or rape, the right of adultery and theft and murder. These rights were crushed, because the little worlds could not exist for even a night with such rights alive.

And as the worlds moved westward, rules became laws, although no one told the families. It is unlawful to foul near the camp; it is unlawful in any way to foul the drinking water; it is unlawful to eat good rich food near one who is hungry, unless he is asked to share.

And with the laws, the punishments—and there were only two—a quick and murderous fight or ostracism [banishment]; and ostracism was the worst. For, if one broke the laws his name and face went with him, and he had no place in any world, no matter where created.

In the worlds, social conduct became fixed and rigid, so that a man must say "Good morning" when asked for it. . . .

The families moved westward, and the technique of building the worlds improved so that the people could be safe in their worlds; and the form was so fixed that a family acting in the rules knew it was safe in the rules.

There grew up government in the worlds, with leaders, with elders. A man who was wise found that his wisdom was needed in every camp; a man who was a fool could not change his folly with his world. And a kind of insurance developed in these nights. A man with food fed a hungry man, and thus insured himself against hunger. And when a baby died a pile of silver coins grew at the door flap, for a baby must be well buried, since it has had nothing else of life. An old man may be left in a potter's field [public burial place for the poor], but not a baby.

A certain physical pattern is needed for the building of a world—water, a river bank, a stream, a spring, or even a faucet unguarded. And there is needed enough flat land to pitch the tents, a little brush or wood to build fires. If there is a garbage dump not too far off, all the better; for there can be found equipment—stove tops, a curved fender to shelter the fire, and cans to cook in and to eat from.

And the worlds were built in the evening. The people, moving in from the highways, made them with their tents and their hearts and their brains.

In the morning the tents came down, the canvas was folded, the tent poles tied along the running board, the beds put in place on the cars, the pots in their places. And as the families moved westward, the technique of building up a home in the evening and tearing it down with the morning light became fixed; so that the folded tent was packed in one place, the cooking pots counted in their box. And as the cars moved westward, each member of the family grew into his proper place, grew into his duties; so that each member, old and young, had his place in the car; so that in the weary, hot evenings, when the cars pulled into the camping places, each member had his duty and went to it without instruction: children to gather wood, to carry water; men to pitch the tents and bring down the beds; women to cook the supper and to watch while the family fed. And this was done without command. The families, which had been units of which the boundaries were a house at night, a farm by day, changed their boundaries. In the long hot light, they were silent in the cars moving slowly westward; but at night they integrated with any group they found.

Thus they changed their social life—changed as in the whole universe only man can change. They were not farm men any more, but migrant men. And the thought, the planning, the long staring silence that had gone out to the fields, went now to the roads, to the distance, to the West. That man whose mind had been bound with acres lived with narrow concrete miles. And his thought and his worry were not any more with rainfall, with wind and dust, with the thrust of the crops. Eyes watched the tires, ears listened to the clattering motors, and minds

. . . **They were not farm men any more, but migrant men.**

struggled with oil, with gasoline, with the thinning rubber between air and road. Then a broken gear was tragedy. Then water in the evening was the yearning, and food over the fire. Then health to go on was the need and strength to go on, and spirit to go on. The wills thrust westward ahead of them, and fears that had once apprehended drought or flood now lingered with anything that might stop the westward crawling.

REVIEWING THE READING

1. What things did the migrant families do to make their journey west more bearable?

2. What happened to those who broke the laws set up by the migrants?

3. **Using Your Historical Imagination.** Of all the changes in their lives the migrant families had to make, which do you think may have been the most difficult for them? Explain your answer.

50
From *F.D.R. My Boss* by
Grace Tully.

The Japanese Attack Pearl Harbor (1941)

By December 1941, World War II had been raging in Europe, Asia, and Africa for more than two years. Americans, many of whom still opposed United States involvement in the war, watched with fear as Germany and its allies, Italy and Japan, grew more and more aggressive.

One special concern was Japanese aggression in East Asia and the western Pacific. In the summer of 1941, after Japan threatened to attack the Dutch East Indies, Roosevelt froze all Japanese assets in the United States and cut off all oil shipments to Japan, a devastating blow to the Japanese, who imported 80 percent of their oil from the United States. The United States then demanded that Japan remove its troops from China and Indochina. The country braced itself for almost certain retaliation from Japan.

Early Sunday morning, December 7, 1941, hundreds of Japanese planes took off from aircraft carriers in the Pacific Ocean, headed for the American naval base at Pearl Harbor in Hawaii. At 7:55 A.M. the planes attacked the American base. Grace Tully, a private secretary of President Roosevelt, recalls the reaction of the White House when news of the attack reached Washington. As you read the following excerpt from Tully's book about her boss, try to determine the greatest fear of those gathered in the White House that Sunday afternoon.

O n Sunday afternoon I was resting, trying to relax from the grind of the past weeks and to free my mind from the concern caused by the very grave tones in which the President dictated that Saturday night message. I was rather abstractedly looking at a Sunday paper when the telephone rang and Louise Hackmeister said sharply:

"The President wants you right away. There's a car on the way to pick you up. The Japs just bombed Pearl Harbor!"

With no more words and without time for me to make a single remark, she cut off the connection. She had a long list of people to notify. In twenty minutes I was drawing into the White House driveway, already swarming with extra police and an added detail of Secret Service men, with news and radio reporters beginning to stream into the Executive Office wing and State, War and Navy officials hurrying into the House. Hopkins [presidential assistant Harry Hopkins], Knox [Secretary of the Navy Frank Knox] and Stimson [Secretary of War Henry Stimson] already were with the Boss [President Roosevelt] in his second floor study; Hull [Secretary of State Cordell Hull] and General [George] Marshall arrived a few minutes later.

Most of the news on the Jap attack was then coming to the White House by telephone from Admiral Stark, Chief of Naval Operations, at the Navy Department. It was my job to take these fragmentary and shocking reports from him by shorthand, type them up and relay them to the Boss. I started taking the calls on a telephone in the second floor hall but the noise and confusion were such that I moved into the President's bedroom.

General Watson, Admiral McIntire, Captain Beardall, the Naval Aide, and Marvin McIntyre were on top of me as I picked up each phone call and they followed me as I rushed into Malvina Thompson's tiny office to type each message. All of them crowded over my shoulders as I transcribed each note. The news was shattering. I hope I shall never again experience the anguish and near hysteria of that afternoon.

Coding and decoding operations in Hawaii and in Washington slowed up the transmission. But the

. . . I hope I shall never again experience the anguish . . . of that afternoon.

The news of the Japanese attack on Pearl Harbor naval base surprised and stunned citizens of the United States.

news continued to come in, each report more terrible than the last, and I could hear the shocked unbelief in Admiral Stark's voice as he talked to me. At first the men around the President were incredulous [skeptical]; that changed to angry acceptance as new messages supported and amplified the previous ones. The Boss maintained greater outward calm than anybody else but there was rage in his very calmness. With each new message he shook his head grimly and tightened the expression of his mouth.

Within the first thirty or forty minutes a telephone circuit was opened from the White House to Governor Joseph B. Poindexter in Honolulu. The Governor confirmed the disastrous news insofar as he had learned it. In the middle of the conversation he almost shrieked into the phone and the President turned to the group around him to bark grimly:

"My God, there's another wave of Jap planes over Hawaii right this minute."

Mr. Hull, his face as white as his hair, reported to the Boss that Nomura and Kurusu [diplomatic representatives of Japan] were waiting to see him at the exact moment the President called to tell him of the bombing. In a tone as cold as ice he repeated what he had told the enemy envoys and there was nothing cold or diplomatic in the words he used. Knox, whose Navy had suffered the worst damage, and Stimson were cross-examined closely on what had happened, on why they believed it could have happened, on what might happen next and on what they could do to repair to some degree the disaster.

Within the first hour it was evident that the Navy was dangerously crippled, that the Army and Air Force were not fully prepared to guarantee safety from further shattering setbacks in the Pacific. It was easy to speculate that a Jap invasion force might be following their air strike at Hawaii—or that the West Coast itself might be marked for similar assault.

Orders were sent to the full Cabinet to assemble at the White House at 8:30 that evening and for Congressional leaders of both parties to be on hand by 9:00 for a joint conference with the Executive group.

Shortly before 5:00 o'clock the Boss called me to his study. He was alone, seated before his desk on which were two or three neat piles of notes containing the information of the past two hours. The telephone was close by his hand. He was wearing a gray sack jacket and was lighting a cigarette as I entered the room. He took a deep drag and addressed me calmly:

"Sit down, Grace. I'm going before Congress tomorrow. I'd like to dictate my message. It will be short."

I sat down without a word; it was no time for words other than those to become part of the war effort.

Once more he inhaled deeply, then he began in the same calm tone in which he dictated his mail. Only his diction was a little different as he spoke each word incisively and slowly, carefully specifying each punctuation mark and paragraph.

"Yesterday comma December 7 comma 1941 dash a day which will live in infamy dash the United States of America was suddenly and deliberately attacked by naval and air forces of the Empire of Japan period paragraph."

The entire message ran under 500 words, a cold-blooded indictment of Japanese treachery and aggression, delivered to me without hesitation, interruption or second thoughts.

"I ask," he concluded, "that the Congress declare that since the unprovoked and dastardly attack by Japan on Sunday comma December 7 comma a state of war has existed between the United States and the Japanese Empire period end."

As soon as I transcribed it, the President called Hull back to the White House and went over the draft. The Secretary brought with him an alternate message drafted by Sumner Welles, longer and more comprehensive in its review of the circumstances leading to the state of war. It was rejected by the Boss and hardly a word of his own historic declaration was altered. Harry Hopkins added the next to the last sentence: "With confidence in our armed forces— with the unbounded determination of our people— we will gain the inevitable triumph—so help us God."

REVIEWING THE READING

1. What do you think those people gathered in the White House feared might happen next?

2. How serious was the damage done to the fleet at Pearl Harbor?

3. **Using Your Historical Imagination.** In the early years of the war—from 1939 to the time of the attack in 1941—many Americans were strongly opposed to the United States entering the war. How do you think most of these people reacted after they heard about the attack? Why would most Americans be particularly concerned that the attack had taken place in Hawaii?

A Hawaiian American in the Pacific War (1940s)

51

From *"The Good War"*: An Oral History of World War Two by Studs Terkel.

If you ask any American who was alive in 1941 where he or she was on December 7 when the news reports came out about the Japanese attack on Pearl Harbor, you can be sure that person will remember. This is especially true of Hawaiians who lived through the nightmare. They were there to see the results of the bombing: 21 American warships damaged, disabled, or sunk; 177 planes destroyed; more than 2,300 Americans killed and more than 1,000 others injured. A large number of Hawaiians—many of Japanese ancestry—were also injured or killed. As you read these excerpts from one Hawaiian's account of the bombing, from an oral history of the war, think about what it must have been like at Pearl Harbor immediately following the attack.

I was sixteen years old, employed as a pipe fitter apprentice at Pearl Harbor Navy Yard. On December 7, 1941, oh, around 8:00 A.M., my grandmother awoke me. She informed me that the Japanese were bombing Pearl Harbor. I said, "They're just practicing." She said, no, it was real and the announcer is requesting that all Pearl Harbor workers report to work. I went out on the porch and I could see the anti-aircraft fire up in the sky. I just said, "Oh, boy."

I was four miles away. I got out on my motorcycle and it took me, five, ten minutes to get there. It was a mess.

I was working on the U.S.S. *Shaw*. It was on a floating dry dock. It was in flames. I started to go

A boat rescues survivors from the burning battleship USS West Virginia *during the attack on Pearl Harbor.*

down into the pipe fitter's shop to get my toolbox when another wave of Japanese came in. I got under a set of concrete steps at the dry dock where the battleship *Pennsylvania* was. An officer came by and asked me to go into the *Pennsylvania* and try to get the fires out. A bomb had penetrated the marine deck, and that was three decks below. Under that

was the magazines: ammunition, powder, shells. I
said, "There ain't no way I'm gonna go down there."
It could blow up any minute. I was young and sixteen,
not stupid, not at sixty-two cents an hour. (Laughs.)

A week later, they brought me before a navy
court. It was determined that I was not service personnel and could not be ordered. There was no martial
law [military rule] at the time. Because I was sixteen
and had gone into the water, the whole thing was
dropped.

I was asked by some other officer to go into
the water and get sailors out that had been blown
off the ships. Some were unconscious, some were
dead. So I spent the rest of the day swimming inside
the harbor, along with some other Hawaiians. I
brought out I don't know how many bodies and
how many were alive and how many dead. Another
man would put them into ambulances and they'd
be gone. We worked all day at that.

That evening, I drove a truckload of marines
into Palolo Valley because someone reported that
the Japanese had parachuted down there. Because
of the total blackout, none of the marine drivers
knew how to get there. It was two miles away. There
were no parachuters. Someone in the valley had
turned their lights on and the marines started shootin'
at that house. The lights went out. (Laughs.)

I went back to my concrete steps to spend
the night there. Someone on the *Pennsylvania* was
walking along the edge of the armored plate. He
lit a cigarette. All of a sudden, a lot of guns opened
up on him. I don't know if he was hit.

The following morning, I went with my tools
to the *West Virginia*. It had turned turtle, totally upside
down. We found a number of men inside. The *Arizona*
was a total washout. Also the *Utah*. There were men
in there, too. We spent about a month cutting the
superstructure of the *West Virginia*, tilting it back
on its hull. About three hundred men we cut out
of there were still alive by the eighteenth day.

It took two weeks to get all the fires out.

How did they survive? [asked the interviewer]
I don't know. We were too busy to ask. (Laughs.)
It took two weeks to get all the fires out. We worked
around the clock for three days. There was so much
excitement and confusion. Some of our sailors were
shooting five-inch guns at the Japanese planes. You
just cannot down a plane with a five-inch shell. They
were landing in Honolulu, the unexploding naval
shells. They have a ten-mile range. They hurt and
killed a lot of people in the city.

When I came back after the third day, they
told me that a shell had hit the house of my girl.
We had been going together for, oh, about three
years. Her house was a few blocks from my place.
At the time, they said it was a Japanese bomb. Later
we learned it was an American shell. She was killed.
She was preparing for church at the time.

My neighbors met me. They were mostly Japanese. We all started to cry. We had no idea what
was happening, what was going to happen.

Martial law had been set in. Everyone had to
work twelve hours, six to six. No one on the streets
after 6:00 P.M. No one on the streets before 6:00
A.M. The military took over the islands completely.
If you failed to go to work, the police would be at
your door and you were arrested. You had to do
something, filling sandbags, anything. No one was
excused. If you called in sick, a nurse would come
to your house to check on you. If you failed to be
there or were goofing off, you went to jail. All civil
liberties were suspended.

There was no act of treason by anyone that I
know of. There were spies, but they were all employed by the Japanese embassy. If they had arrested
the ordinary Japanese, there would be no work force
at Pearl Harbor. There were 130,000 Japanese on
the islands. There'd be no stores, no hotels, nothing.
You'd have to shut the city down. They suffered a
lot of insults, especially by the servicemen. They
took it without coming back.

I tried to get in the military, but they refused. They considered my work essential for the war effort. I was promoted to shop fitter and went from $32 a week to $125. But I kept trying for a year to get in the fight. Finally, I wrote a letter to President Roosevelt. I told him I was angry at the Japanese bombing and had lost some friends. He okayed that I be accepted. I went into the service and went down to $21 a month. (Laughs.)

My grandmother signed for me because I was only seventeen. She said she would never see me alive again. It turned out prophetic because she died one day before I got home. January 1946.

They wanted to send me to Texas for training. I got on the stick and wrote to the President again. I wasn't interested in Texas, I wanted to go into combat. I got an answer from the White House requesting that I be put into a combat outfit. I got thirty days washing dishes for not following the chain of command. (Laughs.)

"When I went into the military, they asked, 'What race are you?' I had no idea what they were talking about because in Hawaii we don't question a man's race. They said, 'Where are your parents from?' I said they were born in Hawaii. 'Your grandparents?' They were born in Hawaii. 'How about your great-grandparents?' I said they're from Europe, some from Spain, some from Wales. They said, 'You're Caucasian.' I said, 'What's that?' They said, 'You're white.' I looked at my skin. I was pretty dark, tanned by the sun. I said, 'You're kidding.' (Laughs.) They put me down as Caucasian and separated me from the rest of the Hawaiians. . . ."

I joined the Seventh Infantry Division in time for the run to Kwajalein in the Marshall Islands. It took six days to take it. We went back to Hawaii. I don't know what we were preparing for, but we practiced and practiced and practiced swimming, some other Hawaiians and me. I said, "Eleanor [Roosevelt] must be coming here." I was taken to the FBI in Honolulu and asked how did I know the

President was coming." I said, "Yeah, I just figured somebody important was coming because we've been practicing this show for two months." They said, "Okay, keep your mouth shut."

All of a sudden one day they told us there'd be a swimming show. We threw oil in the water, set the water on fire, and dove into it. They told us to get dressed and get ready for the parade. We were all searched for ammunition. Not one could have ammunition in his rifle, no pocket knives. But we had bayonets. (Laughs.) As we went past the parade stand, we saw General MacArthur and President Roosevelt.

We knew something was up but we didn't know where we were gonna go. A rumor came down that we were going into Africa after Rommel [General Edwin Rommel, commander in chief of German forces in Africa during the war]. The main body of the Seventh had trained in the Mojave Desert, but was sent to the Aleutians. They had figured on Africa. So we thought for sure it was Africa for us. We got orders for the Pacific. They said Yap.

"I had been made a sergeant by this time because we were given jungle training and I knew the tropics. So they sent me to Alaska. (Laughs.) After three weeks, they had to send me back because I was shaking. It was too . . . . cold. (Laughs.)"

Several nights later, a broadcast came from Tokyo Rose. "Good evening, men of the Seventh Infantry. I know you're on your way to the Philippines."

Several nights later, a broadcast came from Tokyo Rose [woman who broadcasted propaganda messages over the radio from Japan to U.S. troops in the South Pacific]: "Good evening, men of the Seventh Infantry. I know you're on your way to the Philippines." She was right. (Laughs.) We were there from October of '44 until March of '45. Totally combat.

I fought very carefully, I fought low. There were a couple of Japanese boys, our interpreters, who were a little bit heroic. They would climb on board a Japanese tank going by, knock on the things, converse in Japanese, and as soon as the door popped open, they'd drop a hand grenade—boom!

Our next stop was Okinawa. We landed there on April 1, '45. No opposition. Several days later, we got word that President Roosevelt had died. We were all sort of down—boom! They said a man called Truman replaced him. I said, "Who is Truman?" We were there eighty-two days. I did what I had to do. When I saw a Japanese, I shot at him and ducked. Shot and ducked, that's all I did. I was always scared until we took Hill 87. . . .

I was a policeman for fifteen years in Washington, D.C. When I was involved in a hostage situation, I just waited. Eventually, the person gave up. There's no need to be playing gung ho and going in there with guns blazing. I worked always in black neighborhoods. I would not shoot. I would talk and talk and talk. In one instance, there were three men holed up. I took off my gun and I went in. I said, "You guys can kill me, but you're not gonna walk out of here because there's a lot of men waiting for you. You can give me your gun and walk out and do some time, but you're not gonna do it inside of a box." They said, "Man, you're crazy." I said, "I don't think you are." All three of them gave me the gun, and we walked out. It's just that I'm not a killer.

REVIEWING THE READING

1. What evidence of widespread panic does the Hawaiian relate taking place in Hawaii immediately following the attack?

2. What did the Hawaiian have to do to get into active service during the war?

3. **Using Your Historical Imagination.** The Hawaiian tells of his experience after the war as a policeman in Washington, D.C. How do you think his war experience helped him to be a better police officer?

52

From *The Homefront: America During World War II* by Mark Jonathan Harris.

Margaret Takahashi Describes the Internment of Japanese Americans (1942)

Following the Japanese attack on Pearl Harbor in December 1941, many Americans began to suspect the loyalty of the more than 100,000 Japanese Americans who lived on the West Coast. The majority of these Japanese Americans had been born in the United States, and most were United States citizens. By early 1942, however, prejudice and persistent rumors of their possible involvement in sabotage and spying had grown so strong that the government ordered all those of Japanese descent to give up their homes and property and be moved to internment camps. Some Japanese Americans stayed at the camps for just a brief period of time, but others remained in the camps until early 1945 when they were allowed to return to the West Coast.

In the following selection from a book on America during World War II, Margaret Takahashi, a Japanese American, discusses being sent to an internment camp. As you read the excerpts from Takahashi's account, think about what life must have been like for her before the internment order came.

After Pearl Harbor we [Japanese Americans] started to get worried because the newspapers were agitating and printing all those stories all the time. And people were getting angrier. You kept hearing awful rumors. You heard that people were

getting their houses burned down and we were afraid that those things might happen to us. . . . You didn't know when the blow was going to fall, or what was going to happen. You didn't quite feel that you could settle down to anything. Your whole future seemed in question. The longer the war dragged on, the worse the feeling got.

When the evacuation order finally came I was relieved. Lots of people were relieved, because you were taken care of. You wouldn't have all this worry. . . .

You could only take one suitcase apiece, but people who had gone to camp before us were able to tell us what to bring, so we were a little better off than others. My husband bought foot lockers, so our luggage was pretty big and we took sheets and things that the other people hadn't taken. . . .

The day we were taken to camp we had to go to a special designated place to get the bus.

With the children already tagged by United States officials, the Mochida family awaits evacuation to an internment camp for Japanese Americans in 1942.

This friend of ours took me and the baby so that we wouldn't have to walk. Most people just walked. We got on the bus and everybody was just sitting there, and I was thinking, Gee, everybody's so brave, nobody's crying, and I wasn't going to cry either, because Japanese frown on weakness, so I wouldn't look at anybody. And then [a woman] came up and looked in the bus window and she said, "Oh, look at the poor thing, she has a tiny baby." And then I started to bawl, and I bawled the whole way to camp. I felt like a fool, because nobody else cried. They didn't even cry when I cried. . . .

When I think back to the internment camp, I want to call it a concentration camp, but it wasn't. We have a neighbor who escaped from Auschwitz [German concentration camp] during the war, and there's no comparison. In our life it was only four months, and that's not long.

But the evacuation did change our philosophy. It made you feel that you knew what it was to die, to go somewhere you couldn't take anything but what you had inside you. And so it strengthened you. I think from then on we were very strong. I don't think anything could get us down now.

REVIEWING THE READING

1. What were Takahashi's feelings in the months before the internment order came?

2. According to Takahashi, why did most of the people on the bus show no emotion about being sent to the camp?

3. **Using Your Historical Imagination.** What types of stories do you think the newspapers were printing that caused the Japanese American community to be so upset?

An Army Nurse at Bataan and Corregidor (1942)

From *History in the Writing* by Gordon Carroll.

Within hours of their surprise attack on Pearl Harbor, the Japanese had moved on to the Philippines. They bombed and destroyed more than half of the American planes caught on the ground. Japanese troops soon followed with a land invasion. Within a month, American and Filipino troops were pushed back to the Bataan Peninsula and the adjacent island fortress of Corregidor. The troops fought bravely, but they were forced to surrender in April 1942. Corregidor, the last U.S. stronghold in the Philippines, fell a month later. As you read one army nurse's account of those dark days, try to determine why she and the others believed they were safe from future Japanese air attacks.

Conditions at Hospital Number 1 were not too good during the last few weeks we spent there. Patients were flooding in. We increased from 400 to 1,500 cases in two weeks' time. Most were bad shrapnel [shell fragments] wounds, but nine out of ten patients had malaria or dysentery besides. One night we admitted 400 patients, most in worse condition than usual. They'd been left at first-aid stations near the front because of the shortage of gasoline.

We were out of quinine [medicine for malaria]. There were hundreds of gas gangrene [dying body tissue filled with gas] cases, and our supply of vaccine had gone months before. There was no more sulfapyridine or sulfanilimide [drugs used to kill harmful bacteria]. There weren't nearly enough cots so triple-decker beds were built from bamboo, with a ladder at one end so we could climb up to take care of the patients, who were without blankets or mattresses.

There was almost no food but carabao [water buffalo]. We had all thought we couldn't go carabao, but we did. Then came mule, which seemed worse, but we ate that too. Most of the nurses were wearing Government-issue heavy-laced men's shoes. We had to keep our feet taped up to walk in them. Our uniforms had been gone for a long time, so we mostly wore size 32 Air Corps coveralls. We carried steel helmets and gas masks even in the wards, but it was an automatic gesture. We didn't expect to use them.

We went about our work feeling perfectly safe because of the Red Cross roof markings.

We went about our work feeling perfectly safe because of the Red Cross roof markings. When bombers came overhead on April 4, we hardly noticed them. Then suddenly incendiary [fire] bombs dropped. They hit the receiving wards, mess hall, doctors' and officers' quarters, and the steps of the nurses' dormitory, setting fire to all buildings but luckily not hitting the wards. One officer had been confined to quarters with malaria; he was walking outside for the first time when the planes came over. A bomb hit near his bed. Several enlisted personnel wandering outside were killed. The patients were terrified, of course, but behaved well. The Japanese prisoners were perhaps the most frightened of all. Everything was a blur of taking care of patients, putting out fires, straightening overturned equipment.

We remained frightened until two hours later when someone heard the Jap radio in Manila announce that the bombings had been an accident and wouldn't happen again. So after that, we couldn't even leave the hospital for a short drive. We felt safe there and nowhere else.

Life at the hospital went on just the same, perhaps even busier. There was no time off except 30 minutes for two meals a day. Commanding Officer Col. James Duckworth was fine. He announced calmly that no matter how long we had to work, we weren't working as hard as the boys in the front lines. "We're all in the Army. Let's carry on!" he said.

The morning of April 7 we were all on duty when a wave of bombers came over. The first bomb hit the Filipino mess hall and knocked us down before we even knew planes were overhead. An ammunition truck was passing the hospital entrance. It got a direct hit. The boys on guard at the gate were shell-shocked, smothered in the dirt thrown up by the explosion.

Convalescent patients picked us up and we began caring for men hurt by shrapnel. Everything was terror and confusion. Patients, even amputation cases, were falling and rolling out of the triple-decker beds to run. Suddenly a chaplain, Father Cummings, came into the ward, threw up his hands for silence and said: "All right, boys, everything's all right. Just stay quietly in bed, or lie still on the floor. Let us pray." The screams stopped instantly. He began the prayer just as a second wave of planes came over.

The first bomb hit near the officers' quarters, the next struck the patients' mess [dining hall] just a few yards away. The concussion bounced us three feet off the cement floor and threw us down again. Beds were tumbling down. Flashes of heat and smoke burned our eyes. But through it all we could hear Father Cummings' voice reciting the Lord's Prayer. He never faltered, never even fell to the ground,

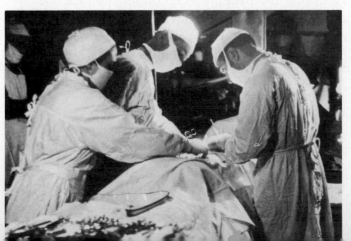

A nurse assists doctors operating in an army field hospital in the jungles of Bataan in 1942.

and the patients never moved. Father Cummings'
clear voice went through to the end. Then he turned
quietly and said: "All right, you take over. Put a
tourniquet on my arm, will you?" And we saw for
the first time that he'd been badly hit by shrapnel.

The next few hours were a nightmare . . .

The next few hours were a nightmare, except
for the way everyone behaved. We were afraid to
move, but realized we had to get to work. One
little Filipino with both legs amputated—he'd never
gotten out of bed before by himself—rolled onto
the ground and said: "Miss, are you all right, are
you all right?" The ward boys all told us, "You go
on outside—don't stay here any longer. We'll take
care of everything." We tried to care first for the
patients most seriously hurt. A great many all over
the hospital were bleeding badly. We went to where
the bomb had hit the ward and began pulling patients
from the crater. I saw Rosemary Hogan, head ward
nurse, and thought for a moment her face had been
torn off. She wiped herself with a sheet, smiled and
said: "It's nothing, don't bother about me. Just a
nose bleed." But she had three shrapnel wounds.

It would be hard to believe the bravery after
that bombing if you hadn't seen it. An enlisted man
had risked his life by going directly to the traction
wards where patients were tied to beds by wires.
He thought it was better to hurt the men temporarily
than to leave them tied helpless above ground where
they'd surely be hit by shrapnel, so he cut all tractions
and told the patients: "Get under the bed, Joe."

We began immediately to evacuate patients to
another hospital. We were so afraid the Japanese
would be back again the next day that even the
most serious cases were moved, because giving them
any chance was better than none. Everyone went—
orthopedic, surgical, medical cases. There were only
100 left the next morning and every patient was
clean and comfortable. We worked all that day making up beds to admit new patients. It never occurred
to anyone that we wouldn't go on as usual. Suddenly,

after dark, we were told we were leaving in 15 minutes—that we should pack only what we could carry. Then we heard the Japanese had broken through and the Battle of Bataan was over. The doctors all decided to stay with the patients, even doctors who had been told to go to Corregidor.

We left the hospital at 9 that night—got to Corregidor at 3 in the morning. The trip usually took a little over an hour. As we drove down to the docks, the roads were jammed. Soldiers were tired, aimless, frightened. Cars were overturned; there were bodies in the road. Clouds of dust made it hard to breathe. At midnight on the docks we heard the Japs had burned our hospital to the ground.

Bombers were overhead, but we were too tired to care. We waited on the docks while the Navy tunnel and ammunition dump at Mariveles were blown up. Blasting explosions, blue flares, red flares, shrapnel, tracers, gasoline exploding—it was like a hundred Fourths of July and Christmases all at once, but we were too frightened to be impressed. As we crossed the water with Corregidor's big guns firing over our heads and shells from somewhere landing close by, the boat suddenly shivered and the whole ocean seemed to rock. We thought a big shell had hit the water in front of us—it wasn't until we landed that we found an earthquake had come just as Bataan fell.

Corregidor seemed like heaven that night. They fed us and we slept, two to an Army cot. We went to work the following morning. Everyone was thoughtful, wonderful. Col. Chester Elmes of the Quartermaster's Corps called us in and said: "I'm going to dress you up. Woo Lee, bring the tape measure." For the first time we had tailor-made overalls that fit.

Months before, patients on Corregidor had filled a few laterals [single beds] only. Now they were in double-decker beds all along the halls and in the main tunnel. There was constant bombing and shelling—sometimes concussion from a bomb outside would knock people down at the opposite end of the tunnel. Emperor Hirohito's birthday, April 29th, was a specially bad day. The bombing began at 7:30 a.m. and never stopped. Shelling was heavy; soldiers counted over 100 explosions per minute. Dive bombers were going after the gun on the hill directly above our heads and the concussion inside was terrific.

Most of the patients were shrapnel cases, but many had malaria and dysentery too. One night 250 patients passed through the hospital for treatment of meat poisoning—they were deathly ill but soon recovered. There were two in each bed, vomiting everywhere. But the worst night on Corregidor was when a bomb lit outside the tunnel entrance on the China Sea side. A crowd had gone outside for a cigarette and many were sleeping on the ground at the foot of the cliff. When the first shell hit nearby, they ran for the tunnel, but the iron gate was shut and it opened outward. As more shells landed, they smashed men against the gate and twisted off arms and legs. All nurses got up and went back to work—surgery was overflowing until 5:30 in the morning. There were many amputations.

Through all those weeks on Corregidor everyone was grand.

Through all those weeks on Corregidor everyone was grand. At 6 o'clock in the evening, after the usual bombing and shelling, 21 of us were told we were leaving Corregidor by plane with 10 pounds of luggage apiece. We don't know how we were selected. Everyone wanted to leave, of course, but morale was splendid. Everyone realized the end was getting close, but none gave up hope.

All Corregidor was under shell fire. We waited for an hour on the dock while medical supplies were unloaded from two seaplanes. Then we went out to the planes in motorboats. The pilot hustled us aboard—said to pile in quickly, not to bother to find seats. He was anxious to get off because we were between Cavite and Corregidor, directly in range of artillery. On that trip we almost skimmed water.

There was so much fog over Mindanao that we had to make a forced landing. A hole broke in the bottom of the ship and water came through. But we did reach the scheduled lake when the fog lifted. They had breakfast ready for us there in Mindanao. Some of us had champagne for the first time since the war started, but scrambled eggs, pineapple and pancakes were also the first we had seen since December. People on Mindanao were just as courageous as those on Corregidor and Bataan. They knew they would be trapped but cheerfully wished us a good trip and happy landings.

At dusk we left for Australia. We had to throw our luggage overboard, and even then the plane barely got off. There is no joy in escaping when all one's best friends are prisoners or dead. But we reached Australia dirty, tired, dressed in overalls we'd worn for four days.

Now we're safe, but the only reaction we notice is wanting to make up somehow, anyhow, for those who didn't get away.

REVIEWING THE READING

1. What two reasons did the nurse have for believing, even after the first air attack on the hospital at Bataan, that the hospital was safe from future Japanese attack?

2. In addition to battle wounds, what other medical problems led to the overload in the hospitals at Bataan and Corregidor?

3. **Using Your Historical Imagination.** What conflicting emotions did the army nurse have after being evacuated from the Philippines? How did she and the others hope to resolve their feelings?

54

From *Hiroshima* by John Hersey.

John Hersey Records the Japanese Experience of Hiroshima (1945)

By the summer of 1945, the Allies had defeated Hitler's Germany. Only the defeat of the Japanese stood in the way of finally ending the long, costly war. The United States had a new weapon—the atomic bomb— and no one knew just how deadly it really was. Only President Harry S Truman could make the decision to use it. Faced with the knowledge that the Japanese would fight to the very end, and knowing that thousands more Americans would die by continuing to fight a conventional war, Truman made that difficult decision that would open the door to the atomic age. On the morning of August 6, 1945, the United States dropped the atomic bomb on Hiroshima, Japan. As you read the following excerpt from writer John Hersey's account of Hiroshima that fateful morning, think about the unknowing decisions made by the Reverend Mr. Tanimoto that allowed him to survive the blast.

The Reverend Mr. Tanimoto got up at five o'clock that morning. He was alone in the parsonage, because for some time his wife had been commuting with their year-old baby to spend nights with a friend in Ushida, a suburb to the north. Of all the important cities of Japan, only two, Kyoto and Hiroshima, had not been visited in strength by *B-san*, or Mr. B., as the Japanese, with a mixture of respect and unhappy familiarity, called the B-29 [bomber]; and Mr. Tanimoto, like all his neighbors and friends, was almost sick with anxiety. He had heard uncomfortably detailed accounts of mass raids on Kure, Iwakuni, Tokuyama, and other nearby towns; he was sure Hiroshima's turn would come soon. He had slept badly the night before, because there had been several air raid warnings. Hiroshima had been getting such warnings almost every night for weeks, for at that time the B-29s were using Lake Biwa, northeast of Hiroshima, as a rendezvous point, and no matter what city the Americans planned to hit, the Superfortresses streamed in over the coast near Hiroshima. The frequency of the warnings and the continued abstinence of Mr. B with respect to Hiroshima had made its citizens jittery; a rumor was going around that the Americans were saving something special for the city.

Mr. Tanimoto is a small man, quick to talk, laugh, and cry. He wears his black hair parted in the middle and rather long; the prominence of the frontal lobes just above his eyebrows and the smallness of his mustache, mouth, and chin give him a strange, old-young look, boyish and yet wise, weak and yet fiery. He moves nervously and fast, but with a restraint which suggests that he is a cautious, thoughtful man. He showed, indeed, just those qualities in the uneasy days before the bomb fell. Besides having his wife spend the nights in Ushida, Mr. Tanimoto has been carrying all the portable things from his church, in the close-packed residential district called Nagaragawa, to a house that belonged to a rayon manufacturer in Koi, two miles from the center of town. The rayon man, a Mr. Matsui, had opened his then unoccupied estate to a large number of his friends and acquaintances, so that they might evacuate whatever they wished to a safe distance from the probable target area. Mr. Tanimoto had had no difficulty in moving chairs, hymnals, Bibles, altar gear, and church records by pushcart himself, but the organ console and an upright piano required some aid. A friend of his named Matsuo had, the day before, helped him get the piano out to Koi;

in return, he had promised this day to assist Mr. Matsuo in hauling out a daughter's belongings. That is why he had risen so early.

Mr. Tanimoto cooked his own breakfast. He felt awfully tired. The effort of moving the piano the day before, a sleepless night, weeks of worry and unbalanced diet, the cares of his parish—all combined to make him feel hardly adequate to the new day's work. There was another thing, too: Mr. Tanimoto had studied theology in Atlanta, Georgia; he had graduated in 1940; he spoke excellent English; he dressed in American clothes; he had corresponded with many American friends right up to the time the war began; and among a people obsessed with a fear of being spied upon—perhaps most obsessed himself—he found himself growing increasingly uneasy. The police had questioned him several times, and just a few days before, he had heard that an influential acquaintance, a Mr. Tanaka, a retired officer of the Toyo Kisen Kaisha steamship line, an anti-Christian, a man famous in Hiroshima for his showy philanthropies and notorious for his personal tyrannies, had been telling people that Tanimoto should not be trusted. In compensation, to show himself publicly a good Japanese, Mr. Tanimoto had taken on the chairmanship of his local *tonarigumi*, or Neighborhood Association, and to his other duties and concerns this position had added the business of organizing air raid defense for about twenty families.

Before six o'clock that morning, Mr. Tanimoto started for Mr. Matsuo's house. There he found that their burden was to be a *tansu*, a large Japanese cabinet, full of clothing and household goods. The two men set out. The morning was perfectly clear and so warm that the day promised to be uncomfortable. A few minutes after they started, the air raid siren went off—a minute-long blast that warned of approaching planes but indicated to the people of Hiroshima only a slight degree of danger, since it sounded every morning at this time, when an American weather plane came over. The two men pulled and pushed the handcart through the city streets. Hiroshima was a fan-shaped city, lying mostly on the six islands formed by the seven estuarial rivers that branch out from the Ota River; its main commercial and residential districts, covering about four square miles in the center of the city, contained three-quarters of its population, which had been reduced by several evacuation programs from a wartime peak of 380,000 to about 245,000. Factories and other residential districts, or suburbs, lay compactly around the edges of the city. To the south were the docks, an airport, and the island-studded Inland Sea. A rim of mountains runs around the other three sides of the delta. Mr. Tanimoto and Mr. Matsuo took their way through the shopping center, already full of people, and across two of the rivers to the sloping streets of Koi, and up them to the outskirts and foothills. As they started up a valley away from the tight-ranked houses, the all-clear sounded. (The Japanese radar operators, detecting only three planes, supposed that they comprised a reconnaissance [exploratory mission].) Pushing the handcart up to the rayon man's house was tiring, and the men, after they had maneuvered their load into the driveway and to the front steps, paused to rest awhile. They stood with a wing of the house between them and the city. Like most homes in this part of Japan, the house consisted of a wooden frame and wooden walls supporting a heavy tile roof. Its front hall, packed with rolls of bedding and clothing, looked like a cool cave full of fat cushions. Opposite the house, to the right of the front door, there was a large, finicky rock garden. There was no sound of planes. The morning was still; the place was cool and pleasant.

The morning was still . . .

Then a tremendous flash of light cut across the sky. Mr. Tanimoto has a distinct recollection that it traveled from east to west, from the city

An American service-man examines the wrecked framework of the Museum of Science and Industry in Hiroshima soon after the atomic bomb was dropped. Few other buildings were standing.

toward the hills. It seemed a sheet of sun. Both he and Mr. Matsuo reacted in terror—and both had time to react (for they were 3,500 yards, or two miles, from the center of the explosion). Mr. Matsuo dashed up the front steps into the house and dived among the bedrolls and buried himself there. Mr. Tanimoto took four or five steps and threw himself between two big rocks in the garden. He bellied up very hard against one of them. As his face was against the stone, he did not see what happened. He felt a sudden pressure, and then splinters and pieces of board and fragments of tile fell on him. He heard no roar. (Almost no one in Hiroshima recalls hearing any noise of the bomb. But a fisherman in his sampan on the Inland Sea near Tsuzu, the man with whom Mr. Tanimoto's mother-in-law and sister-in-law were living, saw the flash and heard a tremendous explosion; he was nearly twenty miles from Hiroshima, but the thunder was greater than when the B-29s hit Iwakuni, only five miles away.)

When he dared, Mr. Tanimoto raised his head and saw that the rayon man's house had collapsed. He thought a bomb had fallen directly on it. Such clouds of dust had risen that there was sort of a twilight around. In panic, not thinking for the moment of Mr. Matsuo under the ruins, he dashed out into the street. He noticed as he ran that the concrete wall of the estate had fallen over—toward the house rather than away from it. In the street, the first thing he saw was a squad of soldiers who had been burrowing into the hillside opposite, making one of the thousands of dugouts in which the Japanese apparently intended to resist invasion, hill by hill, life for life; the soldiers were coming out of the hole, where they should have been safe, and blood was running from their heads, chests, and backs. They were silent and dazed.

Under what seemed to be a local dust cloud, the day grew darker and darker.

REVIEWING THE READING

1. What happened in the life of Tanimoto shortly before the bomb was dropped that allowed him to survive the blast?

2. Why had the police been questioning Tanimoto only a few days before the bombing?

3. **Using Your Historical Imagination.** Although the people in the story survived the bomb, their lives would never be the same. How do you think their lives, and the lives of other Japanese survivors, were changed forever by the dropping of the atomic bomb? Explain your answer.

From *The Homefront: America During World War II* by Mark Jonathan Harris.

55

Defense Worker Rachel Wray Reminisces About Her Wartime Experiences (1940s)

The onset of the United States' entry into World War II in 1941 brought an end to the Great Depression. A decade of economic depression had left the country in short supply of steel, aluminum, rubber, and other raw materials needed to produce weapons, planes, and other war supplies. Unemployment dropped overnight as manufacturers found themselves in need of the hundreds of thousands of workers it would take to meet the demand. With so many men drafted or enlisting for military duty, American women stepped in to do the job at home. An estimated 6 million women took jobs in the factories, most of them working outside the home for the first time. "Rosie the Riveter" soon became a source of inspiration to the men at war. The following selection is from a book on America during World War II. In these excerpts a defense worker, Rachel Wray, describes her experiences on the job. As you read try to determine why Wray's brother and his friends laughed at her for working in the aircraft factory.

I was one of the first women hired at Convair [aircraft factory]. . . . Convair had a motto on their plant which said that anything short of right was wrong, and that stuck with me. I went to work in the riveting group in metal bench assembly. The mechanics would bring us the jobs they had put

together, and we would take the blueprints and rivet what they brought us. . . .

I tackled everything. I had a daring mother who was afraid of nothing, horses, farm implements, anything, so maybe I inherited a little bit of that from her. I remember my brother, who was in the air force at the time, and his friends laughed at me one day, thinking I couldn't learn this mechanical stuff. I can still see them, but it only made me more determined. I think it probably hurt their pride a little bit that I was capable of doing this.

Pretty soon I was promoted to bench mechanic work, which was detailed hand riveting. Then I was given a bench with nothing to do but repair what other people had ruined. I visited a man recently who's seventy-four years old, and he said to my daughter, "All we had to do was foul up a job and take it to her and she'd fix it."

Defense worker Mabel Stark uses a rivet gun to help build a P-38 fighter plane at a Lockheed war plant in Burbank, California.

I loved working at Convair. I loved the challenge of getting dirty and getting into the work. I did one special riveting job, hand riveting that could not be done by machine. I worked on that job for three months, ten hours a day, six days a week, and slapped three-eighths- or three-quarter-inch rivets by hand that no one else would do. I didn't have that kind of confidence as a kid growing up, because I didn't have that opportunity. Convair was the first time in my life that I had the chance to prove that I could do something, and I did. They finally made me a group leader to help break the new women in.

REVIEWING THE READING

1. Why do you think Wray's brother and his friends laughed at her for working in the aircraft factory?

2. What was Wray's job in the factory?

3. **Using Your Historical Imagination.** Most of the women in the factories were working outside the home for the very first time, and almost none had ever worked in a heavy industrial factory. How do you think this experience may have affected the women's lives after the war was over? Explain your answer.

A Black Tank Commander's Story (1940s)

56

From *"The Good War":
An Oral History of World
War Two* by Studs
Terkel.

*Just as they had in World War I and in every
other war, African Americans took up arms for the
United States during World War II. While the military welcomed blacks into service, especially into high-
risk combat jobs, they did not welcome them as equals.
The black soldiers were assigned to segregated units.
Unlike previous wars, however, some blacks did become
officers during World War II. But even then they
were usually put in charge of all-black units. The
following selection, from a volume of oral histories
taken from people who experienced the war, is excerpted from the account of a black tank commander.
As you read the account, consider the discrimination
that the black soldiers were subject to.*

We were the first black tanker group to be used
in combat.

I was twenty-nine when I joined the service
on April 10, 1941. I was sent to Fort Riley, Kansas.
You had the Ninth and Tenth cavalries there, who
established a heck of a record. I might attribute
my success to the training I received from old soldiers
who had no more than a fifth-grade education. Regular army men. I had noticed that every new white
officer who came there was told to observe the old
black sergeants.

They asked if I'd be interested in going to OCS
[Officer's Candidate School]. I said no, I wanted
to do my twelve months and get out. The regimental
commander said, "Do you know any question about
the Field Manual, FM 105-dash-one?" I said yes.
He said, "What are you supposed to do when a

commanding officer requests you to do something?" I said, "Request in that particular case is considered as an order." He said, "Well, I'm requesting that you just sign these papers." So that's how I got stuck and ended up goin' to Officer's Training School. I did that in July of '42. Fort Knox, Kentucky.

I had been strictly an outdoors man. To be inside a building and listen to a monotone all day long, I couldn't take. I did nothing but sleep those first days. The instructor said, "You sleep in my classes, you'll not get anything but a bunch of demerits." I said I didn't want to come here anyway. After six weeks, we had our first examinations. Fifty percent of every OCS class lost in the first examination. I ended up with an average of ninety-six-point-something. So the last six weeks, they just said, Let him sleep. (Laughs.) It came as a result of the training I had gotten in Fort Riley.

I was a lieutenant at Camp Claiborne, Louisiana, until December of '42. The company commander had three platoon leaders ask me questions, to test me. I answered, they were satisfied. I then said that I have questions for them and I'll let them have a month to find the answers. They had searched every field manual and couldn't find them. So I politely told them the answers are in the field manual which they've been waiting to receive. Their manual is obsolete. I said, "This is a lesson for you. Let us work together and we'll accomplish a . . . lot more than we will by trying to trick one another."

It was cold and damp during the winter. Immediately we'd get in the field and the fellas would jump out of the tanks and start building fires. I called all my platoon in and told them, "Now, gentlemen, you know these tanks cost $60,000 apiece. So the first thing for you to do is concentrate on learning how best to use these things. . . . Now I like to play as well as anyone, but when you see me working, that means you work." We worked on that principle and got the job done.

The nearest town was Alexandria. Our place-
ment in camp was down in the sewage area. All
black. When you went to town, you were faced
with nothing but white MPs [military police]. We
had to change that. They required the Negro officer
not to carry a sidearm. Yet the others carried
sidearms. So I went in town with a sidearm. They
questioned me: "You don't need any sidearm." I said,
"Is everybody gonna be without sidearms?" "Oh, no,
no, but you don't need 'em." I said, "I'm performin'
the same type of duty you're performin'. I'm gonna
be equally as well prepared as you." They knew I
was right. I was very foolish, maybe.

They threatened me with charges. I told 'em
my parents would be just as proud of me as a dishon-
orably discharged private as they would if I were a
general. It don't matter to them and it won't matter
to me. But since I'm in this thing, I intend to do
my best according to rules and regulations. And I
do study rules and regulations. After that, we carried
sidearms.

I had experienced so much prejudice in Louisiana that when I got to Europe, it was a joke. (Laughs.)

We went to Fort Hood, Texas, early '44. We
trained against the tank destroyer outfits and consistently made monkeys out of them. They had both
white and black. We established quite a reputation.

In '44, General Patton requested the best separate battalion they had left in the United States.
He wanted 'em for the Third army. We weren't in
a division. Patton had made a statement that Negroes
were incapable of being tankers. The equipment was
too technical. And who should General Patton see
when he went into the armored field? Us. Here we
come, the best they had left in the United States.
(Laughs.)

He viewed us for quite some time. Finally he
said, "You're the first Negro tankers ever to be used
in the American army in combat. I want you to
establish a record for yourselves and a record for

> I told 'em my
> parents would
> be just as proud
> of me as a
> dishonorably
> discharged
> private as they
> would if I were
> a general.

The commanding general of the 71st Infantry Division decorates members of the 761st tank battalion with the Bronze Star medal for heroism in 1944.

your race. I want you to make a liar out of me. When you get in combat—and you will be in combat—when you see those kraut [slang for German] . . . don't spare the ammunition." Of course, the Negroes whooped because here was a white man tellin' the Negroes to shoot white people. Well, that really tore us up. (Laughs.)

The average life of a separate tank battalion was from ten to twelve days. Then they'd just redline it out [eliminate it] and the few men who were left were attached to somebody else. So when there was a bad spot, they'd send the separate tank battalion in the area and the division would just bypass it. You were just gun fodder really. We went 183 days without relief and . . . few replacements.

We had all but ten people in the outfit were black. There were ten whites, officers. Two of 'em were company commanders. One of 'em lasted two days. The other lasted about two weeks. Then there was nothin' but Negro officers and enlisted men on the front from that day on. This was in France, Belgium, Holland, the cracking of the Siegfried Line, West Germany. We finally ended up in Steyr, Austria. Always in combat. No other unit has any record to compare.

In that particular time, we received 250 men from quartermaster units, engineers—types who had never been in combat, had never been in a tank. I had to train these men while we were fighting every day. Those who came through, we kept. The rest, we sent away.

I was captain by then. When the company commander of C Company, Charlie, had been injured—they had lost about eight men killed, thirty-six in the hospital—I took over until the finish of hostilities.

We started out with 750 men. All through the 183 days, we had 35 men killed in action. We had 293 who received Purple Hearts. We had 60 who received Bronze Stars. We had 11 who received Silver Stars. Remember, these awards were granted through the divisions with whom we'd been attached. A division naturally is gonna take care of its own first. So for us to have received that many awards meant to me that any man who received a Bronze Star should have received a Silver Star and any man who received a Silver Star should have received a Congressional Medal of Honor. Because we got only the crumbs. So we must have done a very creditable [good] job. They were very well trained and disciplined. We had a job to do and they did their best.

The German army couldn't see how we could be in so many darned places. We were split into three platoons and the platoon was split into two. We were scattered all over the darn place. To hear the story of the 761st Tank Battalion, it seemed impossible.

On one combat mission, we were having difficulty getting the Germans out of the woods. We kept firing low. Finally I told 'em, "Gentlemen, raise your fire so it will explode up in the trees." That'll send more shrapnel around, also some trees down, and get those people out of those woods. They came out waving white flags and calling, "Kameraden." I told the men to remain in their tanks with the hatches buttoned up, and when the enemy got abreast of 'em, just direct 'em back to the infantry. Well, some guy opened up his hatch a little bit early. The Germans looked and they said, "Schwarzen Soldaten!" Black soldiers! That word just went through the bunch and they started runnin' back to the . . . woods. We figured, We'll be . . . if you're gonna get back to those woods. Finally, they figured they'd better go along with these black soldiers. (Laughs.)

They couldn't understand how we could be just a separate tank battalion. We were in too many places. They had us plotted on their maps. They were very curious. Their major was questioning us: How many divisions of Negro tankers are there? Of course we didn't tell 'em anything.

It was seldom any of this news got to the States. Most people didn't know that we had a Negro tank outfit. The campaign for a Presidential Unit Citation started back in '45. It took us thirty-three years.

Though you have records, the division is not gonna tell you the story. We had discovered that at least twelve other units to which we had been attached had received Presidential Unit Citations. About eighteen had received the French Croix de Guerre. How easy it has been all through the years to conceal the history of the Negro soldier.

REVIEWING THE READING

1. What examples does the tank commander give of racial discrimination in the army during World War II?

2. Why do you think the people back home rarely heard about the bravery of the black soldiers? Explain your answer.

3. **Using Your Historical Imagination.** General Patton was surprised to see the black tank battalion. Why do you think he did not expect them to be good at their job? What do you think his opinion was of them after he saw what they could do in battle? Explain your answer.

America and the Holocaust (1940s)

57

From *The Abandonment of the Jews: America and the Holocaust, 1941–1945* by David S. Wyman.

When Adolph Hitler came to power in Germany in 1933, he began a program of Aryan (white, non-Jewish) supremacy by forcing Jews out of Germany. In 1939, just before the outbreak of World War II, Hitler announced that if war came, he would eliminate all the Jews in Europe. By 1942 Hitler and the Nazi Party had adopted what was called the "Final Solution," designed to "cleanse" Europe of Jews. The Jewish people were subjected to torture and other atrocities, their land and businesses taken from them, and millions of them ended up in concentration camps.

The general public, especially in the United States, did not learn of these atrocities until after the war was over, although it has been argued that Roosevelt and the other government officials did have some knowledge of it. After the war, there were those who believed that the United States could have taken steps that would have saved many of the European Jews. The following selection is excerpted from historian David S. Wyman's book on the Holocaust (Hitler's programs to exterminate the Jewish people). In the book, Wyman outlines 12 programs that the United States could have undertaken. As you read try to determine why, according to Wyman, the U.S. government did none of these things.

W hat could the American government have achieved if it had really committed itself to rescue? The possibilities were narrowed by the Nazis' determination to wipe out the Jews. War conditions themselves also made rescue difficult. And by mid-1942, when clear news of the systematic murder

reached the West, two million Jews had already
been massacred and the killing was going forward
at a rapid rate. Most likely, it would not have been
possible to rescue millions. But without impeding
[obstructing] the war effort, additional tens of thousands—probably hundreds of thousands—could
have been saved. What follows is a selection of twelve
programs that could have been tried. All of them,
and others, were proposed during the Holocaust.

(1) Most important, the War Refugee Board
should have been established in 1942. And it should
have received adequate government funding and
much broader powers.

(2) The U.S. government, working through neutral governments or the Vatican, could have pressed
Germany to release the Jews. If nothing else, this
would have demonstrated to the Nazis—and to the
world—that America was committed to saving the
European Jews. . . .

(3) The United States could have applied constant pressure on Axis satellites [those countries controlled by Germany] to release their Jews. By spring
1943, the State Department knew that some satellites, convinced that the war was lost, were seeking
favorable peace terms. Stern threats of punishment
for mistreating Jews or allowing their deportation,
coupled with indications that permitting them to
leave for safety would earn Allied goodwill, could
have opened the way to the rescue of large numbers from Rumania, Bulgaria, Hungary, and perhaps
Slovakia. . . .

(4) Success in setting off an exodus of Jews
would have posed the problem of where they could
go. Strong pressure needed to be applied to neutral
countries near the Axis (Spain, Portugal, Turkey,
Switzerland, and Sweden) to take Jews in. . . .

(5) Locating enough outside havens, places beyond continental Europe where refugees could safely
await postwar resettlement, would have presented
difficulties. . . . But an American government

deeply concerned about the Jews and willing to share the burden could have used its prestige and power to open doors. . . .

(6) Shipping was needed to transfer Jews from neutral countries to outside havens. Abundant evidence . . . proves that it could have been provided without interfering with the war effort. . . .

(7) A campaign to stimulate and assist escapes would have led to a sizable outflow of Jews. Once the neutral nations had agreed to open their borders, that information could have been publicized throughout Europe by radio, airdropped leaflets, and underground communications channels. . . .

(8) Much larger sums of money should have been transferred to Europe. After the WRB [War

Survivors of the Dachau concentration camp greet liberators from the American 42nd Rainbow Division. Prisoners wearing the striped suits are those who were destined for the crematorium.

Refugee Board] was formed, the earlier, tiny trickle of funds from the United States was increased. But the amounts were still inadequate. . . .

(9) Much more effort should have gone into finding ways to send in food and medical supplies. The American government should have approached the problem far sooner than it did. And it should have put heavy pressure on the International Red Cross and British blockade authorities on this issue.

(10) Drawing on its great prestige and influence, the United States could have applied much more pressure than it did on neutral governments, the Vatican, and the International Red Cross to induce [motivate] them to take earlier and more vigorous action. . . .

> . . . the United States could have applied much more pressure than it did on neutral governments.

(11) Some military assistance was possible. The Air Force could have eliminated the Auschwitz killing installations. Some bombing of deportation railroads was feasible. The military could have aided in other ways without impeding the war effort. . . .

(12) Much more publicity about the extermination of the Jews should have been disseminated [spread] throughout Europe. Allied radio could have beamed the information for weeks at a time, on all possible wavelengths. . . .

In November 1943, [Assistant Secretary of State] Breckinridge Long told the House Foreign Affairs Committee that lack of transportation was the reason the State Department was issuing so few visas. . . . In reality, ample shipping existed. Neutral vessels crossed the Atlantic throughout the war. Three Portuguese liners, with a combined capacity of 2,000 passengers, sailed regularly between Lisbon and U.S. ports. Each ship made the trip about every six weeks. Most of the time, because of the tight American visa policy, they carried only small fractions of their potential loads. . . .

[Another] well-worn excuse for rejecting rescue proposals was the claim that they would detract from the military effort and thus prolong the war.

This argument, entirely valid with regard to projects that actually would have hurt the war effort, was used almost automatically to justify inaction. Virtually none of the rescue proposals involved enough infringement on the war effort to lengthen the conflict at all or to increase the number of casualties, military or civilian. . . .

It was not a lack of workable plans that stood in the way of saving many thousands more European Jews. Nor was it insufficient shipping, the threat of infiltration by subversive agents, or the possibility that rescue projects would hamper the war effort. The real obstacle was the absence of a strong desire to rescue Jews.

REVIEWING THE READING

1. According to Wyman, why did the United States not come to the aid of the European Jews?

2. What two reasons does Wyman say the United States gave for not becoming involved in the Jewish issue? Why does he say that these excuses are not valid?

3. **Using Your Historical Imagination.** Of the 12 programs cited by the author, which one, in your opinion, could have been carried out most easily? Which would have been the most difficult? Explain your answers.

<table>
<tr>
<td>

58

From *Congressional Record*, 80th Congress, 1st Session; and *Congressional Record*, 81st Congress, 1st Session.

</td>
<td>

The Truman Doctrine and the Four Points (1947,1949)

</td>
</tr>
</table>

During World War II, the United States and the Soviet Union were allies. After the war, however, the Soviets were determined to take over the Eastern European countries that they had occupied. The United States opposed this, and the two countries were soon locked into a Cold War. At the same time, communist parties in many European countries began gaining power. President Truman sought ways to end this spread of communism without war.

In 1947 communist rebels in Greece threatened to overthrow the conservative Greek government. Truman asked Congress for $400 million in aid for Greece, stating a plan that became known as the Truman Doctrine. Then, in his inaugural address in January 1949, he outlined his Four Point Foreign Policy, which included his continued support of the European Recovery Program (the Marshall Plan) and America's responsibility to the underdeveloped areas of the world. As you read the excerpts from Truman's address to Congress, in which he outlined the Truman Doctrine, and the fourth point of his Four Point Foreign Policy, consider what Truman thought might happen if the United States failed to provide aid to Greece.

1947

I am fully aware of the broad implications involved if the United States extends assistance to Greece and Turkey, and I shall discuss these implications with you at this time.

One of the primary objectives of the foreign policy of the United States is the creation of conditions in which we and other nations will be able to work out a way of life free from coercion [force or the threat of force]. This was a fundamental issue in the war with Germany and Japan. Our victory was won over countries which sought to impose their will, and way of life, on other nations.

To insure the peaceful development of nations, free from coercion, the United States has taken a leading part in establishing the United Nations. The United Nations is designed to make possible lasting freedom and independence for all its members. We shall not realize our objectives, however, unless we are willing to help free people to maintain their free institutions and their national integrity against aggressive movements that seek to impose upon them totalitarian regimes [systems of government in which all aspects of people's lives are rigidly controlled]. This is no more than a frank recognition that totalitarian regimes imposed on free peoples, by direct or indirect aggression, undermine the foundations of international peace and hence the security of the United States.

The peoples of a number of countries of the world have recently had totalitarian regimes forced upon them against their will. The government of the United States has made frequent protests against the coercion and intimidation, in violation of the Yalta agreement, in Poland, Romania and Bulgaria. I must also state that in a number of other countries there have been similar developments.

At the present moment in world history nearly every nation must choose between alternative ways of life. The choice is too often not a free one.

One way of life is based upon the will of the majority, and is distinguished by free institutions, representative government, free elections, guarantees of individual liberty, freedom of speech and religion, and freedom from political oppression.

> **. . . The United Nations is designed to make possible lasting freedom and independence for all its members.**

The second way of life is based upon the will of a minority forcibly imposed upon the majority. It relies upon terror and oppression, a controlled press and radio, fixed elections and the suppression of personal freedoms.

I believe that it must be the policy of the United States to support peoples who are resisting attempted subjugation [takeover or control] by armed minorities or by outside pressures. . . . I believe that our help should be primarily through economic and financial aid, which is essential to economic stability and orderly political processes.

The world is not static [motionless] and the status quo [present situation] is not sacred. But we cannot allow changes in the status quo in violation of the charter of the United Nations by such methods as coercion, or by such subterfuges [deceptions] as political infiltration. In helping free and independent nations to maintain their freedom, the United States will be giving effect to the principles of the charter of the United Nations.

It is necessary only to glance at a map to realize that the survival and integrity of the Greek nation are of grave importance in a much wider situation. If Greece should fall under the control of an armed minority, the effect upon its neighbor, Turkey, would be immediate and serious. Confusion and disorder might well spread throughout the entire Middle East. . . .

It would be an unspeakable tragedy if these countries, which have struggled so long against overwhelming odds, should lose that victory for which they sacrificed so much. Collapse of free institutions and loss of independence would be disastrous not only for them but for the world. Discouragement and possibly failure would quickly be the lot of neighboring peoples striving to maintain their freedom and independence. . . .

The seeds of totalitarian regimes are nurtured by misery and want. They spread and grow in the evil soil of poverty and strife. They reach their full growth when the hope of a people for a better life has died. We must keep that hope alive.

The free peoples of the world look to us for support in maintaining their freedoms. If we falter in our leadership, we may endanger the peace of the world—and we shall surely endanger the welfare of our own nation. Great responsibilities have been placed upon us by the swift movement of events. I am confident that the Congress will face these responsibilities squarely.

The free peoples of the world look to us for support in maintaining their freedoms.

1949

We must embark on a bold new program for making the benefits of our scientific advances and industrial progress available for the improvement and growth of underdeveloped areas.

More than half the people of the world are living in conditions approaching misery. Their food is inadequate. They are victims of disease. Their economic life is primitive and stagnant. Their poverty is a handicap and a threat both to them and prosperous areas.

For the first time in history, humanity possesses the knowledge and the skill to relieve the suffering of these people.

The United States is pre-eminent among nations in the development of industrial and scientific techniques. The material resources which we can afford to use for the assistance of other people are limited. But our imponderable resources in technical knowledge are constantly growing and are inexhaustible.

I believe that we should make available to peace-loving peoples the benefits of our store of technical knowledge in order to help them realize their aspirations for a better life. And, in cooperation with other nations, we should foster capital investment in areas needing development.

Our aim should be to help the free peoples of the world, through their own efforts, to produce

President Harry Tru-man addresses a joint session of Congress to propose the foreign pol-icy initiative later called the Truman Doctrine.

more food, more clothing, more materials for housing, and more mechanical power to lighten their burdens.

We invite other countries to pool their technological resources in this undertaking. Their contributions will be warmly welcomed. This should be a cooperative enterprise in which all nations work together through the United Nations and its specialized agencies wherever practicable. It must be a worldwide effort for the achievement of peace, plenty, and freedom.

With the cooperation of business, private capital, agriculture, and labor in this country, this program can greatly increase the industrial activity in other nations and can raise substantially their standards of living.

Such new economic developments must be devised and controlled to benefit the peoples of the areas in which they are established. Guarantees to the investor must be balanced by guarantees in the interest of the people whose resources and whose labor go into these developments.

The old imperialism—exploitation for foreign profit—has no place in our plans. What we envisage is a program of development based on the concepts of democratic fair-dealing.

All countries, including our own, will greatly benefit from a constructive program for the better use of the world's human and natural resources. Experience shows that our commerce with other countries expands as they progress industrially and economically.

Greater production is the key to prosperity and peace. And the key to greater production is a wider and more vigorous application of modern scientific and technical knowledge.

Only by helping the least fortunate of its members to help themselves can the human family achieve the decent, satisfying life that is the right of all people.

Democracy alone can supply the vitalizing force to stir the peoples of the world into triumphant action, not only against their human oppressors, but also against their ancient enemies—hunger, misery, and despair.

REVIEWING THE READING

1. What do you think President Truman thought might happen if the United States failed to provide aid to Greece?

2. What resources of the United States did President Truman think the United States could offer to underdeveloped countries? Which American resources did he say were limited?

3. **Using Your Historical Imagination.** How do you think Truman visualized the carrying out of his two plans? What do you think he saw as a long-range end result of the programs he proposed?

59

From *Vital Speeches of the Day*, Volume XXIV, No. 1.

President Eisenhower Intervenes at Little Rock (1957)

In 1896 the United States Supreme Court ruled, in the case of Plessy v. Ferguson, *that racial segregation of public schools was legal if schools for African American students were equal to those for white students. It was nearly 60 years before the Supreme Court overturned the "separate but equal" decision.*

In 1954, in the case of Brown v. Board of Education of Topeka, Kansas, *the Supreme Court unanimously decided that it was unconstitutional for states to maintain separate schools for blacks and whites. In 1957 the school board of Little Rock, Arkansas, under federal court order, agreed to admit nine black students to the all-white Central High School. Arkansas governor Orval Faubus called out the National Guard to prevent the African Americans from entering the school. After the Guard was withdrawn, angry whites blocked the school entrance and threatened the African American students. Finally, President Dwight Eisenhower intervened by ordering U.S. army troops to the school. Eisenhower then went on the radio to explain what had happened and why he took such action. As you read the following excerpts from his speech, try to determine why the president thought it necessary for the federal government to intervene.*

For a few minutes this evening I want to talk to you about the serious situation that has arisen in Little Rock. To make this talk I have come to

the President's office in the White House. I could
have spoken from Rhode Island, where I have been
staying recently, but I felt that, in speaking from
the house of Lincoln, of Jackson and of Wilson,
my words would better convey both the sadness I
feel in this action I was compelled today to take
and the firmness with which I intend to pursue this
course until the orders of the Federal Court at Little
Rock can be executed without unlawful interference.

In that city, under the leadership of demagogic
extremists [leaders who obtain power by means of
strong appeals to the emotions and prejudices of
the people], disorderly mobs have deliberately prevented the carrying out of proper orders from a
Federal Court. Local authorities have not eliminated
that violent opposition and, under the law, I yesterday issued a Proclamation calling upon the mob to
disperse.

This morning the mob again gathered in front
of the Central High School of Little Rock, obviously
for the purpose of again preventing the carrying
out of the Court's order relating to the admission
of Negro children to that school.

Whenever normal agencies prove inadequate
to the task and it becomes necessary for the Executive
Branch of the Federal Government to use its powers
and authority to uphold Federal Courts, the President's responsibility is inescapable.

In accordance with that responsibility, I have
today issued an Executive Order directing the use
of troops under Federal authority to aid in the execu-
tion of Federal law at Little Rock, Arkansas. This
became necessary when my Proclamation of yesterday was not observed, and the obstruction of justice
still continues.

It is important that the reasons for my action
be understood by all our citizens.

As you know, the Supreme Court of the United
States has decided that separate public educational
facilities for the races are inherently [by nature]

Federal troops escort nine black students into Central High School in Little Rock, Arkansas, in 1957.

unequal and therefore compulsory school segregation laws are unconstitutional.

Our personal opinions about the decision have no bearing on the matter of enforcement; the responsibility and authority of the Supreme Court to interpret the Constitution are very clear. Local Federal Courts were instructed by the Supreme Court to issue such orders and decrees as might be necessary to achieve admission to public schools without regard to race—and with all deliberate speed. . . .

The very basis of our individual rights and freedoms rests upon the certainty that the President and the Executive Branch of Government will support and insure the carrying out of the decisions of the Federal Courts, even, when necessary, with all the means at the President's command.

Unless the President did so, anarchy [chaos] would result.

There would be no security for any except that which each one of us could provide for himself.

The interest of the nation in the proper fulfill-ment of the law's requirements cannot yield to oppo-sition and demonstrations by some few persons. Mob rule cannot be allowed to override the decisions of our courts.

REVIEWING THE READING

1. Why do you think President Eisenhower thought it was necessary for the federal government to intervene in the situation in Little Rock?

2. According to Eisenhower, what role does personal opinion play in the issue of school integration?

3. **Using Your Historical Imagination.** Try to imagine that you were present at Cen-tral High School on the day the army troops intervened. What thoughts do you think were running through the minds of the African American students? What conflicting emotions do you think they may have felt?

60

From *Naming Names* by Victor S. Navasky.

Victor Navasky Describes the Costs of "McCarthyism" (1950s)

During the late 1940s a new wave of fear swept across the United States. Several incidents led Americans to believe that communists had infiltrated the highest levels of the U.S. government. Public hearings held by the House Un-American Activities Committee followed, with informers accusing scores of public figures of communist activities or connections. Careers were destroyed virtually overnight.

In 1950 Wisconsin Senator Joseph McCarthy, in an attempt to further his own career, claimed that he knew of 205 "card-carrying communists" who held high positions in the State Department. Although he never produced the names or provided any form of proof, McCarthy attacked and ruined the careers of an untold number of government officials over the next four years. Finally, McCarthy went too far. His irrational tactics became obvious to the public, and the people turned against him. Later that year the Senate passed a vote of condemnation against him, and his star fell as quickly as it had risen. The reputations and careers of McCarthy's victims, however, would never be the same. As you read the following excerpts from journalist Victor Navasky's book on McCarthyism, try to determine the meaning of the term "McCarthyism" as it might be used today.

The social costs of what came to be called McCarthyism have yet to be computed. By conferring its prestige on the red [communist] hunt, the state did more than bring misery to the lives of hundreds of thousands of Communists, former Communists, fellow travelers [associates of hidden communists], and unlucky liberals. It weakened American culture and it weakened itself.

Unlike the Palmer Raids [nationwide raids by Attorney General A. Mitchell Palmer against supposed subversives] of the early 1920s, which were violent hit-and-run affairs that had no long-term effect, the vigilante spirit [Joseph] McCarthy represented still lives on in legislation accepted as a part of the American political way. The morale of the United States' newly reliable and devoted civil service was savagely undermined in the 1950s, and the purge of the Foreign Service contributed to our disastrous miscalculations in Southeast Asia in the 1960s and the consequent human wreckage. The congressional investigations of the 1940s and 1950s fueled the anti-Communist hysteria which eventually led to the investment of thousands of billions of dollars in a nuclear arsenal, with risks that boggle the minds of even those who specialize in "thinking about the

Senator Joseph McCarthy displays photographs of alleged communists at a Senate hearing.

unthinkable." Unable to tolerate a little subversion (however one defines it)—if that is the price of freedom, dignity, and experimentation—we lost our edge, our distinctiveness. McCarthyism decimated [partially destroyed] its target—the American Communist Party, whose membership fell from about seventy-five thousand in 1957 (probably a high percentage of these lost were FBI informants)—but the real casualties of that assault were the walking wounded of the liberal left and the already impaired momentum of the New Deal. No wonder a new generation of radical idealists came up through the peace and civil-rights movements rather than the Democratic Party.

The damage was compounded by the state's chosen instruments of destruction, the professional informers . . .

The damage was compounded by the state's chosen instruments of destruction, the professional informers—those ex-Communists whom the sociologist Edward Shils described in 1956 as a host of frustrated, previously anonymous failures. . . .

It is no easier to measure the impact of McCarthyism on culture than on politics, although emblems of the terror were ever on display. In the literary community, for example, generally thought to be more permissive than the mass media . . . the distinguished editor-in-chief of the distinguished publisher Little, Brown & Co. was forced to resign because he refused to repudiate [give up] his progressive politics and he became unemployable. Such liberal publications as the *New York Post* and the *New Republic* refused to accept ads for the *transcript* of the trial of Julius and Ethel Rosenberg [husband and wife who were tried and convicted in 1951 of passing atomic secrets to Soviet agents; electrocuted in 1953]. Albert Maltz's short story "The Happiest Man on Earth," which had won the O. Henry Memorial Short Story Award in 1938 and been republished seventy-six times in magazines, newspapers, and anthologies, didn't get reprinted again from the time he entered prison in 1950 until 1963. Ring Lardner, Jr., had to go to England to find a publisher for his critically acclaimed novel *The Ecstasy of Owen Muir. . . .* The FBI had a permanent motion-picture crew stationed across the street from the Four Continents Bookstore in New York, which specialized in literature sympathetic to the Soviet Union's brand of Marxism. How to measure a thousand such pollutions of the cultural environment?

REVIEWING THE READING

1. What is the meaning of the term "McCarthyism"?

2. What does Navasky think of the informers used by the government in its attempt to rid the country of communists?

3. **Using Your Historical Imagination.** Navasky says that McCarthyism weakened American culture and it weakened itself. What examples does he give to prove his point? What does he believe to be the only possible good to come out of McCarthyism?

61

From *The Feminine Mystique* by Betty Friedan.

Betty Friedan Discusses the Feminine Mystique (1950s)

Even before the Civil War, women were fighting for equal rights. At a Woman's Rights Convention in Seneca Falls, New York, in 1848, the participants drew up a declaration demanding that women be given all the rights and privileges they deserved as citizens of the United States. Through the years, women fought for and slowly won more rights, although they would not win the right to vote until 1920. The introduction of various labor-saving devices during the 1920s freed women from much household drudgery, and the whole attitude of the Roaring Twenties encouraged women to make their own decisions and lead their own lives. Throughout the 1930s and into the 1940s, the trend continued. More and more women went to college, graduating into all types of occupations. During World War II, women poured into the work force, many of them holding jobs that had formerly been open only to men. After the war, however, attitudes changed.

The following selection is excerpted from The Feminine Mystique, *in which author Betty Friedan talks about the women of the 1950s. As you read try to determine how the values of these women differed from those of their mothers and grandmothers.*

By the end of the nineteen-fifties, the average marriage age of women in America dropped to 20, and was still dropping, into the teens. Fourteen million girls were engaged by 17. The proportion of women attending college in comparison with men dropped from 47 per cent in 1920 to 35 per cent in 1958. A century earlier, women had fought for higher education; now girls went to college to get a husband. By the mid-fifties, 60 per cent dropped out of college to marry, or because they were afraid too much education would be a marriage bar. Colleges built dormitories for "married students," but the students almost were always the husbands. A new degree was instituted for the wives—"Ph.T." (Putting Husband Through).

Betty Friedan, founder of the National Organization for Women (NOW), displays two of the buttons that symbolized the women's liberation movement.

Then American girls began getting married in high school. And the woman's magazines, deploring the unhappy statistics about these young marriages, urged that courses on marriage, and marriage counselors, be installed in the high schools. Girls started going steady at twelve and thirteen, in junior high. . . .

By the end of the fifties, the United States birthrate was overtaking India's. . . . Statisticians were especially astounded at the fantastic increase in the number of babies among college women. Where once they had two children, now they had four, five, six. Women who had once wanted careers were now making careers out of having babies. . . .

Interior decorators were designing kitchens with mosaic murals and original paintings, for kitchens were once again the center of women's lives. Home sewing became a million-dollar industry. Many women no longer left their homes, except to shop, chauffeur their children, or attend a social engagement with their husbands. Girls were growing up in America without ever having jobs outside the home. In the late fifties, a sociological phenomenon was suddenly remarked [noticed]: a third of American women now worked, but most were no longer young and very few were pursuing careers. They were married women who held part-time jobs, selling or secretarial, to put their husbands through school, their sons through college, or to help pay the mortgage.

Fewer and fewer women were entering professional work.

Or they were widows supporting families. Fewer and fewer women were entering professional work. The shortages in the nursing, social work, and teaching professions caused crises in almost every American city. Concerned over the Soviet Union's lead in the space race, scientists noted that America's greatest source of unused brain-power was women. But girls would not study physics: it was "unfeminine." A girl refused a science fellowship at Johns Hopkins to take a job in a real estate office. All she wanted, she said, was what every other American girl wanted—to get married, have four children and live in a nice house in a nice suburb.

The suburban housewife—she was the dream image of the young American women and the envy, it was said, of women all over the world. The American housewife—freed by science and labor-saving appliances from the drudgery, the dangers of childbirth and the illnesses of her grandmother. She was healthy, beautiful, educated, concerned only about her husband, her children, her home. She had found true feminine fulfillment. As a housewife and mother, she was respected as a full and equal partner to man in his world. She was free to choose automobiles, clothes, appliances, supermarkets; she had everything that women ever dreamed of.

In the fifteen years after World War II, this mystique of feminine fulfillment became the cherished core of contemporary American culture. Millions of women lived their lives in the image of those pretty pictures of the American suburban housewife, kissing their husbands goodbye in front of the picture window, depositing their stationwagonsful of children at school, and smiling as they ran the new electric waxer over the spotless kitchen floor. They baked their own bread, sewed their own and their children's clothes, kept their new washing machines and dryers running all day. They changed the sheets on the beds twice a week instead of once, took the rug-hooking class in adult education, and pitied their poor frustrated mothers, who had dreamed of having a career. Their only dream was to be perfect wives and mothers; their highest ambition to have five children and a beautiful house, their only fight to get and keep their husbands. They had no thought for the unfeminine problems of the world outside the home; they wanted the men to make the major decisions. They gloried in their role as women, and wrote proudly on the census blank: "Occupation: housewife."

For over fifteen years, the words written for women, and the words women used when they talked to each other, while their husbands sat on the other side of the room and talked shop or politics or septic tanks, were about problems with their children, or how to keep their husbands happy, or improve their children's school, or cook chicken or make slip covers. Nobody argued whether women were inferior or superior to men; they were simply different. Words like "emancipation" and "career" sounded strange and embarrassing; no one had used them for years.

REVIEWING THE READING

1. How did the values of the women of the 1950s differ from those of their mothers and grandmothers?

2. What types of women were primarily in the work force during the 1950s?

3. **Using Your Historical Imagination.** What event in the history of the United States do you think may have influenced the change in the value system of women in the 1950s? Explain your answer.

62

From "10 Amazing Years, 1947–1957; A Decade of Miracles," *U.S. News & World Report*, XLIII; and *The Affluent Society* by John Kenneth Galbraith.

Two Views of America in the 1950s

For most Americans the years following World War II were years of prosperity and dramatic change. The war had brought to an end the Great Depression of the 1930s as industry raced to meet the manufacturing needs of war, bringing employment to almost anyone who wanted it. When the war ended in 1945, the United States found itself a great world power with a healthy economy. This economic boom continued in the 1950s. In the midst of all this economic growth, Americans took a new look at their value system. Never before had Americans had so many outlets for their leisure time. The home and all that went with it took on new meaning. Most Americans thought they had never had it so good.

The following excerpts are from an optimistic view of America in the 1950s, published in U.S. News & World Report, *and from a more critical view of the era by economist John Kenneth Galbraith. As you read try to determine what Galbraith believed to be the greatest negative change during the 1950s.*

U.S. News & World Report

The last year of an amazing decade is about to end [1947–1957]. These 10 years have been a time of change and accomplishment unmatched in the history of America, or of any other nation.

In one brief, 10-year period, America's face was remade. Vast suburban areas sprang up to receive millions of Americans pressing out from cities. Ribbons of superhighways were laid across the country. A huge expansion of air facilities helped tie the nation into a compact unity.

Whole regions changed their complexion. Deserts were turned into boom areas. Power was harnessed on a stupendous scale to ease the burden of work.

Nearly 30 million added people were provided for, and on a steadily rising standard of living. A car was put in every garage, two in many. TV sets came into almost every home. There was a chicken, packaged and frozen, for every pot, with more to spare. Never had so many people, anywhere, been so well off. . . .

Ten Years Ago. Look back 10 years, and you see how far America has come, how fast changes can occur at this period in history.

As 1947 was ending, the nation contained 144 million people, not the 172 million of today. Television was in its infancy. The four-engine plane was only beginning to appear on civilian airlines. Toll highways were a rarity. The superhighway was little more than a gleam in planners' eyes. Supermarkets had just begun to dot the landscape. The ranch-type house had hardly made a dent in the building market, and split-levels were all but unknown. The "modern kitchen" lacked many of the appliances that are standard today.

Food packing was primitive by modern standards. Nobody had heard of the heat-and-serve dinner. Passenger cars, with few exceptions, lacked automatic transmissions, power steering, power brakes and tubeless tires. Most had only six-cylinder engines. Air conditioning was the exception in average stores and homes. Polio had not been licked. Today's wide ranges of antibiotics and hormones were not available. The company pension was more the exception than the rule. So was hospital insurance. So was the long vacation.

In the 10 years that followed, amazing changes came over America. . . . The things that people enjoy increased immensely in number and volume. . . .

> Television was in its infancy. . . . The super highway was little more than a gleam in planners' eyes.

Home ownership spread until, today, every other family owns its own home. Families themselves have increased 10 million in number, and the average married couple has more children. Physical comforts of family homes were increased to a level not even approached in past decades. Millions of homes acquired their own air conditioning for summer and winter. Automatic dishwashers became standard equipment for millions. Freezers were acquired for even more homes. All kinds of electric gadgets were developed and bought in vast numbers—for disposing of garbage down the drain, for quick preparation of meals, for performing household chores with speed and ease.

People quickly accepted new products and new inventions. TV sets, only a curiosity 10 years ago, were acquired by most American families during the decade. High-fidelity phonographs were developed and sold in huge numbers. So were filtered cigarettes of many kinds. Housewives took to detergents. FM radios caught on. Lawn work was made easier with a wide variety of power mowers. People began to buy tape recorders, boats of glass fiber, instant foods, long-playing records. . . .

People . . . spent record amounts on travel and recreation.

People, more prosperous than ever before, spent record amounts on travel and recreation. More than 8 million civilians traveled abroad. In addition, Americans flocked in record numbers to resorts in the U.S., bought boats, built summer cottages, went to dude ranches, built their own swimming pools, took up fishing and other forms of recreation—spending about 113 billion dollars on these activities in the process.

Recreation became big business. People bought 4 million power boats, 500,000 sailboats. More than 15 million hunters bought guns and licenses, while 4 million took to golf and 18 million bought tackle and went fishing.

Most of the 11 million new homes built during the decade were of the new rambler or split-level designs. More and more had two-car garages. Nearly all had picture windows of some kind. For the first time, the majority were heated by gas or oil rather than coal, had "revolutionized" kitchens. Many had new wall refrigerators, built-in vacuum-cleaning systems, even built-in "intercom" arrangements.

With the growth of suburban developments, many families found they needed two cars to transport all members of the family to schools, shopping centers and jobs. Traffic increased enormously, with a net increase of 25 million new cars on the road. Huge traffic arteries were built. So were thousands of parking garages, to help ease the ensuing parking jams.

At the same time, the big cities began gigantic rebuilding plans during the decade. Billions were poured into these projects. They involved the expressways to clear new routes for commuters, shoppers and freight. They have included huge new civic centers, modern office buildings, new apartment developments, parks and public auditoriums. Belt roads also were begun by many cities to speed service, help heavy industries escape from downtown. . . .

Jobs became more technical, less routine. Demand increased rapidly for engineers, technicians, skilled workers in many fields. The number of jobs created by the technological revolution rose, with 8.3 million more Americans working at paid jobs at the decade's end than at its beginning.

Jobs became more technical, less routine.

Education took on more importance, as a result. Never had such a high percentage of U.S. youths gone on to higher schooling. In this 10-year period, 12.3 million youths acquired high-school diplomas, while 3.2 million went on to get college degrees. . . .

More to Eat. Food production reached a record high, even with a cut in the number of farms and farmers. . . . In the single decade, the figures now show, U.S. farms produced more than 230 billion pounds of meat, 11 billion bushels of wheat, 31

In the 1950s, when gas was inexpensive, many families drove large cars and traveled all over the United States on vacations.

billion bushels of corn—far more than in any other 10-year period in history. . . .

All told, the decade just ending has been a real age of miracles, an unprecedented era of change and expansion, of jet planes and color TV, of great alterations in the face of America, coupled with a technological revolution that promises even greater miracles in the decade that now lies ahead.

John Kenneth Galbraith

A feature of the years immediately following World War II was a remarkable attack on the notion of expanding and improving public services. During the depression years such services had been elaborated and improved partly in order to fill some small part of the vacuum left by the shrinkage of private production. During the war years the role of government was vastly expanded. After that came the reaction. Much of it, unquestionably, was motivated by a desire to rehabilitate the prestige of private production and therewith of producers. . . .

In this discussion a certain mystique [awe] was attributed to the satisfaction of privately supplied wants. A community decision to have a new school means that the individual surrenders the necessary amount, willy-nilly, in his taxes. But if he is left with that income, he is a free man. He can decide between a better car or a television set. This was advanced with some solemnity [gravity] as an argument for the TV set. The difficulty is that this argument leaves the community with no way of preferring the school. All private wants, where the individual can choose, are inherently [by nature] superior to all public desires which must be paid for by taxation and with an inevitable component of compulsion [force]. . . .

The final problem of the productive society is what it produces. This manifests [shows] itself in an implacable [inflexible] tendency to provide an opulent [abundant] supply of some things and a niggardly [scanty] yield of others. This disparity [difference] carries to the point where it is a cause of social discomfort and social unhealth. The line which divides our area of wealth from our area of poverty is roughly that which divides privately produced and marketed goods and services from publicly rendered services. Our wealth in the first is not only in startling contrast with the meagerness of the latter, but our wealth in privately produced goods is, to a marked degree, the cause of crisis in the supply of public services. For we have failed to see the importance, indeed the urgent need, of maintaining a balance. . . .

This disparity between our flow of private and public goods and services is no matter of subjective judgment [personal opinion]. On the contrary, it is the source of the most extensive comment which only stops short of the direct contrast being made here. In the years following World War II, the papers of any major city—those of New York were an excellent example—told daily of the shortages and shortcomings in the elementary municipal and metropolitan services. The schools were old and overcrowded. The police force was under strength and underpaid. The parks and playgrounds were insufficient. Streets and empty lots were filthy, and the sanitation staff was underequipped and in need of men. Access to the city by those who work there was uncertain and painful and becoming more so. Internal transportation was overcrowded, unhealthful, and dirty. So was the air. Parking on the streets had to be prohibited, and there was no space elsewhere. These deficiencies were not in new and novel services but in old and established ones. . . .

The discussion of this public poverty competed, on the whole successfully, with the stores of ever-increasing opulence [wealth] in privately produced goods. The Gross National Product was rising. So were retail sales. So was personal income. Labor productivity had also advanced. The automobiles that could not be parked were being produced at an expanded rate. The children, though without schools, subject in the playgrounds to the affectionate interest of adults with odd tastes, and disposed to increasingly imaginative forms of delinquency, were admirably equipped with television sets. We had difficulty finding storage space for the great surpluses of food despite a national disposition to obesity [overweight]. Food was grown and packaged under private auspices [sponsorship]. The care and refreshment of the mind, in contrast with the stomach, was principally in the public domain. Our colleges and universities were severely overcrowded and underprovided, and the same was true of the mental hospitals.

The contrast was and remains evident not alone to those who read. The family which takes its mauve and cerise, airconditioned, power-steered, and power-braked automobile out for a tour passes through cities that are badly paved, made hideous by litter, blighted buildings, billboards, and posts

These deficiencies were not in new and novel services but in old and established ones.

for wires that should long since have been put underground. They pass on into a countryside that has been rendered largely invisible by commercial art. (The goods which the latter advertise have an absolute priority in our value system. Such aesthetic [concern with beauty] considerations as a view of the countryside accordingly come second. On such matters we are consistent.) They picnic on exquisitely packaged food from a portable icebox by a polluted stream and go on to spend the night at a park which is a menace to public health and morals. Just before dozing off on an air mattress, beneath a nylon tent, amid the stench of decaying refuse [garbage], they may reflect vaguely on the curious unevenness of their blessings. Is this, indeed, the American genius?

REVIEWING THE READING

1. What did Galbraith believe to be the greatest negative change during the 1950s?

2. What irony did Galbraith see concerning the growing number of automobiles and television sets produced and purchased during the 1950s?

3. **Using Your Historical Imagination.** Overall, do you think the changes of the 1950s were mostly positive or mostly negative? Explain your answer.

63

From *Declaration of Indian Purpose*, American Indian Chicago Conference.

A Declaration of Indian Purpose (1961)

American Indians began to lose their native lands almost from the day the first white settlers began to make their new homes in America. Bloody battles followed, but the Indians were no match for the U.S. Government. Treaties were made, then broken. By the late 1800s the Indians had been herded onto reservations, their customs and livelihood shattered.

Even after all Indians were granted American citizenship in 1924, little changed for the poverty-stricken Indians. Ten years later the Indian Reorganization Act was passed by Congress in an effort to return tribal life to the Indians. They were allowed to choose their own leaders and to live with less interference from the government. By 1960 the Indians had begun to demand the return of much of what they had lost. In June 1961, more than 400 Indians representing 90 tribes met in Chicago to discuss the future of the American Indian. As you read the following excerpt from the "Declaration of Indian Purpose" drawn up at that meeting, try to determine what the Indians hoped to achieve by issuing the declaration.

In the beginning the people of the New World, called Indians by accident of geography, were possessed of a continent and a way of life. In the course of many lifetimes, our people had adjusted to every climate and condition from the Arctic to the torrid zones. In their livelihood and family relationships, their ceremonial observances, they reflected the diversity [variety] of the physical world they occupied.

The conditions in which Indians live today reflect a world in which every basic aspect of life has been transformed [changed]. Even the physical world is no longer the controlling factor in determining where and under what conditions men may live. In region after region, Indian groups found their means of existence either totally destroyed or materially modified [greatly changed]. Newly introduced diseases swept away or reduced populations. These changes were followed by major shifts in the internal life of tribe and family.

Members of various Indian tribes demonstrate traditional dances during their 1961 conference in Chicago.

. . . we do
speak out in a
plea for
understanding.

The time came when the Indian people were no longer the masters of their situation. Their life ways survived subject to the will of a dominant sovereign power. This is said, not in a spirit of complaint; we understand that in the lives of all nations of people, there are times of plenty and times of famine. But we do speak out in a plea for understanding.

When we go before the American people, as we do in this Declaration, and ask for material assistance in developing our resources and developing our opportunities, we pose a moral problem which cannot be left unanswered. For the problem we raise affects the standing which our nation sustains before world opinion.

Our situation cannot be relieved by appropriated funds [funds set aside for a specific purpose] alone, though it is equally obvious that without capital investment and funded services, solutions will be delayed. Nor will the passage of time lessen the complexities which beset a people moving toward new meaning and purpose. The answers we seek are not commodities [goods] to be purchased, neither are they evolved automatically through the passing of time. . . .

When Indians speak of the continent they yielded [gave up], they are not referring only to the loss of some millions of acres in real estate. They have in mind that the land supported a universe of things they knew, valued, and loved.

With that continent gone, except for a few poor parcels they still retain, the basis of life is precariously [shakily] held, but they mean to hold the scraps and parcels as earnestly as any small nation or ethnic group was ever determined to hold to identity and survival.

What we ask of America is not charity, not paternalism [treatment as from a father], even when benevolent [kind]. We ask only that the nature of our situation be recognized and made the basis of policy and action.

In short, the Indians ask for assistance, technical and financial, for the time needed, however long that may be, to regain in the America of the space age some measure of the adjustment they enjoyed as the original possessors of their native land.

REVIEWING THE READING

1. What did the Indians hope to achieve with their "Declaration of Indian Purpose"?

2. According to the declaration, in what ways had the lives of the American Indian been transformed?

3. **Using Your Historical Imagination.** Of all the injustices suffered by the Native Americans, what do you consider to be the most destructive to the Indian way of life? Explain your answer.

64

From *Looking Outward: Years of Crisis at the United Nations* by Adlai E. Stevenson.

Ambassador Adlai Stevenson Confronts the Soviets over Cuba (1962)

The Cold War had been steadily growing between the United States and the Soviet Union following World War II. In 1962 it reached a frightening level when the Russians began to install in Cuba missiles capable of nuclear strikes against the United States. On October 22, 1962, President John F. Kennedy made a televised address to the American public about the situation. He then demanded that the Soviet Union close down their Cuban bases and remove all missiles. He warned the Russians that American ships would immediately begin to stop and search all ships approaching Cuba to ensure that no more weapons reached Cuba. Kennedy added that if atomic missiles were fired from Cuba, the Soviets could expect the United States to respond with an all-out attack against them. The entire world braced itself for World War III.

On October 25, United States Ambassador to the United Nations Adlai Stevenson spoke before the United Nations Security Council about the crisis. As you read the following excerpts from Stevenson's speech, try to determine why he displayed so much self-confidence in his position.

I want to say to you, Mr. Zorin [Soviet Union Ambassador to the United Nations], that I do not have your talent for obfuscation [clouding the issue], for distortion, for confusing language and for double-talk. And I must confess to you that I am glad that I do not!

But if I understood what you said, it was that my position had changed, that today I was defensive because we did not have the evidence to prove our assertions that your government had installed long-range missiles in Cuba.

Well, let me say something to you, Mr. Ambassador—we do have the evidence. We have it, and it is clear and it is incontrovertible [undeniable]. And let me say something else—those weapons must be taken out of Cuba!

> . . . Mr. Ambassador— we do have the evidence.

Next, if I understood you, you said—with a trespass on credibility that excels your best—that our position had changed since I spoke here the other day because of the pressures of world opinion and the majority of the United Nations. Well, let me say to you, sir—you are wrong again. We have had no pressure from anyone whatsoever. We came here today to indicate our willingness to discuss U Thant's [Secretary-General of the United Nations] proposals, and that is the only change that has taken place.

But let me also say to you, sir, that there *has* been a change. You—the Soviet Union *has* upset the balance of power in the world. You—the Soviet Union *has* created this new danger, not the United States.

And you ask with a fine show of indignation why the President did not tell Mr. Gromyko [foreign minister of the Soviet Union; later premier] on last Thursday about our evidence, at the very time that Mr. Gromyko was blandly denying to the President that the U.S.S.R. was placing such weapons on sites in the new world.

Well, I will tell you why—because we were assembling the evidence, and perhaps it would be instructive to the world to see how far a Soviet official would go in perfidy [treachery]. Perhaps we

Members of the U.N. Security Council look at aerial photos of Soviet missile bases in Cuba. U.S. ambassador Adlai Stevenson introduced the photos as evidence after Soviet ambassador Zorin denied the existence of the bases.

wanted to know if this country faced another example of nuclear deceit like that one a year ago when, in stealth [secret action], the Soviet Union broke the nuclear test moratorium [agreed-upon delay].

And while we are asking questions, let me ask you why your government, your Foreign Minister deliberately, cynically deceived us about the nuclear build-up in Cuba?

And, finally, the other day, Mr. Zorin, I remind you that you did not deny the existence of these weapons. Instead, we heard that they had suddenly become *defensive* weapons. But today, again, if I heard you correctly, you now say, with another fine flood of rhetorical scorn, they do not exist, or that we haven't proved they exist.

All right sir, let me ask you one simple question: Do you, Ambassador Zorin, deny that the U.S.S.R. has placed and is placing medium and intermediate-range missiles and sites in Cuba? Yes or no? Don't wait for the translation. Yes or No? . . .

You are in the courtroom of world opinion. You have denied they exist, and I want to know if I understood you correctly.

I am prepared to wait for my answer until hell freezes over, if that's your decision. And I am

prepared to present the evidence in this room—
now! . . .

I have not had a direct answer to my question.
The representative of the Soviet Union says that
the official answer of the U.S.S.R. was a statement
carried by Tass [government-run newspaper in the
Soviet Union] that it does not need to locate missiles
in Cuba. I agree—the U.S.S.R. does not need to.
But the question is not whether the U.S.S.R. *needs*
missiles in Cuba; the question is: *Has* the U.S.S.R.
missiles in Cuba? And that question remains unanswered. I knew it would remain unanswered.

As to the authenticity of the photographs which
Mr. Zorin has spoken about with such scorn, I wonder
if the Soviet Union would ask its Cuban colleague
to permit a United Nations team to go to these
sites. If so, Mr. Zorin, I can assure you that we
can direct them to the proper places very quickly.

And now I hope that we can get down to business, that we can stop this sparring. We know the
facts and so do you, sir, and we are ready to talk
about them. Our job here is not to score debating
points. Our job, Mr. Zorin, is to save the peace.
And if you are ready to try, we are.

REVIEWING THE READING

1. Why was Stevenson able to state his position with so much confidence?

2. What proof of Soviet missile sites in Cuba
   did Stevenson offer?

3. **Using Your Historical Imagination.** Ambassador Stevenson addressed his remarks
   directly to Mr. Zorin, although he was
   speaking before the entire Security Council. What do you think he hoped to
   achieve by this?

65

From "I'll Know Victory or Defeat" by James Meredith, *The Saturday Evening Post*, November 10, 1962.

James Meredith Cracks Ole Miss (1962)

In October 1962, five years after federal troops had forced local authorities to allow black children to enter an all-white public school in Arkansas, the federal government had to step in once again. This time, the focus was on helping an African American air force veteran named James Meredith enter the University of Mississippi at Oxford. Following a long court battle that resulted in a federal court order demanding that the university open its doors to blacks, Meredith, accompanied by federal marshals, enrolled at "Ole Miss."

Meredith's presence on campus led to a night of rioting in which two people were killed and dozens of others were wounded. President Kennedy ordered 5,000 federal troops and 12,000 National Guardsmen to the campus to patrol the streets and stop the riots. As you read the following excerpt from Meredith's account of his decision to integrate the University of Mississippi, consider why he thought it was so important that he succeed.

In 1955 I reenlisted. I always had it in mind to come back to Mississippi and study law, but I didn't think I was ready then for the responsibilities I would have to face, so I reenlisted. I was in Japan from 1957 till 1960, and there isn't any doubt that this was the settling-down point for me. I decided not only what I wanted to do, which I have known for a long time in a vague way, but how to go about doing it.

Being in Japan was an amazing experience. Negroes say, "When you're in Japan you have to

look in a mirror to remember you're a Negro,"
and it's true. Japan is the only place where I have
not felt the "air of difference."

I was surprised that the Japanese people were
so aware of the racial situation in America. For instance, I met a boy—I don't suppose he was more
than 12 or 13—and he knew more about Little Rock
than most American kids that age. He was amazed
when I told him I was from Mississippi and that I
intended to go back. This kind of reaction further
convinced me that I would go back to Mississippi
and try to improve these conditions. I was discharged
in July, 1960, and by the end of the month I was
back in Kosciusko [Mississippi].

I entered Jackson State College, a Negro school
in Jackson, and quickly met other students who felt
as I did—that Negroes in Mississippi did not have
the rights of full citizens, including the right to
the best education the state offered. Someone had
to seek admission to the University of Mississippi,
and I decided to do it. But there were many of us
involved. Although the lawsuit was mine, the others
were with me, and I sought their advice on every
move I made.

Someone had to seek admission to the University of Mississippi . . .

As soon as I filed application for admission, I
contacted Medgar Evers, Mississippi field secretary
for the N.A.A.C.P. [National Association for the
Advancement of Colored People], and through him
I asked for N.A.A.C.P. legal aid. Mrs. Constance
Motley, associate counsel of the N.A.A.C.P. Legal
Defense Fund, came to my assistance. The
N.A.A.C.P. was prompt and efficient, and that was
of prime importance. There was a great morale factor
here, and every time we called them, they were
there.

The court fight was long, and there were times
when I wondered if it would be successful. I kept
winning in court, but I didn't get any nearer the
university. Finally, after the Fifth Circuit Court of
Appeals had said I should be registered, I felt the

The hardest thing in human nature is to decide to act.

responsibility was the Federal Government's; it was out of my hands to do anything.

People have asked me if I wasn't terribly afraid the night we went to Oxford. No, my apprehensions came a long time before that. The hardest thing in human nature is to decide to act. I was doing all right in the Air Force. I got married in 1956, and my wife was able to work as a civil servant on the same bases where I was stationed. I had to give this up, this established way of things, this status, and try something new and unknown. That's where the big decision was—not here, last month, but there, a couple of years ago. Once I made that decision, things just had to happen the way they happened.

I think maybe a quote from Theodore Roosevelt that I read somewhere was more important than anything else in helping me make this decision. I think I read it around 1952, and I clipped it out, and everywhere I've gone since then—every place I've lived or everywhere I've worked—I have put that saying in front of me. I guess I must have read it two or three thousand times by now. It says, "It is not the critic who counts. . . . The credit belongs to the man who is actually in the arena, whose face is marred by dust and sweat and blood . . . who at the best knows in the end the triumph of high achievement, and who at the worst, if he fails, at least fails while daring greatly, so that his place will never be with those cold and timid souls who know neither victory nor defeat." At different times different parts of that quotation have been important to me, but when I made the decision to return to Mississippi and later to enroll at the university, the part I kept seeing was the part about "cold and timid souls who know neither victory nor defeat." I didn't want to be one of those.

As far as fear of death or personal injury goes— and I consider this most important for everybody to understand—I put death or the fear of getting hurt in the same category with legal objections to my entering the university, or moral objections, or objections on grounds of custom. They are all on the same level. They are all just ways to keep me out of the university, and no one is any more important than any other. It wouldn't matter if I stumbled and fell and couldn't go to classes or whether I cut my finger and couldn't write for a month or whether I was shot and killed—they're all just things in my way. I might do quite a bit to put a stop to the act of being killed. I have done this several times already—I've taken the advice of the Federal marshals on several occasions, for instance. But this was because, if something happened to me, it would have put everything back as far as the Negroes in Mississippi are concerned. If I have lost an hour's sleep in recent weeks, it has been over some philosophical point, or through apprehension of not succeeding in entering the university, and of discouraging others

James Meredith receives a degree in political science from the University of Mississippi—a year after he became the first African American allowed to register at the school.

from trying if I failed, but not over what might happen to me personally.

I was sure that if I were harmed or killed, somebody else would take my place one day. I would hate to think another Negro would have to go through that ordeal, but I would hate worse to think there wouldn't be another who would do it.

I had an older brother who was scary as a boy. Back home he wouldn't go certain places after dark or walk here or there. I always walked wherever I wanted. I walked four miles to Scout meetings at night, and I always went through all the hollows [valleys] and the places where you were supposed to be afraid to go. I must admit my hair has stood up on my head at times, but I never ran. They used to say, "If you see a 'hant' [ghost] put your hand on it." Most of the time you find it isn't there. I think it's an utter waste of time to worry about dying. It's living that matters—doing something to justify being here on God's green earth. I do what I do because I must. I've never felt I had a choice. There is some urge that I can't explain easily—I guess that's as close as I can come to defining it.

There is something else here, too, and it's hard to say right. People can misunderstand it. But it's this—generally at home I was always thought to be pretty smart. I wasn't particularly proud of it; it was just almost a fact of life. There was an expectation or a more or less acknowledged fact that I was one of the sharpest in the group. I was a champion in my group in Mississippi, but then, when I went to Florida to change high schools, I wasn't a champion at all. I had to fight to keep up. I hadn't been prepared. Since then, one of the biggest things in my life is that I have always felt I was never able to develop my talents. I have felt many times that, given the opportunity, I could develop into practically anything. Many times I have been angry at the world for not giving me an opportunity to develop. I am sure this has been a strong motivating force with me, and I'm sure it is with many Negroes. But that's not good enough. We have to see ourselves in the whole society. If America isn't for everybody, it isn't America.

Through all that has happened I have tried to remain detached and objective. I have had all sorts of reactions to things that have happened, but mostly they have been personal reactions and realistic reactions, both at the same time. When I was in the middle of the force of marshals being gathered to take me to Oxford I thought, personally, how utterly ridiculous this was, what a terrible waste of time and money and energy, to iron out some rough spots in our civilization. But realistically I knew that these changes were necessary. I knew change was a threat to people and that they would fight it and that this was the only way it could be accomplished.

I have tried to be detached and realistic. When we were turned away the first time I tried to register at the university, and especially the second time, at the State Capitol in Jackson, I saw the mobs and heard them jeering, "Go home, nigger" and that stuff, but I never recognized them as individuals at all, even those who showed the greatest contempt for me. I felt they were not personally attacking me but that they were protesting a change and this was something they felt they must do. I thought it was impersonal. Some of them were crying, and their crying indicated to me even more the pain of change and the fear of things they did not know. I feel the people were keyed up by the actions of their leaders. With Gov. Ross Barnett taking the position he did, the people were bound to act that way, and it didn't really have anything to do with me personally. That's the way I saw it.

I might add that I thought the governor put on a pretty good performance. The first time, when he turned us away at the university, he reminded me of Charlton Heston, I believe it was, in a movie about Andrew Jackson. Very dramatic.

> I knew change was a threat to people and that they would fight it . . .

I don't think I have had a real low point in recent weeks. It always seemed to me it was the Government's job to carry out the court order and it would be done. The most annoying time was when there was so much talk about a possible deal between the Federal Government and Governor Barnett. But when the Federal officers told me we were going that Sunday, just a few minutes before we took off to Oxford, the annoyance disappeared.

When we landed in Oxford it was almost dark. We got in a car and I remember seeing a truckload of marshals in front of us and one behind. I went straight to the university and was taken to my rooms—an apartment, I guess you would call it. Since they knew some Government men would be staying with me, I had two bedrooms and a living room and a bathroom. The first thing I did was make my bed. When the trouble started, I couldn't see or hear very much of it. Most of it was at the other end of the campus, and besides I didn't look out the window. I think I read a newspaper and went to bed around 10 o'clock. I was awakened several times in the night by the noise and shooting outside, but it wasn't near me, and I had no way of knowing what was going on. Some of the students in my dormitory banged their doors for a while and threw some bottles in the halls, but I slept pretty well all night.

I was awakened several times in the night by the noise and shooting outside, but it wasn't near me . . .

I woke up about six-thirty in the morning and looked out and saw the troops. There was a slight smell of tear gas in my room, but I still didn't know what had gone on during the night, and I didn't find out until some marshals came and told me how many people were hurt and killed. I had gotten to know these marshals pretty well in recent weeks, and I was so sorry about this. Some supposedly responsible newspapermen asked me if I thought attending the university was worth all this death and destruction. That really annoyed me. Of course I was sorry! I didn't want that sort of thing. I believe it could have been prevented by responsible political leaders. I understand the President and the attorney general were up most of the night. They had all the intelligence at their disposal, and I believe they handled it to the best of their knowledge and ability. I think it would have been much worse if we had waited any longer. Social change is a painful thing, but it depends on the people at the top. Here they were totally opposed—the state against the Federal Government. There was bound to be trouble, and there was trouble.

Social change is a painful thing . . .

Monday morning at eight o'clock I registered, and at nine I went to a class in Colonial American History. I was a few minutes late, and I took a seat at the back of the room. The professor was lecturing on the background of England, conditions there at the time of the colonization of America, and he paid no special attention when I entered. I think there were about a dozen students in the class. One said hello to me, and the others were silent. I remember a girl—the only girl there, I think—and she was crying, but it might have been from the tear gas in the room. I was crying from it myself.

I had three classes scheduled that day. I went to two, and the third didn't meet because there was too much gas in the room. No marshals were in the classrooms with me, nor were they all week.

I have received hundreds of telegrams and more than 1,000 letters, most of them expressions of support. One guy sent me a piece of singed [scorched] rope, and another sent a poem, I guess you'd have to call it:

> *Roses are red, violets are blue;*
> *I've killed one nigger and might as well*
> > *make it two.*

But most of the letters and telegrams have supported me, and some of them have been really touching—letters from 10- and 11-year-olds who think I'm right and offer me their help and that sort of thing.

As far as my relations with the students go, I make it a practice to be courteous. I don't force myself on them, but that's not my nature anyway. Many of them—most, I'd say—have been courteous, and the faculty members certainly have been. When I hear the jeers and the catcalls—"We'll get you, nigger" and all that—I don't consider it personal. I get the idea people are just having a little fun. I think it's tragic that they have to have this kind of fun about me, but many of them are children of the men who lead Mississippi today, and I wouldn't expect them to act any other way. They have to act the way they do. I think I understand human nature enough to understand that.

It hasn't been all bad. Many students have spoken to me very pleasantly. They have stopped banging the doors and throwing bottles into my dormitory now.

One day a fellow from my home town sat down at my table in the cafeteria. "If you're here to get an education, I'm for you," he said. "If you're here to cause trouble, I'm against you." That seemed fair enough to me.

REVIEWING THE READING

1. Why did Meredith think it was so important that he succeed in integrating the University of Mississippi?

2. How did Meredith's experience at the high school in Florida help him see the importance of integrated schools?

3. **Using Your Historical Imagination.** What aspects of Meredith's personality do you think helped him get through the court battles, the threats, and the rejection?

The Reverend Martin Luther King, Jr., Preaches Nonviolence from the Birmingham Jail (1963)

66

From *Why We Can't Wait* by Martin Luther King, Jr.

In 1955 African Americans won a major battle against segregation during a year-long boycott of city buses in Montgomery, Alabama. The boycott began after Rosa Parks was arrested for refusing to give up her seat on a bus to a white man. The strike was led by a young black minister, Martin Luther King, Jr., who urged his followers to fight discrimination through nonviolent resistance.

By 1960 peaceful resistance had gained national support. African Americans, along with many white supporters, conducted sit-ins, marches, and other forms of resistance in cities all over the South. In April 1963 King led a march in Birmingham to protest the city's segregation practices. King and other leaders were arrested and jailed. In jail King received a letter from a group of Alabama clergymen who accused him of being an "outside agitator." As you read the following excerpts from King's response, try to determine how he justified his participation in the protest.

*M*y *Dear Fellow Clergymen:* While confined here in the Birmingham city jail, I came across your recent statement calling my present activities "unwise and untimely." Seldom do I pause to answer criticism of my work and ideas.

. . . I feel that you are men of genuine good will and that your criticisms are sincerely set forth . . .

If I sought to answer all the criticisms that cross my desk, my secretaries would have little time for anything other than such correspondence in the course of the day, and I would have no time for constructive work. But since I feel that you are men of genuine good will and that your criticisms are sincerely set forth, I want to try to answer your statement in what I hope will be patient and reasonable terms.

I think I should indicate why I am here in Birmingham, since you have been influenced by the view which argues against "outsiders coming in." I have the honor of serving as president of the Southern Christian Leadership Conference, an organization operating in every southern state, with headquarters in Atlanta, Georgia. We have some eighty-five affiliated organizations across the South, and one of them is the Alabama Christian Movement for Human Rights. Frequently we share staff, educational and financial resources with our affiliates. Several months ago the affiliate here in Birmingham asked us to be on call to engage in a nonviolent direct-action program if such were deemed necessary. We readily consented, and when the hour came we lived up to our promise. So I, along with several members of my staff, am here because I was invited here. I am here because I have organizational ties here.

But more basically, I am in Birmingham because injustice is here. Just as the prophets of the eighth century B.C. left their villages and carried their "thus saith the Lord" far beyond the boundaries of their home towns, and just as the Apostle Paul left his village of Tarsus and carried the gospel of Jesus Christ to the far corners of the Greco-Roman world, so am I compelled to carry the gospel of freedom beyond my own home town. Like Paul, I must constantly respond to the Macedonian call* for aid. . . .

One of the basic points in your statement is that the action that I and my associates have taken

* Reference to a vision that came to Paul in which a man from Macedonia appeared and asked the apostle to come to that country and help the people.

in Birmingham is untimely. Some have asked: "Why didn't you give the new city administration time to act?" The only answer that I can give this query [question] is that the new Birmingham administration must be prodded about as much as the outgoing one, before it will act. We are sadly mistaken if we feel that the election of Albert Boutwell as mayor will bring the millennium [biblical reference to the period of 1,000 years during which Christ will reign on earth, bringing peace and justice] to Birmingham. While Mr. Boutwell is a much more gentle person than Mr. Connor, they are both segregationists, dedicated to maintenance of the status quo [existing situation]. I have hope that Mr. Boutwell will be reasonable enough to see the futility [uselessness] of massive resistance to desegregation. But he will not see this without pressure from devotees [supporters] of civil rights. My friends, I must say to you that we have not made a single gain in civil rights without determined legal and nonviolent pressure. Lamentably, it is an historical fact that privileged groups seldom give up their privileges voluntarily. Individuals may see the moral light and voluntarily give up their unjust posture; but, as Reinhold Niebuhr [American clergyman and writer] has reminded us, groups tend to be more immoral than individuals.

We know through painful experience that freedom is never voluntarily given by the oppressor; it must be demanded by the oppressed. Frankly, I have yet to engage in a direct-action campaign that was "well timed" in the view of those who have not suffered unduly from the disease of segregation. For years now I have heard the word "Wait!" It rings in the ear of every Negro with piercing familiarity. This "Wait!" has almost always meant "Never." We must come to see, with one of our distinguished jurists, that "justice too long delayed is justice denied."

We have waited for more than 340 years for our constitutional and God-given rights. The nations

We know through painful experience that freedom is never voluntarily given by the oppressor . . .

of Asia and Africa are moving with jetlike speed toward gaining political independence, but we still creep at horse-and-buggy pace toward gaining a cup of coffee at a lunch counter. Perhaps it is easy for those who have never felt the stinging darts of segregation to say, "Wait." But when you have seen vicious mobs lynch your mothers and fathers at will and drown your sisters and brothers at whim; when you have seen hate-filled policemen curse, kick and even kill your black brothers and sisters; when you see the vast majority of your twenty million Negro brothers smothering in an airtight cage of poverty in the midst of an affluent [wealthy] society; when you suddenly find your tongue twisted and your speech stammering as you seek to explain to your six-year-old daughter why she can't go to the public amusement park that has just been advertised on television, and see tears welling up in her eyes when she is told that Funtown is closed to colored children, and see ominous clouds of inferiority beginning to form in her little mental sky, and see her beginning to distort her personality by developing an unconscious bitterness toward white people; when you have to concoct an answer for a five-year-old son who is asking: "Daddy, why do white people treat colored people so mean?"; when you take a cross-country drive and find it necessary to sleep night after night in the uncomfortable corners of your automobile because no motel will accept you; when you are humiliated day in and day out by nagging signs reading "white" and "colored"; when your first name becomes "nigger," your middle name becomes "boy" (however old you are) and your last name becomes "John," and your wife and mother are never given the respected title "Mrs."; when you are harried by day and haunted by night by the fact that you are a Negro, living constantly at tiptoe stance, never quite knowing what to expect next, and are plagued with inner fears and outer resentments; when you are forever fighting a degenerating [humiliating]

sense of "nobodiness"—then you will understand why we find it difficult to wait. There comes a time when the cup of endurance runs over, and men are no longer willing to be plunged into the abyss [bottomless pit] of despair. I hope, sirs, you can understand our legitimate and unavoidable impatience.

 You express a great deal of anxiety over our willingness to break laws. This is certainly a legitimate concern. Since we so diligently urge people to obey the Supreme Court's decision of 1954 outlawing segregation in the public schools, at first glance it may seem rather paradoxical [contradictory] for us consciously to break laws. One may well ask: "How can you advocate breaking some laws and obeying others?" The answer lies in the fact that

The Reverend Martin Luther King, Jr., was jailed in Birmingham, Alabama, after protesting segregation practices in the city.

there are two types of laws: just and unjust. I would be the first to advocate obeying just laws. One has not only a legal but a moral responsibility to obey just laws. Conversely [on the other hand], one has a moral responsibility to disobey unjust laws. I would agree with St. Augustine that "an unjust law is no law at all."

Now, what is the difference between the two? How does one determine whether a law is just or unjust? A just law is a man-made code that squares with the moral law or the law of God. An unjust law is a code that is out of harmony with the moral law. To put it in the terms of St. Thomas Aquinas:*

* Thirteenth-century Christian thinker who taught that governments should support basic human rights and should not go against God's law concerning the worth of the individual.

An unjust law is a human law that is not rooted in eternal law and natural law. Any law that uplifts human personality is just. Any law that degrades human personality is unjust. All segregation statutes are unjust because segregation distorts the soul and damages the personality. It gives the segregator a false sense of superiority and the segregated a false sense of inferiority. Segregation, to use the terminology of the Jewish philosopher Martin Buber, substitutes an "I-it" relationship for an "I-thou" relationship and ends up relegating [putting down] persons to the status of things. Hence segregation is not only practically, economically and sociologically unsound, it is morally wrong and sinful. Paul Tillich [American clergyman and philosopher] has said that sin is separation. Is not segregation an existential [based on experience] expression of man's tragic separation, his awful estrangement [distancing from others], his terrible sinfulness? Thus it is that I can urge men to obey the 1954 decision of the Supreme Court, for it is morally right; and I can urge them to disobey segregation ordinances, for they are morally wrong.

Let us consider a more concrete example of just and unjust laws. An unjust law is a code that a numerical or power majority group compels a minority group to obey but does not make binding on itself. This is *difference* made legal. By the same token, a just law is a code that a majority compels a minority to follow and that it is willing to follow itself. This is *sameness* made legal.

Let me give another explanation. A law is unjust if it is inflicted on a minority that, as a result of being denied the right to vote, had no part in enacting or devising the law. Who can say that the legislature of Alabama which set up that state's segregation laws was democratically elected? Throughout Alabama all sorts of devious methods are used to prevent Negroes from becoming registered voters, and there are some counties in which, even though Negroes constitute a majority of the population, not a single Negro is registered. Can any law enacted under such circumstances be considered democratically structured?

Sometimes a law is just on its face and unjust in its application. For instance, I have been arrested on a charge of parading without a permit. Now, there is nothing wrong in having an ordinance which requires a permit for a parade. But such an ordinance becomes unjust when it is used to maintain segregation and to deny citizens the First-Amendment privilege of peaceful assembly and protest.

I hope you are able to see the distinction I am trying to point out. In no sense do I advocate evading or defying the law, as would the rabid [extreme] segregationist. That would lead to anarchy [chaos]. One who breaks an unjust law must do so openly, lovingly, and with a willingness to accept the penalty. I submit that an individual who breaks a law that conscience tells him is unjust, and who willingly accepts the penalty of imprisonment in order to arouse the conscience of the community over its injustice, is in reality expressing the highest respect for the law.

Of course, there is nothing new about this kind of civil disobedience. It was evidenced sublimely in the refusal of Shadrach, Meshach and Abednego

> Sometimes a law is just on its face and unjust in its application.

* Reference to the biblical story of three Jews who refused to worship the image of their Babylonian conqueror, King Nebuchadnezzar (630–532 B.C.), and were condemned to die in a fiery furnace; saved by their faith in God.

° Reference to early Greek philosopher and teacher who argued against the accepted way of electing rulers in Athens and was condemned to die.

to obey the laws of Nebuchadnezzar, on the ground that a higher moral law was at stake.* It was practiced superbly by the early Christians, who were willing to face hungry lions and the excruciating pain of chopping blocks rather than submit to certain unjust laws of the Roman Empire. To a degree, academic freedom is a reality today because Socrates° practiced civil disobedience. In our own nation, the Boston Tea Party represented a massive act of civil disobedience.

We should never forget that everything Adolf Hitler did in Germany was "legal" and everything the Hungarian freedom fighters did in Hungary was "illegal." It was "illegal" to aid and comfort a Jew in Hitler's Germany. Even so, I am sure that, had I lived in Germany at the time, I would have aided and comforted my Jewish brothers. If today I lived in a Communist country where certain principles dear to the Christian faith are suppressed, I would openly advocate disobeying that country's antireligious laws.

REVIEWING THE READING

1. How did King justify to the clergymen his participation in the protest that took place in Birmingham?

2. How did King respond to the accusation by the clergymen that his actions were "untimely"?

3. **Using Your Historical Imagination.** King advocated obeying "just" laws and disobeying "unjust" laws, yet he said that "In no sense do I advocate evading or defying the law." What do you think he meant by this? Why do you think his idea of nonviolent resistance met with such great success?

President Johnson Defines the Great Society (1964)

67

From a White House Press Release.

When Lyndon B. Johnson became president in November 1963, following the assassination of President Kennedy, he was following one of the most popular presidents in our history. Johnson's first actions in office involved pushing through Congress many of the domestic programs that Kennedy had initiated.

But Johnson had plans and programs of his own as well. As he prepared to run for president in the 1964 election, Johnson chose as his theme for the campaign what he called the Great Society. On May 22, 1964, Johnson gave a speech at the University of Michigan in which he defined the Great Society. As you read the following excerpts from that speech, try to determine why President Johnson chose to give this particular speech on a university campus.

I have come today from the turmoil of your Capitol to the tranquility of your campus to speak about the future of our country. The purpose of protecting the life of our Nation and preserving the liberty of our citizens is to pursue the happiness of our people. Our success in that pursuit is the test of our success as a nation. For a century we labored to settle and to subdue a continent. For half a century, we called upon unbounded invention and untiring industry to create an order of plenty for all of our people. The challenge of the next half century is whether we have the wisdom to use that wealth to enrich and elevate our national life, and to advance the quality of our American civilization.

Your imagination, your initiative and your indignation will determine whether we build a society where progress is the servant of our needs, or a society where old values and new visions are buried under unbridled growth. For in your time we have the opportunity to move not only toward the rich society and the powerful society, but upward to the Great Society. The Great Society rests on abundance and liberty for all. It demands an end to poverty and racial injustice, to which we are totally committed in our time. But that is just the beginning. The Great Society is a place where every child can find knowledge to enrich his mind and to enlarge his talents. It is a place where leisure is a welcome chance to build and reflect, not a feared cause of boredom and restlessness. It is a place where the city of man serves not only the needs of the body and the demands of commerce, but the desire for beauty and the hunger for community.

It is a place where man can renew contact with nature. It is a place which honors creation for its own sake and for what it adds to the understanding of the race. It is a place where men are more concerned with the quality of their goals than the quantity of their goods. But most of all, the great society is not a safe harbor, a resting place, a final objective, a finished work. It is a challenge constantly renewed, beckoning us toward a destiny where the meaning of our lives matches the marvelous products of our labor.

So I want to talk to you today about three places where we begin to build the Great Society— in our cities, in our countryside, and in our classrooms. Many of you will live to see the day, perhaps 50 years from now, when there will be 400 million Americans; four-fifths of them in urban areas. In the remainder of this century urban population will double, city land will double, and we will have to build homes, highways and facilities equal to all those built since this country was first settled. So in the next 40 years we must rebuild the entire urban United States.

President Lyndon Johnson defined his Great Society during a commencement speech at the University of Michigan in 1964.

Aristotle said, "Men come together in cities in order to live, but they remain together in order to live the good life."

It is harder and harder to live the good life in American cities today. The catalogue of ills is long: There is the decay of the centers and the despoiling of the suburbs. There is not enough housing for our people or transportation for our traffic. Open land is vanishing and old landmarks are violated. Worst of all, expansion is eroding the precious and time honored values of community with neighbors and communion with nature. The loss of these values breeds loneliness and boredom and indifference. Our society will never be great until our cities are great. Today the frontier of imagination and innovation is inside those cities, and not beyond their borders. New experiments are already going on. It will be the task of your generation to make the American city a place where future generations will come, not only to live but to live the good life. . . .

A second place where we begin to build the Great Society is in our countryside. We have always prided ourselves on being not only America the strong and America the free, but America the beautiful. Today that beauty is in danger. The water we drink, the food we eat, the very air that we breathe, are threatened with pollution. Our parks are overcrowded. Our seashores overburdened. Green fields and dense forests are disappearing.

A few years ago we were greatly concerned about the Ugly American. Today we must act to prevent an Ugly America.

For once the battle is lost, once our natural splendor is destroyed, it can never be recaptured. And once man can no longer walk with beauty or wonder at nature, his spirit will wither and his sustenance be wasted.

A third place to build the Great Society is in the classrooms of America. There your children's lives will be shaped. Our society will not be great until every young mind is set free to scan the farthest reaches of thought and imagination. We are still far from that goal. Today, eight million adult Americans, more than the entire population of Michigan, have not finished five years of school. Nearly 20 million have not finished eight years of school. Nearly 54 million, more than one-quarter of all America, have not even finished high school.

Each year more than 100,000 high school graduates, with proved ability, do not enter college because they cannot afford it. And if we cannot educate today's youth, what will we do in 1970 when elementary school enrollment will be 5 million greater than 1960? And high school enrollment will rise by five million. College enrollment will increase by more than three million. In many places, classrooms are overcrowded and curricula are outdated. Most of our qualified teachers are underpaid, and many of our paid teachers are unqualified. So we must give every child a place to sit and a teacher to learn from. Poverty must not be a bar to learning, and learning must offer an escape from poverty.

But more classrooms and more teachers are not enough. We must seek an educational system which grows in excellence as it grows in size. This means better training for our teachers. It means preparing

> . . . Our society will not be great until every young mind is set free to scan the farthest reaches of thought and imagination.

youth to enjoy their hours of leisure as well as their hours of labor. It means exploring new techniques of teaching, to find new ways to stimulate the love of learning and the capacity for creation.

These are three of the central issues of the Great Society. While our government has many programs directed at those issues, I do not pretend that we have the full answer to those problems. But I do promise this: We are going to assemble the best thought and the broadest knowledge from all over the world to find those answers for America. I intend to establish working groups to prepare a series of White House conferences and meetings on the cities, on natural beauty, on the quality of education, and on other emerging challenges. And from these meetings and from this inspiration and from these studies we will begin to set our course toward the Great Society.

The solution to these problems does not rest on a massive program in Washington, nor can it rely solely on the strained resources of local authority. They require us to create new concepts of cooperation, a creative federalism, between the national capital and the leaders of local communities.

Woodrow Wilson once wrote: "Every man sent out from his university should be a man of his Nation as well as a man of his time."

Within your lifetime powerful forces, already loosed, will take us toward a way of life beyond the realm of our experience, almost beyond the bounds of our imagination. For better or for worse, your generation has been appointed by history to deal with those problems and to lead America toward a new age. You can help build a society where the demands of morality, and the needs of the spirit, can be realized in the life of the nation. So will you join in the battle to give every citizen the full equality which God enjoins [orders] and the law requires, whatever his belief, or race, or the color of his skin? Will you join in the battle to give every

. . . your generation has been appointed by history to . . . lead America toward a new age.

citizen an escape from the crushing weight of poverty? Will you join in the battle to make it possible for all nations to live in enduring peace as neighbors and not as mortal enemies? Will you join in the battle to build the Great Society, to prove that our material progress is only the foundation on which we will build a richer life of mind and spirit?

There are those timid souls who say this battle cannot be won, that we are condemned to a soulless wealth. I do not agree. We have the power to shape the civilization that we want. But we need your will, your labor, your hearts, if we are to build that kind of society.

Those who came to this land sought to build more than just a new country. They sought a free world.

So I have come here today to your campus to say that you can make their vision our reality. Let us from this moment begin our work so that in the future men will look back and say: It was then, after a long and weary way, that man turned the exploits of his genius to the full enrichment of his life.

REVIEWING THE READING

1. Why do you think President Johnson chose a university campus as the proper place to define the Great Society?

2. What three areas did Johnson define as the places to begin building the Great Society?

3. **Using Your Historical Imagination.** Imagine that you are running for president today. Which of the three areas of concern mentioned by President Johnson still might be areas of concern today? Which of the three areas, if any, is no longer of concern? Explain your answers.

Stokely Carmichael Explains "Black Power" (1966)

68

From "What We Want" by Stokely Carmichael, *The New York Review of Books*, Volume VII, No. 4, September 22, 1966.

As the civil rights movement gained strength in the 1960s, many African Americans became impatient with the slowness of change. Some began to question Martin Luther King's policies of persuasion and passive resistance. Race riots broke out in impoverished black ghettos in cities throughout the country. In the midst of this, a call for "Black Power" emerged. Stokely Carmichael, chairperson of the Student Nonviolent Coordinating Committee (SNCC), a group actively involved in civil rights projects, explained the meaning of the slogan in a 1966 essay. As you read the following excerpts from Carmichael's essay, try to determine why he believed that the civil rights movement was neglecting poor young blacks in urban ghettos.

O ne of the tragedies of the struggle against racism is that up to now there has been no national organization which could speak to the growing militancy of young black people in the urban ghetto. There has been only a civil rights movement, whose tone of voice was adapted to an audience of liberal whites. It served as a sort of buffer zone between them and angry young blacks. None of its so-called leaders could go into a rioting community and be listened to. In a sense, I blame ourselves—together with the mass media—for what has happened in Watts, Harlem, Chicago, Cleveland, Omaha. Each time the people in those cities saw Martin Luther King get slapped, they became angry; when they saw four little black girls bombed to death, they were angrier; and when nothing happened, they were steaming. We had nothing to offer that they could see, except to go out and be beaten again. We helped to build their frustration.

For too many years, black Americans marched and had their heads broken and got shot. They were saying to the country, "Look, you guys are supposed to be nice guys and we are only going to do what we are supposed to do—why do you beat us up, why don't you give us what we ask, why don't you straighten yourselves out?" After years of this, we are at almost the same point—because we demonstrated from a position of weakness. We cannot be expected any longer to march and have our heads broken in order to say to whites: come on, you're nice guys. For you are not nice guys.

An organization which claims to speak for the needs of a community—as does the Student Nonviolent Coordinating Committee—must speak in the tone of that community, not as somebody else's buffer zone. This is the significance of black power as a slogan. For once, black people are going to use the words they want to use—not just the words whites want to hear. And they will do this no matter how often the press tries to stop the use of the slogan by equating it with racism and separatism.

. . . The concept of "black power" is not a recent or isolated phenomenon: It has grown out of the ferment of agitation and activity by different people and organizations in many black communities over the years. Our last year of work in Alabama added a new concrete possibility. In Lowndes county, for example, black power will mean that if a Negro is elected sheriff, he can end police brutality. If a black man is elected tax assessor, he can collect and channel funds for the building of better roads and schools serving black people—thus advancing the move from political power into the economic arena. In such areas as Lowndes, where black men have a majority, they will attempt to use it to exercise control. This is what they seek: control. Where

Stokely Carmichael gives a "black power" salute during one of the many speeches he made during the 1960s.

Negroes lack a majority, black power means proper representation and sharing of control. It means the creation of power bases from which black people can work to change statewide or nationwide patterns of oppression through pressure from strength—instead of weakness. . . .

Integration speaks not at all to the problem of poverty, only to the problem of blackness. Integration today means the man who "makes it," leaving his black brothers behind in the ghetto as fast as his new sports car will take him. It has no relevance to the Harlem wino or the cottonpicker making three dollars a day. . . . As a goal, it has been based on complete acceptance of the fact that in *order to have* a decent house or education, blacks must move into a white neighborhood or send their children to a white school. This reinforces, among both black and white, the idea that "white" is automatically better and "black" is by definition inferior. This is why integration is a subterfuge [deception] for the maintenance of white supremacy. It allows the nation to focus on a handful of Southern children who get into white schools, at great price, and to ignore the 94 percent who are left behind in unimproved all-black schools. Such situations will not change until black people have power—to control their own school board, in this case. Then Negroes become equal in a way that means something, and integration ceases to be a one-way street. . . .

The need for psychological equality is the reason why SNCC today believes that blacks must organize in the black community. Only black people can convey the revolutionary idea that black people are able to do things themselves; they must get poverty money they will control and spend themselves, they must conduct tutorial programs themselves so that black children can identify with black people. This is one reason Africa has such importance: The reality of black men ruling their own natives gives blacks elsewhere a sense of possibility, of power, which they do not now have.

This does not mean we don't welcome help, or friends. But we want the right to decide whether anyone is, in fact, our friend. In the past, black Americans have been almost the only people whom everybody and his momma could jump up and call their friends. We have been tokens, symbols, objects— as I was in high school to many young whites, who liked having "a Negro friend." We want to decide who is our friend, and we will not accept someone who comes to us and says: "If you do X, Y, and Z, then I'll help you." We will not be told whom we should choose as allies. We will not be isolated from any group or nation except by our own choice. We cannot have the oppressors telling the oppressed how to rid themselves of the oppressor. . . .

. . . **we want the right to decide whether anyone is, in fact, our friend.**

But our vision is not merely a society in which all black men have enough to buy the good things in life. When we urge that black money go into black pockets, we mean the communal pocket. We want to see the cooperative concept applied in business and banking. We want to see black ghetto residents demand that an exploiting landlord or storekeeper sell them, at minimal cost, a building or a shop that they will own and improve cooperatively; they can back their demand with a rent strike, or a boycott, and a community so unified behind

them that no one else will move into the building
or buy at the store. The society we seek to build
among black people, then, is not a capitalist one.
It is a society in which the spirit of community
and humanistic love prevail. . . . The love we seek
to encourage is within the black community, the
only American community where men call each other
"brother" when they meet. We can build a community
of love only where we have the ability and power
to do so: among blacks.

REVIEWING THE READING

1. What does Carmichael mean when he
   says that the civil rights movement does
   not speak to poor young blacks in urban
   ghettos?

2. Why does Carmichael believe that blacks
   must organize in the black community?

3. **Using Your Historical Imagination.** In
   his essay, Carmichael states that the press
   is attempting to stop the use of the "Black
   Power" slogan by equating it with racism.
   Do you think this charge is true? If so,
   why do you think the press would do
   this?

69

From *The Arrogance of Power* by J. William Fulbright; and *History of U.S. Political Parties* by Arthur M. Schlesinger, Jr.

Senator Fulbright and President Johnson Debate the Vietnam War (1966, 1968)

In 1964 President Lyndon B. Johnson broke a campaign promise and ordered the U.S. Air Force to bomb selected targets in North Vietnam. By 1968 more than a half million American troops were fighting in Vietnam, even though war had never officially been declared. Johnson chose not to run for reelection in 1968, mainly because of American opposition to his position on the Vietnam issue.

An outspoken opponent to U.S. involvement in Vietnam was Senator J. William Fulbright, chair of the Senate Foreign Relations Committee. The first part of the selection is excerpted from Fulbright's book The Arrogance of Power, *in which he discusses the Vietnam issue. The second part of the selection is excerpted from a 1968 speech by President Johnson in which he reaffirms his administration's position on Vietnam. As you read note how Fulbright's belief that the Viet Cong should be part of the South Vietnam government conflicts with Johnson's stated goals in Vietnam.*

J. William Fulbright

The United States is now involved in a sizable and "open-ended" war against communism in the only country in the world which won freedom from colonial rule under communist leadership. In South Vietnam as in North Vietnam, the communists remain today the only solidly organized political force. That fact is both the measure of our failure and the key to its possible redemption [restoration].

So-called "wars of national liberation" are political wars, whose outcomes depend on a combination of political and military factors. The communist guerrillas in Malaya could not have been beaten without hard fighting, but neither, in all probability, could they have been beaten had Malaya not been given its independence. . . . The major reason for the success of the Viet Cong [pro-communist guerrillas] in South Vietnam has not been aid from the North but the absence of a cohesive alternative nationalist movement in the South. Both the success of the communists in South Vietnam and their failure in India, Burma, Malaya, Indonesia, and the Philippines strongly suggest that "wars of national liberation" depend for their success more on the weakness of the regime under attack than on the strength of support from outside.

Our search for a solution to the Vietnamese war must begin with the general fact that nationalism is the strongest single political force in the world today and the specific fact . . . that in Vietnam the most effective nationalist movement is communist-controlled. We are compelled, therefore, once again to choose between opposition to communism and support of nationalism. I strongly recommend that for once we give priority to the latter. . . . I

Senator William Fulbright (left) and President Johnson (right) often disagreed on policy. Fulbright kept this photo on his office wall. It is inscribed, "To Bill, I can see I haven't been very persuasive," and is signed "Lyndon B. Johnson."

strongly recommend . . . that we seek to come to terms with both Hanoi [capital of North Vietnam] and the Viet Cong, not, to be sure, by "turning tail and running," as the saying goes, but by conceding [granting] the Viet Cong a part in the government of South Vietnam.

Lyndon B. Johnson

Our objective in South Vietnam has never been the annihilation [destruction] of the enemy. It has been to bring about a recognition in Hanoi that its objective—taking over the South by force—could not be achieved. . . .

So tonight I reaffirm the pledge that we made at Manila: that we are prepared to withdraw our forces from South Vietnam as the other side withdraws its forces to the North, stops the infiltration, and the level of violence thus subsides. . . .

One day, my fellow citizens, there will be peace in Southeast Asia. It will come because the people of Southeast Asia want it—those whose armies are at war tonight; those who, though threatened, have thus far been spared.

Peace will come because Asians were willing to work for it and to sacrifice for it—and to die by the thousands for it.

But let it never be forgotten: peace will come also because America sent her sons to help secure it.

It has not been easy—far from it. During the past four and a half years, it has been my fate and my responsibility to be Commander in Chief. I have lived daily and nightly with the cost of this war. I know the pain that it has inflicted. I know perhaps better than anyone the misgivings it has aroused.

And throughout this entire long period I have been sustained by a single principle: that what we are doing now in Vietnam is vital not only to the security of Southeast Asia but . . . [also] to the security of every American.

> . . . we are prepared to withdraw our forces from South Vietnam as the other side withdraws its forces to the North . . .

Surely, we have treaties which we must respect. Surely, we have commitments that we are going to keep. . . .

But the heart of our involvement in South Vietnam under three different Presidents, three separate administrations, has always been America's own security.

And the larger purpose of our involvement has always been to help the nations of Southeast Asia become independent, and stand alone self-sustaining as members of a great world community, at peace with themselves, at peace with all others. And with such a nation our country—and the world—will be far more secure than it is tonight.

I believe that a peaceful Asia is far nearer to reality because of what America has done in Vietnam. I believe that the men who endure the dangers of battle there, fighting there for us tonight, are helping the entire world avoid far greater conflicts, far wider wars, far more destruction, than this one.

REVIEWING THE READING

1. How do President Johnson's stated objectives of the war conflict with Senator Fulbright's opinion that the Viet Cong should be accepted as part of the government of South Vietnam?

2. According to Senator Fulbright, what was the main reason for the success of the Viet Cong in South Vietnam?

3. **Using Your Historical Imagination.** Why do you think that four American presidents—Eisenhower, Kennedy, Johnson, and Nixon—all supported American involvement in Vietnam? What did President Johnson say in his speech that helps you draw your conclusion?

70

From *Everything We Had: An Oral History of the Vietnam War by Thirty-three American Soldiers Who Fought It* by Al Santoli.

An African American GI in Vietnam (1969–1970)

Going to war is especially difficult for those who do not choose the military as a way of life. This problem was compounded for those men drafted into the Vietnam War, which had little public support. The men sent there did not understand why they were there or what they were fighting for. Worst of all, the soldiers returned home to find that no one cared about what they had gone through. The following selection is excerpted from a book of oral histories taken from American soldiers in Vietnam. As you read one soldier's account of his experiences as a rifleman with the 1st Cavalry Division, try to determine why he had such deep-seated hatred for the Vietnamese.

I was up at An Khe for a week to go through the little training school up there that the 1st Cav gives you when you first get in country, and then they ship you out to your unit, which was down in Tay Ninh Province. I didn't expect nothing when I got there, but it was just all the way different. It was an LZ [landing zone] beneath the Black Virgin Mountain.

The first night they sent me on OP [forward observation post] and I was as scared as I've ever been in my life. I just said, "How could I do a year over here?" You know, it was too much. The first night was a strain on me. I could feel it inside. It was worse than being a convict locked up in a prison. We just laid out there. So I said, "If the Cong come, we'll be the first ones to go."

On that mountain was where the VC [Viet Cong] were. There was an American radio outpost at the top, the VC were all up and down the mountain, and we were at the base.

I saw these helicopters land the next morning and I wonders to myself what they is for. They told us to get into the helicopters. I thought, "Oh, we're going to the rear." They put us out there in the middle of the jungle and dropped us off. I was actually bummed out. This was my first time, man, and the helicopter was doing like this and I was so afraid I might fall off because I had two mortar rounds. I finally landed and we started going out on search-and-destroy missions.

> . . . They put us out there in the middle of the jungle and dropped us off.

Just before our first fire fight, nobody told me our OP was out there. I heard something out there and blew a claymore [land mine] on my own OP. Lucky nobody wasn't killed. I took my M-16 [type of rifle] and opened up. The next morning I got chewed out by the company commander. But I didn't know. They don't tell you anything. They just sent you out there.

We got fire fights after fire fights. My first taste of death. After fire fights you could smell it. They brought the guys back wrapped up in ponchos, those green ponchos. The way they put them on the helicopter really just made me think about it all . . . they just threw them up on the helicopter and put all those empty supplies on top of the them. You could see the guys' feet hanging out. I could see those jungle boots. I had nightmares behind them. I can still see those guys . . . I was talking to one guy that morning. His name was Joe Cocaham, he was from New Jersey. They just packed everything up on him and took off. I can remember the guys saying, "I wonder how his family is going to feel." I said, "What are we over here fighting for?"

On Ho Chi Minh's birthday, May 19, 1969, I got wounded in an ambush. I got hit under the chin, over the eye and in the leg. Okay. They sent me back to Tay Ninh. That's the farthest I got back to the rear. Just patched me up. Then as the stitches got well, they cut 'em out and sent me back to the unit. By that time my mind had just snapped. I'd write these letters home saying what to do with all of my stuff, like I was making out a will. Because I had a feeling that I wasn't coming back. . . .

When I got near the deros, or whatever they call it when you come back to the States, sometimes I wished I had died over there with my buddies. I said, "What's back here?" You know, my wife had left.

I got married a couple of months before I got drafted, and they said they couldn't catch up with the paperwork to keep me out of the draft. I was overdue. I was 1-A about a year and a half. I tried to go to school at that time—they was funny about getting into schools—and I tried joining the National Guard, but they was all booked up. I was working for Cleveland Electric Illuminating Company. When I got back everything was changed. The way I feel about life now . . . it's just a bum trip. I have flashbacks and people can't understand me sometimes. I sit by myself and I just think. You try to talk to somebody about it, they think you're out of your mind or you're freaked out. They want to put you in a strait jacket or something like that. That's why I go to these veterans rap groups that they have now every Wednesday. I just blow off the heat that I have built up inside.

About fifteen guys go to them, all different races. And we just sit there and say the way we feel. We just get everything out of our minds. Like Congress and the United States could spend billions and billions of dollars to bring Vietnamese over here now, but they can't even put up a system that's federally funded by the VA or somewhere to help these Vietnam veterans that've actually been having this ten-year relapse. I mean, you could just look at some of them and just tell that they are . . . just gone.

When I got back everything was changed.

Thousands of African Americans served in the Vietnam War.

Most of the guys in the rap group were infantry and Green Berets and Marines. The other day this guy came in. He had lost his arm over there, he had lost his leg over there. And we're talking in the meeting and he told me that he didn't have nothing against the Vietnamese. And I said, I just looked at him, "Man, you've got to be . . . you need help. You done lost your arm and your leg, and you say you got nothing against these people?"

If I see a Vietnamese on the street, I cross and walk on the other side. There are some on the west side, mostly downtown. Sometimes I go downtown to a couple of bookstores or go get fishing equipment, and you can tell them by the way they look, you know. Just a bummed-out trip.

Where we were it was jungle. Completely jungle. And the company commanders and all of them was like gung-ho-type guys. They were lifers, and I just couldn't cope with the service and what they stood for.

In basic training and in AIT [Advanced Infantry Training], they was beating around the bush. They made a joke out of everything, like "We're going to get old Charlie Cong" and all that old stuff. Instead of being down and serious, they used to beat around the bush. We used to sit up in the bleachers and they'd say, "This is how Charlie really works." They couldn't tell me how Charlie really worked. You had to get over there and experience for yourself how Charlie really worked.

The NVA [North Vietnamese Army] tried to overrun LZ Grant. That's when our CO got killed. He was a lifer. Our own helicopter killed thirty of our men. We was on a search-and-destroy mission and we could see all this firing way over there. We knew that was LZ Grant. It was being overrun. We had our strobe lights on and this Cobra helicopter thought it was a mortar tube, so the . . . thing came down, shot two rockets. *Sshhuuu.* . . .

Thinking back on the training, all they told us to do was kill. "KILL! KILL!" "What is the spirit of the bayonet?" "TO KILL!" It was a just a bummed-out trip. And I just didn't go for it, you know. I can remember this one instance where this guy, he was so depressed, he was walking in the boonies [slang for middle of nowhere] and he said, "I'm going home today." I said, "How you going to do it?" "I'm going home today, man. I can't hardly think no more, all this killing and stuff." So he was walking. The next thing I knew, I heard a gunshot. *Boom. Pow.* He had shot himself through the ankle, through the foot. He said, "I finally made it home." And I thought about doing that to get back home.

Mostly I was by myself.

Mostly I was by myself. Some guys over there, they were drug addicts, man. Their mind had snapped so bad that they were taking drugs. They'd get them from guys that would come back from R & R [rest and recreation]. I'd be scared of the NVA soldiers, the VC, and plus I'd have to be scared of my own men. That's too much of a strain. How'd I know this guy might be high or something, sitting up on the bunker, fall asleep, and the VC'd come in and shoot you?

I worked with those ARVNs [South Vietnamese soldiers] for about a month at the end of my tour. That was a good sham [appearance of duty] for me, to go back to the rear and work with them. They weren't worth a cent. In a fire fight those ARVNs would drop everything and run to the rear. That's why I hate them, those Vietnamese. I wish

I'd never see one of them as long as I live, 'cause we was over there fighting for them and they was constantly ripping us off. Stealin' stuff. After I came back from R & R, I brought four suits from Hong Kong. When the luggage went through Tan Son Nhut Air Base, I never saw them again. That was the Vietnamese.

After I got back from R & R, I stayed in a place in Saigon they call Soul Kitchen. That's where all the AWOL GIs used to hang out with mama-san and stuff like that. I hung out down there for a while and I felt like stayin' down there, but I got caught by the MPs and they sent me back to the unit. I got an Article 15 [official reprimand] and I said, "So what." Too much stress and strain. That's rough.

The blacks used to make a shoestring that they braided up and tied around their wrist, and every-where a whole lot of blacks used to go, they'd give a power sign. About six or seven different handshakes. That was about the time that Huey Newton [leader of the Black Panthers, a violent black political group in the 1960s] and all them was around. But for the guys in the bush, the grunts, you know, one of my best friends was a white guy. There was no racism between him and me, nothing like that. That was mostly back in the rear. Out in the bush everybody was the same. You can't find no racism in the bush. We slept together, ate together, fought together. What else can you ask for?

I knew this one guy. . . . We was real close, man, close. He was a Sicilian and I always used to kid him: "Hey, you think I could join the family when we get out of here?" This guy was so close that he should've been my brother, but . . . he died.

I just can't . . . sometimes, man . . . every time I talk about it, it just hurts. But ever since I've been going to these meetings . . . I thought anybody didn't want to listen. But these guys, they listen to me. And if there's any help, you know I need it.

. . . every time I talk about it, it just hurts.

The way I was brought up, they'd say, "If you want something, work for it." And that's what I'm trying to do now.

When I was drafted, I said, "I'll go over to Vietnam to help the people out. That's what everybody wants." But after I got there, I said, "These sons of guns ARVNs are laying back in the rear while we're fighting the war."

During the time I was there my marriage fell apart. It fell completely . . . I got back and I could feel it falling. I said, "I know I'm different. I'm not the high-school chap that you knew." She was my high-school sweetheart. It wasn't the same. I was all the way different. I was short-tempered. Actually, I was violent. I used to go to bars sometimes. I'd take a drink and a guy would call me a boy and I'd just try to light into him. After I had fought for a year and come back to the States, he'd call me still a boy. What more do I have to do?

I can't say now if I was one of the lucky ones. Sometimes I wish I could've just went ahead and died with my friends. I used to say, "I'm only dreaming. I'll wake up one day. I will wake up." But I never woke up.

> Sometimes I wish I could've just . . . died with my friends.

I have nightmares and sweats. I'll be sweating something fierce. My wife will say, "What's wrong with you?" I'll think of something else to say. I've never talked about these dreams with my wife 'cause she can't understand it, you know. She's been a civilian all her life and how would she understand it? The persons I can talk to is the rap group or another Vietnam soldier.

Like they're having this air show down at the lakefront. Yesterday I heard this jet coming over. The way I heard it, it was just like dropping one of those bombs. It brought back another flashback, and that's what I mean about going down there to see one of those planes, because if I feel a flashback coming on, I don't know what I might do. So I tell my old lady, "No. You can go. I ain't going." I didn't tell her why. And I make up an excuse like "I'm going to paint my mother's house."

When I came back to the States, they sent me to Fort Knox. I had several months to kill, so they put me on the funeral detail. That was sickening, man. It was sickening for the U.S. Army to put on a . . . front like they did. It was a twenty-one-gun salute with blank ammo, a bugler and an honor guard, where you folded the coffin flag and gave it to the mother or the child, with the officer saying, "We really are sorry that your son died while defending his country." You see, I was with these guys who never went to 'Nam. Just before the funeral they used to sit back and drink beer and laugh, almost right before the burial, laugh and . . . then they'd say something like this to the guy's family, who were going through all this grief.

One day we went to Pikesville, Kentucky. The family said we was the best thing they could ever do for their son. They invited us in for dinner. They was mostly Appalachian people. They invited us in, we ate, and that was it. But they just didn't know . . . I didn't say anything to them. If I had to talk to them, I'd say, "Let bygones be bygones."

Only thing I can say now is: Have mercy on the younger generation.

REVIEWING THE READING

1. What specific reasons did the soldier give for his extreme hatred of the Vietnamese? How might his situation have contributed to a biased perspective?

2. Why was the soldier sometimes scared of his own men?

3. **Using Your Historical Imagination.** Why do you think the American government did so little to help Vietnam veterans?

"Tucson, Arizona: El Hoyo" by Mario Suarez, in *Arizona Quarterly*, Volume III, No. 2.

Mario Suarez Describes El Hoyo, the Tucson Barrio (1960s)

A community is more than simply a collection of people who live in the same area. Its bedrock lies in the common bond that these people share. Writer Mario Suarez was born and raised in Tucson, Arizona, in a Mexican American neighborhood still known as "El Hoyo" (The Hole). In the following essay, Suarez goes behind the rough, shabby exterior of his home neighborhood to describe the enduring soul of a people who have survived centuries of conflict, hardship, and social strife. As you read the selection, note how Suarez defines the common bond uniting the inhabitants of El Hoyo.

From the center of downtown Tucson the ground slopes gently away to Main Street, drops a few feet, and then rolls to the banks of the Santa Cruz River. Here lies the section of the city known as El Hoyo. Why it is called El Hoyo is not very clear. In no sense is it a hole as its name would imply; it is simply the river's immediate valley. Its inhabitants are chicanos who raise hell on Saturday night and listen to Padre Estanislao on Sunday morning. While the term chicano is the short way of saying Mexicano, it is not restricted to the paisanos [peasants] who came from old Mexico with the territory or the last famine to work for the railroad, labor, sing, and go on relief. Chicano is the easy way of referring to everybody. Pablo Gutierrez married the Chinese grocer's daughter and now runs a meat department; his sons are [chicanos. So are the sons of] Killer

Jones who threw a fight in Harlem and fled to El
Hoyo to marry Christina Mendez. And so are all
of them. However, it is doubtful that all these spiritual
sons of Mexico live in El Hoyo because of its scenic
beauty—it is everything but beautiful. Its houses
are simple affairs of unplastered adobe, wood, and
abandoned car parts. Its narrow streets are mostly
clearings which have, in time, acquired names. Except
for some tall trees which nobody has ever cared to
identify, nurse, or destroy, the main things known
to grow in the general area are weeds, garbage piles,
dark-eyed chavalos [youngsters], and dogs. And it
is doubtful that the chicanos live in El Hoyo because
it is safe—many times the Santa Cruz has risen and
inundated [flooded] the area.

In other respects living in El Hoyo has its advantages. If one is born with a weakness for acquiring
bills, El Hoyo is where the collectors are less likely
to find you. If one has acquired the habit of listening
to Octavio Perea's Mexican Hour in the wee hours
of the morning, with the radio on at full blast, El
Hoyo is where you are less likely to be reported
to the authorities. Besides, Perea is very popular
and sooner or later to everybody "Smoke In the
Eyes" is dedicated between the pinto beans and white
flour commercials. If one, for any reason whatever,
comes on an extended period of hard times, where,
if not in El Hoyo are the neighbors more willing
to offer solace [comfort]? When Teofila Malacara's
house burned to the ground with all her belongings
and two children, a benevolent gentleman carried
through the gesture that made tolerable her burden.
He made a list of five hundred names and solicited
from each a dollar. At the end of a month he turned
over to the tearful but grateful senora one hundred
dollars in cold cash and then accompanied her on
a short vacation. When the new manager of a local
store decided that no more chicanas were to work
behind the counters, it was the chicanos of El Hoyo
who, on taking their individually small but

. . . living in El
Hoyo has its
advantages.

collectively great buying power elsewhere, drove the manager out and the girls returned to their jobs. When the Mexican Army was enroute to Baja California and the chicanos found out that the enlisted men ate only at infrequent intervals, it was El Hoyo's chicanos who crusaded across town with pots and beans and trays of tortillas to meet the train. When someone gets married, celebrating is not restricted to the immediate friends of the couple. Everybody is invited. Anything calls for a celebration and a celebration calls for anything. On Armistice Day there are no less than half a dozen good fights at the Riverside Dance Hall. On Mexican Independence Day more than one flag is sworn allegiance to amid cheers for the queen.

. . . Anything calls for a celebration and a celebration calls for anything.

And El Hoyo is something more. It is this something more which brought Felipe Sanchez back from the wars after having killed a score of Germans with his body resembling a patch-work quilt to marry Julia Armijo. It brought Joe Zepeda, a gunner flying B-24's over Germany, back to compose boleros [music for Mexican dances]. He has a metal plate for a skull. Perhaps El Hoyo is proof that those people exist, and perhaps exist best, who have as yet failed to observe the more popular modes of human conduct. Perhaps the humble appearance of El Hoyo justifies the indifferent shrug of those made aware of its existence. Perhaps El Hoyo's simplicity motivates an occasional chicano to move away from its narrow streets, babbling comadres [old women] and shrieking children to deny the bloodwell from which he springs and to claim the blood of a conquistador while his hair is straight and his face beardless. Yet El Hoyo is not an outpost of a few families against the world. It fights for no causes except those which soothe its immediate angers. It laughs and cries with the same amount of passion in times of plenty and of want.

Perhaps El Hoyo, its inhabitants, and its essence can best be explained by telling a bit about a dish

called capirotada. Its origin is uncertain. But, according to the time and the circumstance, it is made of
old, new or hard bread. It is softened with water
and then cooked with peanuts, raisins, onions,
cheese, and panocha [a coarse sugar made in Mexico].
It is fired with sherry wine. Then it is served hot,
cold, or just "on the weather" as they say in El Hoyo.
The Sermenos like it one way, the Garcias another,
and the Ortegas still another. While it might differ
greatly from one home to another, nevertheless it
is still capirotada. And so it is with El Hoyo's chicanos. While being divided from within and from without, like the capirotada, they remain chicanos.

REVIEWING THE READING

1. To whom in El Hoyo does the word "chicano" refer?

2. According to Suarez, what are the practical advantages to living in El Hoyo?

3. **Using Your Historical Imagination.** How
   does the "something more" of El Hoyo—
   the bond among its inhabitants—compare
   to the sense of community where you
   live?

From *Washington Journal: The Events of 1973–1974* by Elizabeth Drew.

72

Elizabeth Drew Recounts the Vote to Impeach President Nixon (1973)

The controversial events usually lumped under the heading of "Watergate scandal" eventually brought down the Nixon presidency. These events included burglaries, political "dirty tricks," and attempted cover-ups of criminal acts. Political writer Elizabeth Drew wrote about the Watergate scandal at the key point in the sequence of events that forced Nixon to resign. In the following excerpts from her book about that time, Drew describes the fateful day that the House Judiciary Committee voted to impeach President Nixon. As you read consider the reaction of the members of the committee who voted for impeachment.

At seven o'clock, the roll is called on whether or not the House Judiciary Committee will recommend to the House that the President be impeached. . . . And, no matter how seemingly inevitable [unavoidable] this vote has been for some time now, no matter how well we know the outcome, there has been no way of preparing ourselves for this moment. More than any of the several other moments when the emotional reverberations [shocks] outran the intellectual anticipation, this one has stolen up on us, taken over, leaves us sitting here feeling stunned, drained, almost disbelieving as the clerk calls the roll and the members cast their votes. The room is utterly still except for the call of the roll and the sound of cameras clicking. The moment has taken over the members; they know what they are doing, and they are physically, mentally, and emotionally spent [drained]. They have been through a long period of strain. No other group in the Congress has ever had to go through anything like this. One can barely hear the members as they respond to the clerk.

First the Democrats. Even those for whom this is not a difficult vote are somber as they respond "Aye"—perhaps in part because they know they should be. Mann, for whom this has not been easy, stares into space as he says "Aye." His voice is all but inaudible [can hardly be heard]. Again there appears to be tears in his eyes. Father Drinan, his long, thin face looking stern and sober, ever more like an El Greco painting, quietly says "Aye." Barbara Jordan, usually of full voice, also responds quietly. Ray Thornton looks at the ceiling, closes his eyes, and says, softly, "Aye." They are impeaching Richard Nixon. They are setting loose an unimaginable course of events, and they know it.

Representatives Barbara Jordan and Charles Rangel (right), members of the House Judiciary Committee that voted to impeach President Richard Nixon, discuss a point with the Committee's chief counsel, John Doar (left).

The first vote cast with a loud certitude [sureness] is Hutchinson's "No." Hutchinson smiles—the only one who does. . . .

Rodino, who casts his vote last, undramatically says "Aye." The clerk announces, "Twenty-seven members have voted aye, eleven members have voted no." All twenty-one Democrats—including three Southerners—and six Republicans have voted to impeach the President for the cover-up.

The vote on the article as amended is a ceremonial vote now, but it must be taken, and again it is taken solemnly. This time, Rodino's voice cracks as he speaks the final "Aye." The room is utterly silent, and then, at a few minutes after seven, Rodino announces, "Article I . . . is adopted and will be reported to the House."

Hamilton Fish comes out of the committee room holding his wife's hand. Some members are being interviewed on television. Barbara Jordan, preparing to be interviewed, is having difficulty composing herself. Some members—Rodino included—went into the anteroom behind the committee room and wept. There is a small group of observers, dressed in casual summer clothes, standing quietly outside the Rayburn [Congressional Office] Building. When Barbara Jordan comes out of the Rayburn Building, several in the group applaud. She smiles and waves vaguely. Reporters have gone back to the pressrooms to file their stories. It is good to have something that must be done.

The Capitol grounds are very quiet tonight. Across the way is the Supreme Court Building. Could it really have been only three days ago that the Court ruled against the President? The committee members have taken the first step—the hardest step, making it easier for those who will follow. They didn't walk away from it; they became the definers. But there doesn't seem to be much of a sense of triumph on anyone's part tonight. Perhaps this will be written of in the future as a moment of triumph—

"the system worked"—but that is not how it feels now. There is a feeling of sadness, and exhaustion, at what everyone has been through. A feeling, too, of foreboding about those unimaginable next steps. It is a drained feeling. When history records events, it tends to leave out this kind of human emotion.

REVIEWING THE READING

1. How many Republicans (President Nixon's party) were on the committee, and how did they vote?

2. How does Drew describe her emotions, and what seemed to be the emotion of the committee after the vote was taken?

3. **Using Your Historical Imagination.** What evidence is there in the reading that, as Drew wrote, "the moment had taken over the members of the committee"?

73

From "A Vision Beyond
Time and Place" by N.
Scott Momaday, *Life*,
July 7, 1971.

N. Scott Momaday Describes the Indian Vision (1970s)

*N. Scott Momaday, a member of the Kiowa tribe,
is a professor of English literature at Stanford University and the author of a prize-winning novel about
Native Americans,* House Made of Dawn. *In
the following excerpts from an article written in the
1970s for* Life *magazine, Momaday offers a description of the "native vision" of the first Americans. As
you read the selection, consider what Momaday says
are the elements of the Indian point of view.*

When my father was a boy, an old man used
to come to my grandfather's house and pay
his respects. He was a lean old man in braids and
was impressive in his age and hearing. His name
was Cheney, and he was an arrowmaker. Every morning, my father tells me, Cheney would point his
wrinkled face, go out, and pray aloud to the rising
sun. In my mind I can see that man as if he were
there now. I like to watch him as he makes his
prayer. I know where he stands and where his voice
goes on the rolling grasses and where the sun comes
up on the land. There, at dawn, you can feel the
silence. It is cold and clear and deep like water. It
takes hold of you and will not let you go. . . .

I often think of old man Cheney, and of his
daily devotion to the sun. He died before I was
born, and I never knew where he came from or
what of good and bad entered into his life. But I
think I know who he was, essentially, and what his
view of the world meant to him and to me. He
was a man who saw very deeply into the distance,
I believe, one whose vision extended far beyond

the physical boundaries of his time and place. He perceived [saw] the wonder and meaning of Creation itself. . . .

Once, in the first light, I stood where Cheney has stood, next to the house which my grandfather Mammedaty had built on a rise of the land near Rainy Mountain Creek, and watched the sun come out of the black horizon of the world. It was an irresistible and awesome emergence, as waters gather to the flood, of weather and of light. I could not have been more sensitive to the cold, nor than to the heat which came upon it. And I could not have forseen the break of day. The shadows on the rolling plains became large . . . in a moment . . . then . . . dark and distinct again as they were run through with splinters of light. And the sun itself, when it appeared, was pale and immense [large]. . . . It is no wonder, I thought, that an old man should pray to it. It is no wonder . . . and yet, of course, wonder is the principal [main] part of such a vision. Cheney's prayer was an affirmation of his wonder and regard. . . .

N. Scott Momaday is a leading contemporary Native American poet and writer.

This native vision, this gift of seeing truly, with wonder and delight, into the natural world, is informed by a certain attitude of reverence and self-respect. . . . In addition to the eye, it involves the intelligence, the instinct, and the imagination. It is the perception not only of objects and forms but also of essences and ideals, as in this Chippewa song:

> As my eyes
> search
> The prairie
> I feel the summer
> in the spring

. . . [The singer] beholds what is there; nothing of the scene is lost upon him.

Most Indian people are able to see in these terms. Their view of the world is peculiarly native and distinct, and it determines who and what they are to a great extent. It is indeed the basis upon which they identify themselves as individuals and as a race. . . . When old man Cheney looked into the sunrise, he saw as far into himself, I suspect, as he saw into the distance. He knew certainly of his existence and of his place in the scheme [design] of things.

In contrast, most of us in this society are afflicted [infected] with a kind of cultural nearsightedness. Our eyes, it may be, have been trained too long upon the . . . artificial . . . aspects of our environment; we do not see beyond the buildings and billboards that seem at times to be the monuments of our civilization, and consequently we fail to see into the nature and meaning of our own humanity. Now, more than ever, we might do well to enter upon a vision quest of our own. . . . And in this the Indian stands to lead by his example. For with respect to such things as a sense of heritage . . . investment of the mind and spirit in the oral traditions of literature, philosophy, and religion—those things, in short, which made this vision of the world—the Indian is perhaps the most culturally secure of all Americans.

REVIEWING THE READING

1. To what did "old man Cheney" pray?

2. What does Momaday identify as the essential characteristics of the Indian vision of life?

3. **Using Your Historical Imagination.** What does Momaday say the Indian vision has to teach most of us in modern society? What does he mean when he says we need to go on "a vision quest of our own"?

President Ronald Reagan Delivers His First Inaugural Address (1981)

74

From *Public Papers of the Presidents of the United States, Ronald Reagan, 1981.*

In November 1980 Ronald Reagan won a resounding victory over President Jimmy Carter in Reagan's first presidential bid. Two months later, on January 20, 1981, he delivered his inaugural address. As you read the following excerpts from that address, consider in what direction Reagan says he intends to lead the country.

These United States are confronted with an economic affliction of great proportions. We suffer from the longest and one of the worst sustained inflations in our national history. It distorts our economic decisions, penalizes thrift, and crushes the struggling young and the fixed-income elderly alike. It threatens to shatter the lives of millions of our people. . . .

In this present crisis, government is not the solution to our problem; government is the problem. From time to time we've been tempted to believe that society has become too complex to be managed by self-rule, that government by an elite group is superior to government for, by, and of the people. Well, if no one among us is capable of governing himself, then who among us has the capacity to govern someone else? . . .

We hear much of special interest groups. Well, our concern must be for a special interest group that has been too long neglected. It knows no sectional boundaries or ethnic and racial divisions, and it crosses political party lines. It is made up of men

President Ronald Reagan tells the nation of his plans as he delivers his inaugural address. Vice President George Bush is seated behind the president.

and women who raise our food, patrol our streets, man our mines and factories, teach our children, keep our homes, and heal us when we're sick—professionals, industrialists, shopkeepers, clerks, cabbies, and truck-drivers. They are, in short, "We the people," this breed called Americans.

Well, this Administration's objective will be a healthy, vigorous, growing economy that provides equal opportunities for all Americans. . . . Putting America back to work means putting all Americans back to work. Ending inflation means freeing all

Americans from the terror of runaway living costs. All must share in the productive work of this "new beginning," and all must share in the bounty of a revived economy. With the idealism and fair play which are the core of our system and our strength, we can have a strong and prosperous America, at peace with itself and the world. . . .

It is my intention to curb the size and influence of the Federal establishment and to demand recognition of the distinction between the powers granted to the Federal Government and those reserved to the States or to the people. . . .

It is no coincidence that our present troubles parallel and are proportionate to the intervention and intrusion in our lives that result from unnecessary and excessive growth of the government. It is time for us to realize that we're too great a nation to limit ourselves to small dreams. We're not, as some would have us believe, doomed to an inevitable decline. I do not believe in a fate that will fall on us no matter what we do. I do believe in a fate that will fall on us if we do nothing. So, with all the creative energy at our command, let us begin an era of national renewal. Let us renew our determination, our courage, and our strength. And let us renew our faith and our hope.

REVIEWING THE READING

1. According to Reagan, what is the major problem confronting the country?

2. What does Reagan say is to be his response to this problem?

3. **Using Your Historical Imagination.** What do you think Reagan means by his reference to a "new beginning"?

75

From *Women in Modern America: A Brief History* by Lois W. Banner.

Lois Banner Evaluates the Gains of the Women's Movement (1980s)

In 1963 Betty Friedan published The Feminine Mystique. *In this important book, Friedan gave voice to feelings shared by many women around the country concerning "the problem that has no name." This problem centered around the fact that, at that time, women's roles were virtually restricted to the home and family. Although it appeared that women were happy in carrying out their duties as wives and mothers, many women felt unfulfilled and did not know why. Friedan's book provided answers to their questions and, more importantly, let women know that they were not alone in these feelings. Out of this the women's movement, calling for the social, political, and economic equality of the sexes, was born.*

Since the publication of Friedan's early book, the women's movement has achieved advances for both men and women in many areas of life. In the following excerpts from her book on American women, historian Lois Banner explores some of these advances and evaluates the situation of women in the 1980s. As you read the selection, note how American attitudes concerning housework have changed since the 1970s.

Indications of increasing equality for women are strong within the nation. Growing numbers of women, for example, are moving into the professions. In 1970, 4.7 percent of all lawyers and 8.9 percent of all doctors were women. By 1979, these percentages had risen to 12.4 percent and 11 percent, respectively. By 1981, the percentage of women doctors had risen to 22 percent and 30.2 percent of the nation's law-school graduates for that year were women. The percentage of women being awarded engineering degrees increased from 0.8 percent in 1971 to 10.4 percent in 1981. More women, too, are winning political office. In 1969, there were 301 women state legislators nationwide; in 1981, there were 908. In 1975, 5,765 of the nation's elected officials were women; by 1981, the figure stood at 14,225. And advances are being made in breaking down many sex-segregated occupations [occupations traditionally male-dominated or female-dominated]; 47 percent of all bus drivers and bartenders are now women. . . .

Striking gains also have been registered by black women, who have moved in impressive numbers into employment areas traditionally dominated by white women. These gains were one of the greatest successes of the civil rights movement. In 1965, 24 percent of all black women were white-collar workers, compared with 62 percent of all employed white women. By 1981, these figures were 46 percent for black women and 66 percent for white women. Most importantly, black women abandoned the category of domestic service, with which they had been identified for a century. In 1965, 30 percent of all employed black women were domestic workers; by 1977, the figure had dropped to 9 percent. In many instances, immigrants from Mexico and Latin America—part of the migrant exodus to the United States in the 1970s and 1980s—came to replace them.

Yet major evidences of discrimination against women remain. The work force is still, for the most part, segregated by sex. In 1979, 70.8 percent of all noncollege teachers were women; 80.3 percent of all clerical workers were women, and 96.8 percent of all nurses were women. Such sex segregation still underlies wage discrimination; in 1982, women still

> . . . major evidences of discrimination against women remain.

Sally Ride was the first woman astronaut to travel in space, aboard the space shuttle Challenger, *in June 1983.*

made about 57 cents of every dollar men made. The majority of college undergraduates are women, but the vast majority of faculty members are male. More than one-third of all candidates for the M.B.A. degree (Master of Business Administration) are women, but only 5 percent of the executives in the top 50 American companies are women. Out of the 435 members in the House of Representatives, 19 are women; two of the 100 senators are women. Over the last decade, the greater incidence of poverty among women has increased precipitously [sharply]. Bureaucrats and scholars routinely discuss the "feminization of poverty"; 81 percent of all welfare recipients in the United States are women.

It cannot be denied, however, that the broad social changes affecting women's lives throughout America's modern age have recently followed a revolutionary direction, prompting some analysts to predict that the traditional ways in which Americans have lived will presently cease to exist. Census data consistently reveal that . . . the age of first marriage is rising, more and more individuals are living alone, the divorce rate is rising, and women, especially married women and women with preschool children, are increasingly moving into the work force. In 1965, about 39 percent of all American women were employed for remuneration [pay] outside the home. In 1982, the rate stood at 52 percent, and it is expected to rise to 65 percent by 1995. Surveys revealed that only 19 percent of all Americans continue to live in the tradition of the legendary American family, in which the husband works and the wife stays at home with the children. . . .

On the one hand, Americans seem overwhelmed by the new social trends, by the incidence of divorce and the breakdown of the family, by the danger of nuclear war and the seeming inability of government administrators to solve the nation's economic difficulties, by women's new threat to traditional definitions of masculinity. On the other hand, many Americans seem willing to . . . applaud the extension of equality to women. In 1980, polls showed overwhelming support for women's . . . right to political office. For the first time in the nation's history, a majority of Americans indicated that it made no difference to them if a man or a woman was the mayor of a town, a lawyer, a doctor—even "their own boss." A majority of the respondents to a survey on these issues conducted by the President's Advisory Committee for Women believed that husbands and wives should share financial decision making as well as household chores and care of the children. Such thinking represents a profound shift from the mid-1970s, when most Americans polled on this issue still defined housework exclusively as women's work. Responses to the 1980 survey indicated that most Americans still believed there were advantages to being a man, but their stance did not stem from sexist [prejudiced] motives. Rather, they felt that women must still cope with a double standard that impeded [blocked] their progress in most areas of their behavior.

What the future holds is difficult to predict. Once before in America's modern history, with the attainment of suffrage and the movement of women into the work force, equality for women seemed in sight, only to dissipate in the face of a depression and a war. But the feminist revolution of the last 20 years has so permeated [penetrated] the national consciousness that it is difficult to visualize its demise, holding out, as it does, a different and more humane way of life for men as well as women — for all Americans.

REVIEWING THE READING

1. According to Banner, what evidence is there that discrimination against women still exists?

2. How have American attitudes concerning housework changed since the 1970s?

3. **Using Your Historical Imagination.** In what ways has the women's movement helped men?

The Man with the Guitar (1980s)

76

From *La Raza: The Mexican Americans* by Stan Steiner.

By the 1970s and 1980s, the problem of illegal immigration from Mexico to the United States had become a major concern. Estimates of the number of illegal aliens entering the country each year varied from 50,000 to 250,000. The situation was complex. Some Americans, even some Hispanic Americans, resented the new immigrants because they competed for jobs. On the other hand, many United States farmers depended on the illegal aliens for cheap agricultural labor. The immigrants themselves were driven by harsh economic realities to look for work in the United States. Sometimes exploited and abused by persons on both sides of the border, they nonetheless chose to take their chances north of the border. The following selection is excerpted from an account of the illegal immigrants by Stan Steiner. As you read consider the significance of "the man with the guitar."

It is four o'clock in the morning on the Mexican border. The lights of the Border Station flicker on the deserted streets. A truck parks in a dark alleyway. The driver lights a cigarette, and waits. Hundreds of people with small bundles move noiselessly past the yawning border guards. The driver spits contemptuously at the ragged ones. These are his human cargo.

One by one the men and women crawl under the loose tarpaulin on the back of the truck. No one talks. When the truck is full the driver stomps out his cigarette and roars northward. He drives one hundred, two hundred, three hundred, four hundred miles without stopping, except for gas. The local city ordinances along the way are not gracious to truckloads of Mexicans. He knows the police will not stop him if he does not stop.

Inside the truck there may be thirty or forty men and women. The stagnant air is nauseating. Even the breeze under the tarpaulin of sweetly sick desert dawn does not help. . . .

Going to the fields, in every truck I have been in, there is a man who can sing. He may have a harmonica or he may have a guitar. It doesn't matter. If he sings at that lonely hour he sings to himself.

> When I left Hermosillo
> My tears fell like rain,
> But the little red flower
> Consoled my pain.
>
> I am like a coyote
> Who eats poppies, and goes
> Trotting off sideways—
> Where? Nobody knows.

The migrants are put in windowless trucks and the doors are locked. Where are they going? They do not know. They do not all get there. In San Antonio one locked truck was abandoned on the highway in the summer of 1968. The men and women who were imprisoned inside—more than three dozen—cried out for hours until their lungs gave out, pounded on the steel walls that muffled their shrieks until their fists were bloodied. When help came, several had died. They had suffocated in the truck that was to deliver them to jobs in the fields.

> The Brave men have died.
> Every good man passes.
> The shameless are left—
> Who eat corn mush.

The open, rumbling trucks of the *coyotes* [transporters of illegal aliens] and the old buses, abandoned by the regular companies, are not all that bad. Like the village buses of ancient vintage in old Mexico

. . . in every truck I have been in, there is a man who can sing.

they wheeze through the deserts of the Southwest.
Every year one or two of these fail to make it across
the railroad crossing, somewhere on a country road,
and the campesinos [farm workers] are flung out,
like chickens, to die beside the highway.

One ordinary morning in the little town of
Calexico, in the Imperial Valley of California, there
are twenty-three trucks and old buses waiting for
their human cargoes. In one hour, from 4:00 to 5:00
A.M., Dr. Samuel Yellen, a city councilman from
nearby Brawley, using a hand counter, clocked those
who crossed the border at that single customs station.
He counted 1,404 campesinos, in that dim, predawn
hour. "These are poor people," says Dr. Yellen. "In
Mexico the farm workers earn fifteen cents an hour,
those who are lucky enough to get jobs. The corporations—Litton Industries, Fairchild Camera, Hughes
Aircraft—who have factories south of the border
pay their workers as little as two dollars a day. So
naturally these poor people think that working for
fifty cents an hour in the United States is paradise.
It's worth the suffering, they think."

And so they come, singing of sorrows and nos-
talgia. The exodus goes on. It is the same in every
border town, on every morning, from Brownsville
to Tijuana.

"The most deprived classes of Chicanos are constantly replenished by new immigrants, both permanent and temporary, from Mexico," says Hector
Abeyta, the director of California's Manpower Opportunities Project of the U.S. Department of Labor.
"Almost all of the immigrants are from the poorest
people in that country, who came north in search
of opportunity.

"Mexican Americans have a higher proportion
of foreign born than any other ethnic group in the
United States," Abeyta says.

It is whispered in the barrios [Mexican neighborhoods in large cities] that tens of thousands of
people are neither citizens nor legal residents of

the United States. "They jump!" says Eduardo Perez, a community leader of East Los Angeles. "They disappear. They vanish into the barrios. They live like anyone. They don't hide in this Disneyland of the U.S.A.," says Perez. "They are bold."

The old *corrido* [traditional ballad] says:

Who puts water in his wine
Makes it thin and weak;
Who never has known life
Of living may not speak.

And yet the emigrant is fearful. The rites of passage across the border of legality are Kafka-like. One young man, a Chicano student at UCLA, says, "Kafka would be at home here. If Kafka had more *macho* [masculinity], more passion, he could be Mexican. He knew what he was writing about when he compared a man to a cockroach.*'La Cucaracha'— that's us."

*Reference to a story by Franz Kafka in which a man awakes one morning to find that he has been transformed into a cockroach.

"La Cucaracha" was the hymn of the Mexican Revolution, but the man with the guitar sings it differently. He *is* a cockroach. He is invisible. Not only the memory of his illegality, but the ever-present reality of deportation [forced return to Mexico].

It is officially guessed that as many as 40,000 Mexican citizens come to Los Angeles alone yearly. (The population of San Antonio is estimated to increase by 50,000 every year.) One barrio leader of East Los Angeles says that he unofficially guesses the annual influx in that city may be 100,000. He is asked, Why, if this is so, is the population of the barrios not many millions? "The border is a two-way street," he says. "Maybe 100,000 come; maybe 100,000 go."

Once he has crossed over, he is in jeopardy. He may be "cowed and thankful" for his family's safe arrival. "After all, isn't he, the Mexican immigrant, a guest, an *ensimado*, and an *arrimado*, a parasite?" writes Antonio Gomez in *Con Safos:* "Is it not unthinkable for a guest to complain about the lodgings

and odd jobs that his host has given him? What voice does a guest have in operating the host's household?"

The migrant is ridiculed by the Chicanos. The young Los Angeleans sometimes refer to the newcomer contemptuously as "TJ." Literally the nickname means that he comes from Tijuana. Where he crosses the border does not really matter so much as his awkward manner, unfashionable dress, and servility [submissiveness]. He is cowed by the affluence [wealth] of the city and overwhelmed by the speed

Mexicans are crossing the border into the United States at Tijuana. The sign in the background reads, "Stop! Street no exit."

An emigrant to the barrios has to know how to laugh at his dilemma.

of the freeways. The poorest of the poor, the TJ has no choices. He must accept the lowest jobs, live in the worst barrios, suffer the insults of both Chicano and Anglo. He has only his family to help him. Life is precarious and work is scarce.

An emigrant to the barrios has to know how to laugh at his dilemma.

> I went to the border
> To see who knew me:
> And at eleven that night
> The police arrested me.
>
> They arrested me
> In the American style:
> As if I was a criminal
> With pistol in hand.

He is jailed for "being a fighting cock," the emigrant of the *corrido* laments. In his cell he is offered "a recipe of the House of Congress," the warrant for his arrest. "Do you know why you're in prison?" asks the judge. He doesn't. The emigrant replies seriously, putting on a formal manner, "I don't expect a temple or crystal palace." But the judge is not amused; he sentences the emigrant to jail, and to himself the emigrant thinks, I have been arrested "because of my stupidity." He laughs at himself.

> I come from Morelia
> Dreaming of the dollars,
> Bought shoes and a hat,
> Even put on trousers.

Hundreds and thousands of *vaciladas* [migrant songs], *corridos*, ballads, serenades . . . and popular tunes tell of the journey of the migrants and of living in the barrios. In the life of an "unlettered people," words are music and history is sung. "Wherever you go, you shall go singing," Huitzilopochtli, the war and sun god of the Aztecs, had commanded. It is still so. The odyssey of the migrants into the urban cities is rewritten by every man with a guitar.

"Out of poverty, poetry; out of suffering, song," is the old Mexican proverb. Songs are the true history of the migrations of La Raza.

> Now I am confused.
> I am a shoemaker.
> But here I am a camel,
> With a pick and shovel.

> What good is my trade
> If machines are faster;
> When I make two shoes,
> They make one million.

> They told me the money
> Lay in the streets
> Like girls and theatres—
> A utopia of sweets.

Laughter of the *vacilada* is cruel, yet not bitter. "It hurts. Like the old clown, we laugh on the outside and connive on the inside," says Eduardo Perez. The song of the *vacilada* is the song of irony; it has many meanings. It is the tale told by the *corrido*, set to music of a madrigal, with the moral of a hallucination. . . .

He is complex, the man with a guitar. He is the troubadour of the exodus. The *corrido* and *vacilada* are the Mexican spirituals of the barrios.

And yet these songs are as different as the sunrise and the twilight. The *corrido* is a musical fiesta of barrio life and love and death, the newspaper of those who do not read, sung in the cantina and plaza by the village chronicler. Its melody is familiar to all, every verse is as rounded and predictable in form as a tortilla, and every line is rhymed. The *vacilada* is a blasphemy. It is the song of the refugees from the dying villages. Sung by the urban villagers, on the highways and in the barrios, its words have the mocking tone of a Mexican Bob Dylan, haunting and questing. Nothing of how a *vacilada* will end is known when the singer begins, except that it will end in a tragicomic way. It always does. Even death is mocked, not lamented. The singer twists the words any which way he wishes. The melody is unsettled and nervous, with lines that rhyme and lines that conflict.

Strangely, the words of the *corridos* that the man with the guitar sings sound more and more like those of the *vaciladas.* . . .

Like the troubadour of old he goes down the road not quite knowing where he is going. He knows only he has nowhere else to go. He goes singing.

In the back of a truck or in a broken bus he rides with his family. He goes into the fields or into the cities. Wherever he goes he momentarily becomes a nonentity [nobody], one of the unknown and nameless ones who leave their identity behind and seek a new life. He is invisible. There is safety in not being seen, in the ghetto, in the barrio, where he is one of many in what seems a hostile and unfriendly society.

He may sing to himself:

Where am I to go? Where?
The road is here.
The road to the Gods.
Well, who counts men here?
Here where all lack a body?
At the bottom of the sky?

REVIEWING THE READING

1. Who are the "coyotes"?

2. Why does the author say that Mexican immigrants residing in the United States are invisible?

3. **Using Your Historical Imagination.** What does the author suggest is the role of the "man with the guitar" among the illegal immigrants from Mexico?

Corridos: Songs of Exodus

From *Aztlan: An Anthology of Mexican American Literature,* edited by Luis Valdez and Stan Steiner.

The ballads, or corridos, of the Mexican Americans tell of their history and of the spirit of a people. Following are two corridos, one about leaving Mexico, the other about returning.

An Emigrant's Farewell

Goodbye, my beloved country,
Now I am going away;
I go to the United States,
where I intend to work.

Goodbye, my beloved mother,
the Virgin of Guadalupe;
goodbye, my beloved land,
my Mexican Republic.

At last I'm going,
I bear you in my heart;
my Mother Guadalupe,
give me your benediction.

I go sad and heavy-hearted
to suffer and endure;

my Mother Guadalupe,
grant my safe return.

Mexico is my home-land,
where I was born a Mexican;
give me the benediction
of your powerful hand.

I go to the United States
to seek to earn a living.
Goodbye, my beloved land;
I bear you in my heart.

For I am not to blame
that I leave my country thus;
the fault is that of poverty,
which keeps us all in want.

Deported

I shall sing you a song
of all who were deported,
who came back speaking English
from those wretches.

They are shoved around anywhere
and have to beg their way.
It's a pity to see them
with nothing to eat.

They set out for the north
with high hopes and eagerness,
but they work in the fields
like any field hand.

They go to pick cotton
and get on very badly;
they work on the track
or with shovel or with pick.

So they deserve that and more,
those poor countrymen,
for they knew that this land
is for the Mexicans.

They lop off their mustaches
and chew their tobacco;
it seems the thing to do
and they don't have a cent.

Francisco Jiménez Describes the Circuit (1980s)

77

"The Circuit" by Francisco Jiménez, in *Arizona Quarterly*.

Writer and educator Francisco Jiménez was born in Jalisco, Mexico, in 1943. When he was four years old his family moved to California, where jobs were available for migrant workers. The family moved from place to place during the years in which Jiménez was growing up, and he tells what this experience was like in his short story "The Circuit."

Jiménez worked as a janitor while attending Santa Maria High School to help support his family. He graduated from high school in 1962 and was offered three college scholarships. Eventually, Jiménez earned a doctoral degree from Columbia University. He is presently a professor in the Department of Foreign Language at Santa Clara University. As you read this story, determine why "The Circuit" is such an appropriate title.

It was that time of year again. Ito, the strawberry sharecropper, did not smile. It was natural. The peak of the strawberry season was over and the last few days the workers, most of them braceros [contract farm laborers], were not picking as many boxes as they had during the months of June and July.

As the last days of August disappeared, so did the number of braceros. Sunday, only one—the best picker—came to work. I liked him. Sometimes we talked during our half-hour lunch break. That is how I found out he was from Jalisco, the same state in Mexico my family was from. That Sunday was the last time I saw him.

When the sun had tired and sunk behind the mountains, Ito signaled us that it was time to go home. "Ya esora [It's time]," he yelled in his broken Spanish. Those were the words I waited for twelve hours a day, every day, seven days a week, week after week. And the thought of not hearing them again saddened me.

As we drove home Papá did not say a word. With both hands on the wheel, he stared at the dirt road. My older brother, Roberto, was also silent. He leaned his head back and closed his eyes. Once in a while he cleared from his throat the dust that blew in from outside.

Yes, it was that time of year. When I opened the front door to the shack, I stopped. Everything we owned was neatly packed in cardboard boxes. Suddenly I felt even more the weight of hours, days, weeks, and months of work. I sat down on a box. The thought of having to move to Fresno and knowing what was in store for me there brought tears to my eyes.

That night I could not sleep. I lay in bed thinking about how much I hated this move.

A little before five o'clock in the morning, Papá woke everyone up. A few minutes later, the yelling and screaming of my little brothers and sisters, for whom the move was a great adventure, broke the silence of the dawn. Shortly, the barking of the dogs accompanied them.

While we packed the breakfast dishes, Papá went outside to start the "Carcanchita." That was the name Papá gave his old '38 black Plymouth. He bought it in a used-car lot in Santa Rosa in the winter of 1949. Papá was very proud of his little jalopy. He had a right to be proud of it. He spent a lot of time looking at other cars before buying this one. When he finally chose the "Carcanchita," he checked it thoroughly before driving it out of the car lot. He examined every inch of the car. He listened to the motor, tilting his head from side to side like a parrot, trying to detect any noises that spelled car trouble. After being satisfied with

. . . Everything we owned was neatly packed in cardboard boxes.

the looks and sounds of the car, Papá then insisted on knowing who the original owner was. He never did find out from the car salesman, but he bought the car anyway. Papá figured the original owner must have been an important man because behind the rear seat of the car he found a blue necktie.

Papá parked the car out in front and left the motor running. "Listo [Ready]," he yelled. Without saying a word, Roberto and I began to carry the boxes out to the car. Roberto carried the two big boxes and I carried the two smaller ones. Papá then threw the mattress on top of the car roof and tied it with ropes to the front and rear bumpers.

Everything was packed except Mamá's pot. It was an old large galvanized pot she had picked up at an army surplus store in Santa Maria the year I was born. The pot had many dents and nicks, and the more dents and nicks it acquired the more Mamá liked it. "Mi olla [My pot]," she used to say proudly.

I held the front door open as Mamá carried out her pot by both handles, making sure not to spill the cooked beans. When she got to the car, Papá reached out to help her with it. Roberto opened the rear car door and Papá gently placed it on the floor behind the front seat. All of us then climbed in. Papá sighed, wiped the sweat off his forehead with his sleeve, and said wearily: "Es todo [That's all]."

As we drove away, I felt a lump in my throat. I turned around and looked at our little shack for the last time.

At sunset we drove into a labor camp near Fresno. Since Papá did not speak English, Mamá asked the camp foreman if he needed any more workers. "We don't need no more," said the foreman, scratching his head. "Check with Sullivan down the road. Can't miss him. He lives in a big white house with a fence around it."

When we got there, Mamá walked up to the house. She went through a white gate, past a row

> . . . I turned around and looked at our little shack for the last time.

of rose bushes, up the stairs to the front door. She rang the doorbell. The porch light went on and a tall husky man came out. They exchanged a few words. After the man went in, Mamá clasped her hands and hurried back to the car. "We have work! Mr. Sullivan said we can stay there the whole season," she said, gasping and pointing to an old garage near the stables.

The garage was worn out by the years. It had no windows. The walls, eaten by termites, strained to support the roof full of holes. The dirt floor, populated by earthworms, looked like a gray road map.

That night, by the light of a kerosene lamp, we unpacked and cleaned our new home. Roberto swept away the loose dirt, leaving the hard ground. Papá plugged the holes in the walls with old newspapers and tin can tops. Mamá fed my little brothers and sisters. Papá and Roberto then brought in the mattress and placed it on the far corner of the garage. "Mamá, you and the little ones sleep on the mattress. Roberto, Panchito, and I will sleep outside under the trees," Papá said.

Early next morning Mr. Sullivan showed us where his crop was, and after breakfast, Papá, Roberto, and I headed for the vineyard to pick.

Around nine o'clock the temperature had risen to almost one hundred degrees. I was completely soaked in sweat and my mouth felt as if I had been chewing on a handkerchief. I walked over to the end of the row, picked up the jug of water we had brought, and began drinking. "Don't drink too much; you'll get sick," Roberto shouted. No sooner had he said that than I felt sick to my stomach. I dropped to my knees and let the jug roll off my hands. I remained motionless with my eyes glued on the hot sandy ground. All I could hear was the drone of insects. Slowly I began to recover. I poured water over my face and neck and watched the dirty water run down my arms to the ground.

I still felt a little dizzy when we took a break to eat lunch. It was past two o'clock and we sat underneath a large walnut tree that was on the side of the road. While we ate, Papá jotted down the number of boxes we had picked. Roberto drew designs on the ground with a stick. Suddenly I noticed Papá's face turn pale as he looked down the road. "Here comes the school bus," he whispered loudly in alarm. Instinctively, Roberto and I ran and hid in the vineyards. We did not want to get in trouble for not going to school. The neatly dressed boys about my age got off. They carried books under their arms. After they crossed the street, the bus drove away. Roberto and I came out from hiding and joined Papá. "Tienen que tener cuidado [You have to be careful]," he warned us.

After lunch we went back to work. The sun kept beating down. The buzzing insects, the wet sweat, and the hot dry dust made the afternoon seem to last forever. Finally the mountains around the valley reached out and swallowed the sun. Within an hour it was too dark to continue picking. The vines blanketed the grapes, making it difficult to see the bunches. "Vamonos [Let's go]," said Papá,

Experienced grape pickers in the California fields can often pick as much as 60 cases per day, earning about $36.

signaling to us that it was time to quit work. Papá then took out a pencil and began to figure out how much we had earned our first day. He wrote down numbers, crossed some out, wrote down some more. "Quince [fifteen]," he murmured.

When we arrived home, we took a cold shower underneath a waterhose. We then sat down to eat dinner around some wooden crates that served as a table. Mamá had cooked a special meal for us. We had rice and tortillas with "carne con chile [dish made of meat, beans, and red peppers]," my favorite dish.

The next morning I could hardly move. My body ached all over. I felt little control over my arms and legs. This feeling went on every morning for days until my muscles finally got used to the work.

It was Monday, the first week of November. The grape season was over and I could now go to school. I woke up early that morning and lay in bed, looking at the stars and savoring the thought of not going to work and of starting sixth grade for the first time that year. Since I could not sleep, I decided to get up and join Papá and Roberto for breakfast. I sat at the table across from Roberto, but I kept my head down. I did not want to look up and face him. I knew he was sad. He was not going to school today. He was not going tomorrow, or next week, or next month. He would not go until the cotton season was over, and that was sometime in February. I rubbed my hands together and watched the dry, acid stained skin fall to the floor in little rolls.

When Papá and Roberto left for work, I felt relief. I walked to the top of a small grade next to the shack and watched the "Carcanchita" disappear in the distance in a cloud of dust.

Two hours later, around eight o'clock, I stood by the side of the road waiting for school bus number twenty. When it arrived I climbed in. Everyone was

. . . The grape season was over and I could now go to school.

busy either talking or yelling. I sat in an empty
seat in the back.

When the bus stopped in front of the school,
I felt very nervous. I looked out the bus window
and saw boys and girls carrying books under their
arms. I put my hands in my pant pockets and walked
to the principal's office. When I entered I heard a
woman's voice say: "May I help you?" I was startled.
I had not heard English for months. For a few seconds
I remained speechless. I looked at the lady who
waited for an answer. My first instinct was to answer
her in Spanish, but I held back. Finally, after struggling for English words, I managed to tell her that
I wanted to enroll in the sixth grade. After answering
many questions, I was led to the classroom.

Mr. Lema, the sixth-grade teacher, greeted me
and assigned me a desk. He then introduced me to
the class. I was so nervous and scared at that moment
when everyone's eyes were on me that I wished I
were with Papá and Roberto picking cotton. After
taking roll, Mr. Lema gave the class the assignment
for the first hour. "The first thing we have to do
this morning is finish reading the story we began
yesterday," he said enthusiastically. He walked up
to me, handed me an English book, and asked me
to read. "We are on page 125," he said politely.
When I heard this, I felt my blood pressure rush
to my head; I felt dizzy. "Would you like to read?"
he asked hesitantly. I opened the book to page 125.
My mouth was dry. My eyes began to water. I could
not begin. "You can read later," Mr. Lema said under-
standingly.

For the rest of the reading period I kept getting
angrier and angrier with myself. I should have read,
I thought to myself.

During recess I went into the restroom and
opened my English book to page 125. I began to
read in a low voice, pretending I was in class. There
were many words I did not know. I closed the book
and headed back to the classroom.

Mr. Lema was sitting at his desk correcting papers. When I entered he looked up at me and smiled. I felt better. I walked up to him and asked if he could help me with the new words. "Gladly," he said.

The rest of the month I spent my lunch hours working on English with Mr. Lema, my best friend at school.

One Friday during lunch hour Mr. Lema asked me to take a walk with him to the music room. "Do you like music?" he asked as we entered the building.

"Yes, I like corridos [ballads]," I answered. He then picked up a trumpet, blew on it and handed it to me. The sound gave me goose bumps. I knew that sound. I had heard it in many corridos. "How would you like to learn how to play it?" he asked. He must have read my face because before I could answer, he added: "I'll teach you how to play it during our lunch hours."

That day I could hardly wait to get home to tell Papá and Mamá the great news. As I got off the bus, my little brothers and sisters ran up to meet me. They were yelling and screaming. I thought they were happy to see me, but when I opened the door to our shack, I saw that everything we owned was neatly packed in cardboard boxes.

REVIEWING THE READING

1. When migrant workers were employed, what hours did they often work?

2. Why did the narrator wait until November to start school at Fresno, California?

3. **Using Your Historical Imagination.** Why is "The Circuit" an appropriate title for a story about the life of a migrant family?

Presidential Candidates Bush and Dukakis Debate the Issues (1988)

78

From *Presidential Debates Between Governor Michael Dukakis and Vice President George Bush*, compiled by Federal News Service.

Beginning in the 1960s with John Kennedy and Richard Nixon, the televised presidential debate has become a fixture of all United States presidential campaigns. Critics claim that these media events fall short of the live give-and-take of a real debate—that they are really more of a joint press conference held by the candidates. Nevertheless, the televised debates are perhaps the only chance voters get to see the candidates side-by-side in live action, fielding questions from reporters. Political polls consistently show that the televised debates strongly affect voters' opinions. The selection below contains excerpts from the beginning, middle, and end of the second debate between George Bush and Michael Dukakis, which took place in Los Angeles, California, on September 13, 1988. As you read consider who seems to give the more impressive responses.

MR. SHAW: Good evening. On behalf of the Commission on Presidential Debates I am pleased to welcome you to the second presidential debate. I am Bernard Shaw of CNN, Cable News Network. My colleagues on the panel are: Anne Compton of ABC News; Margaret Warner of *Newsweek* Magazine; and Andrea Mitchell of NBC News.

The candidates are: Vice President George Bush (applause), the Republican nominee; and Governor Michael Dukakis, the Democratic nominee. (Continued applause, cheers.)

For the next 90 minutes we will be questioning the candidates following a format designed and agreed to by representatives of the two campaigns. However, there are no restrictions on the questions that my colleagues and I can ask this evening, and the candidates have no prior knowledge of our questions.

By agreement between the candidates, the first question goes to Governor Dukakis. You have two minutes to respond.

Governor, if Kitty Dukakis were raped and murdered, would you favor an irrevocable death penalty for the killer?

GOV. DUKAKIS: No, I don't, Bernard, and I think you know that I've opposed the death penalty during all of my life. I don't see any evidence that it's a deterrent, and I think there are better and more effective ways to deal with violent crime. We've done so in my own state, and it's one of the reasons why we have had the biggest drop in crime of any industrial state in America, why we have the lowest murder rate of any industrial state in America.

But we have work to do in this nation; we have work to do to fight a real war, not a phony war against drugs. And that's something that I want to lead, something we haven't had over the course of the past many years, even though the Vice President has been, at least allegedly, in charge of that war. We have much to do to step up that war, to double the number of drug enforcement agents, to fight both here and abroad, to work with our neighbors in this hemisphere. And I want to call a hemispheric summit just as soon after the 20th of January as possible to fight that war.

But we also have to deal with drug education prevention here at home. And that's one of the things that I hope I can lead personally as the President of the United States. We've had great success in my own state, and we've reached out to young people

> . . . I've opposed the death penalty during all of my life. . . . there are better and more effective ways to deal with violent crime.

and their families and have been able to help them by beginning drug education and prevention in the early elementary grades.

So we can fight this war and we can win this war, and we can do so in a way that marshals our forces, that provides real support for state and local law enforcement officers who have not been getting that kind of support, do it in a way which will bring down violence in this nation, will help our youngsters to stay away from drugs, will stop this avalanche of drugs that's pouring into the country, and will make it possible for our kids and our families to grow up in safe and secure and decent neighborhoods.

MR. SHAW: Mr. Vice President, your one-minute rebuttal.

VICE PRESIDENT BUSH: Well, a lot of what this campaign is about, it seems to me, Bernie, is to a question of values. And here, I do have, on this particular question, a big difference with my opponent. You see, I do believe that some crimes are so heinous [evil], so brutal, so outrageous—and I'd say particularly those that result in the death of a police officer— those real brutal crimes, I do believe in the death penalty. And I think it is a deterrent. And I do believe we need it, and I'm glad that the Congress moved on this drug bill, and it finally called for that, related to these narcotics drug kingpins. And so, we just have an honest difference of opinion. I support it, and he doesn't. (Applause) . . .

> . . . I do believe that some crimes are . . . so brutal, so outrageous . . . I do believe in the death penalty.

MR. SHAW: Anne has a question for you, Mr. Vice President.

MS. COMPTON: Let's change the pace a little, Mr. Vice President. In this campaign, some hard and very bitter things have been spoken by each side, about each side. If you'd consider for a moment Governor Dukakis in his years of public service, is there anything nice you can say about him—(laughter)—anything you find admirable?

VICE PRESIDENT BUSH: Hey, listen, you're stealing my close. I had something very nice to say in that—(laughter).

Ms. COMPTON: Somebody leaked my question to you?

VICE PRESIDENT BUSH: No, look, I'll tell you what—no, let me tell you something about that. And Barbara [Bush] and I were sitting there before that Democratic Convention, and we saw the Governor and his son on television the night before, and his family and his mother who was there. And I'm saying to Barbara, "You know, we've always kept family as a bit of an oasis for us. You all know me, and we've held it back a little." But we use that as a role model, the way he took understandable pride in his heritage, what his family means to him. And we've got a strong family and we watched that and we said, "Hey, we've got to unleash the Bush kids." (Laughter.) And so, you saw ten grandchildren there jumping all over their grandfather at the—at the convention. You see our five kids all over this country and their spouses.

And so, I would say that the concept of the Dukakis family has my great respect, and I'd say that—I don't know whether that's kind or not, it's just an objective statement. And I think the man—anybody that gets into this political arena and has to face you guys everyday—(laughter)—deserves a word of praise because it's gotten a little ugly out there, it's gotten a little nasty. It's not much fun sometimes. And I would cite again Dan Quayle. I've been in politics a long time and I don't remember that kind of piling on, that kind of ugly rumor that never was true printed. Now, come on. So, some of it's unfair, but he's in the arena. Teddy Roosevelt

used to talk about the "arena"—you know, daring to fail greatly or succeed. No matter—he's in there.

So, I salute these things. I salute those who participate in the political process. Sam Rayburn [late Democratic Congressman] had a great expression on this. He said, "You know, I hear all of these intellectuals out there griping and complaining and saying it's negative coverage." Rayburn says, "Yeah, and that guy never ran for sheriff either." (Laughter.) Michael Dukakis has run for sheriff, and so has George Bush.

Presidential candidates George Bush (left) and Michael Dukakis (right) discuss questions posed by a panel of journalists during the 1988 presidential campaign.

MR. SHAW: Governor—(applause)—a one-minute response, sir.

GOV. DUKAKIS: I didn't hear the word "liberal" or "left" one time. (Laughter) I thank you for that.

VICE PRESIDENT BUSH: That's not bad; that's true.

GOV. DUKAKIS: And doesn't that prove the point, George, which is that values like family, and education, community—

VICE PRESIDENT BUSH: That's where you want to take the country.

GOV. DUKAKIS:—decent homes for young people— that family in Long Island I visited on Monday, where—Lou and Betty Tulamo (phonetic) bought a house for some $19,000 back in 1972, they have seven children. They're all making good livings; they can't live in the community in which they grew up in. Those are basic American values. I believe in them; I think you believe in them. They're not left or right, they're decent American values. I guess the one thing that concerns me about this, Anne, is this attempt to label things which all of us believe in. We may have different approaches, we may think that you deal with them in different ways, but they're basically American. I believe in them, George Bush believes in them, I think the vast majority of Americans believe in them, and I hope—

MR. SHAW: Governor.

GOV. DUKAKIS: —the tone we've just heard might just be the tone we have for the rest of the campaign. I think the American people would appreciate that. (Applause) . . .

MR. SHAW: Andrea Mitchell has a question for you, Mr. Vice President.

MS. MITCHELL: Mr. Vice President, Jimmy Carter has called this the worst campaign ever. Richard Nixon has called it trivial, superficial and inane [foolish]. (Laughter.) Whoever started down this road first of negative campaigning, the American people, from all reports coming to us, are completely fed up. Now, do you have any solutions to suggest? Is there time left to fix it? There are 26 days left. For instance, would you agree to another debate before it's all over—(applause)—so that the American people—(cheers)—so that the American people would have another chance before election day to compare you two?

VICE PRESIDENT BUSH: No, I will not agree to another debate. (Applause.) The American people are up to here with debates. They had 30 of them. We had 7 of them. Now we got three of them. I am going to carry this election debate all across the country in the last—whatever remains of the last 3-1/2 weeks or whatever we have. And the answer is no. I am not going to have any more debates. I've spelled out my position.

In terms of negative campaigning—you know, I don't want to sound like a kid in a schoolyard— "He started it." But, take a look at the Democratic convention—(laughs)—take a look at it. Do you remember the senator from Boston chanting out there and the ridicule factor from that lady from Texas that was on there? (Laughter.) I mean, come on. This was just outrageous. But, I'll try harder to keep it on a high plane.

But, let me—if you could accept a little criticism. I went all across central Illinois and spoke about agricultural issues in about seven stops. We had some fun—Crystal Gayle and Loretta Lynn with us and they got up and sang. We went to little towns and I talked agriculture. And not one thing did I see, with respect, on your network about my views on agriculture and not one did I read in any newspaper. Why? Because you're so interested in a poll that might have been coming out. Or because somebody had said something nasty about somebody else. And, so, I don't know what the answer is. I don't—somebody hit me and said Barry Goldwater said you ought to talk on the issues more. How can Barry Goldwater, sitting in Arizona, know whether I'm talking on the issues or not, when we put out position paper after position paper—he puts out position paper after position paper—and we see this much about it because everyone else is fascinated with polls and who's up or down today and who's going to be up or down tomorrow. So, I think we can all share, with respect, in the fact that maybe these—the message is not getting out. But, it's not getting out because they're too few debates. There will be no more debates. (Applause.)

MR. SHAW: Governor Dukakis, you have one minute to respond, sir.

GOV. DUKAKIS: Well, I can understand, after the vice presidential debate—(laughter)—why Mr. Bush would want no more debates. (Boos.) That's my five seconds, George.

Andrea, I think we both have a responsibility to try to address the issues. Yes, we have fundamental differences. I think a great many of them have come out today. And I think if we get rid of the labels and—I'm not keeping count, but I think Mr. Bush has used the label "liberal" at least 10 times. If I had a dollar, George, for every time you used that label, I'd qualify for one of those tax breaks for the rich that you want to give away. (Laughter.) Isn't that the point?

Most Americans believe in basic values—we have differences about how to achieve them. I want to move forward. I want this nation to move forward. I'm concerned about the fact that ten percent of our manufacturing and 20 percent of our banking and nearly half of the real estate in the city of Los Angeles are in the hands of foreign investors. I'm concerned about what that does to our future. I'm concerned about the fact that so many of our securities are in the hands of foreign banks because of those massive deficits.

But, those are the issues on which we ought to be debating, and if we'd just—

MR. SHAW: Governor—

GOV. DUKAKIS: —put away the flag factories and the balloons and those kinds of things and get on

to a real discussion of these issues, I think we'll—
(applause)—

MR. SHAW: Andrea—

GOV. DUKAKIS: —have a good 26 days. . . .

MR. SHAW: To each of you candidates, regrettably,
I have to inform you that we have come to the
end of our questions. That's a pity. Before I ask
the candidates to make their closing remarks, on
behalf of the Commission on Presidential Debates,
I would like to thank all of you for joining us this
evening. Governor Dukakis, yours is the first closing
statement, sir.

GOV. DUKAKIS: Twenty-eight years ago, as a young
man, just graduated from law school, I came to this
city, came clear across the country to watch John
Kennedy be nominated for the presidency of the
United States, right here in Los Angeles. I never
dreamed that someday I would win that nomination
and be my party's nominee for president. That's
America. That's why I'm proud and grateful to be
a citizen of this country.

> . . . I never dreamed that someday I would . . . be my party's nominee for president. That's America.

    Twenty-six days from today, you and millions
of Americans will choose two people to lead us into
the future as president and vice president of the
United States. Our opponents say, "Things are okay.
Don't rock the boat. Not to worry." They say we
should be satisfied. But I don't think we can be satisfied when we're spending $150 billion a year in
interest alone on the national debt, much of it going
to foreign bankers, or when 25 percent of our high
school students are dropping out of school or when
we have two and a half million of our fellow citizens,
a third of them veterans, who are homeless and
living on streets and in doorways in this country
or when Mr. Bush's prescription for our economic
future is another tax giveaway to the rich. We can
do better than that. Not working with government

alone, but all of us working together. Lloyd Bentsen and I are optimists and so are the American people. And we ask you for our hand—and for your hands and your hearts and your votes on the 8th of November so we can move forward into the future.

Kitty [Dukakis] and I are very grateful to all of you for the warmth and the hospitality that you've given to us in your homes and communities all across this country. We love you, and we're grateful to you for everything that you've given to us. And we hope that we'll be serving you in the White House in January of 1989. Thank you, and God bless you. (Applause, cheers.)

MR. SHAW: Vice President Bush, your closing statement, sir.

VICE PRESIDENT BUSH: Sometimes it does seem that a campaign generates more heat than light. And so let me repeat, I do have respect for my opponent, for his family, for the justifiable pride he takes in his heritage.

But we have enormous differences. I want to hold the line on taxes and keep this, the longest expansion in modern history, going until everybody in America benefits. I want to invest in our children, because I mean it when I say I want a kinder and gentler nation. And by that, I want to have child care where the families, the parents have control.

I want to invest in our children . . .

I want to keep our neighborhoods much, much better in terms of anti-crime. And that's why I would appoint judges that have a little more sympathy for the victims of crime and a little less for the criminals. That's why I do feel if some police officer is gunned down that the death penalty is required.

I want to help those with disabilities fit into the mainstream. There is much to be done. This election is about big things, and perhaps the biggest is world peace. And I ask you to consider the experience I have had in working with a President who has revolutionized the situation around the world. America stands tall again and, as a result, we are credible and we have now achieved a historic arms control agreement. I want to build on that. I'd love to be able to say to my grandchildren, four years after my first term, I'd like to say, "Your grandfather, working with the leaders of the Soviet Union, working with the leaders of Europe, was able to ban chemical and biological weapons from the face of the Earth."

Lincoln called this country the last, best hope of man on earth. And he was right then, and we still are the last, best hope of man on earth.

And I ask for your support on November 8th, and I will be a good President. Working together we can do wonderful things for the United States and for the free world. Thank you very, very much. (Applause, cheers.)

Lincoln called this country the last, best hope of man on earth.

REVIEWING THE READING

1. How would you describe the technique used by Governor Dukakis in his response to his first question on the death penalty?

2. What conclusion can you draw about the campaign from the candidates' answers to the question posed by Anne Compton?

3. **Using Your Historical Imagination.** In your opinion, who made the better impression in this televised debate?

79

President William J. Clinton Delivers His Inaugural Address (1993)

In the 1992 presidential election Bill Clinton won more than twice as many electoral votes as George Bush. Clinton, however, received only 43 percent of the popular vote, while Bush won 38 percent and Ross Perot received 19 percent. As you read this excerpt from Clinton's inaugural address, consider the message he presents to a divided electorate.

When our founders boldly declared America's independence to the world and our purposes to the Almighty, they knew that America, to endure, would have to change. Not change for change's sake but change to preserve America's ideals. . . . Each generation of Americans must define . . . what it means to be an American. . . .

Today, a generation raised in the shadows of the Cold War assumes new responsibilities in a world warmed by the sunshine of freedom but threatened still by ancient hatreds and new plagues.

Raised in unrivaled prosperity, we inherit an economy that is still the world's strongest but is weakened by business failures, stagnant wages, increasing inequality. . . .

We earn our livelihood in America today in peaceful competition with people all across the Earth. Profound and powerful forces are shaking and remaking our world. And the urgent question of our time is whether we can make change our friend and not our enemy.

This new world has already enriched the lives of millions of Americans who are able to compete and win in it. But when most people are working harder for less, when others cannot work at all, when the cost of health care devastates families and threatens to bankrupt our enterprises great and small, when the fear of crime robs law-abiding citizens of their freedom, and when millions of poor children cannot even imagine the lives we are calling them to lead, we have not made change our friend.

We know we have to face hard truths and take strong steps, but we have not done so. Instead, we have drifted, and that drifting has eroded our resources, fractured our economy and shaken our confidence. . . .

. . . we know we have to face hard truths and take strong steps.

Thomas Jefferson believed that to preserve the very foundations of our nation we would need dramatic change from time to time. Well my fellow Americans, this is our time. Let us embrace it. . . .

To renew America we must be bold. . . . We must invest more in our own people—in their jobs and in their future—and at the same time cut our massive debt. . . . And we must do so in a world in which we must compete for every opportunity.

It will not be easy. It will require sacrifice. But it can be done and done fairly. . . .

We must do what America does best: offer more opportunity to all and demand more responsibility from all. . . .

To renew America, we must meet challenges abroad as well as at home. There is no longer a clear division between what is foreign and what is domestic. The world economy, the world environment, the world AIDS crisis, the world arms race— they affect us all.

Today, as an old order passes, the new world is more free but less stable. Communism's collapse has called forth old animosities and new dangers. Clearly, America must continue to lead the world we did so much to make.

While America rebuilds at home, we will not shrink from the challenges nor fail to seize the opportunities of this new world. Together with our friends and allies we will work to shape change. . . .

The American people have summoned the change we celebrate today. . . . You have changed the face of Congress, the presidency and the political process itself. . . .

. . . But no president, no Congress, no government can undertake this mission alone. My fellow Americans, you, too, must play your part in our renewal.

I challenge a new generation . . . to a season of service; to act on your idealism by helping troubled children, keeping company with those in need, reconnecting our torn communities. . . .

In serving, we recognize a simple but powerful truth: We need each other and we must care for one another.

Today we do more than celebrate America, we rededicate ourselves to the very idea of America: An idea born in revolution and renewed through two centuries of challenge; . . . an idea infused with the conviction that America's long, heroic journey must go forever upward.

REVIEWING THE READING

1. According to Clinton, what is the major issue that Americans must address?

2. Based on this speech, how do you think Clinton defines what it means to be an American?

3. **Using Your Historical Imagination.** How do you think Clinton would define the role of the federal government?

The Republicans' Contract with America (1994)

80

From Newt Gingrich's speech after his election as Speaker of the House of Representatives

The 1994 elections gave the Republicans control of Congress for the first time in 40 years. In his opening speech, the new Speaker of the House, Newt Gingrich, summarized the provisions of the Republicans' Contract with America, which some 300 Republican candidates for the House of Representatives had signed. As you read this excerpt from Gingrich's speech, consider the proposed changes.

This may seem particularly appropriate to say on the first day because this will be the busiest day on opening day in congressional history. I want to read just a part of the "Contract With America," not as a partisan act, but to remind all of us of what we're about to go through and why, because those of us who ended up in a majority stood on these steps and signed a contract, and here's part of what it says, quote:

"On the first day of the 104th Congress, the new Republican majority will immediately pass the following major reforms aimed at restoring the faith and trust of the American people in their government:

"First, require all laws that apply to the rest of the country also apply equally to the Congress.

"Second, select a major independent auditing firm to conduct a comprehensive audit of Congress for waste, fraud or abuse.

"Third, cut the number of House committees and cut committee staffs by a third.

"Fourth, limit the terms of all committee chairs

"Fifth, ban the casting of proxy votes in committees.

"Sixth, require committee meetings to be open to the public.

"Seven, require a three-fifths majority vote to pass a tax increase.

"Eighth, guarantee an honest accounting of our federal budget by implementing zero baseline budgeting."

. . . We then said, thereafter, "within the first 100 days of the 104th Congress, we shall bring to the House floor the following bills, each to be given full and open debate, each to be given a clear and fair vote, each to be immediately available for inspection."

We made it available that day. And we listed 10 items: a balanced-budget amendment and line-item veto; to stop violent criminals, emphasizing among other things an effective, enforceable death penalty; third was welfare reform; fourth was protecting our kids; fifth was tax cuts for families; sixth was a stronger national defense; seventh was raising the senior citizens' earning limit; eighth was rolling back government regulations; ninth was common sense legal reform; and tenth was congressional term limits.

REVIEWING THE READING

1. What reforms in the Contract apply to Congress?

2. Which of the ten items in the legislative program affect the ability of Congress to balance the budget?

3. **Using Your Historical Imagination.** Do you think the proposed term limits would make Congress more democratic? Explain your answer.

Photo Acknowledgments

Front Cover: HRW Photo

Table of Contents: Page iii, The Bancroft Library, University of California—Berkeley; iv (t) State Historical Society of Wisconsin; iv (b), v (t), Museum of the City of New York; v (b), Denver Public Library Western Collection; vi, Library of Congress; vii (t), Austin Public Library, Austin History Center; vii (b), Wide World Photos; viii (t), United States Geological Survey; viii (b), U.S. Army; ix, Wide World Photos; x, John Goodwin.

Page 5: Texas Memorial Museum; 10, Nawrocki Stock Photo; 17, 23, The Bettmann Archive; 28, Historical Pictures Service; 32, Culver Pictures; 41, California Historical Society; 46, 52, Historical Pictures Service; 61, The Kansas State Historical Society, Topeka; 63, 65, Library of Congress; 67, Texas Tech University, Southwest Collection; 69, Culver Pictures; 74, Library of Congress; 80, Culver Pictures; 86 (l), 86 (r), Historical Pictures Service; 95, Anita McLean, Courtesy of University of Texas Institute of Texan Cultures; 98, Museum of the City of New York; 104, Culver Pictures; 109, The Bettmann Archive; 117, 123, 126, 130, Historical Pictures Service; 133, The Bettmann Archive; 139, 144, Historical Pictures Service; 149, 155, The Bettmann Archive; 160, Historical Pictures Service; 165, New York Public Library; 169, The Bettmann Archive; 175, Culver Pictures; 179, Historical Pictures Service; 190, Culver Pictures; 195, 198, The Bettmann Archive; 202, Culver Pictures; 207, Courtesy National NAACP Public Relations Department; 212, Library of Congress; 218, The Bettmann Archive; 225, Wide World Photos; 228, 229, 1, The Smithsonian Institution; 2, Carnegie Library of Pittsburgh; 3, Lee Boltin; 4, 5, Nawrocki Stock Photo; 6, Ford Motor Co.; 7, Culver Pictures; 8, Minnesota Historical Society; 9, AT&T; 232, UPI/Bettmann; 241, Barker Texas History Center, University of Texas at Austin; 247, Library of Congress; 252, FPG International; 256, UPI/Bettmann; 259, Culver Pictures; 263, 268, The Bettmann Archive; 278, 284, UPI/Bettmann; 290, Wide World Photos; 295, FPG International; 299, Wide World Photos; 308, 311, UPI/Bettmann; 316, Bettmann Archive; 321, UPI/Bettmann; 328, FPG International; 332, Wide World Photos; 335, 339, UPI/Bettmann; 346, Cornell Capa/Magnum; 351, Wide World Photos; 356, 361, 371, UPI/Bettmann; 377, Wide World Photos; 383, Bob Adelman/Magnum; 387, Wide World Photos; 393, Philip Jones Griffiths/Magnum; 403, 407, 410, Wide World Photos; 414, NASA; 421, Alex Webb/Magnum; 425, Organization of American States; 426, Marilu Pease/Monkmeyer Press; 431, Rene Burri/Magnum; 439, Wide World Photos.